BROTHERS

OF THE

WIND

THE JOURNEY TO
HERE AND THERE

KEN NOEL and NEAL CHAPPELL

We dedicate the book to the life and memory of Mihály Iglói, the successful Hungarian and American track coach.

And to Sándor Iharos, István Rózsavölgyi, László Tábori, Jim Beatty, Jim Grelle, Bob Schul, Dave Martin, Bobby Seaman, Nick Kitt, Jerry Laird, Tom Brown, Jack Marden, and Ray Schnore who showed exceptional courage and physical abilities to reach unprecedented levels of human accomplishment. With Frank Wolfgang, Merle Magee, Joe Douglass, Charles Grant, Joe Szurcik, and other athletes who couldn't handle Igloi's demands, they contributed and grew through participation.

And to the memory of Coach Harold Zimmerman at West Chester High School. He provided encouragement and guidance in critical teen years beyond the reach of most other role models available daily. The desire to make Coach Zimmerman's final year of coaching his most rewarding drove our exceptional cross-country and track performances.

Without everyone's strength and help, we could not have written this book.

CONTENTS

ACKNOWLEDGMENTS

To our parents and ancestors before them.

To our brothers and sisters, most of whom left the world too soon.

We are thankful for the collective members of the OPHR, Eddie Green, the Velasco family, Don Dansby, Tony and Marilyn (Conkle), Joe Friedberg, Tom Huntsman, Gene Zubrinsky, Peggy Kredel, Bob A., Susan Peters-Koch, Gillete and Vicki Renneckar, Mel and Debbie Pender, Dylan Langan and Steve Martinez, Hedy Hedgewig Gibson, Paul and June Drayton, the Sims family, the Edwards family, Jack and Donald Chappell, Vicki and Dave Garcia, Nancy and Terry Qureshi, and Walt Van Zandt and the WVJS Running Club, and the Las Vegas Running Club.

The abundant use of material from *The Revolt of the Black Athlete* was granted by Professor Harry Edwards, UC Berkeley Professor Emeritus.

To Dr. David Matza for recruiting and supporting Ken at U.C. Berkeley.

To Andi for coming to the rescue.

Having Leila as a goal audience made the trials and struggles of writing bearable.

The book title and subtitle have special significance as the contributions of Neal Chappell and Eddie Green respectively.

INTRODUCTION

Where to begin is a political question.

The ebb and flow of human progress features events starkly defining our humanity. Through the ages, many such events influenced literature portraying the classical conditions of human existence. In the literature, the differences between each individual's life are mostly related to unequal distributions of the tragic and the glorious—the triumphs, failures, or lack thereof, experienced. With great unpredictability, vastly different lives unify on diverging and converging paths—so long as they successfully cultivate fundamental ties spanning them. Because of our profoundly diverse population, this has been a decidedly American phenomenon. Therein the bond of the brothers of the wind exists.

Neal:

Our life courses unfolded as parallel lines extending over the horizon, growing separated but converging in every expansive view. It was uncanny that fellow students envisioned a lifetime of selfless connectedness in the youthful endeavors of classmates like Kenny and me. Their envisaging proved prophetic, although such a relationship didn't surface in our teenage thinking. To wit, our peers predicted a literal partnership of running together along a shared path while making no similar intuitive predictions for others.

STILL CHAMPS

Neal Chappell and Kenneth Noel have just won the Olympic Crown for the United States for riding bicycles backward and uphill over Mount Everest. (Garnet and White Class of 1956 Yearbook Prognostication)

Garnet and White's crew got it right! They identified future foci for us, and their prognostication metaphor applied to most people we knew. Our existence and advancement occurred in a nation inundated with racist pitfalls and contradictions. Economic class, ethnocentrism, sexism, ableism, and other relational phobias exist. Considering respective starting points, our journey compared to winning an Olympic Crown as projected in the yearbook. Staff members recognized our vital connection as a pair of individuals. We saw in each other courage and a willingness to sacrifice to overcome barriers. We tied bonding to surviving in settings primed for our destruction and bent on maintaining existing social stratification.

The Prefontaine Classic Oregon Track Club event aired on May 25, 1997, hosted by Larry Rawson, Craig Masback, and Dwight Stones, NBC's resident experts. Prior to announcing events, they identified New Zealand's Arthur Lydiard, along with Bill Bowerman at Oregon University, as starting the early 1960s jogging craze in this country. The state of track, according to them, relies on two or three pioneering minds. Those theorists reigned as founders.

The broadcasters' statements struck a nerve, triggering a moment of puzzlement. We had learned of the Kiwi guru, and Percy Cerutty, from Australia, as training geniuses. We knew more about Mihály Iglói's (Iggles, Mihái) skills in designing hellish workouts and the Hungarian émigré's ability to motivate and develop world-record performers. (Hailing from close to Philly, we took the liberty of calling him "Iggles" from our appreciation of the Philadelphia Eagles.) The Santa Clara Valley Youth Village (SCVYV) team members, following Iglói, saw no reason to position any coach above the others. Television announcers exercised their sports commentator positions to create or recreate a chronicle complying with their broadcast's programming aims. Their TV pronouncements are often taken as gospel when not correct. The contributions from Auckland and Eugene were vital to increasing the popularity of running. However, the history goes back to Paavo Nurmi, Emil Zatopek, and other Europeans. There was an uptake in Americans exercising after WWII. Browning Ross, Fred Dwyer, Fred Wilt, and Horace Ashenfelter, on the mid Atlantic coast, dominated eastern seaboard road racing in the 1940s and 1950s.

The blossoming American involvement in running, exercising, and physical fitness came with vital foundations in place. For those making the pilgrimage to San Jose, California, the seminal influences were Cerutty, Lydiard, and Iglói, with their 1950s and 1960s methods. Oregon's impact continued trends into the 1970s. Devotees moving there made San Jose the center of distance running in the United States. The commanding figures responsible for nourishing those roots were Mihái and Bowerman. They developed workable strategies to raise performance levels to ever-increasing heights. Of course, they needed dedicated followers. They required talented athletes to demonstrate the validity of their theories. Such record-setters as Jim Beatty (the first person to run a mile under 4 minutes indoors), 1964 Olympic champion Bob Schul (5000 meters), Billy Mills (1964 10,000 meters winner), and Jim Grelle keyed his group. Bowerman credited Iglói as an architect behind the emerging fashionable running era. He used Mihály's techniques but never connected directly with him. He related drawing on the Hungarian Coach in one instance:

Dale Ransom at North Carolina was with me on the NCAA rules committee, and he told me once: "Iglói will be here (at UNC), and I expect I'll learn a lot." After the Hungarians had been there six weeks, I phoned Ransom and asked, "So did you find out anything from the Coach?" He replied, "I haven't found out a damn thing. He won't talk to me." Then Dale said, "I have an idea. I'm going up in the bell tower with binoculars and watch him." He did and sent me notes on the work they were doing. So we added what Mihái called his sets—600, 400, 200—very productive, but I never actually got it from him. (Lost citation)

We present our story as Iglói's disciples, who were involved in elevating and carrying America's "fitness" movement from the late 1950s until today. Jogging came of age in the 1960s and became essential to a healthy lifestyle, changing the culture's general features. In a more profound sense, we achieved the rebirth of understanding self and the wonder and value of an active life. Our journey seeks the joyous excitement of "being" regardless of circumstances. So, it's right to relate:

Over time, we learned about possibilities to improve prospects by arming ourselves with the universal tools for change, such as activism in resistance to the degrading impacts deliberately fostering perversions like poverty, homelessness, sexism, racism, and disintegrating families.

The ultimate value of how we lead our lives rests in navigating to heightened consciousness. Change, eradicating adverse conditions, and positively embracing our humanity could be accomplished under the worst systems of oppression (slavery, caste, colonialism, or imperialism) with protracted struggle. We learned the necessity to resist and attack the status quo despite barriers and setbacks encountered in facing the uphill obstacle-laden pathways over political, social, and economic "Mount Everest(s)." Personal growth can happen for some people, even when condemned by birth (in an elitist class structure with racism) to a life of struggle. That fight was akin to riding bicycles backward over the highest mountains to achieve our just measure of status and our potential as human beings. In complex modern societies, with their complicated dynamics, individual interactions, and relationships, there are many obstacles and ways to go up and over. It helped to have pursued and embraced a calling that functioned like religion without being burdened by immersion in superstition. (Stevie Wonder: "When you believe in things you don't understand, you suffer.")

CHAPTER
ONE

Beginnings and Early Transitions – Kenny

*People subjugated over time eventually develop
a need to individually and collectively destroy
themselves and a need to individually and collectively
re-create themselves. All too often, their sad fate has
been limited to one or the other, to self-destruction
or to re-creation. In some instances, however,
people achieve the good fortune of doing both.*

Neal:

For Kenny and me, participation in the nation's fitness and jogging explosion began after he hitchhiked from Florida's panhandle, arriving in San Jose, California, on Wednesday, October 5, 1960. He did little running after graduation in 1956. Before that, as high school runners, we started a collective that included exercise as an essential daily feature. We were dedicated, motivated, and consumed with things related to running. When possible, we ran everywhere. Running transformed into a timesaving routine as our quest for logging higher mileage proceeded. I carried this passionate mindset to The University of North Carolina (UNC), eventually landing under Mihály Iglói. His achievements placed him among the top international track coaches, so he made loving it as a way of life even more special.

Kenny:

When I was seven years old, every Coonville (eastside) resident knew that I was fast. None had equal or better speed, including many older boys. My ability gained notice because Gerald (Gerry, GT), my brother, recruited neighbors, forming "The Four Marines," a relay team named for the 1945 Pacific War's last campaign. Accounts following the Marine Divisions' (1st and 6th) battles dominated news reports when they launched an operation to conquer Okinawa. Combat stories filled newscasts preceding the expected invasion of Japan (Operation Downfall). Military successes resulted in massive casualties affecting every element of our lives. People survived by working hard at myriad enterprises; a war economy's requirements produce extraordinary times. Nearly everything was rationed except water.

Our rented house's left wall separated us from the Negro American Legion/ Foreign War Veterans Hall. They were in the corner storefront at 301 East Miner Street, formerly housing grocery markets and failed restaurants. Since Japan's December 7, 1941, sneak attack on Pearl Harbor, veterans' organizations staged regular fundraisers, supporting our troops fighting tyranny. Veterans provided a link to past international conflicts. Vets marched in parades, performed patriotic ceremonies, and provided for needy members. Old soldiers marched wearing vintage (Spanish-American War or World War I) uniforms, many of which sported campaign ribbons, medals, and citation insignias for heroism. Negro vets were not spared the impressive range of physical and mental disabilities from engaging enemy fighters. Their appearances honored service personnel's nobility, making selfless contributions benefiting our entire country. For this youngster, seeing old Negro warriors created pride and hope for eliminating racism. We were all looking for positive racial images, and honoring the nobility of Negro veterans was extremely impactful. We hungered for actions showing our representatives contributing to successful combat. I seized on using them to feel self-worth and value my race. Dorie Miller was an extraordinary, courageous United States Navy sailor. He earned a Navy Cross for bravery during Pearl Harbor. He stands as our first to earn a top combat honor. His courage received massive newspaper publicity. The Philadelphia Tribune made him an iconic figure that energized support for our fighting men.

Popular items for Negroes pictured Miller. Coonville households displayed several items depicting him. Dorie Miller's picture calendars graced our living room and kitchen walls, showing his image each month. Photos pictured a large, dignified Black man in a white uniform. A hero's medal graced his proud chest. Looking at him each day gave me satisfaction. Colored people spoke about Dorie because he belonged to us. He represented everything we needed in order to claim involvement in avenging Japan's attack. Vets' activities in their converted hall lifted spirits, even with abundant battle-related afflictions. They are our heroes.

Our Veterans' Post held monthly fundraising nights featuring card games and slot machines. Since we lived next to their meeting hall, they hid slot machines in our basement to protect them from police raids while not being used.

Like most families, we sacrificed mightily to support our troops. We collected rags, paper, glass, and discarded metal with Gerald's wagon. Kids in each neighborhood did that. Six houses east, Mr. Harmon's junkyard hummed doing recycling work. The entire population delivered scrap materials, loading enormous trucks transporting recyclable material for re-manufacturing. Our contributions grew significantly because Uncle Tommy (Brown) and Mom's cousins (Pennock and Dallas Hammond, for example) were "Red Ball Express" drivers. She received mail from the Netherlands, Belgium, and France. Many letters came from former classmates. John Jr. (Boardley), her half-brother, became a Tuskegee Airmen after graduating as an engineer from Hampton (Virginia). Word arrived from him twice a month.

"The Four Marines" had no trouble defeating challengers, racing against other ethnic enclaves. I was younger than my competitors. We always won our relays circling the block. 200-yard sprints based on our ages got staged on Hoopes Bro & Darlington Spoke Wheel Factory's powdered cinder walk. It was catty-corner to our rented East Miner Street house. Youthful winning laid the foundations for sports to emerge as a motivating influence. Soon, I represented our recreation center against other playgrounds in age group contests. I lacked the maturity to understand such matters, while my passion's metaphysical properties caused feeling valued and fed deep desires to escape from soft oppression.

During the races, competitors' and spectators' alike were left in awe of my speed. It gave me satisfaction, but did nothing to generate social equality. On most occasions with our relay team, ever-present inter-ethnic conflict disappeared from cooperative sports events. I realized our interaction was complicated. For specific moments, we transcended prejudices. Now, holding several degrees, I'll postulate that passions discovered early made vital connections to my essential being, influencing who I am. An internal peace found by dedicated runners fosters a sense of "freedom." This FREEDOM reaches the core being. Grasping one's existence and humanity creates an ultimate manifestation. It encourages intrinsic motivation essentials like self-mastery, performing superior in valued activities, and sharing competency to help others. That manifestation encompasses our complex hopes, dreams, trials, struggles, triumphs, defeats, and allows us a healthy and empowered path to act in the world.

Many past conditions shaped quests for acceptance into problematic subconscious issues. Paths ahead for minority youth filled with negative possibilities, raising the likelihood of short-circuited journeys on uncertain courses having violent conclusions. Survival beyond childhood depends too much on narrow escapes and lucky near misses in the face of weak planning without affirmative action. Some happenstances grew transformative or life-shaping. As early as 1943, near-death events kept happening. For example, I dashed to within a hair's breadth of flying off an eight-story apartment house on vacation in Harlem trying to save a German Shepherd.

HARLEM LIFE

Children only living in their dreams
No sense for what's not as it seems
Sans belief in self, believing in others
No models to follow — sisters and brothers
Venturing forth with faith in the living
Finding each night comes no forgiving
No rest, no peace, no happiness there
Somewhere? Nowhere? Oh, where?

Butch Little, 1943 (adopted from the internet)

I turned five on March 3, 1943, and Daddy took Gerald and me to Aunt Elsie's for a summer in Harlem. She's his younger sister. It counted as the first days away from my parents, except for spending three frightful nights in Chester County Hospital for tonsil surgery. Their apartment building had a basement pawn shop in front. There sat a dark-skinned giant in a rocking chair. A foul-mouthed parrot guarded steps going down through the door. There was assorted dirty, used stuff on display. Exposure to a talking bird surprised me! Aunt Elsie only permitted listening once. Its colorful language eclipsed all I'd thought possible! Our New York trip had four unforgettable events. We visited Coney Island before Chas. P. left, and I rode on his shoulders into the Atlantic Ocean up to his neck. Not being swimmers, we chanced to drown. I had never seen the ocean, so mental pictures of braving waves on Daddy's shoulders created irreplaceable memories. It was unanticipated to embrace a known risk. I continued being a risk-taker, loving ocean depths. (Now, as an adult, spearfishing is a favorite activity.)

Gerald and I expected an exciting, memorable Harlem vacation. Aside from problems returning to Elsie's from a multi-block movie trip, a troubling event arose on the roof looking over apartment building tops. Our first ascent above the seventh floor was taking Queenie, their German shepherd. Crinkled heat waves rose from hot, black tarpapered roofs when stepping out on a boiling sun-baked day. Pigeons sat perched on our roof's edge, topping a 10-degree incline for three feet before a seven-floor drop to the sidewalk. As she cleared the stairs, birds squatted unconcerned. Rocketing at them, the dog reached full stride in a flash. I saw Queenie's pursuit as carrying her to a horrible death.

I sprang forward to halt her charge into the open air for a bone-shattering landing. Gerald tackled me at the angular rise's base! Short khaki pants we both wore got smeared, rolling on black oily tar paper. At nine, Gerald discerned that grabbing Queenie meant plunging to the sidewalk. His reaction saved me. It was an unsolvable puzzle. How did GT calculate such danger to trigger intercepting me? He never yelled a warning before his deft tackle stopped me! That's how Gerry was. He figured out what to do when excellent decision-making is critical. I never considered Queenie was taking me with her while distressed over her death. Uncle Jimmy forbade us from seeing her battered corpse.

OPINION: There must be an answer to the question I put forth on how someone so young (nine) saved me in the blink of an eye. Consider that all humans have the capability, with our brain, nerves, and muscular systems, to analyze sensory data and act on our conclusions with beginning-to-end processing, perhaps at the speed of light. Humans' ability to function positively under any trying circumstances depends on the types, quality, and frequency of involvement we've had with the myriad ingredients of our immediate and extended environment. Thus, there are differences in the size and diversity of the realm of possibilities available as tools. It matters whether the experiences were voluminous, if interactions in their world were far-reaching, and if the theatre of the social had enough diversity. Those are vital in deter-mining one's inventory of tools for dealing with problem conditions. There are creative mechanisms helpful in expanding the individual's repository of responses. Pursuing roles in the realms of play, games, individual and team sports, music and dance, reading and similar discovery, travel, study and development of academic skills, and close interaction (particularly hands-on) with nature are some of the most valuable methods for maximizing the arsenal of coping mechanisms. Someone's instant discernment that a dog chasing pigeons would fly off the roof displays a critical level of data analysis. Not realizing the futility of trying to stop the pet showed the limits of my repository and processing capability. An emotional response guarantees self-destruc-tion if completed. Fortunately, Gerry had prepared in all the important ways to save me from a fatal decision. His path to promoting and bring-ing to fruition a miraculous potential defies explanation by the most significant thinkers. Most of what we do is antithetical to that process. The list of inhibitors is lengthy (fast food, poisoned water, television, unbridled capitalism, poverty, prejudice, racism, cowardice, arrogance, and insecurity, to mention a few).

(Letter from Aunt Elsie about events in Harlem in 1943)

344 Manhattan Ave
Apt 5A
NY. 26 NY.

Dear Helen & Bro.

Received your letter also money. Have Helen and Pat ready by the 31st of July. I'm going to bring the cow boys home and get Helenlory and Pat. I am feeling as well as can be expected after losing my dog. Jim just bought me another dog. But it is too young to take away from its mother yet. Kids are well and enjoying themselves. Jim's Cousin took them over to his house and his wife and the kids had a little party. They took them to see the soldiers. Mary is crazy about Kenny. We call him droopy drawers and Gerald sass-box and they answer to their names. Kenny is just like an old man but he still thinks he's a bird jumping off tables and radiators. They are really enjoying themselves. I just got them some ice cream and they are eating it now and they ain't thinking about bed. They don't want to come home. They miss the dog so much. But they was tickled pink when I took them to see the new puppy. Well so long.

from Nloris

P.S. Just got a letter from Thomas, and he got his gold cross from me on his birthday. His wife told him how good Bro. was to her.

On August 1, 1943, a race riot exploded in Harlem before returning home. It began because the police shot Robert Bandy, a colored soldier. While arresting a Negro woman, Officer James Collins reacted when Bandy intervened. Robert struck Officer Collins, and then kept walking, refusing an order to halt. Rumors spread—a bullet between the shoulder blades killed a soldier protecting his mother. Aunt Elsie let GT and me climb onto an exterior fire escape, watching people fighting. This opportunity for reckless behavior was our last. Grownups battling it out looked small, viewed from high as if merry kindergarteners were dancing. Combatants appeared nondescript since most men wore hats and jackets. On seeing the fighting, we reacted by dropping half-bricks, trying to clobber unlucky souls. After a short period, Daddy arrived. He pulled us inside, holding his belt. After sound beatings, we hustled out of Harlem by subway to Penn Station for trains to Philly. I escaped falling off a tall building in New York and joined a riot! There were more narrow escapes in coming of age. An example was a Saturday afternoon when a fishing lure thrown on a casting rod came within an eyelash of blinding me.

Becoming Athletes and Sportsmen

Before junior high school, we only did athletics for casual play. Our parents expressed little interest in amateur leagues or local teams. We didn't get encouragement to support entering organized athletics. Chas. P., though, had been an accomplished baseball player. That was his passion. He abandoned aspirations to play in the Negro Professional League, opting for construction work and marrying Mom. (Her grandfather refused to let her marry a ball-player.) On weekends, he taught us baseball skills. After playing semi-pro, there had to be visions of his sons as professionals. Since I was born "wrong-handed," he converted me to throwing right-handed. We practiced catching while he pitched, but only because it pleased him. Practicing went on, but we did not wish to join organized baseball. We were more capable than most but varied our activities. Coached by local college athletes interning at playgrounds, we did soccer, wrestling, or gymnastics every summer. The first intern taught gymnastic high-bar routines. Foot speed, a foundation for most sports, made for standout performances in different communitywide competitions. Not immersing in baseball, football, or basketball allowed us time to investigate wild food resources throughout unpopulated territory past our town's borders.

Our next discovery mission was exploring forests, grasslands, and streams while hiking in unexplored areas. We often trotted from Barnard Street, heading in new directions striking our fancy. Those days were before the regional government exploded. Open spaces, rolling hills, farms, and woodlands extended for miles. Black Angus bull attacks were frequent challenges whenever crossing horse corn patches or grassy pastures. The ill-tempered behemoths charged at intruders. We confused them by split-ting, separating objects in their field of view, and stopping them. The rural countryside had many swamps, creeks, and lakes. Specific locales offered eels or frog legs starting at town boundaries. As dedicated woodland Indian lore fanciers, we spent most summer waking hours investigating uncultivated lands and practicing local Native hunter-gatherer skills gleaned by reading. We hunted or fished when not trapping small animals. Longbow hunting expertise came with practice, including using handcrafted spears, throwing knives, constructing animal snares and traps, and learning how to shoot a 22-caliber rifle and a shotgun. We had read James Fenimore Cooper's *The Last of the Mohicans*, *The Deerslayer*, and *The Pathfinder*.

While committing to running for traveling, we had equal enthusiasm for exploring nature's wealth. Those pursuits were fun, provided food and modest income selling animal skins, and engendered an incentive to conserve time by jogging round-trip. I matured when able to capture dinner with GT.

Introduction to GT's interests started with a twenty-minute run to bag sunfish in the Township dam's rushing overflow. We relied on bare essentials, twine, hooks, and worms dug from the moist ground by the waterway using sticks. We passed pleasant ideal summer afternoons yanking panfish from pools under Chester Creek's bridge leading to West Chester's nearest reservoir. Snagged fish catapulted amidst kids jumping while bellowing. Soon, we adopted more studied methods to hook dinner. We researched angling to learn how species lived. Other children kept pursuing their quarry using rudimentary tools. We formerly waited for bites, yanking so hard that the bright-scaled creatures sailed onto the muddy bank. No one finessed catches. Soon, I worked odd jobs (mowing lawns, yard work) to buy manufactured gear and magazines for studying proven angler methods. There were large perch, but how do we entice them to bite? Oversized sunnies don't stay long if there's commotion from children throwing stuff or yelling.

Prime motivation became locating "hogs." Learning their behavior from the pros was the best path. Research reading *"Field and Stream"* or *"Sports Afield"* magazines provided information. Various writers told expert stories about defeating crafty trophies. Armed with their accounts, we identified habitats for dominant aquatic animals. We eased alongside Chester Creek's flow, invading farmland. Penetration into pastures, avoiding landowners, and harvesting one-pounders hidden in deep pools behind miniature falls maintained freezer stocks. The effort to strip downstream regions succeeded.

My role was spotting hiding places for pulling out lunkers. One quiet evening, we relaxed as Gerald announced completing our quest. That milestone finished working Township Line Reservoir's effluent. Excellent catches now lived beyond barbed wire-topped chain-link fencing. We graduated from snatching no-limit perch to bagging large bass inside secured grounds. It's more challenging since off-limits signs populate this watershed's border. It looked easy for poachers to get busted by patrols. Our determination to tap new resources triggered midnight expeditions. Unrivaled preferred ventures became traversing four miles to the spillway undetected. Traveling undetected by cops or sheriffs through Devil's Hour into dawn took great stealth. Then, we managed forays violating restrictions but not drawing 24/7 guards' attention. We had to return, ready for school, without anyone knowing. We race there and back to arrive on time. After midnight, we crawled out our third-story bedroom window on a 12-inch wide ledge to Jerry Harmon's roof. Neither our parents nor authorities discovered this practice. We traveled unseen along Philadelphia Pike's recessed edge after clearing alley networks! Early morning operations encountered no traffic.

Restricted waters promised largemouth bass, smallmouth bass, and one-pound crappie. Our hauls measured up to the accounts in magazines. We advanced beyond worms to artificial bait and, through trial and error, proved lures that work in the dead of night. We gained intimate knowledge of fish and small game as resources and, from many forays, found sure spots for catching any resident species.

Civic leaders announced a summer tournament in 1950, allowing reservoir access for a single day. It bodes well because we know how to catch resident species! We spent many nights plying those shores, and we were the only commoners who went there. Today's wealthy, influential people always had exclusive, protected hunting and fishing, mimicking nobles' medieval lifestyles. As far as we figured, clandestine forays compared to Robin Hood outwitting Nottingham's Sheriff. Our eagerness to enter that sultry afternoon defied restraint. Any prizes, we reasoned, were ours.

We had already learned where to locate big fish and what attracts them.

We had success casting Pflueger's #2 Luminous Tandem Spinners. They were ceramic, featuring razor-sharp miniature grappling hook tailing. Glow-in-the-dark paint-coated wings release light underwater, fluttering and swimming deep with wiggling feathered tails. Catches often come down to casting into the right spot. No one else is using site-tested bait. There's no sleeping as the competition approaches. After the jog along Paoli Pike, turning down Airport Road, we settled into a familiar spot, waiting for their starting signal. A fire truck's siren blasted to begin seconds before the worst disaster occurred. Gerald cast long over the wind-blown, rippling water. The line tangled on the reel, back lashing at whip-cracking speed. We both ducked away from a familiar dangerous phenomenon.

Then, a sharp white-hot pain flashed across my left eye as if stabbed by our handmade spears. For the greatest possible horror, a treble hook slammed into my face! Having a 6-inch faux ornament hanging from my eye was shocking. Screams echoing anguish emitted, skimming over the lake. They continued at length, not diminishing or pausing from panic. My immediate assumption concluded total sight was gone! The dangling lure pulled at skin folds like costume jewelry piercings. I was sure and screamed, "My eye! My eye! I can't see! I can't see!" Wails spilled forth until Gerald said to open them and stop. (I had shut both eyes as tightly as possible.) A prong speared the upper and lower eyelids, stapling them. What were the odds? Distress from wounds was imaginary, hurting less than the tetanus vaccine medics shot in my arm right there.

Though a gathered crowd thought it justified, such a childish response grew embarrassing. So, I pulled myself away from unwarranted despair enough to feign bravery before a concerned audience. I've enjoyed plenty of luck, both misfortune and good fortune. The medics on duty rejected removing something sharp near my eye. Firefighters and nurses refused to snip the tine's shaft, then pull it free. We saw different-sized snips in their toolbox and asked them to do it! An ambulance rushed me to Biddle Street Memorial Hospital. The emergency entrance required pushing through a gaggle of curious people. Several medical personnel marveled at my freak predicament, no doubt providing the subject for their dinner conversations.

Nurses expressed amazement at a boy so near losing his eyesight. It either astonished or horrified them. An hour ago, I was a terrified kid, and now, my thinking shifted to treatment costs. The last thing I needed was people calling me "One-Eyed Kenny" until I died. That was a total disaster! I felt anxious over wasting scarce funds in a backdrop of fussing emergency room personnel. Voluminous chagrin haunted me for a while. Given family economics, self-loathing didn't end. That comes with an advanced understanding of forces at work, including dealing with societal institutions, personal history, and systemic victimization. It wasn't near to becoming my state of consciousness. The struggle to grow up remained to do something positive and significant.

The same psychological complex developed when subjected to a presumptive "impact" tonsil removal. For someone that young (four years old), it caused a most painful separation from my parents. Those were sad hours, feeling abandoned. Mom's comforting protection proved no longer immutable. Doctors prescribed a tonsillectomy after failing to identify why I was shockingly skinny with water blisters spreading over me. Any effort not to scratch or break them was a losing proposition. We wrapped them in clean rags for absorbing discharges as a precautionary measure. If they popped under wraps, loose skin lay empty until drying into a crusty, itchy scab. We tried various ointments for treating scabs. Adding wheat germ to breakfast cereal was the most satisfying. No treatments had noticeable effects, but eating wheat germ is good.

Pre-tonsillectomy hospitalization turned devastating once Mom departed that night. There was a big insecurity problem in seeing only whites on staff. I'm afraid to be alone with them, no matter how mightily they try to comfort me. I recognized their heroic efforts. Yet, it was a frightening prospect! It's impossible to fathom their caring. There is no basis for trusting any white person for safety or personal welfare. To that point, no positive interactions had ever occurred involving white people where I could see it. Jews were the exception. Fear was a condition Jim Crow set in motion and reinforced. Reasons existed to distrust whites because no welcome contact occurs outside our community. The evening descended, creating anxiety that I'd never see another morning. There was only hope my family would return for me while crying myself to sleep with eyes fixed on where mom exited. Late into the evening, nurses paid extra attention to helping me dismiss fear. It's laying there locked on, blaming myself for being sick—needing surgery. I was the cause.

Mom arrived before they wheeled me in for anesthesia. Ether was the primary substance used. Instructions were to count backward, starting at 21. Drops of chemicals fell into gauze placed over the nose and mouth. On reaching 11, each number flashed as a picture in my drug-controlled brain. Figures formed as red or yellow dots on a brown-orange circular disc, looking like an Ishihara color blindness test. A pungent acidity bubbled as static electricity tingled through me. The multicolored puzzle spun, gathering speed and pulling me into bottomless darkness. A severe sore throat woke me. Sensory impressions of anesthetic drugs repeated over thirty years as a prominent instigator for reoccurring nightmares. They were "bone cell" dreams because whenever I awoke from them, empty feelings of invasions draining leg bone cores, altering me in invisible unexplainable ways, lingered. Pungent ether vapors flooding my brain assaulted my olfactory senses, inducing visions forming numerals sweeping into swirling hallucinations. Awake, I felt anesthesia's effects in both legs' marrow, propelled by an adrenaline rush. After a frightening night surrounded by pale-faced strangers, experiences launched a repetitive dream.

Eight years after enduring that tonsillectomy, a menacing triple-barbed fishing lure flapped against my left cheekbone. In a hospital bed, after the object's removal, wasting hard-earned funds on something avoidable, I continued costing sizeable extra money through sickliness and being accident-prone. I saw myself as flawed and guilty, with a keen awareness of costs. Why didn't they clip the piercing and use a medicated Band-Aid? They administered the tetanus vaccine there. The doctor wanted me to stay overnight. They treated me nicely, bringing a great lunch. When the medical personnel left, I slipped on pants under the sheets—eased out of bed, and walked out the front door. A few stitches aren't good reasons for hospitalization. I proceeded, wary on the streets, afraid they'd send the cops, forcing me to return. Nobody asked for the story at home, so I said nothing. We didn't care who won the grand prize in our first contest from that point forward, and competition existed only with our quarry.

Sharpless' 1.6 square mile estate to the northeast was great for outdoorsmen forays. Their holdings encompassed more acres than encompassed West Chester. The property had an English-style Manor House built in 1907 by Philip M. Sharpless (1857-1944), an inventor manufacturing Sharpless Tubular Cream. The Sharpless family had been prominent since 1750. Their estate spanned an idyllic tree-covered country setting. The property made a perfect domain for proving ourselves as practitioners of native survival techniques. These "royal forests" contained animals to shoot or snare for meat or fur, and hills surrounded three stream-fed lakes with canoes. Conveniences for wealthy owners provided wonders for us. Since marshy shorelines were overrun with giant bullfrogs, their legs were ubiquitous in our diet.

Bow hunts brought rabbit meat to the dinner table. We trapped mink, weasels, and martins, bagging fur in the winter to sell. For our prime pursuit, we fished there year-round. There was an endless amphibian supply during summers. Sharpless clan members never appeared but hired wardens guard the estate to prevent poaching. They harkened back to Verderers (judicial officers) in English royal manors. By being woods savvy and outrunning people, any efforts chasing us failed. Success harvesting wildlife established a love of nature and appreciation for pursuing a minimalist lifestyle. It was an essential contributor to personal characteristics melding with social, economic, and political pursuits as well as being an outdoorsman and lifetime runner. Kids around town called Gerald "Nature Boy." It fits as a label, for he concentrated his boyhood development on embracing nature and becoming an accomplished woodsman. His approach was to read, study, and practice indigenous people's and frontiersmen's subsistence methods.

James Fenimore Cooper's novels were biblical essentials. Gerry would act once he researched proven techniques for accomplishing goals. The "Nature

Boy" nickname came from *The Boy with Green Hair,* a movie screened in 1948. That same year, Nat "King" Cole popularized "Nature Boy." The song stayed #1 on Billboard's charts for eight weeks that summer. The film was a parable about the ravages of war, its impact on children, our world's future—and the necessity to change the path of human destiny. As the younger brother, his status impressed me. The behavior creating his notoriety raised wild lands to greater importance for me. Those places were a fountain of deep-rooted appreciation for him. The natural land's forces bring spiritual renewal. (Valuing research for preserving the natural environment formed his foundation for compatible life pursuits. He graduated Phi Beta Kappa in Nuclear Physics from Drexel Tech, specializing in solar energy development.) He freed himself from Jim Crow to the greatest extent possible, setting his humanity beyond spiritual penetrability.

IZDEAL

Violent self-defense is the destroyer of self-doubt and creator of self-doubt (for the other). It frees both from ultimately destructive needs.

Both of us were ready to pursue discovery into properties past West Chester State Teacher's College. A freeway opened four miles south, bypassing WC. We longed to know the details of those lands before the new highway. Sweltering heat stalled under clouds, then breaking into sunshine. We recognized that this day promised no rain and gave no respite from soaring temperatures. It was visible in the wavering air, shimmering above shoulder height. Today we carried full army canteens next to Bowie knives. If hungry, foraging in vegetable plots sufficed. Raw corn, onions, carrots, and ripe tomatoes' flavors exploded with the addition of salt from our pockets. Whitewashed huts formed a compound on the right, emitting the sweet smell of manure-filled mushroom beds. Animal compost vapors infused the steam from cooking mushrooms, bringing visions of Grammuddy's (our grandmother) cannery labors. She came from work smelling like the warm, moist, fertile bedding for spawning delicious fungi. To our family's delight, she supplied more mushrooms than we deserved to eat.

When the asphalt curved due east, turning its tail to the passing sun, we continued into a dense, evergreen wooded parcel. Daylight dissolved fast as air-cooled by 10 to 15 degrees upon entering thick groves. Overpowering terpene molecules helped chill the shade, providing welcome relief from the early heat when walking into the country. Sound muffled inside tree alcoves harmonized a dark coolness. Eerie changes added to impressions of invisibly silent moving. We chose a tunnel path formed by wind-bent stunted firs, bowing to sun power, accommodating kindred species. Relentless resident game footsteps wore crisscrossed trails under canopies. We noted places for traps to harvest fur skins for sale.

We observed caution emerging from our pine tree soundproof chambers formed by undisturbed pine needles layered underneath surface-enveloping branches. Steps into light hit as if forcing wide a vacuum-sealed compartment. Then, it was getting sucked into green pastures. Moisture puffs rose from wet ground, evaporating last night's drenching rain. Machine-gun fire thunderstorms swept through on lacey-stringed lightning, dropping bucket-load showers. In loving the outdoors, we transformed into "Pathfinders," moving through gullies and streambeds, crossing tracts bracketed by "No Trespassing" or "Private Property" signs hung to scare obedient intruders. It doesn't deter Lenape ancestors' ghosts. On rare occasions, farmers spot and threaten us. Sometimes they send their dogs, though never slowing or stopping our discovery treks. As we slipped undetected, crossing early crops and grazing lands, approaching road construction, a distant popping sound came closer. That we picked up no regular cadence drew speculation. Increasing noise beckons, continuing, although there are no worthy discoveries. No inviting habitat remained, stretching to the bypass.

Four hundred forty yards ahead, a restaurant stood in a hollow formed by the northbound off-ramp from Route 202's overpass. A maggot-filled garbage heap festered in the brush behind this hamburger joint's construction, ending at a clearing's edge to the northeast. "202 Drive-in," their handmade poster said. Uncompleted exposed framing extended the building into cemented cinder block layers. As we crept toward popping sounds, we discovered a crouching man firing a .22 at rodents scrambling on his refuse heap. Targeted giant steel-gray rats came into focus.

We made a disturbance so as not to startle him, and avoided emerging with his gun thrust in our faces. He owned the drive-in with Cormay, his wife, and he demanded we use his given name. Mike was Gerry's size—welterweight or light-middleweight class. A broken-nosed, battered face displayed prizefighter toughness. A complete set of teeth were there. He topped out a muscular tad short at five feet five, his bald patch framed by sparse brownish hair wisps. He was personable—talkative, outgoing—prone to mischief. This guy stood out as blasting without aiming. Hails of bullets don't discourage voracious rodents one iota. As their comrades fell, they never hesitated to devour chosen morsels, including live wounded fellows. He offered us a turn with the rifle, smiling too quickly. To us, it wasn't genuine, much too sly, intended to deceive. Gerald started plugging vermin, not missing a shot, even though the gun was inaccurate. He had a .22 with a peep sight, so we shot at an expert level. Mike suggested entering the building for a milkshake.

He narrated a drive-in tour. As we readied to leave, Izdean offered Gerry a job. It's easy to see there wasn't a need for me, a seventy-pound preteen. Gerald started helping to do construction and kitchen duties. I felt awkward, excluded, and of no value. Soon, I also worked there. It was cleaning up, operating a potato peeler, or cultivating flower beds framing walkways. It constituted working for nothing, but I ate more hamburgers, fries, and milkshakes than average. The buttered pecans in the walk-in freezer eased my resentment about the meager pay. They were expensive and delicious, so I kept both pockets full.

Mike enjoyed goofing around at other people's expense. From professional boxing, he exhibited a mean streak. Izdeal delighted in bullying—trying to diminish victims—to get them pissed. He insisted on acting out grandiose demonstrations, treating GT better than me. Abundant transparent behavior impressed me as silly. His specialty was ordering me to labor without breaks. What he intended was no mystery, but we never grasped its humor. Why did he think it was funny? Nothing about his comic shtick ever rose to more than pitiful. On occasions where Cormay protested a stunt, it pissed him off—threatening her. We expected conditions to improve over the summer, but they never did. His surname was Izdean, but we used part of it, referring to him as "Izdeal," as a reflector for noting questionable ways by our determination. We used a nickname as enduring reminders of degrees to which someone warrants acceptance, trust—or not. A telltale warning flashed in his tiny pupils. If you came close, light reflected, picturing windows into a residence for cruelty.

Mike always talked under his wife's clothes, grabbed her ass, and caressed her tits in front of us. He prodded GT to do the same whenever she wore shorts or halter tops. His demonstrable need to embarrass and humiliate disturbed us. Threats and testing were a concern, frequently accompanying his devious suggestiveness toward her. Maybe he assumed that our thinking worked as his, especially a 16-year-old like Gerald. Cormay was a gracious woman who loved decorative displays and flower arrays. We had nothing but respect for her. After a month, Izdeal ordered me to plant a new peony patch. That was his only effort to please her. Beaten down by a scorching day, he whispered for her to fetch three iced drinks. He excluded me. I observed her feeling terrible, accepting what her husband wanted. If she looked upset, she better not act against his commands. We recognized his penchant for volatility, including abusiveness. He directed them to recline in lawn chairs, enjoying refreshments and ordered me to keep working by voicing detailed planting instructions. The air temperature was intolerable. There was no shade. To work, digging soil in smothering conditions, bordered on insanity! In that temperature and humidity, being outside defied sound judgment! His willingness to stand there ordering me was puzzling, pointing to his deranged mind. For another thing off-kilter, he spewed orders embellished with harsh criticisms.

Flower placements provided a phony reason for Mike's anger. He stooped, pointing to particular spots where new plants belonged. I stalled there, hugging the shovel, as he screamed instructions filled with abundant profanity. He said, "It's not right, you stupid little son of a bitch! Why in the hell can't you do it? You're the dumbest fucking asshole I've ever seen!" This moment was the first time I ever got called a son of a bitch, or cursed at in any way. My parents never swore for any reason.

The blinding noon glare washed over me. It reflected intense heat off his balding head while kneeling, his lips near to kissing the earth. That was bravado to show an earnest project connection. Such unwarranted treatment shocked and hurt. Less than five feet tall and weighing seventy pounds, I qualified as puny. Seconds passed before my shovel's blade followed a solar beam's brilliant course, plunged, then rebounded off Izdeal's reflecting bare scalp.

As an undersized kid, I lacked the strength to execute a lethal strike. (Not that I tried to kill him. My purpose was connecting.) It required power to bring the curved edge into his neck, decapitating him (as involuntarily visualized). The recoil off his bald pate showed my best effort and didn't crush him as desired. It wasn't a swing arcing in a man's hands or sweeping, simulating an executioner's ax to sever his offending noggin. Scenes unfolded in my mind's eye as an out-of-body experience.

Motion occurred in slowed frames seeing myself as a dispassionate observer standing alongside an unfolding event. Everything else stopped. Birds had their songs suspended in air. Sweet notes froze in the blue skies above, forming musical compositions hanging by their ethereal elegance. Cormay sat immobile beside my brother as if frozen in disbelief. No wind or traffic noise penetrated as tight vehicle lines rushed past a few yards away.

The drama played a thousand times over in a few moments. Too weak to make complete contact, I "choked up" on the handle to raise it, which reduces efficiency. It rebounded similar to a trampoline when the flat head connected. Strange that Izdean's scalp didn't burst open, splattering blood and wetting plants and soil. That I could run to Barnard Street before an ambulance arrived is more than reasonable. Because of age, size, and his abuse, I'd avoid punishment.

Reality returned when he remained conscious enough to stand up, recovering himself. I dropped the shovel to run, not gauging the damage.

Surrounding sounds restarted, puncturing the rage-induced world's silencing upon stepping onto Route 202. Safety at home waited over two scared miles away. Yes, he chased me, but upon reaching the highway, people were present. What could he do? While I raced along 202's gravel shoulder in tears, it wasn't long before his banged-up 1940's Ford pulled alongside. He apologized for his mistreatment, begging me to stop and return. Ice cream offers sounded childish, a naughty boy trying to make up for mistreating another child. He anticipated trouble if I arrived home, distraught, to tell Daddy.

My legs kept rolling and each stride increased satisfaction from standing up against abuse. I weathered an assault and protected myself by responding with aggression. Afterward, this incident remains a metaphor for self-defense. "When your tolerance gets breached, pick up a shovel, and bust 'em in the head."

Later, Mike rang our doorbell, apologizing in the aftermath. Head bandages were visible under an unaccustomed hat; I didn't care. What a valuable lesson in growing to understand the world! He drove in town at times, and whenever coming within hailing distance, he sought my recognition. For me, he was not worthy. Once showing vulnerability to someone, they lose me if they take undue advantage, earning shunning forever. There's no hesitation in taking risks to discover a decent person. I never feared suffering abuse or betrayal, but it only can happen once.

My social life changed after Gerald enlisted in the Navy, and his direct positive influence ceased. Following him had allowed for substantially avoiding systematic racism's designs and its instigated mistakes. My maturing moved me onto a common cohort male path when GT's guidance no longer prevailed. Our unsolicited burden was struggling to survive constant negative encounters with racist individuals and ever-present attacks of Jim Crow practices, preventing realizing self-worth. To a great extent, adverse social conditions deny entering acceptable pathways to valued societal positions. Many channels point to terrible outcomes without consistent, rewarding avenues to follow. Sinister cultural features act to dissipate energy and suppress efforts to improve. They maintain racial segregation and frequent indeterminate contact, suffering discrimination. I'd go to prison (or worse) unless I found other workable institutional supportive intervention (religion, military, or education).

CHAPTER
TWO

Beginning and Early Transitions—Neal

Our lives are spiritual because we are
runners in the greater sense.

Neal:

I arrived as a West Chester High School student after six years at Episcopal Farm School. Mine is a personal story of childhood struggle, survival, and achievement that other kids didn't experience. It's a complicated journey, with the early years affected by World War conditions. Wartime made up an innocent, unsettled period. Most of the time, I lived with my mother in Chester, Pennsylvania's checkerboard cityscape of European ethnic enclaves. Different ethnicities dominated neighborhoods on my daily journey to1st-grade at Fifth Street Elementary. Extensive sections were Polish, German, and Negro. Stints in that port city interspersed with periods of living with the Fryes, my adopted "grandparents." They were located eight miles out on Highway 252. Their house was on Providence Road near Baltimore Pike in

Media, Pennsylvania. Experiences in Media were fantastic and nurturing in significant ways! Mr. Frye was a model of male strength, stability, and valuing human kindness. My adopted grandparents and their neighbors supported me in every way imaginable. As a young child, I was eager to learn everything.

Adults read to me non-stop. They doted on me so much, and with my mother teaching me, I entered elementary reading books and writing sentences. These supporters were hell-bent on sending me into the world as an avid reader. Unexpected skills sent teachers to verify my ability. During her Chester Heights Primary School reading class, I remember the first teacher, Mrs. Willis, saying, "Put down the booklet and turn the page. What does it say?" "It says, 'Johnny has the dog, and here comes the cat,'" I responded. When flipping pages, Mrs. Willis asked, "What are you doing, looking at the pictures?" I said, "No, I'm reading." She instructed, "Turn the page and tell me what it says." I said, "Johnny likes the cat." Mrs. Willis concluded I read above that book level and needed advancing.

For the last half of that school year, after staying in Delaware County, Unc brought me to West Goshen, where his place straddled West Chester's boundary. (The early part of that school year was in Chester.) Since starting primary education, schools were similar. I thrived on competition, throwing either hand up to answer every question or pestering teachers with meaningful inquiries. There weren't personal or social problems, but sometimes, enthusiastic classroom dominance was considered borderline disruptive behavior. More than probable, boring slow-paced lessons caused those reactions. They moved me from 2nd to 3rd grade and into 4th-grade reading, and teachers stationed me in front for reading to classes. When kids talked or didn't pay attention, I told teachers on them, encouraging them to take responsibility for keeping order and making other children stay focused.

Despite an unsettled existence outside school, it felt good to be sharp, skipping 2nd grade while advancing two reading levels. So I stayed in West Goshen with Unc for another year through 3rd grade. During this period, the school was great! Adopted grandparents' support continued in West Goshen, with Uncle Coty and Aunt Jessie taking the reins. That Unc "rode the rods," as they say, during the Great Depression proved a boon. He gained street knowledge and then shared it with family children. Other uncles contributed to rapid early development while Mom worked multiple jobs, but even then, her support prevailed. She remarried before my 4th grade started, and we moved to Thornton, nine miles south. At Glen Mills Elementary, serious competition arrived, and she was determined to be top in the class. Madelyn was her name, and she was driven to vie for perfect grades. Our connection focused on beating each other, so both of us thrived. That was my initial exposure to an ever-heightening classroom competition, and I liked it.

Mom's Thornton relatives included a gaggle of cousins near my age. Connections with my stepfather's family swelled our group that much more. With close family so near, I felt secure for the first time. Mom's full-time presence indicated we wouldn't move soon. Of course, my brothers became long ensconced at Episcopal Farm School (EFS), an academic-oriented boarding school off Route 100 north of West Chester. It sustained a small student body of 110 boys. After mom remarried and had security, I was slated to be there later. Family adults considered it best to have her third son (me) spend his pre-teens and teens at the boarding school.

Experiences with daily exercise occurred through efforts to earn candy, ice cream, soda pop, and extra food money. In those days, riding on the local milk truck delivering was a typical kid's hustle, bringing in a few coins. I finished deliveries fast by racing to and from customers' houses. Afternoons passed playing and buying sweets. The most consequential job, however, was exercising neighborhood dogs. I ran them to Cheyney State, a nearby Negro College occupying Bob Cheyney's former farm, for a nickel each. It was the earliest of the Historical Black Colleges and Universities. I ran the dogs east on Thornton Road, then north on Cheyney Road, going another mile to the campus. Acres of idyllic landscaped grounds were perfect for letting dogs play free. There was sizeable demand, as neighbors knew I liked handling pets. Several animals needed to exercise four or five afternoons each week. Amazing things happen because of exercising people's pets. It's not only getting conditioned by running four miles round trip, but leading dogs made effortless fun! During this practice, I met Bill O'Shields, the Cheyney Wolves track coach. He counts as my initial track coach. O'Shields saw me jogging often enough to start conversing. He was puzzled seeing me. Even alone, I'd head over to while away afternoons watching his athletes undergo demanding workouts. There were two national-class sprinters. Walter Womack drew particular attention. He combined sprinting and 440-yard dash training. Coach O'Shields was ahead of his time, leading his profession in designing and teaching sprinting techniques. I didn't know this, but the team's training regimen fascinated me. They mixed slow-distance training with repeated sprints and sprint starts. Womack's workouts were extensive, more intense than others. Tall, slender, and muscular, he did effortless sets of sustained sprints. One day in August 1948, watching practice, I noticed the Coach wore a colossal belt buckle with five large circular rings over the words "1948 Olympics." I asked, "Where did you get that?" That's when I discovered that O'Shields coached the 1948 U.S. Olympic sprinters. He explained his long history of developing world-class athletes. His sprint accomplishments extended back to Tuskegee College in 1930s Alabama. Coach O'Shields educated me about national-level coaching through many conversations, naming a string of world-class sprinters. Mozelle Ellerbe, his Tuskegee sprinter, won the 1938 and 1939 National Collegiate Athletic Association (NCAA) 100-yard sprint championships in 9.7 seconds. WWII meant there were no 1940 or 1944 Olympics. In 1940, Ellerbe won Penn Relays' 100-yard dash in 9.6 seconds. Ellerbe's and others' careers were casualties of worldwide conflict, postponing global athletic competitions. Because of his openness and accommodation, I greatly admired Coach O'Shields. A renowned track person befriended me, and because of our relationship, my first EFS English Class paper covered the 1896 Olympic Games. (His legacy continues with Cheyney Pennsylvania State University dedicating the Bill O'Shields' track stadium.) In September 1948, after summer ended, they enrolled me in the boarding school.

There were frequent articles in the *West Chester Daily News* about Coach O'Shields' success coaching sprinters. The press usually referred to him as "the cagey coach." That made me also refer to him as a "cagey coach." He heartily laughed whenever I said "Cagey Coach O'Shields" before asking him a question. I imagine it seemed strange and funny coming from an appreciative little kid. Our relationship grew much closer due to an incident at the college gymnasium during my first Christmas vacation home from EFS. It was a freezing day with lots of snow on the ground.

A bunch of guys from the neighborhood and I planned to spend Saturday afternoon playing basketball. The outdoor courts, however, were buried under snow. We decided to see if Cheyney's gym was open. Making our way to the campus trudging through the snow, we found all the gym doors locked for Christmas vacation. Nevertheless, an unlocked window allowed me (the skinniest kid) to get inside and open a side door. We played several half-court games of three-on-three before turning the lights on, which brought campus security to see who was there. In simple terms, six white kids had broken into the gym at the Negro school. Coach O'Shields entered the gym as the security officers were about to call the sheriff and have us arrested. (Fortunately, he lived on campus across from the athletic facilities and decided to walk over and see what the security officers were doing.)

The coach recognized me in the group and told the officer, "I know that boy, so it's ok." So we got no heat! He told them we could continue playing and leave when he finished his office work, secured the building, and went home. He told me he would have opened the gym for us if I had asked. That's the kind of guy he was. The next time I saw him during that Christmas vacation, he invited me to the annual Philadelphia Inquirer Indoor Track Meet at Philadelphia's Convention Hall. We made this a yearly event for the two of us. He picked me up, drove into the city, and treated me to dinner at the Horn and Hardart automat lunchroom on Broad Street downtown. The whole day was a big deal for a young kid living in a country town.

I considered it a memorable bonding experience, almost a ritual event. It felt like the coach took me under his wing and adopted me when it came to running. He did everything possible to educate me and enhance my budding interest in track and field. Everybody knew him at the indoor meets, especially the coaches and the world-class sprinters. The most notable occasions were when coach O'Shields introduced me to Harrison Dillard, hurdles world record holder and 100-meter Olympic champion, and 4 x 100-meter relay champion in 1948, and Barney Ewell, 100-meter silver medalist, and 1948 Olympic 4 x 100-meter relay champion. At the indoor meets, he taught me about the strengths and weaknesses of runners as we watched their races. These were invaluable experiences for any young boy interested in running. I must say that the foundation of my interest in running at the highest level came from my relationship with the "cagey coach."

Transition to Episcopal Farm School

I was put in 5th grade in 1948 though I was only nine years old. EFS was for lads living without fathers—many died in the wars. An Episcopalian priest founded the school in 1918. It incorporated Glen Loch land alongside U.S. Route 30 near Exton, Pa. As a practitioner of strict behavior control and possessor of a strong work ethic, the founder got labeled the "Colonel." That moniker harkened to Napoleon as "The Little Colonel." The culture shock I experienced at the school was immense. While proclaimed essential for learning and growth, firm martial order felt cruel and unsettling. Harsh punishment counterbalanced newly-minted-teachers' sympathetic support. They instilled an ethic of hard work; forced labor is a more accurate description. An excellent teaching staff, promoting high academic performance and teamwork, formed the upside. I found efforts "creating an environment providing context for revealing life's spiritual dimension and cultivating moral values" hollow and overbearing.

Before my arrival, their site grew to over 2,000 acres, a sizeable self-sustaining agricultural enterprise. Each boy made economic contributions by working half days plus full-time one day each weekend, including holidays and summers. Housing comprised eight cottages arranged topping hills near academic buildings above U.S. Interstate 30 (Lincoln Highway). I often sat alone atop Chapel Lane Hill overlooking our demarcated confinement bordering Route 30. There were daydreams of traveling coast to coast through exciting settlements connecting its path in quiet moments away from toiling under harsh supervision. I fought tears and feelings of abandonment all too frequently, wondering if getting the hell out of there would ever come. I longed for freedom, exploring distant cities with endless traffic in both directions. It's the only motorway crossing the country. Geography lessons taught that. I lay hidden by the hill's tall grass when I got beyond feeling forlorn, visualizing future freedom. Warmed by absorbing sunbeams, I saw myself as a free spirit gliding with ease alongside Lincoln Highway, end to end. My imagined start was in Philadelphia, finishing in San Francisco, California—even then, I saw future endeavors connected to running! Passion for feeling physically free by running and the effort that entailed provided a driving force!

(Funny that now the Lincoln Highway, which I wanted to traverse as a child, passes behind my house in Lake Tahoe. It has turned into a bike path we run weekly from May to December! Weird!)

Fifteen internees (my word) occupied each two-story cottage, sleeping upstairs without heat. Housemothers managed each cabin, and academic instructors lived in an area off-limits to us. Together with the college-prep curriculum, we explored time management alongside basic farm practices performing as adults. Church life centered in the stone-hewn Chapel of Atonement, built in the 1920s. Three religious meetings occurred weekly, and staff or guest speakers give Tuesday lectures. There was an entire Eucharist ceremony on Wednesdays and all-hands prayer sessions on Sunday mornings. Attendance at faith gatherings was mandatory. We committed to religious dictates but didn't have to become church members. We were beggars, but residence fees weren't cheap.

The school's founding faith is Episcopalian, so that's their religious orientation. None of us could identify an Episcopalian from a Baptist. All students attended Chapel (assembly) each week. They sent everyone to Whiteland Congregation's worship on adjoining church grounds on Sunday afternoons. The group wore suits or blazers—neat and clean—walked up Chapel Lane to populate weekend services. Steady Bible study offerings, Jesus, and God-talk prevailed, but they did not jam joining down our throats. We were free to choose to undergo baptism.

JC transferred the following year, finishing high school and graduating from West Chester. He never stated being keen on leaving southeastern Pennsylvania's small-town setting, thus limiting his life. Soon, he sought his fortune as a soldier. I could have gained plenty with more of his mentoring. Having Donald helped, for sure. It would have been better, though, if JC stayed. Other teenage relatives lent support but were soon gone as the Marine Corps had priority. Upon landing on the Farm, contact with relatives remaining in Thornton ceased. That help ended.

Any sense of life based on the security of close family connections faded. I felt destiny played a role. There's no scheming or planning an escape because I was supposed to be there. At nine years old, who knew? Really! Unknowable reasons existed for becoming a "boarder" rather than staying at Uncs or the Fryes. There's nothing to figure out when Donald and JC went away. That made it "normal" or "inevitable" since they were doing it! Why should things change? Simple logic kept me going, making sense. A vital realization came over me—my future children aren't living in a world like this!

The first eight years of growing up blurred because of non-stop difficulties without extended families buffering 100 percent. I was too immature to understand shuttling between different homes, plus adopted grandparents. Daily interpersonal contact appeared ordinary. An un-clarified dissatisfaction existed (if I'm aware) between our parents. JC provided any information I got about John. He told the story:

The first housing we had was the Colonial Apartments on Orange Street in Chester, Pennsylvania. We were moving every six months and our dad became an alcoholic. World War II was in full swing. It was all over the newspapers that the Japanese bombed Pearl Harbor. Who knew where that was? Our father was abusive, lazy, and condescending. He was good looking and had a nice singing voice, which easily charms lots of ladies. He made good money building ships at the Chester Shipyard for the war. The first thing he did with each paycheck was buy a new shirt and matching tie. He put them on and came home drunk. He refused to give mom any money. Year after year, it's the same crap! My mother worked her ass off to keep us fed. John (our father) always had a new girlfriend and a new shirt with a tie. Don't forget that during the war most of the men were getting drafted. There are lots of women around without men. With a wife and three kids, the draft left him on the home front as the big man around! He frequently whipped up on me and Donald! Mom, at least, knew how he was and wouldn't let him go near Neal.

One of the bad things about Chester was the water. Down the road about a mile from where we live there's a spring with water coming out of a pipe. John kept some gallon glass jugs for the water in our place. He wanted them kept full. We had to walk down to the spring for water every day. If the jugs weren't full when he got home after work, we got a beating. He gave me his pocket knife and told me to go cut a switch. I thought to myself, "that's one hell of a deal!" I start notching the switches so they easily broke. When they broke he'd say, "Bring me my belt." He used the heavy leather to finish the job. We'd dance around and around until he got tired. He didn't bother Neal because he's the baby. You can't call it discipline. It's abuse! He comes home drunk, reaches into his pocket and gives me a quarter to go buy some Bromo-Seltzer. It's the most popular antacid of the day and my father uses it nonstop. I go to the drug store and bring home the Bromo. Then he pours himself a pint of water, drinks it all down and tells me to go fill the jug. Oh dear mom! She has to put up with a lot of crap! As soon as possible, Donald and I are gone most of the time. We're in the streets somewhere trying to make a little money however we can.

Mom kept Neal a considerable distance from John. I can tell you, she didn't want another child when Neal was conceived. She already had two and, like a hillbilly bastard, John kept insisting on another. He has to have his nookie and get her pregnant. She did everything to prevent it. Nothing worked. The whole family dysfunction was hard to describe with clarity. After Neal's birth, mom worked ironing shirts in the local laundry. She walked to work in Media, Pennsylvania and it seemed like it's 5 miles. We were living in "The Heights" section where she walked down the railroad tracks to work. Mom ironed shirts all day. She had baby Neal, but she couldn't keep him with her at work. It's lucky that she finds Mrs. and Mr. Frye across the street from the laundry. With Neal situated that close to work, mom could see him during her morning and afternoon breaks. That made life feel a bit more normal for him. The Fryes are an old retired couple. They are well educated former teachers that, in effect, adopt Neal. Donald and I are fending for ourselves in the streets and Neal was growing up with the Fryes. Individually, the Fryes are perfect citizens and fit Neal's needs—concerned, gentle, and caring adopted grandparents. Their days are spent joyfully teaching him everything. He's reading newspapers at three and a half years old. They absolutely adore him. He's so lucky to have them! Their attentiveness with Neal makes all the difference in the world for his survival and growth.

Mom married dad because he was good looking and a slick talker. He was a charming hillbilly from North Carolina! She was young and had never been out of Thornton. Her upbringing in Thornton was very much like what Neal experienced at EFS—not much of a life. Nobody in Thornton ever went anywhere. People, particularly girls, made it to 8th grade, didn't go to high school, and never left the area. Dad must have gone there in the '30s looking for work. There wasn't much work in Carolina except for the textile mills and tobacco factories. John's half-sister, named Baker, lived in Thornton. I surmise that he came to Thornton to see his sister and got acquainted with the Smileys. Mom—Mildred May Smiley—was most likely looking for a way to get out of a futureless place. She lived in a house that was built in 1900. You got married to get out of being confined in a small town in those days. Her job was janitoring at Westtown School and she had a brand new 1931 Ford. I still have the papers on it. The first thing John did is got drunk and wrecked the car. He crashed about 14 automobiles in the next few years. I was with him in one of those. He was going along hell-bent on Lenape Road to Lenape Amusement Park 10 miles on the other side of West Chester. We slid off the road into a tree. I was thrown head first into the windshield at 6 or 7 years old. The state police come along and I was hurt and crying. I cried out, "My daddy's drunk! My daddy's drunk! Get me out of here! I want to go home!" Daddy said, "Jacky, Jacky, don't talk like that! You'll get me in trouble!" So he slick talked me! We end up at the courthouse in West Chester. A doctor examined me and they lock him up. I don't remember how I got back home. Some of those cars he destroyed while running moonshine because you have to drive like that. The autos he drove had storage tanks for whiskey underneath the running boards. When I got older, I went down to North Carolina where he was living like a hermit. He was in a shanty in the back of the family property. I guess he cooked good enough to keep himself happy and fat. Every time he got a few dollars it's spent on whiskey. There isn't much more to know about our father.

Any elderly relatives that might help maintain reliable extended family support were dead. Unc, whose real name is Wilmer "Coty" Smiley, kept everyone afloat, taking responsibility and sustaining his strong-willed nephews. Family members called him Unc, but he was more than that. His family-owned a general store and he created a home life, giving us stability. Unc and Aunt Jessie had children, too, and they shared their good fortune.

Moving to Episcopal Farm School was a foregone conclusion when it was time to advance my development. In the 1940s and 1950s, little about boarding school environments impacting youthful innocence was known or understood. Even though many were aware of similar homes portrayed by Charles Dickens's classical writings describing conditions in Victorian England, advocating societal reform, our populace didn't question mid-20th century American renditions. Although it never occurred to us, we lived as indentured servants. As entrapped submissive child workers, we didn't entertain reasons not to be there. Nothing got labeled hardship or injustice. Under the school authorities' punitive eyes, we had no choices. It was a given we'd do our duties without fail or reasoned departure. To psychologically soften physical acts, he's called "baldy" when beyond hearing range. Bald and short, he sports an enormous belly. At gatherings, attending principals promote the school's founding as helping wayward youth (headed toward perverse behavior). That's true for a minuscule number. All in all, experiences were positive enough that appreciative graduates returned as volunteers, giving back to the school.

Most of those guys were like Donald, doing three major sports. He bitched about laboring on crops but saw positives. Status as a jock was his whole thing! That kept him mentally together. His view was, "I'm playing basketball. I'm leading the six-man football squad. I'm breaking school track records. All's good!"

Donald smashed Bob Hessenthaler's ten-year mile record. "He set it in 1938, and I broke it by 37.6 seconds." One hundred twenty-two points scored playing six-man football gave him the East's top-scorer title. When he was 16, he fled to public school.

After graduating from WC, Jack joined the Army. Not long after the Korean War started, he wanted to go over there to fight. But they sent him to a spy training school in New York, and from there, he spent three years in Germany during the Cold War. I think they called him a Morse code interceptor or something. He joined, and I didn't know why. Within two years, Donald entered the Navy. Neither JC nor Donald ever confided their vision.

Child laborers provided the school's solid economic foundation. Every boy toiled, cultivating Katahdin potatoes, milking, maintaining chicken and egg production, hauling hay, and feeding hogs and goats. Our unenviable task was managing sickening, sweet-smelling manure streams from farm animals. Such unpalatable work fell on Nins. Officials overlooked daily indenture requirements compared to written and frequently proclaimed humanistic aims. Our work failed to put money in individual pockets. Boarders can't have bank accounts or share profits. In offering education combined with labor-intensive child farming by teenagers and pre-teens, there's little doubt the founder thought his creation was a righteous home for deprived boys. Otherwise, socially and economically underprivileged children lack a secure, stable environment for healthy development. Administrators use every opportunity to make it known their boys have the potential for achievement but come from challenging backgrounds, making them worthy candidates to reap the benefits of their rigorous college preparatory program. Ordinary life circumstances put such opportunities beyond average reach. This mantra was repeated at gatherings, meetings, and assemblies. I didn't see how those conditions applied to me. If the boarding school was so great, WHY DOESN'T THE HEADMASTER'S SON ATTEND HIS SCHOOL? Instead, Charles Jr. attended Philadelphia's Academy Prep School (PAP). Speculation on why Junior chose PAP leaned toward ensuring everyone received equal treatment. Learning among an inmate population could make certain administrative situations difficult for a schoolmaster's son. Harsh treatment of other boys could cause reprisals.

Junior played baseball, trying out with Major League clubs. He opted to help his father as Assistant Master and future Master. Junior realized in the '60s that continuing youth servitude wouldn't receive local citizens' favor. Society had outgrown indentured servant-supported businesses. So, he sold land to raise money and quit providing cream to Breyers Ice Cream Company. Perhaps, attending Philadelphia Academy Prep, Junior realized he was facing a different future, managing forces socially transforming the 1960s and needing to improve his inheritance. Charles Jr. finds wealthy classmates at PAP who become donors or fundraisers. (He made rich contacts that couldn't happen at EFS.) Reverend Snyder's dream of doing good work and saving underprivileged kids was commendable, but everyone paid through their labor. Their operation wouldn't do well otherwise. Big profits bought more acreage, livestock, equipment, and top-notch faculty.

I followed my siblings, who got summarily written off as "street urchins" during their pre-teens. Following them, I was similarly labeled. Before becoming teenagers, they shined shoes at train stations, meeting Philly commuter trains into the night. They worked the bars after late trains ended, and nobody controlled their school attendance. Mom couldn't change anything as she worked Chester Linoleum factory's night shift and added other part-time jobs. Our father wasn't around and beat my brothers when he was there. Mom ensured nothing happened to me. Those two deserved it, but it wasn't good. Little normalcy existed before any boarding opportunity was "normal" for the Chappell triumvirate.

Eventually, they booted JC out. He holds it's no wonder they gave me such treatment:

I messed it up for Neal. I had never heard of anyone getting kicked out of there. I was insolent, insubordinate and impertinent. I always went out of bounds and questioned what was going on. I was born and raised on the cheap streets of Chester, Pennsylvania. I used to take my shoeshine box and go anywhere I wanted. I know how to make a nickel and how to survive. When I was shipped out to EFS, I was belligerent. Like the "Eastside Kids," I was used to being on my own. I got to West Chester High School because the Father booted me out of EFS. I was glad to get out of there and live in Thornton. I was glad to not be milking cows and lugging racks of potatoes.

After eight years and being sent to toil at a farm labor camp, consider my fortune. Conditions appeared as those described in classical literature decrying homes confining rebellious children. Administration, policies, and practices creating strict religious overtones mirrored an early English industrial revolution approach. This feature included organizing as "forms." Public education systems' grades 7th through 12th corresponded to forms 1 through 6. The youngest residents were under ten. Before entering Forms, they labeled us "Nins," short for nincompoops, because little kids are too unthinking to perform tasks acceptably. Under tight control, I was the youngest on any crew. Everybody's assigned responsibilities occupy every hour: Work, classes, sleep, exercise, showering, dining room, and study hall. Sundays, during morning services, many youngsters dozed off with butts aching on hard-surfaced pews. Form 6 church monitors whacked nappers awake.

Boys from broken families who received court referrals were taken for free as the church patrons paid for it. My mom didn't pay for Jack or Donald, but Harvey contributed for me after she remarried! We were free laborers. (News circulated about pedophiles at "boarders" facilities elsewhere. They kept moving them whenever abuse surfaced. Those issues didn't occur here.) The "Colonel" beat boys while claiming he hurt more than our screaming pleas. That's as far as it went. You started in the workforce, no matter how small. Spring mornings, it was picking peas, with afternoons spent herding. I was too weak to milk cows but I picked Katahdins. You cleaned stalls at any age and pitched hay bales onto flatbeds if they were dry. Two boys grabbed opposite ends of bundles, heaving them.

Nursery jobs tending plants were prized assignments because you didn't do much. If you ever landed nursery duty, you stayed there because you knew the details of plant cultivation. Otherwise there was all kinds of work: Cleaning—dorms (you did every inch) chicken barns, pigsties. We did everything, including "pumping udders." They added hand-milking at 11. The mature stalwarts (6ths) collected milk. Our business sold everything.

Pigs trucked to Habbersetts were processed into bacon, sausage, and an Amish delicacy called "scrapple." Milk products went to the Supreme Company or Breyers ice cream factory. Ten-gallon dairy cans, brimming with unpasteurized milk, got lined by the road in the mornings—thirty-two cans every day, seven days a week. Fat content had to qualify for Breyers through reporting measured levels. Sometimes it had mastitis—not suitable commercially. We ended up drinking it. Raw milk's my favorite, and I drank plenty.

Experiences before leaving mom included delivering milk for products and loose change. In Media, Pa, we siblings begged delivery men for free items. Tuesdays and Thursdays, I helped one driver fill orders. He had me racing to houses delivering bottles. He'd give five cents for the day, asking if I wanted a Lincoln, a Washington, or an Indian. Later, when Mom remarried, we moved close to Homestead Dairy in Thornton. Their delivery man put me to work.

Education activities went from 8 until noon. Showing up for work late was a severe problem. There's no recovering lost freedom because of frequent tardiness. Eventually, all my vacations got confiscated. You can't earn complete summers off anyhow. Half of us go the first 45 days and half the next 45. Those collecting enough demerits stayed there to work. Chucking potatoes qualified as among the least desirable jobs. Digging machines uprooted spud rows. Boxes got set yards apart that were yours. Upon reaching the end, I moved the other guy's container in order to get shorter rows. Such work was dirty, and packed boxes were heavy lifting. We picked spuds by the tons.

Summers brought different crops than cold months. It never ended. You'd think there was less work in winter weather. Hens and silage served as year-round mainstays. Livestock wintering indoors wanted out, but their feed was inside.

Our weekend's greatest fun was breaking the rules by riding sows. Leading rule-breakers fashioned "piggyback belts" using dried pigskin strips. Those who dared climbed into the swine yard and straddled them while looping the strap under their middle. They're smart, immediately banging against the pen's side rails. Gray mottle-haired sows were as big as 200 lbs. They're faster than you'd think. While bucking and spinning, they tried rubbing you off against the rough-cut sideboards.

Like professional bull riders, I avoided getting splinter-filled legs after crashing against rough-cut rails or being tossed into the mud, slop, and putrid urine-soaked manure by hoisting and lowering my legs. Hog shit is the worst. Legs pin-cushioned with wood splinters and coated with shit were real health risks. You don't mess with sows when they have piglets. The last thing you want is a pig-bite bacterial infection! Boars were easy. As "King Swine

Jockey," I collected the most demerits while setting untouchable riding-time records. Livestock numbers included two breeding bulls. They're unique breeds, registered, and worth hefty rental fees. Both bulls commanded top reproduction service fees.

As Chief Herdsman, Ronnie Peete's dad whipped the crap out of me for leading cows to far reaches in the fields. Plus, he reported against me, so they docked more time. His brother hated me for bad-mouthing his dad. Ronnie, though, was a good kid. They had another boy, too. Older guys claimed their mate was Dave's birth father. Rumors painted a former fellow as Peete's wife's lover. Old man Peete thought keeping us in line was part of his job. He stretched his responsibility from taking care of the herd to dogging us. Old man Beecher was kind, though holding a similar position. Few of them ganged up on us. When messing up our tasks, we suffered penalties. Academic instructors were top university grads—Harvard, Yale, Princeton, and Penn. They didn't know what they were walking into by teaching undisciplined souls.

Episcopal Farm School didn't approach being an elite eastern private academy. As a parallel, picture the days of "Boys Town" and near to being an orphanage. Our work ethic proved more rigid than other similar enterprises. We rose at 4:30 am for work, hand-milking over 150 Guernsey's, then on to more tasks tending other animals. Additional backbreaking duties included bare-handed cleaning and composting animal waste. These requirements got categorized as "worst." Stripping cows' teats before sunrise topped the responsibilities. Next was fieldwork. Each became routine soon, so labeling them as "worst" soon came to an end. The entire workload became standard when given sufficient repetition. The idea that some things were worse than others soon disappeared. Over time, I learned that not making our traveling teams hurt worse than getting whippings. Those were changes in outlook occurring while institutionalized.

Depending on our specific jobs, studies melded into accommodating shifts. They taught college prep subjects under strict discipline matching military academies. Unlike public education, there was no "recess." Fieldwork, cleaning barns, and then AP studies after lunch (unless you have night duty). Otherwise, they encouraged various forms of exercise. Everyone had labor and study details, looking ahead to each day's 2 hours of physical training. Six-man football and cross-country were the fall sports, with basketball in the winter and track after February.

My first taste of athletic competition came here. Jack and Donald encouraged running because they enjoyed it. They pushed and pulled me into it. Both of them were runners, with Donald having more success. They understood the advantages afforded those showing talent in athletic participation.

Nevertheless, it was Jack's hell-hole, so he wanted out. They deemed him a troublemaker and were glad to get him to leave. Jack quipped, "I never got very far running because I'm not 6'2" and 140 lbs."

As for sports participation in rural Thornton, folks were deep into Little League and Pony League baseball before being sent away. My stepbrothers starred in high school. Phillies' scouts gave them tryouts in the 1940s when all Pennsylvania towns had clubs. They played for Thornton, with me as junior batboy. Baseball's a big deal. Harvey Martino, mom's new husband, attended games with other locals. Their teenagers went to WCHS and played ball. There's no hardball at The Farm. But, either way, there weren't summers off. When home again, small-town baseball had declined. The Batboy connection lasted a couple of seasons, but ties were severed after I moved away. By 1950, our town was changing. They stopped supporting summer leagues. Like their hallmark pastime, small settlements disappeared, too.

Spending half a summer home was possible with good behavior, if not losing leave because of farm rules infractions. For me, however, it wasn't long before I lost every minute of leave. We got a one-week winter vacation with half the boys taking Christmas week. The rest go home the following week, including New Year's. Farm duties meant only half the troops could leave at one time. Half of us always stayed. Those pulling Christmas duty were home for the New Year. That's how they established balance. A Glen Mills doctor endorsed my having a chest cold on one occasion. Although required, I hadn't reported back from vacation but got seen at the Downingtown High versus

West Chester basketball game. This extended stay increased dorm-mate burdens because others covered my absences.

On January's return, catching hell awaited! The teacher, a tough guy, said in homeroom: "Well, Chappell, did you catch that flu you got exposed to?" He spoke with greater volume as though getting sick avoids farm responsibilities on purpose, implying I disrespected deprived brethren. An extra week of vacation indicates you were not caring. By adding time off, I used seven fellow mates' leave days. Oh, man! That stuff gets guys upset! There's spring break, Thanksgiving, Christmas week or New Year, and partial summers! That's it! Losing days hurts those covering errant holiday absences!

We all wanted to find a sport to express our talent and gain respect. Younger kids seek peer approval by supporting cohorts and upper-level classmen pursuits. Everybody attempted sports. Two role models in extra-curricular activities drove my excelling at whatever I cared to do. Donald had a significant influence. A solid runner, he insisted I work out all the time. His encouragement and protection made success easier. His reputation among older fellows helped, so my getting accepted was in many respects because of him. Donald sought an outstanding athlete's advantages and groomed me. Running and other physical activities gave us freeing outlets each day. As a jock, I received greater appreciation than non-athletes. That steered me toward valuing the sport for sure. Expectations that positive social dynamics apply didn't exist because I hadn't played organized sports. The Thornton Batboy stint and my friendship with Bill O'Shields were it.

Because of Jack's former presence, his era's remaining fellows continued giving me a pass and I got their acceptance. He was a rebel—never a rat. "Guts" and "brains" were essential brokering commodities at our male bastion. There's always acceptance if you have "guts" or "brains." Either quality puts people in a different category. The Chappells had brains and guts to spare from Chester's tough neighborhoods. They diligently showed me "the way." When Mom remarried, both their influences were already gone. They had settled at the Exton farm (school). Donald wasn't with me there long before enrolling in WCHS. Cross-country created more excellent value for me.

Perhaps the administration became fed up with Donald, as with JC. They probably told him to go. Neither commented nor offered information. Both of them signed into military service. Letters arrived every month. With me there, they were off roaming, busy guarding Europe and Asia. Donald became a merchant seaman.

Coming of Age at EFS

An uplifting event happened when the school's best runner, a senior classman, surprised by asking me to join in mile repeats over our dirt 440-yard oval. We wore the affordable Keds sneakers, as spiked shoes were too expensive. Above everyone's expectations, I finished in 6:21.6. As a nine-year-old new arrival, that's an incredible achievement garnering enthusiastic spectator acknowledgment. Those understanding the talent required for a good four-lap time stood impressed. It was a seminal transformative moment, starting my ongoing mission. That performance established being a runner as my defining personal character, setting a life journey in motion. Year after year, running success progressed.

My best dropped to 6:06 as a ten-year-old 6th grader, and then lowered by sixteen seconds (5:50) one year later. Next, they put me in our top group, resulting in a breakthrough 5:15 3rd place against Westtown Prep. That scored three senior high points. The effort provoked unprecedented encouragement from our science master (read "teacher") who was also our coach/trainer. A single person's responsible for physical education. He teaches the sciences and reprimands the hell out of us on principle. An earlier era Farm grad, before an Armed Forces stint, he later went into teaching, taking on mentoring athletes. After I won third against a Quaker preparatory school, and after chemistry students were seated, he began a spiel. "Well, Chappell, it seems perseverance has paid off for you." That's an actual compliment. This guy never tossed congratulations around. His praise defined it as exceptional. His comment stuck. It matters that one cares and gives 100%.

Our former PE instructor was at the Penn Relays when I ran as a WC senior, and he saw our stirring Suburban Relay victory. Our chat, this time, differed from when he was on my case before, but he was sometimes encouraging.

Peer attention made dedicated workouts enjoyable while gaining flexibility and escaping daily drudgery. It's nice to look forward to afternoons. A consuming improvement quest started, and associations became firm between running and everything else. At an unanticipated juncture, athletic ability pointed toward becoming a "way of life." Success followed against interclass competitors and onto varsity competition accompanying maturing. During early Christmas and summer, I hung out with Mom. When she did things with Harvey, our backup plan became staying at Unc's. Days, otherwise bringing the loneliness of a solitary person, turned satisfying by doing long runs. "Boarders" have no friends inside or outside. I enjoyed doing Cheyney's hills and getting Coach O'Shields' tips whenever in Thornton. His explicit routines, increasing speed, and endurance were vital for filling gaps and gaining positivity, improving my stunted outlook. Consistency leads to satisfaction. It increased favorable recognition from most others within farm confinement.

Another insight was embracing unwavering cohort connections. Intragroup fidelity was different at the farm. Above everything, dorm mates are "family." Staff members were parental figures. Compared to other public institutions, holidays and time away was minimal. Days get noted by marking calendars, as occurs in asylums or prisons. Indeed, priceless days get taken away as punishment when breaking the rules. If speaking out of place, arriving late for assignments, or going beyond property perimeters without passes, that warranted losing precious free time. Herein rested brotherhood bonds. I learned the lesson when I was spotted off-bounds, swimming. They stood me in front during morning assembly, pressuring me. I blurted out that I wasn't alone, saying, "Others were there, so why only blame me?" Well, Donald's head dropped while sitting in the next aisle. He rose, staring while yelling "shut up!" It didn't hit me before; you can't snitch. You don't rat out people. It's where my sense of camaraderie was born, if that's the right word. You need complete allegiance, or we'll be in trouble. So, I'd never squeal on anyone again, ever.

Above other values, there's no "ratting." You never jeopardize your compatriots. Our "no ratting" convention ensured shared disciplining. The larger body receives punishment when infractions aren't given to a single perpetrator. This practice of withdrawing privileges hits everyone associated with an offense. It's easy seeing how losses of leave time mounted. They dinged me for frequent rebellions, as well as sanctioning wider misdeeds. Responses administered extend beyond reduced "time away." Sentences were often thrashings with a one-inch wide belt, whipping my ass through thin pajamas at bedtime. In self-defense, many donned two pairs, increasing "padding," dampening blows. For me, there are three pairs whenever lashings come. Administrators considered every norm violation as deserving punitive action. They carried it out, for sure. Their list of violations was short but controlling and unreasonable. Top offenses included not doing assignments, talking back, or disrespecting adults. Tardiness on tasks counted as a significant violation. We couldn't have conversations or make noises that others heard after lights out. More infractions included talking during lectures, falling asleep during Sunday services, and slipping off the grounds to hang out at Exton Crossroads.

Back-talking housemothers seeking compliance or 'shirking' responsibilities guaranteed whippings. Judgments were terrible when they resulted in cleaning animal dwellings. The minor infractions were failing Sunday dorm checks, mostly not dusting rooms. Lateness in attending important occasions hit me big because there were no excuses. Sometimes, they caught me out after curfew. Furlough cuts were the primary administrative response to rebelling. They often resorted to switching, but not by Principals alone. When caught crossing property lines, we lost time available to go home. So much lateness cost me that in spades. Breaking residence cottage restrictions got the same, or maybe a hiding that punishes special misdeeds. If failing inspections, violators could receive more work instead of Saturday or Sunday off. If you talked during homework in the library after dinner, an instructor came up behind you, grinding a knuckle into your head. That was called "eggnogging." They never hesitated to slap the crap out of your head.

The beating frequency per individual was low. Across our general populous, thrashings had wide distribution. That nobody escaped disciplining rendered it a permissible experience. There wasn't cause for feeling persecuted or resentful. Psychological damage prospects don't appear bothersome under such practices. Everyone understood behavioral limits, and subjects knew each penalty. Simply because the population experienced harsh enforcement, discipline executions were fair. It makes little sense to consider punishment bias-based.

Top administrators executed whippings, but each adult could knock our heads off without hesitation. They did it with impunity. They had the final decision on all points. That uneducated and crude hired hands acted as overseers disturbed me. They didn't connect with education. It happened whenever cattle wandered during my field-watching. We knew the tough ones by nicknames. Newer educators were helpful adults but careful about leaning too far toward our favor. Bullies were one thing we didn't encounter. There were no dangerous characters. Nobody ran away or committed criminal acts. Fights were rare, as strange as that might be for minors in confined spaces. We shared confinement, interacting with equal-status fellows. When unsupervised, it's with same-age kids, so mean upper-level students can't bully us. Ever-present concern was over losing summer or holidays off. That's their cruelest, most painful judgment. It created absolute emptiness, even though other people were present around the clock. Realization came right before falling asleep. They gripped my guts when hearing train whistles and seeing the faraway glow of other settlements through the darkened window. Those feelings continued while lying there, puzzled over what in the hell was happening in the world beyond. What would happen if I were out there past distant hills? During silent periods, related ideas surfaced from subconscious reservoirs. They came with heartache attached. Conditions could be worse if I understood life's nascent abnormality. I didn't know it, but Jack did in being here before me. I wondered why life went the same for each of us. Multiple factors of being poor are not satisfactory reasons. It wasn't good! We were born into the wrong world.

There are no overstating outdated Episcopal Farm School experiences. They reproduced conditions characteristic of institutions treating 19th-century English waifs. Monotonous meals lower the quality of life, but every morsel must get eaten. Scarce comforts magnified adverse labor requirements, strict discipline, the administration's corporal punishment penchant, and unyielding judgments. Adolescents in this setting face more substantial peer pressure than in other institutions. No "ratting" was our common standard for maintaining collective security. Teamwork was an ironclad survival condition. Fitting in and bonding with roommates as reliable actors count big time! We learned cohort loyalty—an invaluable code.

Perseverance and allegiance add two team foundations. From those notions and seeing athletics bringing relief from work being something to look forward to daily, I froze them in conscious thoughts. Besides that, acquiring other extracurricular skills was imperative. There were tricks we relied on to help us live better than was intended. We were sometimes able to get extra keys and enter locked areas. That enabled sneaking into pantries to supplement skimpy meals with purloined food. We spent dark hours creeping through buildings. When they bagged someone, they suffered significant repercussions. Anyone accosted got branded guilty. They allowed no questioning or hearings. The biggest thing was not implicating others.

During early residency, my brothers were very helpful, of course. As noted, too soon, Jack and Donald entered military careers. They left me there solely sustained by athletic involvement, and their departures rendered sports more meaningful than ever. Education was rigorous, featuring mandatory study halls for college-level programs that weren't too troublesome. Positive identity continued developing through competing against other educational institutions as regular fulfilling experiences.

Two-hour physical exercise breaks were all the more welcome after tending cows, showering for class, then doing more slaving after midday before attending study hall at night. It was a swath of self-determination in our regimented existence. Their magazine, *The Maroon & Grey*, had a favored feature series called "Then" and "Now." A popular edition covered the 1942 football squad's glory season. Their times were simpler! The best 1954 article addressed public perceptions of our group. "In those days, weekends weren't free. Sandra Barr's parents welcomed several boys at their home on occasions. They treated us as indistinct teenagers." That describes plenty, considering we existed as captives. We did everything possible to appear normal in public. Most "Maroon & Grey" magazine information was current. Who did what, etc.? Outside observers didn't comprehend the broader meaning of socialization inside.

As the middle boy, Donald had a better position to grasp the complexity of circumstances, arrangements, and struggles. He knew the situation before and during our respective tenures, and looking at them shed light on the positive and negative possibilities I faced. They laid the groundwork for learning the ropes for more than remaining afloat, and I succeeded as they couldn't. Donald perceived they battled as orphans without an orphanage's security.

Going into EFS was the next best thing to an orphan's home for us. We are all beggars, but the school wasn't cheap. We earn our keep and mom pays $400 for each of us. That was a lot of money in those days. I think it was worth it to Harvey Martino to have all of us safely out of his way. It also gives our mother some invaluable peace-of-mind. Immediately prior to entering the farm school, we are located in Wallingford close to Media. We are barely surviving there when World War II breaks out. By that time the family was well on the way to falling apart. Soon, Neal's situation was akin to living in foster homes. Lucky for him, some of them aren't all bad. Under the circumstances, one of them, namely Mrs. Frye's, was a real blessing for him. We move to Chester Heights and mom was walking several miles to and from work at the laundry in Media. Neal can't be at the job with her so she's found someone to take care of him. These were some of the best times for Neal because he got to walk down the railroad tracks with mom almost all the way to her job. They would spend the time talking while he was skipping along and throwing rocks. They did this going and coming twice a day as she dropped him off and picked him up at the babysitter's. Every night, Neal eagerly recounted his adventures of the day for us. The one thing we could see was he got better at throwing rocks and talking everyday. He told us everything about the days at the Fryes. Turns out, the sitters, Mr. and Mrs. Frye, all but adopted him. He's with the Fryes lots of the time because we move around frequently and can't consistently pay the rent anywhere. This gives him a little more stability because the rest of us move frequently. That's how it was when my mother gets divorced around the end of the war. Fortunately, that coincides with our uncle in West Chester taking us in for a spell. While we are staying with our uncle, something transpired between our mother and Harvey Martino, a building contractor living in Thornton. He has known our mother since she was a child. His wife died and he has four children. One thing for sure was he knew my mother needed help. It appears that they worked out some agreement and married. We never knew what the particulars of the agreement were. Mom was almost forty years old and Harvey was in his mid fifties. By that time, Jack was already at EFS and I am not far behind him in going there a year later in 1946. Neal arrives two years later. I am there for five years, but Jack was kicked out, more or less. He lasted only a couple of years and moved on to West Chester High School and graduated in 1950.

At EFS, we have one athletic coach for everything. He was also Dean of Men and has a hundred other jobs. We never get any coaching at all. Whatever we do was learned on our own. We watch other people, particularly the older kids. Coming off the streets helps because it makes Jack and me tough. On the streets, we have to go out and get what we want. In our pre-teens, with no father in our lives and our mother always working, we get up at 7:00 in the morning and work odd jobs. Sometimes I delivered milk and butter until two in the afternoon for fifty cents. There aren't many men around because of the war and there was a guy who drives a delivery truck for Homestead Dairies. I work with him running bottles of milk to people's doors and bring back the empties. I run back and forth from the truck delivering milk all day. After spending the day on the milk truck, I deliver newspapers. When that was done, I come home and buy something to eat on the way. There was never any food at home and a hot dog cost five cents. When my mother goes to work, Jack and I take our shoeshine boxes and hit the streets. Later, I work on a different milk wagon where the guy has a horse. It's one of those special Belgian horses that are bigger than a regular horse. When deliveries are finished, he lets me sit on the horse and ride down the street. The kids from school think that was the neatest thing! As a big shot riding a majestic horse, I deliberately ignore them! Soon we are evicted from the place in the projects. Our next move was to Uncle Coty's (Wilmer Smiley) place in West Chester. We stay in the attic above the third floor. Eventually, Uncle Coty puts a store in the house. That was about September of 1946. Jack was already at EFS and soon Neal goes to live with our mother who recently re-married. Harvey Martino in Thornton was her new husband. That's when Neal attends Glen Mills Elementary School—not the Glen Mills Reform School down the road. Harvey Martino doesn't like Neal. The reason was mostly that Neal was a real smart little snippy kid. Harvey was already an old man and Neal was mostly obedient. But, when Harvey tells him to do something, Neal always responds with a snide remark and insists on getting in the last word. That's why Harvey doesn't like him! Neal has no idea how much he gets on Harvey's nerves. Harvey likes me and I mostly do what he wants without arguing. Jack and I know what work was because we've hustled all of our lives.

As athletes at EFS, we have to learn on our own and follow the example of the other kids. I happened to like running. I don't know why.

We work like men on the farm. We go to school for only half of the day. In my case, classes are in the morning. After noon, I work in the fields until 4 p.m. The farm has 2000 acres of potatoes to be tended. The crops and pastures stretch as far as you can see. During September and October, the harvest season, we plow the fields so the potatoes come to the surface. The whole damn school turns out to pick them! Income from the potato crop was largely what keeps the school running. We also have fields of barley, wheat, and hay. There are 200 cows to be milked by hand every day. Fourteen boys milk the herd of Golden Guernsey cows. All of us develop strong hands. We live in cottages with 15 boys in each. Shriver, the Headmaster that we call the "Colonel," runs the place like a military base. It's boot camp! The beds are always made and the place was spotless top to bottom. We do it all; slaughtering animals, helping with the cooking, and doing all of the cleaning inside and outside. The Colonel was a world class fundraiser bringing in tremendous amounts of money from the outside. His main tactic was working through the women in wealthy families. We sell milk to the Supreme Dairy, a big local dairy. We sell potatoes to the grocery stores. With all of the extra milk, we make our own butter at the school. We sell large quantities of milk. The whole operation at EFS was self-sustaining. We get up at four in the morning and milk the cows. We get back to our cottages at 7:30, have breakfast, shower, and go to school. Then, the day crew cleans the stables. We all do a turn at everything. One of the worst jobs at 12 or 13 years old was dealing with the potatoes. The plants grow high and the rows extended far into the distance. We are definitely doing the work of men. A major task was pulling mustard plants that threaten to crowd out the potatoes. Miss pulling mustards one week and it's double the work the next week. Otherwise, the mustards suck all the nutrition away from the potatoes. It's one of the hardest jobs—miserable work! We bale hay and straw and load it on trucks. As for my positive attitude as an inmate on the farm, I was slick. I am good at getting around duties I don't like. For some reason, I am a pretty fast runner. Agility was a strong quality and I take to athletics very well. An important outgrowth of my athletic ability was having the favor of certain people that allow me to avoid the most difficult jobs. I was also a mean "mother" from being on the streets in Chester. I have to deal with people trying to steal my shoeshine box. I carry a butcher knife and would cut them in a heartbeat. With my frame of mind, nobody messes with me. I am vicious. In a fight, I beat the opponent as long as I can. Big or small, size doesn't matter to me. That was the attitude that comes out in football. EFS plays six-man football because there aren't enough boys for regular football. The teams are categorized by weight. I was a terror. Everybody likes me because of my viciousness on the football field. We have two undefeated seasons. One of those years, I scored 122 points. That's a hell of a lot of touchdowns. They always wrote me up in the paper because I was good. I play on those teams until going to West Chester High School.

As I said, I liked running. One of my favorite things was to race the potato truck back to the school from the fields about a mile away. When the work was done and the boys loaded on the truck, I run and try to beat the truck back to the barnyard. My advantage was cutting across the fields and over the hill while the truck sticks to the road. With that kind of frequent workouts, I get pretty good at running. I do well when I'm on the track team in the 8th grade. I do it with no training. That makes me realize I am a good runner. The next year, I practice on my own without a coach and do well. Neal latches on to me when he comes the following year. That's when he starts running. I won ten out of eleven one mile races that year. Still, we don't know anything about running. We just do it! I broke one record at EFS. A guy named Bob Hosinteller held the one mile record. I broke it by 37 seconds. My participation in several sports makes it easier for

Neal coming along behind me. Anyway, Neal doesn't stay at EFS long enough to do any damage to my record. That's largely because when Jack gets out of the Army he doesn't like the way things are going for Neal. He's pissed off. Neal's still at EFS. Jack comes home, gets his car, drives out to EFS and takes Neal out of school. He did it against Harvey Martino's wishes. It was 1953. I quit school at EFS and went to play football at West Chester High. I was already known there because of my six man football career at EFS. At West Chester, Dick Flagg was all everything. Buddy Bulotta was another one. I'm new at the school in 1950 and make the varsity team for the last three games of the season. Bobby Irons played the same position as me. He's real fast and tricky, but shies away from contact most of the time. Horse Lawson comes on the team the next year. The best thing about West Chester football was that Elmer Haupt was coaching. Reagle became the head coach after him. I contracted pleurisy in the 11th grade and that knocked me down. I made the football team and played against Lancaster High School. There were other problems, as well. All of it led to my quitting school and joining the Navy after the 1951 football season. I wanted to join the military earlier since Jack was already in but mom wouldn't sign. When turning 18, I dropped out of school and went to the train station! I landed in Korea and actually got a Purple Heart. Jack was ticked that he never got there! I married Barbara Jones (class of 1953) when I got discharged in 1955. Her mother always worked at Kaufman's department store.

As for Neal surviving at EFS and becoming a runner, first and foremost, he was real smart and always real slick. He came to EFS two and one half years before I left. In the 9th grade I'm on the varsity for football, baseball, and track. Neal followed me around the track and I was the best runner. With coaching, I would have been even better. I really didn't like the school because all the rules and regulation were contrary to the freedom of my previous life on the streets in Chester, Pa. Early on, I knew that Neal could run. I also thought that he could become a great runner because he paid unusually close attention to the workouts I was doing and joined in on some of it. *(He watched, did what I was doing, and did it right! He was a little skinny runt. I didn't realize how strong he was going to be. All of a sudden he got into it and thought it was a neat thing to do!)* Then he went over to West Chester and got involved with the runners there and that coach, Zimmerman. Somebody told him he had potential. It might have been me letting him know how good he was doing. When I'd tell him he was looking good, he'd do a few more strides. I'd tell him about his form and he listened. He wanted to lean back a little. I got him to correct that. I told him about arm swing and how that impacted his legs. The most important thing I told him about was running smooth—eliminating bouncing and wobbling. There were little things like how to hold your hands to avoid tightening up. When he was at West Chester, I saw him a couple of times. I was in the Navy. I watched him run and told him what he needed to do. I gave him praise and encouragement. He doesn't jump in with a passion, but eases his way into it. He knows he can do it and does so without putting a lot of pressure on himself. He ends up with a real nice stride. Before that, he has a little hop.

Zimmerman was looking for Neal when he showed up at West Chester in the fall of 1954. He already knew of me and wanted me for cross-country when I came there. I, however, was more interested in football. When track season came, I had the damn pleurisy that just about killed me. I was weakened and sapped of strength for quite a few weeks. I was on the team and had run indoor track in the winter. I was on the relay team with Horse at the Convention Hall as part of the Inquirer Games in Philadelphia. I ran the fastest relay leg that night. I only ran in one outdoor meet. It was against A.I. Dupont in the first meet of the season. I may have gotten 3rd place.

I also pole-vaulted with a bamboo pole. I could do 10 feet 6 inches, but it took a toll on my pleurisy-ridden body. Eventually, I was not able to continue working out. I rested for the summer and went out for football in the fall of 1951. However, the sickness had taken its toll on my body. I was with Herb Scott and Bobby Irons. They were good guys. This was a good place for Neal to come to next year.

One thing going on in my life that I was sensing was a diminished intensity of commitment to schoolwork. It took several years at EFS to lose my drive for academic superiority, but I recognized the gradual decline. I was always on the honor rolls there in the first four years, and then it started souring. I abandoned the intense desire to do well in school. A highly restricted order can do that. It's a shame because coming into EFS. I had an urge for learning drilled into me by teachings from (adopted) grandparents and support from the rest of the family after that. It got me started the same way at EFS and took years to fall away, but it eventually fell by the wayside. If there was anything there to like, it was history. A few teachers were kind to me, and I hated just as many. Whatever love I had for competing in classes in the first years was increasingly dissipated by the time I got to the middle of junior high school.

By my sophomore year, nothing was imperative except to "beat the system" in whatever way. Throughout my tenure, I was a swift learner and mastered the ins and outs of survival by thwarting or manipulating the system. Before long, it all caught up with me, and they stopped allowing me to "regain lost time" or to use other mechanisms to avoid chastisement for transgressions. By then, they knew I was the highest offender in beating the rules and slammed the door on it. With one swipe, they took away all my time to go home. They told me I wasn't getting any more time off and was on restriction all year with no time at home. The only time I could leave the boundaries was for long mileage runs and some competitions. It would destroy me if they took that away.

I knew that in the coming two years, nothing could turn around. There wasn't enough time because I had already forfeited all the breaks for the following years. Only a miracle could save me.

West Chester High

Our 1953 cross-country program included a dual meet against West Chester High's Warriors. Although expecting they'd win, our leaders, two seniors, performed superior yet only placed third and fourth. Those are not sports' worst finishes, but how easily two younger Warrior sophomores outran our seniors surprised me. Disbelief practically drowned us. No way should two youngsters out of Junior High beat our seniors. What an eye-opening outcome! Stark silence on the return bus ride framed questions. Those sophomores' accomplishments signaled future possibilities. They planted seeds, and I wondered whether remaining at Episcopal Farm allowed reaching my potential. How much would Warrior sophomores improve over subsequent seasons? Where would I rank compared to them by graduation if they keep improving?

On May 6, 1954, an unexpected earth-shattering event occurred four days after my fifteenth birthday. Roger Bannister destroyed complacency toward running by becoming the first man to do a mile in under four minutes. Cabin mates gathered, our ears pressing a shared radio as British news reported an accomplishment until now thought impossible. Commentators proclaimed Banister's feat the most remarkable sporting achievement of the century, but I'm not sure others listening felt as moved. A 3:59.4 mile was magical, an accomplishment convincing me that running offered what I wanted in terms of identity, and I wanted to be another Bannister. Roger's revolutionizing possibilities regarding running and how human evolution continues occurred before the fall semester.

Meanwhile, changes affecting my family had progressed by June 1954. Developments launched a new chapter and I escaped institutionalization to enter West Chester High, where I joined several outstanding runners. That's a tremendous change after six years in virtual lockdown. Jack's return from his U.S. Army Cold War travels delivered the catalyst. His arrival in the parking lot out of the blue shocked me! He exited his new car with an aggravated expression and asked, "Why the hell are you still here?" I stared quizzically, without answers, because I never thought I had a choice. "Here's where I'm 'supposed to be.'" There's only one way of seeing it; they programmed this for me. "Pack your bags and meet me near the front entrance; I'm hauling you out!" What he was after lived inside his head. I "owed" the damn place all of 1954's vacation. Shriver's son and assistant (who we nicknamed "Dutchy") had come to my room and lectured me that "there was no way I could 'work off' the time as I had done in some years past by extra hours on-campus jobs. "There's no recovering from being late for classes and work!" You couldn't get full summers anyhow! Those getting similar penalties stayed the whole season. So I was gonna be stuck there milking cows for the entire year! Good thing Jack got there on graduation day, so there were many adults, etc., on the campus, and no one noticed us sneaking out. Jack's intentions of getting me out of there were decisive, if not dramatic:

> I just got back from overseas. I had two years in Germany and got discharged. I got back to Thornton, bought myself an Oldsmobile, and was getting ready to go to some kind of school—college or something else. I wasn't sure what I wanted to do. I said to mom, "Where is Neal?" I thought by now he would be living at home.
>
> She said, "Well, he is still at the Farm School."
>
> I thought: "Oh my god! I've been halfway around the world and halfway to who knows where and he's still out there!" I jumped in my car and drove out to his cottage at EFS. I said, "Neal, get your shit, we're getting out of here! What the hell are you still doing here?" He had been there for the entire year because he had lost all of the possible vacation time. We threw his stuff in the car and headed for Thornton.

I tried figuring out events right there, but no other choices emerged. Why does my brother opposing my situation astound me? I was here when he left and still here when he returned! Where the hell else is there? While looking shocked, I blurted out, "What do you mean? I lost summers off because of penalties! You can't just walk out!" I heard, "Bring everything and wait at the bell tower."

In 30 minutes, I jumped in as the car kept rolling, then sped away. It took fifteen minutes to gather everything. That shows the poverty of possessions they held over us. It's unbelievable!

I can't refuse to follow my oldest brother! He's not asking Harvey's permission to move me. We're headed to Thornton, hauling my stuff. How the hell could that work? I've never done much without my parents, okay? Nobody logged me out of EFS! Harvey's approval means nothing! When I left the farm in 1954, my Personal Independence Day arrived! According to JC, that room in Thornton was mine. Mom didn't, and Harvey couldn't object. What could he say? JC wasn't taking crap after being a Cold War warrior. Harvey accepted, keeping quiet. He didn't speak because keeping me away was wrong. That's clear. In six years, he had become a doddering old man. He's less and less capable of commanding Mom. Jack explained:

I told mom I've got to get Neal out of that place and into West Chester High School. It's like jail. It's like being in prison. I told her, "There was no social life." I've been around the world, and my kid brother was still in that prison. It's not much different from being in the service. Everything was on time—meals, classes, work and sleep. You're not allowed to leave the place. There's no childhood, no social life. He had never met a girl. That's weird! I was contrary. I used to sneak off bounds and go down to Exton to fool around. Getting Neal out of there just seemed so necessary to me. When we got home, things just straightened out. Everything worked out. He had to learn the routine of going to West Chester High School. That was a real point of change in his life.

I thought hard. When Jack returned with great awareness after three years of touring the world, he intended to grant me the strength and determination he claimed for himself. He transferred freedom from an unjust fate's grip to me. After fifteen years, getting freed physically, cognitively, and emotionally and achieving positive self-awareness meant escaping the past where only others know what's best. I never felt empowered to question. Under these implacable conditions, thinking didn't happen. Farm experiences groomed me into not seeking something better. JC snatched me, only giving instructions to enroll at WC. The future of my having ordinary freedoms of youth, some self-determination, and being a typical teenager—began in that moment.

The transfer was good fortune at a critical juncture. Since too many transgressions meant zero vacation, fleeing there worked well. I moved forward after massive restrictions without knowing public system differences or interacting with girls. Interacting with brethren from backgrounds different from the norm of "problem fellows" left plenty to learn about others. (Once again, participation in sports opened the way for improving my life. That's the next chapter.) Jack's view was correct in significant ways:

Neal was living like an orphan child in an institution for a very long time. His term at Episcopal Farm School started much earlier than that of either Donald or me. We were already teenagers when we arrived. We also arrived together. Since he's now fifteen, from the age of eight he lived as if both of our parents were dead. In those critical years, he had no friends who had a normal existence. He had never gone to another child's home other than as a guest of charity. He hadn't spent time outside of confinement at EFS, especially at night. He hadn't spoken to a girl in an environment that supports friendships. He had never had a date or been where those kinds of opportunities existed. Holding a girl's hand or dancing never happened in his world. That would have been nice! At the least, it's normal to be able to do that; to have those choices. He needs to be in a much different place, but has no way to understand or even think that. His response to my insisting that he leave EFS on the spot told the tale.

JC insisted I go to WCHS. He, however, didn't know the enormity of the gains possible in the new environment. They go beyond building an eclectic collection of friends or being where girls are available. Most notable were the benefits of joining a contingent of committed runners. To enter their track and cross-country programs, incorporating and eclipsing social opportunity where deficiencies had endured most of my life, proved the best of fortunes. That's my miraculous development. Here's the perfect place at the right time. Two principal reasons were John Roger Williams (aka Cap'n Jack or JR) and Kenny Noel (sometimes pronounced Nole, sometimes Noël, it doesn't matter which). Arriving there provided another instance of the transforming importance of place. (Importance of "place," in this case, became locating my pathway of focus and salvation in pursuing happiness.) It was a life-changing occurrence.

I didn't generate expectations from experiencing teenage life's attractions and wasn't used to goals other than farm work. We followed the almanac, the farm's business plan, relying on military-style discipline and pursued elite prep school-style tutelage. Pointing out adverse features is not claiming there weren't gains under farm conditions. Their academic curriculum was first-class. For me, however, the rest spelled disaster. Over time, touted possibilities promoting spiritual elevation struck me as rationalization due to the lack of fulfilling socializing roles and relationships. It required my brother to experience foreign lands, then return and understand my reality as if it were himself. That realization provoked him to rip me from bondage without a clear vision of where life was going. His action accomplished more than expected because JC placed me with everything I needed.

CHAPTER
THREE

Delinquency or Rebellion

For the psychological health of the oppressed,
it's important for the oppressors to know THEY
cannot be trusted. An inevitable dictate of the
oppressed condition is formulating and committing
irrevocable actions against the oppressor.

Kenny:

Mom was hard, tending toward the extreme. When caught doing wrong, we got the hell beat out of us. There were frequent whippings as a pre-teen. They meant nothing to deter delinquency. Whenever violating norms, I expected ass whippings. Most available objects qualified for administering lashings. Her preferred tools were half-inch diameter leather treadle belts, 3 feet long, we called straps. They came off her pedal-operated sewing machine because she sewed clothing when not cleaning homes or doing maid service for super-rich people like the DuPonts. Broken flywheel belts joined her punishing instruments' collection on a nail beside the kitchen door. Physical discipline was aimed toward forcing general obedience to Jim Crow. Corporal punishment might influence others, but it amounted to my parents' doomed attempts at preventing major rebellion. Before beatings, she ordered us to choose a strap, which heightened our pain.

She made us strip naked, waiting in line more often than not. It couldn't happen with Daddy (Chas P.) home because he'd interfere. At that point, issues turned into arguments he always lost, tearfully apologizing. Before my teens, I believed whippings were meaningless regarding a purpose. Their rationalized intent was to preempt behavior that would attract cops, forced self-control, and avoided street deaths. Fear caused Negro families to rely on corporal punishment, hoping to prevent children from misbehaving and developing attitudes of resistance as they aged. It continued because slavery's oppressive intolerance remained in supporting white supremacy. I couldn't stomach watching my sisters, Madelyn (Pat) and Helen (Dup), getting whipped. While very young, I took the blame for their rule-breaking and started shielding them. Nothing traumatized me more than witnessing or hearing their fright-filled pain. Protecting them became vital. Responsibility came from our sibling relationship and got enhanced by teaching them reading, and their eagerness to learn culminated in my taking responsibility for protecting them. Daily school work reinforced sibling bonds and valuing education.

I understood being honest, doing right, and being well-behaved. Those values became prominent in socialized children's thinking. That my family demanded good behavior made absolute sense. Part of me wanted that. However, earning adult appreciation and rewarding righteousness were impossible unless acceding to Jim Crow. Those in power insisted on preventing equal social participation, no matter what. Such societal changes didn't happen while my parents were alive, nor has it come in sufficient measure later. As with so many others, I was born where accepting racism brings self-hating through swallowing depredations at every turn. The only respite is around our people under the Negro enclave's limited security. Life, relatively speaking, is a prison without bars and inadequate tools for rectifying debilitating conditions. Conforming and being full-fledged humans were contradictions sustained by whites' informal and formal enforcement of Jim Crow at critical points. Theaters, for example, had segregated seating. That contorted practice probably sounds strange, but it had the desired effect of inflating white people's value in their eyes and universally diminishing Blacks.

Our families feared that non-conformity might bring incarceration, death by police, or government execution. They argued for promoting calm, reserved behavior and not displaying distress underlying our social position's precarious nature. Inequality's stifling demands were preexisting conditions. Past the primary grades, systemic controls included policing, where officers knew kids' names on sight. In knowing names, they knew addresses. Facial recognition enables managing rebellious behavior more artfully. Enough ability to eliminate most conflict was impossible. Protecting my sisters from violence proceeded unabated over the ensuing years, as the alternative was living as a craven coward.

Benign powerlessness hurt plenty. Systemic abuses flooded our daily lives, making childhood obedience a matter of giving up self-respect while accepting disrespect from others. Some practices identified very early, including deliberately denying resources like swimming pool access, made Blacks less than others. Learning to swim required courting the danger of jumping into the Brandywine River. Girls never learned. Too many barriers created emotional concerns about staying alive. Institutional processes created formal and informal harmful practices while not causing troublesome disruptive notice from perpetrators, victims, groups, and organizations. Surface appearances indicated accepting second-class citizenship when none exists underneath. Protection against societal mistreatment or help to resolve related issues didn't exist. From seventh grade on, white instructors never approached viewing society's injustices or addressing necessary changes for Negroes to become equal. Before, at our segregated primary school, teachers dedicated their lives to influencing children toward self-liberation while staying within white power limits and avoiding criticizing unfair conditions.

They didn't pursue instruction to instigate progress, grow past present-day arrangements, or eliminate injustice. Their nurturing efforts aimed at building ourselves and our race while shying from open opposition to prevailing deprivation. White power shackles us by limiting access to resources, reducing opportunities for success, and allowing no greater expectations.

By September 1951, well before 1954's Supreme Court ruling against legal separate but equal public education (Brown v. Board of Education), Helen, my youngest sibling, integrated High Street School. West Chester's education board planned to end segregation well before the court decision. Town administrators' actions surprised people, raising aspirations about seeking change. Unexpected segregationists protested out front! Helen encountered problems with racist staff and several unreceptive, misguided kids. There were threats from a red-haired teenage cracker who had recently arrived from Tennessee. During mid-summer, strangers (Magrubbers) moved several doors to the left across from us. While they unpacked, the sound of their heavy southern drawl signaled probable trouble.

The boy was big at fifteen, though in elementary. In those days, there were "Special Classes" where teenagers stayed until they were legal to hold jobs at sixteen. This grown hillbilly threatened Helen, who was integrating third grade. Child abuse happened in supporting white supremacy. Considering her feelings at dinner, I resolved to end the overt threats, as sure as the sun also rises. I escorted her the next day. My plan to bring gang members to battle proved unnecessary because the local government banned demonstrations. Tuesday, several blocks in each direction were empty. Events had frightened Leonard Yates enough to reenter segregation at Coonville. I determined to go after that Appalachian cracker as soon as possible. He needed instantaneous convincing this wasn't Confederate territory.

I headed uptown on Saturday when Magrubber and an older sister came through the alley carrying groceries. Once I barred their route, they both froze—looking into a wrathful face. I attacked him because his arms were empty—he could run. Palpable panic marked his blood-drained freckled face as I pummeled him. She stood there shrieking! Once beating him down, she fell next. This lesson proved successful because Helen's tenure remained uneventful. It's satisfying how the hillbilly changed, falling into line. Direct violence proved most effective in thwarting cowardly bullies. I wasn't a tough or a neighborhood bully. A heightened determination to resist maltreatment is an apt characterization.

Problems couldn't diminish in our lives because of peckawood Walter's harassment. We fought on sight because he yelled "nigger" at Pat on seeing her. He looked hokey wearing purple-blue plaid shirts above wrinkled gray pants, fitting as ragged cuffed "high-waters." Walter acted oblivious to his obvious unwholesome conditions. This poorest of the poor absorbing racial supremacy was the ultimate misguided state. When traveling east or west on Barnard Street, he'd call out, "Hey niggers!" leaning from their alley rental's window! Patsy nicknamed him "Horsey" because his elongated jaw was filled with big horse teeth. Horsey hurled direct insults at us while ignoring other Negroes. Fights were daily during 1954, so his mother watched regular confrontations. She must have known about Walter's constant race-baiting and never called the cops. He battled hard, showing no trepidation. Clashes continued until mid-1955. I encountered him one hot summer morning in High and Barnard's vast granite Methodist courtyard. Their rectory complex's quad looked like a medieval castle jousting list. A parapet wall adorned the sanctuary roof, enclosed on several sides. What an ideal setting for staging our decisive battle!

I pounced, flooring him. Blows landed having little effect. At a critical point, horse's teeth sunk deep into my left pinky finger, biting hard while absorbing punches. Failing to pull away my bleeding appendage, I continued, "no holds barred." A 12-inch pipe pulled from my pocket served that purpose. Blood spurted everywhere from successive sharp strikes across Horsey's ear, forcing him into a fetal position. His friend stood frozen, shivering in scorching summer sun rays while gripping two tiny plastic airplanes before scooting south along the sidewalk.

Meanwhile, several old white women exited one tiny chapel with small handkerchiefs covering gray hair. They begged me to stop—for Christ's sake!

Plea's for mercy fell on deaf ears, bent on ending continued fighting's causes. There won't be another abusive word directed at Madelyn, I vowed! Problems ceased after working him over with that iron pipe. In later encounters, he never again uttered "nigger" aloud. Trouble, however, doesn't end here.

Before starting my senior year, I got arrested and convicted of two assaults. The rub was I only committed one of two crimes charged. Maybe such distinctions shouldn't matter, but it raises injustice. The rib-breaking blow at issue occurred during fighting started by a bog-trotter gang (Irish). Is it unfair if they only arrest us concerning altercations? It's not surprising that only Blacks got jailed. Did the injured boy say it happened unprovoked—that he wasn't kicking Gator's ass? Or did the cops not bother to ask? You can bet they didn't care. It was the same old blatant racism. From numerous experiences, we knew policing processes operated against us.

The latest battle took place at West Chester College's football opener. Glenn Killinger, their legendary coach, produced winning programs. Enough encounters showed the campus' and its teams' racist nature. Angry contacts were routine. Whenever meeting players, we clashed. They often had advantages, wearing pads and helmets. They played great, so we seldom missed home contests. Friday night games evolved into annual gang forays. Once climbing fences to get inside, mini-scrimmages took place on the grass beyond the end zone seating. Tackling in street clothes turned too rough for the other boys. They quit every time. On this occasion, they resorted to using fists. I wasn't there at the start. An honest description is, "I exited the bleachers, put a foot into an ofay's side, and then returned to the stands to continue watching the game." Yeah, that kid crumpled over on broken ribs, and my polished new footwear helped police identify who did it. An unconnected beating Saturday night raised the police's ire. Someone whipped Mayor Mullin's son using a static strap. Undisclosed witnesses identified me.

Uncovering who fingered me failed. Kids all over town looked at him as a blatant open-vocal Nazi. His enemies list couldn't get any longer. They busted me, lying that Saturday night's assailant wore shiny boots. My father questioned my innocence claim. I denied everything because Mayor Mullin's son never graced my victims' list. Two detectives stood convinced by testimony about the football game incident, so they added Saturday. Their view concluded that I pursued a weekend terror campaign. Their false accusation alleging two assaults justified my denying Friday night's rib-breaking episode. Chas P., sensing one truth, said so. However, owing him honesty, dwelling on guilt on both charges continued my lying. There is no questioning or permitting juveniles to speak. We languished in custody over Labor Day.

Ernie Gardener (Gator), smallish, skeletal-chested, quiet, and younger, shared the lock-up. His needing help drew me into brawling. Bog-trotters pinned him against cyclone fencing behind the grandstands. On sweeping the grounds, I ran over, jump-kicking one nondescript gangster, breaking several ribs. After eliminating one attacker, Ernie handled his other assailant. This scene typifies our condition! "You wander into unbalanced battles; you step in, breaking some ribs, before continuing socializing as though nothing happened!" Seated again, not further interested, it felt playfully innocent. Fights become inconsequential given the historical hostility between ethnic groups. Aren't these engagements typical clashes? Police never acknowledge Negroes as victims exercising self-defense. They chose sides, carrying out systematic injustice.

A kid was already there after repeatedly running away from home. White runaways were typical juvenile home internees. Other whites I'd known going to "Juvy" committed depravity, such as bestiality or sodomy. Stories circulated through WCHS should that occur. Justice administrators' children spread the word about schoolmates getting busted on sexual depravity charges. There was at least one every year. This fellow had been there twice, adjusting well to soft imprisonment. What we took from him was embracing self-containment, suiting this place. Juvy being the harshest consequence possible, he was unfazed in familiar detention. We were not so blessed and assumed larger problems lay ahead. Realistic options offered few breaks. This kid's manner suggested lowering anxiety until reaching court. Before the trial day, sensing outcomes was impossible. Decisions must be harsh. There's an injustice to face.

That year's Labor Day Parade marched past Juvenile Hall on Monday. My mother and father were devoted colored Elks officers, so I played trombone in their band, performing in every annual holiday pageant. Negro social clubs throughout greater Philadelphia staged yearly parades, so we marched in each. Elk's events provided summer fun and travel. No funds existed, so mismatched uniforms were fashionably shabby. Most of us wore white shirts and black slacks. Half sported peaked caps or heavy wool trousers with shiny stripes. Displaying different uniforms helped keep the focus on the music's unmatchable power. It was soulful and grand. Years before, our leading people boasted credentials as renowned Dixieland Jazz musicians. They got swept up over Chicago, Memphis, and New Orleans nightclub stints. Yes, it's a ragtag look, but our sounds were glorious! Disparities of mismatching appearances joined unparalleled musicianship, raised appreciation, added extra flavor to our performances, and stimulated audience reception.

Audiences wanted our version of "Red River Valley." It's an unlikely anthem done by assembled jazz musicians, making it more striking. As we strutted past dignitary-packed reviewing stands, folks exploded off sidewalks. They merged into gyrating masses, boogying their hearts out. When Wilbur Jones blew his battered trumpet's square-shaped mouthpiece planted at his mouth's corner, with the hat cocked sideways, gatherings became large moving celebrations. Jazz and blues tunes became marching music for mobile parties. Everyone gets pulled into collectively interpreting life's soul-based rhythms – vis-à-vis self-expression. At parades, eastern seaboard sister organizations showed appreciation. Whenever pausing before VIP grandstands, other bands' lead players hustled to blend into our group. Legends moved front and center. Crowds got serenaded by Dixieland icons performing inspiring solos.

Those memories were why this year's parade elevated stress in confinement. Being in custody as bands marched past didn't instigate remorse but brought reflective thoughts. Racially limited promising features of our challenging existence were slipping beyond reach. This realization did nothing to alter behavior but sparked consciousness. Meaningful citizenship, based on participation, comes with freedom. As our prospects stand locked up, even limited opportunity trickles into the sewer. Incarceration interrupts chances for betterment while suspending personal growth. Our future stood uncertain because there was no telling what the wrathful justice responses were. By maintaining Jim Crow, they limited representations of full citizen status to mouthing the Constitution's and Bill of Rights' words, not by acting to ensure living without oppression.

Both my parents warned me non-stop to stay out of trouble. I told them if arrested, they should let me face it alone. Our political reality (past and present) made all violent actions self-defense. Mom heeded my words just as much as I refused her advice. Later engagements had to be low-key because Daddy was too sensitive, gentle—too forgiving. Contact during my imprisonment meant sending him into depression. He'd spend present and future family resources to free me. She understood us both. It's better for his mental health if he doesn't see me in jail.

WCHS opened three days into September, so classes proceeded before Friday's hearing. Juvenile prosecutions were always perfunctory proceedings. For juveniles going to court, determining guilt and sentencing decisions happened before trials. Once forming judgments, they forbid explanations or leniency pleas. Behind his polished mahogany magistrate's desk, Judge Blakely asked if anyone wanted to speak. The only person coming forward was Mr. Zimmerman, WCHS's revered coach since 1925. He handed the clerk an envelope, nodding while turning to leave without glancing my way. It appeared that Zim knew Blakely. As the state education administration's most beloved individual, someone of his stature appearing on my behalf created hope.

Zim's letter in hand, Judge Blakely rose, ordering a ten-minute recess by striking his gavel. Returning with verdicts, I stepped forward to hear, "considering favorable letters from educators and civic leaders with no prior offenses, you will receive a three-year suspended sentence with three years' probation. This decree requires leaving West Chester after graduating, until you are twenty-one. The court is allowing graduation, but you must show proof of signing into the military one week after your eighteenth birthday, ensuring you are leaving here." That's it; probation, avoiding prison. Air Force enlistment would show compliance.

Ernie's case's adjudication was shocking. Not a single soul submitted references helping him. Gator's record showed no prior offenses, but Blakely ordered three years in Pennsylvania's regional reform institution. His ruling struck cruel unfairness, so different from mine, triggering extreme guilt. My light sentence appeared to cost him possibilities for living decently. Family, friends, and acquaintances projected he'd shatter serving that much prison time. Ernie was too gentle and couldn't mount the survival-level viciousness required. After so many years, he'd return home irredeemably degraded. Maybe it was better having Irish gangsters beat him.

When Judge Blakely delivered my probation, Ernie and his mother probably thought he'd get off lighter. Indeed, our crimes weren't equal. Gator should have received less punishment. He was younger at fifteen, up on one count, while I had two. Upon hearing my fate, we primed their hopes to suffer injustice's cruelest dagger. His sentence delivered immeasurable heartbreak. She collapsed, near losing consciousness. Utter agony kept her from passing out after such a crippling blow. I saw great despair brought on by profound misfortune. Together, they sank to the lowest of lows. This desperate scene induced guilt in me because there was no hope, no saving or altering his fate.

Irreparable psychological damage engulfed them before justice's last words struck. They inexplicably freed me, but my friend received a monstrous penalty. There could be no ready explanation. Half that year went by wrestling to understand our treatment disparity. Figuring out why our treatment ended so lopsided required more time. Key factors must have been unassailable favorable character witnesses and political influence. Chas P. worked his heart out as the Negro's Democratic Party contact in a Republican municipality. It helped in getting Republican representatives to influence sentencing. Democratic favors earned delivering Negro votes were used to save me. Daddy stayed quiet after spending every drop of his hard-earned political capital.

Several favorable factors contributed to my puzzlement regarding the reasons explaining a lenient outcome for me. School officials (Harold Wingert, WCHS's Principal, and Mr. Zimmerman (Zim), track coach) submitted glowing references. These men were our region's most highly regarded personalities. "Zim" was revered statewide. While founding Pennsylvania's Interscholastic Athletic Association (PIAA), they named him State Track Association Director. Bipartisan support from government influencers and achievements in athletics matched my good citizenship record. I loved school, so there's excellent citizenship. My unique attraction to running (which I also loved) guaranteed each day was special. I perceived (vaguely) that physical gifts offered advantages, potentially helping me.

Explaining Ernie's imprisonment required comprehending second-class citizens' lives growing up in northern towns where powers practiced discrimination as egregiously as anywhere in the south. Inherent to "northern Jim Crow," most activities, outlooks, and relationships maintained great dichotomies in intimate, controlled settings. There were no drawn lines or printed signs warning or declaring restrictions governing people of color. Yet, constraints were everywhere. We often misread un-displayed limits framing our devalued existence. So, we spawned a continuous need for system keepers reinforcing lower social position limitations. These were insurmountable obstacles preventing people from becoming whole. Even as unenlightened youths, we knew this. I felt soul-deep defenselessness because deprivations were daily affronts. They triggered shame-inducing incidences exploiting and affirming powerlessness. From birth, uncertainty in normal behavior grew unabated through early socialization. Negative status prevailed as racist ideas and practices comprised constraints against which we struggled. These conditions exhausted efforts at progressing without positive returns. In this perpetual struggle, the future promise dissipated, our humanity diminished, and opportunities for valuing ourselves met destruction, including intra-group destructiveness. Anytime venturing into neighborhoods outside Coonville, we expected insults, leading to confrontations. On reaching puberty, we sought physical altercations to show we were unconquered. Weekly invasions of other ethnic spaces turned combat into political resistance (opposing Jim Crow) and self-defense.

Throughout my youth, the local government touted its historical roots as key to carrying out the American Revolution. Origin stories celebrated the Turk's Head Inn at the crossroads to Wilmington and Philadelphia, forming the settlement's hub dating from 1762. With Brandywine Battle Field's proximity, within walking distance going southwest, there's Valley Forge's fabled 1777-78 Continental Army winter encampment 10 miles northeast. Drum beats of the revolutionary war's relevance continue steadfastly sounding as a force influencing the borough's daily life. Markers showing "George Washington (or Marquis de Lafayette) slept here" dotted roadsides and red brick sidewalks. Authorities insisted Negroes should be proud, even inspired, by being in the presence of current caretakers inheriting glorious history. Some folks tried but failed to show that people of color warranted representation in this epic saga. At frequent celebrations, declarations proclaiming Britain's defeat ignored our people as contributors. Under continuing oppression, our revolutionary involvement alongside white folks goes unstated. An odd question was how and why racial separation prevailed everywhere, except in public education, after the primary level. The answer remains unknown! "Chester County was home to a diverse patchwork of religious communities, anti-slavery activities, and free Black populations, all working to end the blight of slavery during the Civil War era." (Dane E. Tilghman) Layered beneath accepting African bondage were productive anti-slavery forces stemming from Quaker beliefs. The Society of Friends' durable humanistic ethic operated alongside racism. Prominent local anti-slavery actions date from 1834. That's when Rachel, who escaped near Baltimore, settled in West Chester, marrying a free Negro. Slave hunters had county sheriffs enforcing the 1850s Fugitive Slave Act. They captured her after several years. Most accounts hold she fled further north, freed by the presiding town magistrate's wife. Relying on Underground Railroad networks, they reached Canada. Rachel's story has been among familiar narratives of "a time with the Underground

Railroad in full operation" around Philadelphia. (See Dr. Edwin Fussell's: Underground Railroad in Chester County, Pennsylvania.)

Many writings noted operations freeing slaves worked well, even lacking ways of identifying, transporting, or caring for runaways. Abolitionists plucking Africans from bondage relied on darkness, guiding stars, allies, and people's humanity. Their covert operations broke laws, exposing people involved to life-threatening dangers and defying armed bounty hunters. Torture scars on escapees displayed enduring misery and reinforced abolition's noble mission, giving reasons to disregard personal welfare. Fugitives often survived severe floggings where bloody masses raised by enmeshed interwoven scars mimicked enormous bird nests grown on their backs. Pictured examples exhibited grim numbers of lashes; none were below one hundred. Those wounds told beholders what they needed to know about indescribable suffering.

Embracing this history, we had annual "underground railroad" tours through prominent Quaker residences, starting in Mrs. Spann's fourth grade. We didn't see current residents recognizable as friends. None looked like abolitionists from reference materials or oatmeal box images. They still avoided identification. Children passed entire mornings absorbing vibes in dim-lit chambers which sheltered escapees on their trek toward secure havens further north. Eating prepared beans on bread—"slave meals"—in rooms carved into hard dirt was eerie. We huddled as did Africans occupying those exact cellars a hundred years before, feeling desperate peoples' spirits seeking salvation. Their presence remains from determined expressions of faith, courage, and perseverance. Frightening descriptive narratives accompanied each station visited. Most objects shown were unforgettable, like restraining devices designed to suppress the desire to escape. Among the artifacts were heavy shackles that slavers welded on captive's legs, sometimes attaching additional weights. They had spiked iron collars that fastened around captive's necks as punishment after attempts to flee. Torture instruments caused physical and emotional effects. Their deliberate designs opened flesh wounds by attaching bulky weights. Eyewitness accounts hardened abolitionists' resolve against slavery's inhumanity. Books explaining cruel practices weren't available to classes other than those displayed in these preserved pockets of desperation. Textbooks didn't mention the unspeakable harshness our ancestors experienced. From intimate exposure to history at 10, I wondered if this country would ever allow the elimination of degradation. Having hope on our path was near impossible. Many righteous souls existed, but depending on others to free us wasn't reasonable.

Our family knew our great-grandmother hid in similar "safe house" networks when stealing away from Virginia to Reading, Pennsylvania, fifty miles due north from Mason's and Dixon's Line. That's where Sarah, Daddy's mother, took her first breath in 1876. Born in 1901, he resembles Granny Hewlett. They often called her "the African." Recounting the oral history, Daddy described bounty hunters searching. Fake lawmen failed to discover chambers 20 feet below ground in Bethel A. M. E. Church's bowels on Tenth Street. Curators opened underground chambers shored by massive timbers descending through four stages, revealing platforms at each level that provided living areas. Granny hid there for over thirty months—until pursuers stopped searching. Based on popular belief, impressions of her presence inhabit that space forever. I imagined hiding, overwhelmed with fear, while being hunted by southern plantation owners leading their minions. They were acting under Fugitive laws. When visiting shelters under homes, I felt unexplainable spiritual connections.

Besides primary education practices, West Chester's YMCA represented an excellent example of segregation's paradoxes, self-contradictory institutions promoting logically unacceptable claims. Norman Bell, an over-age teammate, got me into setting bowling pins at the "Y," where white schoolmates holding memberships attended with their families. We serviced their games but couldn't display familiarity. Both sides acted like they didn't know each other. How much crazier can it get? There were popular claims that a private estate donated its building based on a supposed agreement stating only Caucasians could belong. They claimed being handcuffed by unassailably justified Jim Crow practices while professing to believe Jesus' teachings!

Everyone saw their indoor swimming pool as the most problematic feature. Unless barred, we'd share the same waters. Negro boys, seeing their girls in bathing suits, cross the line. What revolting possibilities!

Prohibitions applied to bowling, swimming, or even lingering near their building. Although we never wanted memberships, working there while denied membership prompted discussions, with racism reaching everywhere. Management manipulated bowling lane assignments, keeping us from getting people known as generous tippers. They ensured white employees earned more money. (The same practices existed as caddying at nearby golf courses where Negroes couldn't join.) Bosses justified giving less desirable customer assignments by criticizing our performance, even as customers praised us. Beyond doubt, Bell and I were untouchable at this job, far above other "pin boys." Most bowlers delighted in trying to "whack a nigger with rubber-banded duckpins." They enjoyed watching us evade flying pins, especially if we got hit! Action mimicked what they called "Coon Dodging." In our view, we two skinny niggers are faster than hell at resetting pins, too quick to get clipped. Should that happen, we pretended being unfazed.

The YMCA, an institutional pillar, epitomized sanctuaries where Christian democracy's hypocrisy maintained gross contradictions. Even small kids understood it as wrong. How could racism escape being a sin if one embraced Jesus' teachings? It was willful because there was no effort to acknowledge issues or problems. I doubt there's anyone who doesn't know how hurtful it was. Shared awareness existed, recognizing their discriminatory business under a phony guise that the U.S. Constitution and Bill of Rights ideals include all citizens. Such monumental mass obfuscation is unspeakable.

In literature, characters often achieve their shape by living through insecure, unsettling childhoods, which applies to me. These characters wished their living circumstances improved to where envisioned acceptance becomes real. This need for acceptance influences positive character development. Classical literature portrays this personality as romantic. This world wasn't suiting me. At five years old, tragedy, disappointment, and negative happenstances overwhelmed my introverted child's sense of lacking security. When learning in childhood, masses of people fear and hate you without prior contact; coping with adverse effects takes considerable mental adjustment. It launches empty cognitive accommodations by creating romantic views of the future, hoping people change for righteousness.

Childhoods that require struggling to fit in beyond being hated objects means becoming openly antagonistic toward harmful social practices. The truth about conditions creates an undeniable necessity to oppose the status quo. The culture's romanticized childhood yearnings remained the ultimate purpose of struggles, making confronting reality more difficult. Powers perpetuating shattering our humanity always sought to capitalize on promoting romanticism.

By extension, Calvinist-grounded religion supporting the selling of unbridled corporate capitalism's bogus virtues to the masses mutes possibilities for progress. Except for Chas P., the rest of us attended church on Miner Street. Dupe (Helen) was too little. Based on his constant comments, our father had no time for preachers' business. His favorite expression on Christianity went, "I wouldn't give a wooden nickel to see Jesus Christ ride down Market Street backward naked on a donkey." Anti-religion pronouncements contrasted with employing biblical sayings and singing spirituals in his better-than-average tenor voice. There were two grueling bible training hours each week. But my friends and I tried sneaking into the recreation center's playground every Sunday. Getting caught happened without fail, but rare escapes brought immeasurable satisfaction. Those busted during children's service were captives requiring additional bible discussion. Saint Paul Baptist services proved less flamboyant and superstitious than Coonville's other churches. It's a sedate outlook focused on practical issues rather than afterlife preparations.

Reverend J. C. Clark's sermons were more a business manager or teacher-style presentation than preaching. Delivering Southern style, soul-bearing wasn't his standard offering. Usual actors included stern deacons wearing black suits with white gloves. The Senior Choir was regal in gold-trimmed blue robes, white hats, gloves, stockings, and shoes, Church mothers presided. Their supporting soundtrack's faithful humming, grunting, or amen(s) added color. Salient points generated clapping as punctuation. Seeing these folks as other than ordinary neighbors wasn't easy to conjure. If settling into God's temple transformed them, my eyes were blind to it. People acted judgmentally. I consider it disturbing because there were no secrets in living so close together. Signature worship occurred upstairs, where elegant upholstered pews awaited adult congregations on Wednesday nights and Sundays. Side walls exhibited biblical paintings between golden curtains. Exquisite drapes surrounded stained glass windows.

You couldn't eat mom's eggs, sausage, and pancake breakfast on Sundays unless you attended services. Before turning twelve, I set an unbreakable record by eating 22 large flapjacks drenched in pork drippings. She cooked while we ate and ate. No religious motivation existed to justify suffering through preaching until thirteen. After hundreds of Sundays caring about what Jesus said, secular applications took precedence over spiritual indulgence.

Reverend Clark's sermons had no lasting impact on me. Soon, I started sampling services at other denominations. Checking several services to discover differing benefits, they were similar. I wasted time! Local preachers said nothing that confronted oppression. Their beliefs soft-pedaled how things were. Ministers assumed if you entered, they had you. It was their real purpose. You committed because everyday tribulations offered no respite. People relied on prayer plus faith in religious mysteries, seeking psychological comfort and stability in white domination's milieu. That's like having blind faith in the notion that "all men are created equal," becoming the social standard. It was structural functionalism at its best. Religious presentations, Black or white, never created sought-after change. They primarily advocate salvation after death. There, I learned something freeing!

Coonville

Coonville's the term racists used instead of Nigger town. That being the case, Negroes employed it affectionately, mocking racist stupidity. We use terms like Coonville and our culture's uniquely embracing Nigger that whites can't understand. Other ethnicities call Gay Street Elementary "Coonville College" to denigrate us as unsuitable for educating past sixth grade. Using their labels conveys affection for the institution, subtly rejecting colonization's destructive aims. These ways of managing language are essential to our revolutionary struggle.

Developing gifts, like loving school, the outdoors, and sports, came from following Gerald. His influence in seeking formal learning before preschool defies overstatement. Before turning four, sneaking to the crossing at Gay and Adams and following him was simple. Neighborhood kids could travel unaccompanied because grown-ups were surrogate parents. Several times, they allowed Gerry to usher me home before returning. Administrators approached my mother, allowing early enrolment into kindergarten. They granted permission to start before the usual age. Officials didn't give qualified status for funding recreation center classes. Eastside's segregated recreation center has existed since 1938. They limited our elementary education by denying funding, so added taxes served white people. Gay Street's square red brick structure, framed by cut stone, housed levels one to six. It has more than adequate class space, but restricting our development didn't matter. School property occupied an entire city block with quiet streets on three sides. Students entered the building's west side through doors facing Adams Street. Chain-link fencing along Penn Street protected the property's eastern half. This street was different since it marked our Jewish enclave. Gay Street's grounds were strategic because, on weekdays, Jewish children gathered at Chestnut and Penn, boarding buses transporting them to Auditorium school. They rushed over to our playground and joined in seasonal games upon returning. It appeared they were going to private school, but they attended an all-white elementary school.

(Recent history notations describe Gay Street School as "housing white and African American students during a time when segregation was prevalent...") "Coonville College" was a popular derogatory name for Gay Street School throughout town. Everybody used the label. Also, "Coonville" was our residential quarter. The elementary charter accommodated grades 1-6. The government decided that teaching Negroes before first grade wasn't worth the investment. Knowledgeable resolute representatives organized an early learning program by gathering eastside residents' funds supervised under Charles Melton Sr., an astute mulatto politician. Because of his extreme stuttering, our people called him "Scats." He was the colored Elks' "Exalted Ruler" and our titular leader.

My initial term went well since reading, writing, and keeping up with older children were easy. Their morning and afternoon programs allowed me to attend both sessions. Later, early enrolment brought other problems. The harassment started in September. I was too young, so officials refused advancement to Gay Street School. Kindergarten continued for another year. Soon, former mates began chasing me. They decided that not advancing with them made me slow-witted, thus a perfect target for bullying. Their turning against me was devastating.

It was 1942, and World War II roared full tilt. Harmon's junkyard covered half our block along Miner Street. They chased me past trucks lined end-to-end, hauling recyclable war-use materials. Dodging between trailers, I ran into my house or veered to duck into our backyard outdoor toilet sitting over Goose Creek's polluted waters. The creek carried waste from stabled horses that pulled Mr. Harmon's scrap-collecting wagon. They unloaded constant streams of breath-stealing urine-saturated manure. Animal waste-laden water swept through Hoopes Brothers & Darlington wagon wheel factory across Franklin Street, carrying off chemicals expelled from treating wooden wheels. Locked in our outhouse, I screamed for Mom and "Grammudy" (granny).

Day after day, I cried while running, scared they'd hurt me. Begging Gerald to make them stop had no results. He, at nine, refused to threaten little kids. His advice was "stop running." My father added that by choosing to stand up, they'd quit. Before long, that decisive moment arrived. Since none could approach my speed, catching me wasn't happening. When they corralled me—what then? Their threats prompted me to flee, even though we were neighbors. They bullied on the way home from school but we played together later. Without planning, I stopped at the front steps well ahead of my pursuers. Even with outrunning by a mile, going inside didn't happen this time. I waited for my tormentors. There wasn't an exact reason except for accepting my fear! While discussing who would get the fun of hitting me, I struck Audrey Spreel. He was shorter, a few months older. I recognized an opportunity with the smallest kid blocking my path to safety. My straight right knocked out two front teeth before trampling over him through our front door. It was anticlimactic—my fear had vanished on stopping to await their assault.

Now, doubt evaporated, too. The next day, no bullies showed. Rising in self-defense succeeded, as my family predicted. Additional effects of bringing clarity for valuing me, as the first steps, were transformative lessons, such as standing up—resisting bullies. Most children need this understanding, as it befits their circumstances. This stance especially applies when knowing you won't win; holding your ground beats future cowering. Fighting your hardest is best, even when you can't win. Defending yourself includes acting intelligently. After clearing those hurdles, the remaining elementary time was ideal. Though my brother left after second grade, Gay Street remained a safe, nurturing space. Freddy Smith, another fourth-grader, and I disagreed over marbles once. Fisticuffs lasted thirty seconds. After Mr. Fugett's detention, there was more punishment at home. A disputed game of marbles and a shared punishment spawned our lasting friendship.

Coonville's administration, faculty, and staff lived close to students and parents. Families have known each other since before World War II. Negroes interacted everywhere in our quarter, especially at Sunday services. Teachers didn't lecture or teach social justice at length, but there was comfortable closeness minimally pushing against practices denying human rights. Mrs. Gibson, Mr. Anderson, Mrs. Waddleton (a refined super-intelligent squat, rotund woman), Mrs. Ricketts, Mrs. Spangler, Mrs. Robinson, Principal Fugett, and his staff lived in our homogeneous community. Irreverent students called Mr. Anderson "Baldy." Miss Waddleton was "Miss Waddle

Duck" behind her back. Spencer and I were her favorites. Mrs. Waddleton invited us for tea starting in the summer. She set out her fine china and served cookies while delivering encouraging words about working hard through college. Our teacher encouraged us to select books from her wall-to-wall library. My choices were a complete Sir Walter Scott collection alongside anthologies of Shakespeare's plays. Mrs. Waddleton's gesture raised expectations that heightened enthusiasm for entering Biddle Street Middle School at summer's end. We felt immense pride, treated as worthy students within her orbit.

Before starting seventh grade in 1950, summer's transition to integration encountered difficulty when an incident occurred at the Junior High gymnasium entrance. It happened on the way to our library. For years we consumed several books each week. I followed Gerry's lead after moving across town. Exploring research materials in numbers required wagonloads of historical novels, texts, and magazines. Trudging through winter snows, it was a matter of tying boxes on his American Flyer sled. He instigated becoming an avid reader. Weekly trips started after leaving Coonville to live with Grammudy. Before, it required traveling through hostile territory. Our route changed after moving. Now, it's a straight shot north on Church Street, all neutral territory.

West Chester Junior High School

I encountered some white boys playing stickball during summer's next solo library trip. Midday boiled, but the shady sunken gymnasium quad where Church crosses Chestnut remained cool. Their noisy enjoyment caused me to linger, watching from the street. They called out, offering a turn at bat. Before long, tension arose as my batting ability, defense, and quickness dictated play. Soon, the older one announced a halt. They called him Mickey (Rodeback) or "Boss." He stood taller, with olive skin under long dark hair. I had seen him hanging around uptown, wearing a leather jacket and jeans over boots. My best guess: he was aspiring to be a tough character at 14 years old. On my way out, Mickey queried, "Youse wanna fight?"

"No," I answered.

He commanded, "Wells, youse gotta go couple'a rounds wid wunna deese guys afore youse kin go."

That's an interesting unsurprising development. Such sudden prospects couldn't faze me. Challenges loomed for Coonville's youngsters crossing turf boundaries. Otherwise, the eastside ghetto is our encapsulated safe zone. Colored girls, for example, never entered other ethnic communities. This self-appointed fledgling overseer demanded fighting for freedom. His demand meant taking on their chosen champion or more. It could mean defeating one, then getting beaten by the bunch. In any event, it's nothing fearful. Escaping those punks posed no problem because I already showed catching me was impossible. From surviving in Coonville, boys stayed combat-ready, leaving me unmoved. Mickey's followers encircled me. Most were very excited over the looming possibilities. They jumped around while shadowboxing as if conducting radio's Friday Night Fights. Sizing up Jimmy Price, their champion, he looked my age, muscular but shorter, probably three to five pounds heavier. His tiny head had very blond crewcut hair framing cherubic features. Based on his sturdy build, I expected a tough contest. Most important were avoiding being grabbed and remaining on my feet. Jimmy's history of using his fists posed an uncertainty. Surely, I'd done more fighting. Coonville featured strong neighborhood ties and frequent fights. Most of us, from eight onward, were warriors. Customary boyhood stature required a willingness to war. There weren't drawbacks to fisticuffs, but there were consequences for declining to defend one self. Avoiding "fairs" (one-on-one fights) brought a whipping before getting sent outside to face opponents. Normal exposures were why I faced a dozen hostile white boys without feeling stressed. The key was they weren't brandishing weapons. Fistfights happen among people sharing expectations for what is acceptable during ensuing violence. It is a street/playground culture promoting mutual respect among boys. Regardless, we lived together, enjoying basic harmony, even experiencing black eyes, bloody noses, or busted lips. Differences in social conditioning applied to going against strangers—outsiders. Those are circumstances without shared views governing clashes between antagonists. One must assume a stranger's intent is projecting power, inducing fear, and destroying opponents' will. This contest was between Blacks and whites. It's representing our races. Are there concluding thoughts before combat? "This 12-year-old nigger can dish it out." "I can defend myself!" "I won't kowtow to a bunch of Dagos!" "It takes more than this baby-faced punk, backed by other cowardly lackeys, to fuck me up!" We started dancing, jabbing, and clinching. Gashes opened over Jimmy's left eye—straight rights blunted desperate charges. Blood trickled down his cheek in thin lines. I moved too fast. With their boy's cuts oozing red, Rodeback moved between us. On his signal, several cronies grabbed both my arms. Stepping back, Mickey ordered Jimmy to slug me. He mimed gut-punching. Jimmy refused, so Mickey did it himself. His act falls within likely possibilities whenever outnumbered on somebody else's turf. We'd give non Negroes similar treatment, except they'd never venture inside Coonville. No white person ever walked those streets without being escorted. Negro teens never hesitated to cross ethnic boundaries, fighting when accosted. After Rodeback's punch, lackeys followed him into their enclave off Chestnut Street. Mild abdominal stress resets my library trip to jogging south on Church Street toward home. A strange feeling arises while trotting through our segregated town's center after being assaulted by an Italian gang. This incident is a warning for transitioning to desegregation. My inner voice says, away from segregation's protective cocoon, I must bring a more serious warrior mentality than before. Mid-summer's transition from elementary school encountered telltale problem interactions, likely previewing the future. Hostilities with other groups getting viewed through racial conflict lenses are unsurprising. My brother advised me to "be patient. We'll trap Mickey alone," he said. In encountering frequent physical threats, we always handled them ourselves.

Trips to the gym were perpetual reminders of my Rodeback gang run-in. Based on last names, Jimmy Price sat near me in homeroom. I generated no ill feelings toward him. Even though defeated, he balked at hitting me with both arms held. If recognizing or remembering me, it never arose. Catching Rodeback is on file with memories to finish in a future encounter. Since forming our gang, he's disappeared. Failure to avenge unfair incidents lingers as unfinished business. We don't leave such issues unaddressed. No matter how time passes, such cases don't fade away. That's an expectation developed in surviving racist attacks under attending conditions.

Integration followed graduation from Coonville. Other than Jews, there wasn't close contact with whites. Soon, it became clear I was not ready for integration! I faltered in the uncomfortable setting! Upon entering integrated schooling, social insecurity made fitting in difficult. Most other prior school-mates adjusted, but I didn't understand how! Trying to follow their lead, and adapting a different racially determined ambiance, wasn't working. As an example of disturbing white school cultural anomalies, cliques were typical. That differed from the security, familiarity, and confidence encouraged by faculty nurturing at Gay Street Elementary. Diminished classroom involvement characterized my plight. Junior high personnel were white, which made engaging difficult. Though it might appear minor, teacher-assigned seating meant relegation to each class' back row anonymity. Throughout elementary school, I took part in lessons, seated up front. Now, attentiveness disappeared, along with feelings of belonging! Soon, sports competitions against other middle schools became my only source of satisfaction. Gym instructors recognized my potential track contributions as superior, thus pointing in a meaningful direction. Sports recognition is more accessible than performing in other areas because above-average athletic ability in service to our school triggers collective appreciation.

At Biddle Street, I experienced shifting emphasis without grasping its impending importance or future meaning. Changing focus to other than academics was implicit in an immediate playground incident. Robert Erinhart (the wealthiest kid on campus) ripped my brand new shirt while playing "Capture the Flag." My mother just finished making it. She beamed when I wore new clothes. Someone carelessly destroying her creation pissed me off. I had never felt such a passion for clothing. Erinhart, being super-rich, fueled powerful feelings. Great privilege caused his attitude of superiority. Although bigger than me, Richard lost our obligatory fistfight after school. He battled well but lacked street brawling exposure. In my mind, fighting was avoidable. He should have paid for ripping my shirt. Circumstances occurred during games, absent racial cross purposes, allowing negotiating reasonable conclusions without hurting each other. Richard declined an amicable resolution, favoring fighting to settle it. After beating him, I insisted on collecting five dollars every Monday until further notice. Since he'd bragged about a $25 weekly allowance, giving me five wouldn't hurt. Unannounced, Richard moved to an elite private academy near his parent's country estate. Anyhow, six payments satisfied his debt. In reality, continuing unending threats wasn't comfortable.

On another occasion, soon after school started, an attack from a big white boy triggered a serious escalated response. While strolling, unaware, through the second-floor corridor to English, I was stunned by paralyzing pain dead-center between my shoulder blades. It mimicked a bayonet stabbing, taking several seconds to shake. Spencer, my best friend since kindergarten, walking beside me, saw it. Two boys passed laughing while I regained equilibrium. Spencer named Moose, by far the biggest guy we had ever seen at that age. Strange, but this act was our first interaction. Neither Spencer nor I had met them, so hitting me was beyond fathomable justification! It certainly isn't the way we'd choose to meet! (Is it ordinary that big white guys abuse small colored guys? I wondered.) This assault misses being funny, as does any bullying! Should attacks by strangers be taken as humorous? Our people aren't playing that way! Any humor escaped me! We followed as they celebrated.

The next period's room had front and back doors. One has direct hallway access, while the other entered/exited inside a stairwell. With my antagonist(s) about to go downstairs, I dashed through our room, silently emerging behind them. They descended two steps before my fist landed dead-center between Moose's shoulder blades. To my delight, his reflex was like being stabbed (the involuntary arching back, plus crying out from unanticipated sharp pain) before tumbling down several metal-edged concrete steps. There were a few moments of silence. Then, fuming, looking for me, Moose exploded into Mrs. Weir's room seconds later as she prepared roll call.

His scraped face exhibited painful, growling, fierce determination. Wet red color spread around his left ear. Through tears, both eyes were flaming red, enraged. Beside the teacher's desk, I waited with her heavy wooden chair raised over everyone's heads, expecting blinding anger intent on smashing me. There's space for slamming it into him. I don't think he'd survive that, but if so, it's mayhem from there. Just in time, Mrs. Weir yelled at him to stop. I was wrong in expecting him to ignore a white female teacher's orders when she screamed, "You get out!" English lessons proceeded after her stern look at me. She barely audibly mumbled, "I don't want to know what happened." I slid into my exit door seat. He's not coming back!

My fracas showed something interesting. Mrs. Weir had a unique feel for our world as pre-teens and, maybe, for Negroes. Displaying sympathy and support was unusual. Among the teachers, she accepted me despite my reluctance to interact. Every Negro football player rose to defend, knowing nothing. Nothing reached the administration's ears. Having hostilities die at that moment worked out best. Later, Spencer and I didn't even mention it. There was no need to dwell on such happenstances.

Spencer and I understood such incidents get answered in kind since all battles are open-ended. Hostilities conclude when adversaries realize they face future perpetual fighting. These seventh-grade scenarios exemplified ongoing travails with achieving cursory tolerance in Jim Crow's only integrated sliver. Experiencing attacks by white boys having fun, racist or not, only added to the difficulty of adjusting. How could I understand why issues fell on me? My friend is much smaller than me, so why wasn't he attacked? Why me? Integration meant my destruction, while many considered it a welcome change. Above other avenues for acceptance, embracing sports becomes my most workable response. Problems remained unaltered beneath surface appearances.

Junior High School Sports

Junior high's track team grew into a reliable sanctuary, where good and bad experiences, combined with sprinting and hurdling, shaped core attitudes

that influenced my development. My sacrificing personal interests in supporting teams, plus an eventual hard-nosed approach to competing, were due
to positive and negative occurrences. The long-anticipated arrival of days
for donning their steel-trimmed blue uniform proved an elating time. It
launched me into an era when talented kids' names appeared in area newspapers reporting sports excellence. That's the most practical way to gain public
notice. It gave visibility to representing the town through the present into
later years. I sought a hero's mantle, producing value extending across Daily
Local News' circulation. My elevated wishes arose from needing to escape
internalized bonds of the consignment to segregated society's lowest-status
population, where treatment as pariahs destabilized innocent minds. One
should remember that most situations bringing success or failure come in
tandem. A much-expected promising career began with an unadulterated
execution error. It's a reason to radically revise expectations and define effective responses to possible adverse issues.

Failing mattered immeasurably as a 7th-grader displacing the 8th-grade
relay foursome's slowest runner. They were entering their second year
together, so members weren't welcoming. Two were Delbert and Joey,
well-liked Boyer twins, and Joey lost his spot. Being younger and untested
in competitions made my reception chilly! Our early season test came at
Downingtown's Chest-Mont Relays. The 4 x 110 put me on the third leg,
usually the weakest position. Pottstown held the inside, with Coatesville
ahead on my right as the stick passed from Leon Purnsley.

When powering into full stride, passing Coatesville, the kid struck
my hand, knocking our baton onto the ground. Years of dreaming about
winning championships shattered. Shame devastated me. In one instant,
blowing by our rivals, I approached emerging hero status. A fateful moment
later, much-awaited success crashed. My debut failed in the worst way.
During the remaining hours in Downingtown, I languished alone—crying.
Our 30-minute return bus ride went by with me sobbing on its long back
seat. Nobody sat near me. Unending shame overflowed. Family comments
over dinner did not help. Solace only came earlier from Coach Labin. To

diminish my coping difficulties, a weekend of doing nothing helped. I realized future competitions required becoming combative. Being prepared as an ultimate aggressor was necessary. Deep shame taught me that only others should cry. I have to be pushing, hitting, tripping, or spiking opponents. It etched into my subconscious mind! I would never have another disaster. More opportunities remained for showing our talent, and we experienced no losses after that. Season's accomplishments boasted the Chest-Mont League Championship record. Phoenixville's standard, there since 1940, was erased. How great was that?

In 1952, I moved to anchorman, finishing unbeaten at 80 yards. Our foursome won every 4 x 110. My final term concluded by winning the District's 100-yard dash and coming from behind in the relay. Bala Cynwyd's touted anchor became distraught earlier after losing at 100 yards. Since we had never met before, it was his first loss. He'd shown up cocky as—owning victory by being there. I frowned at such bravado displayed by someone so young. Talking shit happens, but this kid acted way too cocky! Living in wealthy suburban Philadelphia Townships influences people to think that way. Their upper-middle-class attitude assumed superiority. Maybe it's about wearing top-quality uniforms. Yeah, checking our opposition's characteristics was standard. He cried again after getting embarrassed in the relay. Dominic Fallini handed off almost even, so we won with no problem. I bumped "hot shot boy," passing in the curve.

After failing the inaugural athletic challenge by dropping the baton, physical contact with others became a trademark expression. Bumping people can happen in any race. Physical contact communicated control, I wanted them to feel me—a signal that fair play ideals were insignificant. Bala Cynwyd's anchorman stood beside his parents, obviously shaken, while they complained to officials about me. They argued throughout our victory lap, while we wore gold medals and carried our big trophy.

MIDDLE SCHOOL TO HIGH SCHOOL

1953 Cross Country

WCHS Coaches decided against my playing football. They conferred, making plans before school opened. Of course, such organizing escaped our adolescent awareness. At tryouts, Coach Halsey said that Mr. Zimmerman denied permission. After P.E. class, Mr. Zim called me to his office to explain. (His cautiousness was correct for someone 6 feet tall and 115 pounds. My legs were so skinny I felt self-conscious.) Already being on his radar meant something. Coaches said to try cross-country. Thoughts of racing, other than sprinting, hadn't entered my mind.

I went out for cross-country, still desiring to partner with Snake, who wasn't interested in competing in sports. A solid solution was assisting Spencer as football equipment manager. Traveling to games on the team bus put me dead center in our most crucial athletic program. I latched onto a way to visit every county settlement, possibly bringing opportunities for meeting girls. Distance races on Fridays didn't produce social contacts. There is nothing sexy about cross-country. Legitimate school-related jobs dampened parental controls, enabling me to escape curfews. Following daily practice, I restocked uniforms and reorganized equipment. Most cross-country meets were on weekdays, while football games were Saturdays. One scheduling exception was traditional Homecoming on Thanksgiving Day against Tredyffrin/Easttown from Berwyn, Pennsylvania. Working alongside Snake served well in providing more freedom.

Expectations for me being good at more than 100 yards were low. I identified as a short-distance guy. Much to my surprise, the increasing mileage became satisfying. Racing wasn't all that bad, either, because I wasn't putting pressure on myself to excel. Soon, with low expectations, there were glimmers of progress toward closing the gap our leaders created. Incremental improvement in endurance began showing heretofore unperceived potential. I wasn't considering becoming a distance runner. The confidence gained while improving in each competition advanced until staying with the leaders was comfortable on good days. Jack Williams, another sophomore more capable of longer distances, started leading us to outperform juniors and seniors. That accomplishment seemed a bit norm-defying rather than legitimately manifesting talent. He never revealed intentions of becoming our best runner. I had no thoughts or desire to get there. My place improved to fourth, earning West Chester's coveted "W" athletic award.

Those beating us throughout our sophomore season are seniors, but we are close. Watching Jack's achievements inspired improvement. By midseason, performances gradually closed in on staying at the front. That potential snuck up on me without conscious intent or noticeable trying. We began making mental notes about those finishing ahead on other teams. They were graduating before us. Our upward trajectory heightened interest, and sophomores leading brought more future promise. Our competition against Episcopal Farm School (EFS), a private boarding school educating single-parent needy boys, constituted October's coming-out party. Scheduling them served as filler without affecting Ches-Mont League standings. We saw it as ideal for testing our improvement—racing with nothing to lose. Our team expected to win, but they had two seniors considered better. EFS's pair ran together beside Jack and me. It was a challenging pace, elevating breathing to stressful points on hilly paths. We pushed from a half-mile out to finish first and second. Jack cruised in with me on his heels. We didn't know Neal Chappell, an EFS sophomore, would eventually transfer, raising WC to unprecedented heights, starting our junior year!

1954 Track Season

1954 turned into a random developmental experience. Unexpected successes in cross-country raised high-scoring possibilities in more track events. My champion sprinter/hurdler record in eighth and ninth grades got ignored after doing so well at longer distances. My interest in doing 440s was limited to relays. Having no specialty squandered opportunities to grow formerly-demonstrated sprinting potential. Others picked events expecting to improve. For me, the utility contributor's role continued, hoping to garner points against opponents at different distances. Sprinter's speed and distance running endurance left me undecided about where to concentrate. The lack of training, plans setting goals, or achieving noteworthy performances over prior seasons made becoming a standout performer difficult. I wanted an event to win championships in 1956. 1954's season concluded and I lettered in mile runs, 880s, and 440s. It remained puzzling what to take on as my signature event. I wasn't an outstanding performer for the first time since elementary school, and getting accustomed to that wasn't easy.

CHAPTER
FOUR

West Chester High School (WCHS or WC)

*Inside and outside his lair, the Children
of the Gray Fox are special.*

Neal:

I left Episcopal Farm School (EFS), moving to Thornton in 1954. Destiny had me riding West Chester High's school bus for eleventh grade. Surprisingly, Harvey doesn't bother me much, living at his house, and was known as "that damn boy." He used my brothers' labels. "Get that damn boy to mow the lawn!" or "Get that damn boy to take out the trash!" Some time prior, wintering at Unc's, Harvey Martino visited, often having late-night chats with Mom. Sneaking up close and listening, I heard them discussing what would happen to her boys when they married. They agreed to focus on my future. Was it now time to go with Jack and Donald? He and Mom were marrying at 53 and 37, if I remember correctly. Guess her marriage concession was placing me in Episcopal Farm School, too. She sacrificed by marrying an old man who provided security until I'm grown. Becoming his wife, she negotiated a solid, safe spot, guaranteeing our survival. This notion held up long term. Soon, Harvey's health deteriorated, and he slowed quickly with age. He grew impotent concerning me. Sure, life works that way. Ailing, he no longer had the strength to hassle anybody. He didn't want me there. His children, adults with families, didn't get involved.

Harvey never got ready for me in his world, given his age when marrying Mom. He counted on being alone with her. Yes, I was gone as much as possible, but if home, everything fell to me—the garden, the yard, the house. Jack (JC), who pulled me from EFS into WCHS, attended Wilmington, Delaware's Goldey-Beacom Business College, with DuPont's offspring. He focused on having fun driving his 54 Mercury. Cars were status symbols, and wealthy kids flaunted them. Amazing what they cost! Neither he nor Donald offered advice on social situations.

Our new public school's instruction began late because West Chester Junior High occupied the building's east side, causing schedule changes. Now, at this joint site, we had a pep rally. It celebrated football, yet our fall session hadn't started! Recent days were spent with Uncle Coty in Goshen, sleeping there. Attending Friday's assembly was an unfamiliar experience. With our band playing fight songs and cute cheerleaders doing routines with polished precision, such gatherings typified public high schools. It was fascinating! What an eye-opening new experience! Social environment-wise, I'm light-years beyond EFS.

Meanwhile, our official opening is Monday! Walking back to Unc's, hearing Mr. Zimmerman's marked nasal-toned shout, "Hey Chapel, what are you doing?" was shocking. (He always called me Chapel, not Chappell (French pronunciation).) You weren't practicing today." Can you believe he recognized me among so many kids? Everyone paused, hearing Mr. Zim's distinctive voice. He has a gentle hands-on way. Navigating in-between boy and girl groups, he grabbed my arm. "You need to attend the workout on Monday!" Students watched, listening. *How the hell does he know me*? I didn't get how he recognized me, let alone could name me. Something unusual and exciting was underway! *Who is he, and what is this?* He taught both older brothers, but none of us looked alike. I blurted out an involuntary "yes, sir" when Mr. Zim ordered picking up my uniform.

On Monday morning, I walked to Montgomery Avenue's school bus entrance, where West Chester's phase began igniting an enhanced running career. Before practice, there was a team meeting inside the locker room. There was no hesitation to love it! It's about fellows connecting! That's it! I'm taken in by them, feeling comfortable! I must become an established club member to thrive in this bigger picture. Without joining an in-house group, you're an outsider, not welcome. Different clubs represented shop people, snotty girls, jocks, cheerleaders, Future Farmers, student government representatives, and marching band members. Practical organizations existed, managing everything happening. I only wanted cross-country (XC) and track. It becomes our thing—what we do!

Williams (Jack, JR) and Noël (Kenny) constitute known quantities on my arrival, but no one else. Then, having similar schedules, we shared some classes while making up our running program's backbone. So, bonding soared without effort. Kenny and I chose class schedules supporting workouts. Leadership with teammates grew from elevating their running by displaying knowledge about training, teaching racing tactics, and showing courage (guts), manifested on difficult racecourses. On or off the roads, we showed dedication ensuring everyone reached their potential. That gained respect for our leadership. So, there's a single team mind understanding what improving requires. Those not paying the price quit. So once younger members embraced valuing guts and commitment, speeding up collective performances went easier.

Our early training focused on sticking together, elevating everyone's allegiance, and performing well. Public recognition through news coverage coupled with morning announcements helped our cause. Principal's assemblies praised our most recent conquest. We elevated cross-country significance. "Zim's boys" meant plenty; being under his wing had many privileges. Nobody questioned our coming or going. Our adopted routines favored supporting extracurricular schedules. Absence and tardy rules didn't apply to us. We earned exemptions from physical education. People must have realized we dedicated ourselves to producing something special. Zim was an institution himself. With affection, we referred to him as the Gray Fox.

When leaving EFS, WC students are strangers, except for two cousins— Victor, and Sarah Smiley. That changed on finding Kenny and JR. (We met once before, competing against them while at EFS.) They also are juniors. There were other outstanding youngsters. I already knew those two names and their talent. This group made a hell of a force! We have to do this! One kid, Bobby, lived near me and got cajoled into joining. On Krapf buses, he heard sales pitches every morning. Some seniors hung on as okay performers. JR, Kenny, and I were much more talented as training progressed. It's our show. A few older guys (seniors) are unknown characters. They're lucky to compete. I quickly came to know each of the youngsters behind us, and they respected us. Next year, we're three veteran upperclassmen, with five juniors reinforced by four promising sophomores. That's a hell of a lineup! Naturally, there are many newspaper write-ups. Recognition comes with winning everything!

One by one, people peeled off, going home together after training. Giunta split into ritzy north-central housing, then Norman Bell. Kenny swung west on Barnard Street before Jack went west on Union Street. Conversions explored life, walking across town, end to end, and tightening personal connections. Great value came from strolling the Borough's length, particularly building bonds and enhancing relationships. Sharing life's fundamentals after practice, walks, and accompanying conversations created lifelong brotherhood foundations. My idea of us as "Brothers of the Wind" sprang from there. Approaching High Street's last traffic signal, I'm left thumbing rides traversing country roads entering nightfall.

While other fellows arrived home, I hitchhiked seven more miles. You can't catch Krapf's school buses because transporting kids stops after 3 p.m. No public transportation serves Thornton. Winter darkness descended fast, but trekking alone offered no other choice, and no other options existed. A gay college professor gave me frequent lifts. His courses were favorites among many athletes, and he gave them good grades! He was a welcome resource getting me to Wilmington Pike's crossing with Dilworthtown Road.

More than anyone, old Sam Cheney stopped. He drove an ancient Ford pickup truck, and he chatted non-stop. His mouth went faster than a hummingbird's wings. Faking understanding sufficed! Drivers let me out on Route 322 at Dilworthtown Crossroads. Another ride covering Glen Mills Road into Thornton was necessary. Mom's new husband's house was ten minutes away after catching rides down Delaware County's country lanes. Anybody driving Dilworthtown Road picked me up because only locals traveled there. Everyone knew me, making hitchhiking safe.

Strolling with my track compatriots uplifted me—it was glorious! With this dedicated group, I dwelled in a spirit of freedom, fulfilling my sense of belonging and reaching depths EFS couldn't produce. Life's possibilities were better with accessing abundant choices connected to frequent, fulfilling social contacts—something lacking until now. This new environment nourished my soul, bringing a positive outlook. Negotiating less restrictive environments constituted a blessing. Our exchanging intimate thoughts and feelings, scheming, gazing out classroom windows surveying expansive athletic grounds, planning upcoming outings, and walking after workouts fed into running becoming our most satisfying life interest. Beyond WC's existing ethos, my most valued EFS viewpoint was steadfast loyalty to those sharing your condition. One mustn't forget that surviving means keeping solid relationships with your mates—protecting each other. Other cooperative values learned before remained undetermined. Earlier academic discipline had dissolved to the degree that recapturing that fire was impossible. Academic achievement doesn't start again when no longer critical to a new lifestyle. So, I never carried books. Kenny understood well! More significantly, we focused on extracurricular activities by choosing classes enabling easy passing grades. Scheduling subjects together and occupying back row seats was our MO. We spent hours looking out windows, dreaming, or plotting against competitors. Ideas of high school constituting college preparation escaped us from histories of contending with unfavorable social circumstances.

1954 CROSS-COUNTRY

Kenny:

Cross country was my saving grace. Joining 1954's Warrior thinclads fostered a quick, thorough transition with full social acceptance. Regular practices provided rewards and established purpose with built-in, high satisfaction, promoting achievement. Not only were we set on improving, but also on dominating future competition. Judging from race results, only those grad-uating might beat us. Mission Numero Uno was becoming elite as soon as possible. Sticking with our best would get me there. Practices started with cruising over Goshen Road's race course at varying intensity levels, either forward or backward. Inside the stadium, more single-lap repeats using different tempos ended days. Against Downingtown, our first fall season outing, my small gap with compatriots narrowed, settling solid among our top five. A bigger question was, to what extent can improvement occur beyond here? Our vision is that the Warrior's first perfect record is doable. We looked long-range while working hard. Capn Jack was in front against Downingtown's Whippets, pulling us into 1954. Our approach of forming tight groups was more important than running faster. We dared look ahead, expecting an undefeated 1955 campaign.

1955 TRACK

Neal:

An unforeseen achievement capped my inaugural track season when we tied Coatesville as League Champions. The Red Raiders dominated Ches-Mont's A section by winning seven straight times. Sharing the title shocked everybody because the dual meet performance was average, landing midway against six squads, counting wins and losses. Our relay foursome ran Penn's Winter Carnival suburban section preliminaries in February, and we failed to advance to the next round. Adequate 440 talents weren't there, and the sixth-place finish felt consistent with our current ability. With one senior, we achieved another milestone, eclipsing West Chester's 4 x 880 records.

A correct description is calling us average. Week-to-week, Jack, Kenny, and I expected to blossom much later, lurching through spring trying to figure out signature events. No standout successes occurred among us running 440s, 880s, miles, and scoring points. Kenny had corresponding results doing similar combinations with adding 220s. Efforts yielded nothing notable. Our problem was never doing specific training, enough racing, or achieving results showing superior possibilities doing different distances. Cap'n Jack (Williams) chose the 120-yard hurdles and the mile run. Both events proved productive with victories. His physical makeup featured better-than-average speed and high endurance. His leg spring converted into a bounding stride. No wonder he hurdled well! He earned his 1956 specialty after finishing fourth in District 1's mile run. Such decision-making stayed unsettled for Kenny and me. Our lot was "try some sprints, some middle distances, and then wait until next season, sorting things out." Our ultimate interest remained to look forward to September 1955, launching Mr. Zimmerman's most successful x-country program performance ever. Our ultimate goal was to be a top-three team at Cobb's Creek Country Club's District 1 Championship in Philadelphia, capturing PIAA qualifier spots going to Happy Valley. Oddly, there were no verbalized thoughts until that day.

1955 CROSS-COUNTRY

Kenny:

Juvenile Court, people surmised, allowed me to finish school after being convicted because of sports. I connected as an asset to the high school and respected authorities. With me available, we could predict an undefeated cross-country campaign. A large part of the court's leniency was the positive relationships I had with coaches since seventh grade. I assumed they spoke to Judge Blakeley, supporting me without being asked. WCHS benefited plenty after my avoiding imprisonment. It was Zim's final year, so our teams worked toward making this his most successful.

Neal:

1955's XC squad won all eight scheduled dual contests. Dominating weekly, our top guys took turns winning. Races got choreographed, so Chick, Bobby, and Petey had each crossed first. Rather than teammates tying, planned solo victories spread individual recognition. Our final home meet was one I wanted to win, and I planned my concluding cross-country scenario, waiting until then. We staged going undefeated by timing the race's finish as football's homecoming halftime featured act.

There was high theatrical value because many students attended games with football fans, families, and news reporters. What an opportunity to demonstrate our talent to the assembled school and town! The resounding spectator response blew us away when we entered our packed stadium. Yeah, we weren't competing for selfish glory. I took comfort in Kenny announcing that if someone else tried winning, he'd stop them. I believed him because he would do anything. During one long run traversing Riggtown, a white guy who threatened his sister crossed our path. Saying nothing, he knocked him down, rejoining our group moments later. That said plenty. An unexpected acknowledgment was cheerleaders forming a reception aisle. Organized cheers lent surprising spirit, including dancing, and waving Garnet and White Pom-Poms. My waiting until our Phoenixville meet became an unparalleled, rewarding choice. Sunday's Daily Local News sports page covering our undefeated campaign included my picture. Their comprehensive article had me feeling great! My WCHS experience was as far as I could be from farm-labor-driven boarding school life.

It was late October, with x-country completing. We seniors, facing our last league race, loved these tests, their challenging pace, required endurance, and shared grit. In such contests, we cherished the moment starter's guns fired, supporting each other until everyone's home generated heartfelt appreciation. West Chester State College's manicured grass had painted chalk line stalls separating paddock spaces, caging 60 starters. We arrived at station #3 long before starting, intending to command the event. The usual nervousness before every significant challenge climbed above normal.

Along with the Championship as conclusion to a perfect season, it was Coach Zimmerman's Ches-Mont X-Country farewell. Individuals sought to honor him by winning. Anxious nerves subsided once mates showed readiness and willingness, intending to compete all-out. An undefeated record predicts typical execution will win. After several minutes, visualizing the upcoming battle subsided. We ran through feared oxygen debt, dashing toward establishing ourselves, fronting a charging mass. JR, in the lead, comforted following mates while we positioned familiar characters to prevail. Soon, Kenny pulled alongside him. Our reliable front-running captains signaled regular performances, assuring good scoring. We (veterans) warned against going out uncontrolled. Rookies always did it, even with abundant warnings. Starting too fast didn't prevent them from achieving expectations. Over time, you can grow into it. The increasing effort helped improve every week. Uncharacteristically, Pete Giunta, our stellar junior, surged ahead. Our collective thought, "While he's no threat, maybe today will be his best—if he's not too ambitious!" What an encouraging omen on an already pleasant sunny day! The weather was picture-book, perfect for stadium crowds enjoying ball games. Brilliant days can cause one's mind to wander beyond immediate tasks.

A factor that helped us focus was long-standing rivalries getting put to rest. Numbers of individuals were familiar actors. For the respective team's seniors, our histories were closing. Previous confrontation's competitive antipathies were being rendered passé. These thoughts swirled within us, assembled, waiting to charge across open ground. They had a path cutting through split openings, exiting campus at the reach's far end. The course proceeded along West Chester State's northern boundary onto country roads looping south before curving east toward a symbolic triumphant return via their campus' "Historic Quadrangle." The college's grand entrance funneled out, crossing sprawling grass fields onto a cinder practice oval requiring three-fourths of a circuit. We preach being physical and exercising self-protection. Within mad dashing mass starts, protecting your position dictates behavior. There is elbowing or pushing encroachers, avoiding tripping. Once through the gates, a small group formed, comprising several strong opponents. Jogs on weekends make the course familiar, giving us a home-field advantage.

Our Co-Captains lost no competitions except against each other or teammates by design. When challenged, they take first and second. On this occasion, among those who could win, I stayed near the pace, leading the trailing pack. Positioning remained stable, traversing the college perimeter, gliding past apple orchards, and then grinding up bordering western hills. Before 2 miles, a single rising lane gradually leveled off while curving east to skim the campus's southwest edge. Starting up New St., Petey (Giunta) eased ahead without attracting attention. He won't keep going so fast! Eight of us, now intent on winning, drew together. He created an insurmountable gap before our senses returned. Focusing on each other, the usual pain of demanding tempos never surfaced. Then, reality hit us! Pete surged 90 yards ahead with 880 left! Our tempo increased, charging to close the gap. But success wasn't likely. Only luck favoring us, his miscalculation, or both could allow overcoming Giunta's lead. Misfortune had its way when, on the verge of an upset, disaster struck Giunta. He missed the poorly marked turn for re-entering campus! Once he recovered, we chasers had drawn close within several strides. Among our closing group, victory belongs to whoever had more leg speed. No one in District 1 could stay with Kenny, now near the end where endurance wasn't a factor. Reporters described a great contest where outcomes got determined at the very end. "The Race For First Place, Won By West Chester's Noël, was thrilling." Sportswriters saw those last moments as I did, trailing on their heels.

Kenny:

To finish as the team and individual champion, with Cap'n Jack (Williams) second, comported with this year's promised success. Pete Giunta was fourth, with Neal fifth. First place secured Daddy's bet plus bragging rights over Ron Houghton, his white Berwyn friend. Ronnie's father challenged his son would take me. Chas P. had never mentioned an upcoming personal contest! Ronnie came in third in an earlier race, but Jack and I appeared to need a desperate sprint on his home course. Not taking control before the last 100 yards gave observers a false impression of being a competitive contest. Comparing other race results, he couldn't challenge us. Actual jousting was only between our teammates. While cruising in, we agreed on tying. Curious, no one noticed we always had a two-to-one advantage over an opposing team's best runners and a reason for confidence.

Over most of the course Pete Giunta, No. 3 man among the Garnet and White harriers, set the pace. He was in the front when the pack returned to Wayne Field with a little more than a half-mile of course ahead. He led over the back stretch of the track, down over the soccer field and up the terrace to the tennis courts. Close on his heels all the way was Ron Houghton of the Conestoga team.

Coming back to the track for a final quarter-mile lap, Williams was in front, with Houghton still second, Noel third and pacemaker Giunta pounding along in fourth place. ...

At the first turn, Noel moved up to take first place and Houghton passed Williams to remain second. Just before the last turn, however, Williams passed Houghton and was just a stride or two behind Noel coming down the stretch. Houghton finished third with Giunta closing in for a safe margin in fourth place.

Houghton's mistake was following rather than forcing a fast tempo. Setting a pace and depleting our kick was his only chance. In this moment of mental lapse, Giunta sped out fifty yards without us noticing. He approached, stealing my title! Unfortunately or not, with less than a half-mile remaining, Petey missed the last turn. We called out, turning him back. Three of us pulled even with him moments after he returned to the course. From there, victory was mine because I had sprinter speed. I apologized before sprinting with

300 left (I considered waiting until 220 to go). After receiving our awards, I chastised our youngster (Petey), calling him a sneaky disrespectful ingrate who attempted to steal my crown. (25 years later, our undefeated season received acclaim as 1956's defining class achievement.)

The local competition ended after Jack and I finished 5th and 7th in District 1, earning trips to the State Championship. 1955's State qualifying run courted disaster. Stats showed we were shoe-ins for seats on the bus to Happy Valley, and Neal and Petey had better-than-average possibilities. Racing across pristine fairways began predictably with Abington's Clark and Englebrink, along with Lower Merion's Dose, pushing the tempo beyond our ability. They're suburban Philadelphia's best, but we saw them as other than invincible. Our strategy was to follow off their pace, looking to overtake them, pressing the second circuit. While trailing, we watched the battle churning over immaculate groomed fairways.

Warring with each other might expend enough energy to allow us to move into contention. Halfway to finishing, the leaders' turnover markedly increased. After rounding a north-end maple grove, we exited onto a narrow trail cut through trees with intact green plumage. It's October, well into the time when leaves show autumn reds, oranges, and yellows. Our animal core detects autumnal sunlight's subtle changes on late fall days, presaging winter. October's ambiance turned on an anxiousness to run, peaking as cross-country ended. After crossing wooden bridges over Cobb's Creek, the path converted into rough utility road ruts heading south. It became a challenging freak point because an inch-thick chunk of tree root glommed on my right spike upon entering the second loop. Staying side-by-side with Jack, concentration faltered while struggling to dislodge an unbalancing piece of wood before spraining an ankle, breaking bones, or stumbling to the ground. Going through half of my career's most important race with some foreign object stuck on a spike had a problematic impact. This mishap caused a rush of fear and questioning fate. *Why me? Why now? Should I stop to remove it? Should Norman Bell, head student manager, pluck it off when we passed him? Would using help disqualify me? Can I make the top ten with something hobbling me? What else should I do besides continuing while hoping it'll break apart?* My decision became moot because I was afraid to stop and restart; placing meant persevering with an object threatening injury. The increasing pace wasn't wise because elevating force through the remaining distance could injure me. Only more significant accidents could threaten the state's qualifying with our lead. I slowed sufficiently to prevent injury. Amid everything, the reduced effort ended in securing the top ten. After crossing the line, we waited for Neal, Giunta, and Harris. Hopes of other teammates earning slots at Penn State failed. In seventh, I wondered how the District race would have turned out had a destabilizing object not crippled me. Two charges performing at the state level put that feather in Zim's cap. Neither of us ran worth a damn fighting subzero temperatures with knee-deep "Happy Valley" snow. Under icy conditions (they sprayed water that immediately froze), Zim argued against running. They delayed for hours, waiting until heavy snowing quit. He allowed us to run after we accepted dropping out if conditions worsened. We had never been so frozen! It was freezing where warm-up runs only wasted energy! He felt more than satisfied with us getting that far. Our success launched their legacy of special WC teams. We hoped they'd continue long after we left. Accomplishments resulted from respect for Zim along with regard for each other.

Neal:

Our closing 1955 act was at Marcus Hook Lions Club's Invitational. Our biggest problem was contending with their petroleum vapor-filled air. How could residents stand it? Conestoga, our chief rival, had captured successive titles. Winning another would mean they own the Mayor's trophy. If defeating our traditional opponents denies them permanent trophy possession, we get a double-layered triumph. Spoiling their quest dominated the pre-race discussion. We proved ready, taking first, second, third, and the Invitational crown. Giunta followed in seventh before Jerry "Chick" Stine, thirteenth, completed our team scoring. (Chick transferred from St. Agnes Catholic School, a refugee Kenny pulled from baseball. He later played pro.) 26 vs.

49 is a convincing margin. Personal funds bought our post-season Pancake House breakfast. That's icing on the cake for Mr. Zimmerman's tenure.

1956 TRACK

Kenny:

After three months indoors, snow still covered surfaces before sunny days allowed outdoor workouts. Having ended distance training, I transitioned to sprint work because no competent dash people joined. My best performances were at 440 yards, but I racked up 220-yard first places each week. The Ches-Mont Relays in Downingtown, Lower Merion Relays, Penn Relays, and the League meet headlined 1956's slate. Dual schedules comprised head-to-head competitions between Chester County and Montgomery County public institutions. Additional meets were against Delaware teams. We (seniors) spearheaded dominating opponents by winning multiple running events. Williams and Noël were consistent names appearing in news coverage, notching numerous wins. Neal's (Chappell) name appeared each Sunday for winning 880s. Reporters asked Zim about season prospects. He responded, "Outside of Noël, Williams, Chappell, and a few others, we don't have much." An early write-up hailing competition with Conestoga said, "Jack Williams and Ken Noël score track 'triples.' Most exciting for the day was the 880 won by Neal Chappell, who kicked at the finish to snap the tape."

Our outing with Coatesville continued trends, with the following reporting:

West Chester out-pointed the Coatesville Red Raiders on the running strength of Ken Noel, Jack Williams, both triple winners, and Neal Chappell who copped his third consecutive 880. Noel out bid the opposition for 100-yard dash honors and bested the field in the 220. The 440 was the senior's third jewel for the day. Jack Williams won the high hurdles, mile, and low hurdles.

Next week's sports page addressing Downingtown's meet results stated,

In the dashes, hurdles and middle distance events, West Chester banked on the tireless efforts of senior Ken Noel and the matchless grace of Jack Williams. Neal Chappell, the 880 star, went against a strong field. Ken Noel and Jack Williams, fleet co-captains, snapped three tapes each and Neal Chappell won his fourth straight 880.

Major triumphs came in showcase 4 x 880s. Reporting said, "There was a win at the Downingtown Relays with Ken Noel, Bob Harris, Neal Chappell, and Jack Williams running in that order. The foursome repeated with first at the next week's Lower Merion Relays." Their invitational had more prestige than other track events outside Philadelphia. Local news gave an account:

West Chester won the two-mile relay with Jack Williams running anchor after a lead by Ken Noel, Bob Harris, and Neal Chappell. They broke the school record set last year (1955) by the team of Ken Noel, Dominick Falini, Jack Williams and Norman Bell.

An unlikely Penn Relays' result delivered an unprecedented mid-season highlight bolstering Coach's legacy. No venue equaled Penn's intense competition attended before enthusiastic crowds. Their boys' 4 x 440 series was an international pinnacle. None was more dramatic than how ours unfolded. We trailed on initial legs but maintained contact with frontrunners, with Bobby Harris passing to Jack Williams. Still behind everybody, I never lost real-time visions of winning. JR went into fifth place, handing off to Neal. We were closer than this stage at Downingtown. They were right where we wanted them, as Neal moved past 4th and 3rd, a stride behind 2nd! He had enough strength to push me through the baton zone faster than other teams. With the baton in hand, I settled within an arm's reach from Downingtown, with Coatesville leading through the first turn. It felt like Neal threw me on their tail! Side-by-side, hugging the curve, they forced my throttling back.

They drew apart on the back straight and restrained energy pushed me past another one onto the Coatesville anchorman's shoulder. It seemed like using magic! Invisible forces had taken control! We scurried like greyhounds after frightened rabbits that were too slow; I closed fast, exerting no extra effort. Pure momentum took me past them both before entering the turn. Our strategy, drafting before passing so others did the work, proved unnecessary. No potential control problems arose when processing essential measures (distance, speed, prior contacts with these athletes, and transpiring effort) for prevailing over the remaining 150 yards. Bathed by relief, I relaxed.

As we entered the back straight, spectators rose, creating an increasing resounding roar circling within the packed stands. Thundering cheers penetrated my consciousness, progressing around Franklin Field, keeping pace with us. Penn has great spectator responses, erupting during dramatic contests! In these moments, seconds before finishing, the crowd noise peaked. Their encouragement's volume brought spiritual satisfaction as they voiced tribute for moving from last to first, improving through every stage, and improbable third and anchor legs were poised to win.

Their finishing tape broke over my chest, synchronized with a mop of red hair splashing on the ground beside me. A reddened face plunged, kissing the cinder surface alongside my trailing right foot. Sustained spectator roaring accompanied my last strides, cresting as Tredyffrin Easttown's (Conestoga) runner closed with each step. Genuine drama raised into climax! Drowned under so much noise, I sensed no one closing. No matter, Coach Zimmerman's concluding Penn outing ended victoriously. Joy, consuming us, abounded. Such an unlikely win; celebrating our mentor was foremost because he cared about us.

News columns praised West Chester's first Penn championship.

FIRST CHAMPIONSHIP

West Chester rewarded its retiring coach, Harold Zimmerman, with the Ches-mont League title in 3:37.3 -- the school's first championship since the event was inaugurated into the relays in 1951 — by rallying to overtake Coatesville. The victory quartet, anchored by Ken Noel, also included Bob Harris, Jack Williams and Neal Chappell.

APRIL 28, 1956 WIN FOR ZIM

Warriors Cop Ches-Mont Mile On Penn Track

Out to give veteran coach Harold I. Zimmerman another memory to cherish after his retirement in June, his current mile relay quartet won the Chesmont League mile, a schoolboy highlight of the Penn Relay Carnival in Philadelphia Saturday afternoon. Beaten by Coatesville at the Chesmont Relays in Downingtown a week earlier, the Garnet and White combine bettered the time of that effort to beat out the Red Raiders and Pottstown. The winning time at Penn was 3:37.3. In Downingtown, it was 3:42.

Actually the Warrior thin-clads were given their stiffest opposition by a quartet from Conestoga High. The Pioneer runners came in second but were disqualified for crowding on a turn. This placed the Coates second, Trojans third and Downingtown fourth.

Bob Harris led-off for the Garnet and White Saturday and was followed by Jack Williams and Neal Chappell before Ken Noel came up with a great anchor lap to nab the victory. These same runners won the two-mile relay at the Lower Merion Relays last Saturday. The winning time Saturday was only three-tenths off the Carnival record for the Chesmont mile, set at 3:37 by Avon-Grove High in 1954.

PENN RELAYS SYMBOLIC "BROTHERS OF THE WIND"

The "Brothers of the Wind" are naked like a blank slate as they approach Ben Franklin on the seat of knowledge, wisdom and human achievement. The last in line carries the baton of human progress behind his back to hand off to generations yet to follow in their footsteps. With their ascension in victory, the completeness of our Darwinian existence is captured in a single relay on an oval track. We (as students and dedicated runners) are all "Brothers of the Wind" in pursuit of human excellence.

For me, the remaining outdoor racing unfolded a pace until another surprise at the League Championships. After five years, hosting Ches-Mont's track and field finals created many memorable moments. Having them here allowed Mom and Chas P. to watch together for the first time. It was a rare opportunity to close my career there, serving long as proving grounds! With one lap, my signature event, 100s and 220s, fell to me because no others could score. Two miles of walking from home to the stadium raised thoughts reviewing my multi-year running history that reached notable peaks in cross-country. 1954 was miles; 440-yards and 880-yards marked 1955. Each season, they required me to switch events where needed.

In 1956, no sprinters joined, so I was a short-distance guy. In seven dual meets, I took four 100s and got second three times while undefeated in the 440s and 220s. No one proved competitive with me at 220 yards, but I was the slowest 100-yard final qualifier, and being slowest gave me lane eight. It's a poor lane, with a chest-high five-inch diameter iron rail inches away. It blocked lower-level bleacher access, and anyone near the edge had restricted movement. I rejoiced at getting through prelims with a chance at placing sixth.

Pottstown's and Phoenixville's sprinters dominated the hundred. Favorites crouched in center lanes, poised to burst out after the starter barked directions. After coming "set," we're off hurtling over packed cinders upon the gun blast. The best specialists staged a heated battle, attacking each other stride for stride down center lanes. After eighty yards, flashes of disbelief hit because my senses said I was in front! Indeed, they'll pass this straining torso before it's over! Out of the picture, banished to Lane 8, competitors missed seeing me. I would wager nobody experienced so much surprise as I. In third place, a Native American from Pottstown collapsed, disappointed over losing. I'm shocked that someone reacted so distraught. How could he be so sure about winning before racing? I wasted no time crossing into the stands and embracing my proud parents. Both parents watching after competing for so many years was most gratifying! Daddy circulated, collecting money owed by people wagering against me. He won a fool's bet. Happy money losers exchange boisterous talk, enjoying my unlikely success. Monumental upsets are priceless. As a prohibitive 440 favorite, it's an easy run while saving for the 220 or mile relay. Maybe three individual titles will generate sports headlines and scholarships across eastern Pennsylvania.

No threats existed in the 220, and it promised to be a more comfortable win than the quarter. Others weren't strong enough to challenge. A "hat trick" might bring scholarship offers, but expectations remained relatively low. Inquiries should have come, but none had. When an announcement blared, calling 220-yard contestants, Coach Zimmerman approached, letting me know final event decisions were mine. State rules restricted athletes to three races. I'd succeeded twice. Zim communicated favoring the relay without saying it. We shared quiet contemplation, looking across abandoned infield space. Field events had ended. Nothing remained to be considered because I'd decided on anchoring one more time.

Outsiders might find this unusual, but the team came first. Relay members were Penn's quartet—Williams, Harris, Chappell, and me. Mile relays express ultimate engagement on the track. JR destroyed our school, stadium, and League one-mile run records earlier. He was ready for his fastest leadoff ever.

Neal deserved a gold medal, and judges cheated him out of an 880 championship, making relay gold even more meaningful. He hadn't lost a half-mile this year. Later, finish-line pictures showed him winning. The conversation afterward expressed great disappointment:

The unfolding of the first lap is a blur of different runners surging to the front and we were twelve guys elbowing each other for positions on the inside lane. After a full lap of this physical combat, I knew my best tactic was to get out of the crowd and control the race from the front. It took some extra effort, but once I gained the lead position, it was a matter of holding it to the finish. There was no pressure until I entered the home stretch. Closing in on the finish line with every stride, I could hear the approach of Baxter, from Coatesville. As he got close enough, I also felt him pushing and coming into the fringe of my personal space. We were a few yards from the finish and I just gutted it out. I crowded to the inside edge of his lane kept my right shoulder and arm in front of him to break the tape. It was shocking, unbelievable, when the judges called him the winner! There was no way to record and prove the actual finish. Some track meets had photo finish equipment, but it was too expensive for us. Without such equipment, there was no basis for protesting a decision. All they said was the guy from Coatesville was wearing red shorts and that was what caught their eye. Funny but the picture that made it into the newspaper showed me in front as the winner. I can only say it was very disappointing and my only loss in League competition. There was no way I could feel other than robbed! There was little solace to be drawn from all my teammates feeling the same way about it.

I was in disbelief that he only has silver! Jack has gold and silver, and I have two golds.

Since Neal's nearing his WC journey's end, the 4 x 440 is his only gold medal shot. A gold medal around his neck meant more to me than an easy third victory running 220 yards! Expecting his best relay performance, I envisioned a more decisive win than at Penn. Our grand vision is triumphing before the home crowd. That evaporated after JR got clipped, falling while leading after 180 yards. I brought that baton home last with no regrets. Electing the relay brought great personal satisfaction because making such an unselfish choice carried goodwill over our lifetime.

With Co-captain Jack, I earned entry to the Pennsylvania State Championship at the District I Meet. He captured his specialty (mile) while breaking school and district marks again, while I ran second in the quarter-mile. We made it through preliminary rounds in Penn State's Friday trials and semifinal heats and placed sixth in our respective Saturday finals. For running at WC, 1955 and 1956 proved banner years. Most unusual, but never noted, was being undefeated in the 220 and claiming Ches-Mont 100-yard and 440-yard dash titles. There was my 2.5-mile Ches-Mont Cross-Country win alongside Championship sprinting. No officials or reporters knew of anyone capturing both sprint and distance running championships. Successfully mixing those races had never occurred. After two years away, I pulled off an improbable resurrection of speed. Fast-twitch muscles got resurrected just in time. An athletic rediscovery meant more than claiming starring positions. It included attitude adjustments deflecting segregation's impacts that had caused insecurities managed by combative reactions. It was like resting between the middle rounds of a prize fight. Personal scores remained to settle before reaching a Jim Crow court defying liberation and closing our senior year.

CHAPTER
FIVE

Destroy the Yard Niggers and Leave No Unfinished Business!

Every generation must sacrafice to lift the next one higher, even if that is all it can do.

Kenny:

Our successes created little consequence for the present and future, with only individuals changing. On the inside, there's no escaping who I am. Defiant behavior under Jim Crow makes me a juvenile delinquent. Under the circumstances, championship running attracted attention and distracted people from seeing that negative realities existed. But it was critical that I didn't fall in with those confused or blinded by athletic ability, translating that as social achievements. I didn't fool myself that much. I couldn't let daily contradictions and degradation result in accepting conditions causing mental illness or self-destruction. Therefore, life bent toward resistance. In our world, confronting slavery's vestiges, destroying lingering manifestations, plus erasing its internalized locks on each victim's human spirit, is necessary. Those are fundamental reasons for resisting.

Though living on the verge of formal imprisonment, criminalized acts of rebellion remained in daring to violate juvenile court probation. With full awareness of my precarious position, I dismissed controls by internal constraints. In established routines, there were frequent occasions requiring that I fight dehumanization. Walking to school, for example, was not an innocuous practice. Penn Street landscaping, from Chestnut to Washington, had a degrading feature. Front yards with lawn jockeys lined two blocks, ending at Stadium Alley. Their existence made innocent walks injurious. (Black students call such figurines "Yard Niggers.") For three years, we faced multiple totems symbolizing America's racist history and current representations of slavery, in the form of these Jim Crow caricatures, twice daily. They carried out covert destructive purposes demeaning Negroes. A route negotiating the train tracks offered a dangerous path, avoiding insulting countenances. But railroad tracks were not a realistic choice for our sisters.

"Yard Niggers" are the most offensive, racist images depicting us. Their stunted chimpanzee bodies had giant heads with massive protruding foreheads shading bulging eyes—looking ready to explode. Most pictured ears are as big as average hands, and each has swollen bright red lips under flaring nostrils. In mocking poses, hailing an era where slaves raced horses, they stared at us from presumptuous tranquility guarding manicured, green-carpeted lots. These projected representations assault our sensitivity and feelings of self-worth, symbolizing powerlessness. Such depictions exemplified an inability to protect ourselves from voluminous degradation. Residents often doubled down with twin statues gracing walkways.

W.E.B. Dubois writes that propagating ugly stereotypes is an instrument for terrorizing Blacks. It is orchestrating unrelenting disparagement. Scholars regarded Jockos as tools for intellectual and psychological intimidation. Distorted faces and bodies characterize Negro physical inferiority in racist cultures. They show whites don't value nonwhites as individuals or productive society members. Social science studies hold that perpetuating these images attacks an individual's well-being. Scholarly conclusions explain that assaults using stereotypes were relentless sources of denigration warranting resistance. After years of absorbing insults, accessing educated analyses taught us that not executing defensive actions is acting against ourselves. We needed change, but political officials, teachers, administrators, school staff, and students lacked sufficient consciousness to interpret and remove those racist symbols. These folks regularly saw those statues. Many viewed them when coming and going to work. It was past the time for decisive action!

Walks with white schoolmates along Penn Street's otherwise pristine yards were uncomfortable. We took great pains faking not paying attention to Yard Niggers, displayed with feigned neighborly politeness. If while walking along, we acted as though they aren't there, maybe our white friends wouldn't notice. Like whistling by Gay Street Graveyard, magical thinking might keep offending symbols from asserting more presence. It might have been enlightening to ask white companions their opinion vis-à-vis those demeaning depictions! One problem with asking was admitting awareness, which calls attention to "Jocko" symbolism penetrating our consciousness, elevating the shame of oppression.

In contrast, J. Oscar Dicks Stadium, where my most satisfying moments played out, lay behind those offending dwellings. Second-class status decreed accepting them before our births. After that, each time, it was a matter of suppressing judgments.

I suggested not finishing our careers, leaving youngsters facing this perpetual gauntlet of Old South insults. Helen, a ninth grader, was joining Patsy, traveling that offending path down Penn Street. Freddie's two sisters and brother faced this pantheon of insulting caricatures. In fairness to Coonville kids entering West Chester High School, we couldn't let those demeaning displays continue past summer. If only those before us struck decisive blows and changed it! Six personalities ruled in formulating rebellious actions pursued after coming together in Junior High. Those with nicknames earned respective monikers. Snake, for instance, was skinny and dark-skinned. He was dangerous in confrontations but among three National

Merit Scholars in 1956. His score was second-highest. Hindu possessed an aura of mystics—subdued always. He, too, won National Merit Scholarship recognition. Genie appeared and disappeared mysteriously. His "good hair" connected with girls. Stone-Jaw lived up to his nickname. He was a consummate fighter of average size. His combat record was perfect.

We planned on destroying every Yard Nigger with simple tools, smiting those demons—busting them into pieces was the ultimate solution. In romantic visions, it's no different from batting frozen drinking glasses. Six-foot-long two-by-four boards were perfect. Snake joined me in stealing them from an unlimited supply of stacked wood at Hoopes Brothers & Darlington's Franklin Street wood shed. They were hard and limber enough to shatter cast-iron figures with single blows. Objects shattering from vibrations, as depicted for structures and different cartoon creatures, came to mind. It's an apt association in that our existence was cartoonish. We were not of our creation. With that, we tried passing as legitimate beings with fleeting marginal success. Our appointed cadre left during "Coonville" Community Center's monthly dance, proceeding up Penn Street on Friday evening. Freddie dropped us at the north end in his '51 Ford. We ran south across lawns, covering both sides in two groups, swinging lumber. Calculations worked in a dispassionate blur. So much for what many white people considered giving their neighborhood an "Old South ambiance!"

Relieved by cleansing destructive action, we rode back, savoring thoughts in sweet silence. That told me it meant more than perceived. One more collection of open displays mocking our existence vanished from the degrading cultural fabric. News reports erased any uncertainty around accomplishing our mission. A Saturday West Chester Daily Local News story delineated Friday night's destruction on Penn Street. Law enforcement blamed rogue fraternities from West Chester teacher's college. With their racist bent, it's a bonus that West Chester State frat boys received credit. After so many years of tolerating northern Jim Crow, were we taken for granted as docile? Or were they ignorant of the racist history behind those statues? Official explanations worked well because blaming fraternities fed into my next night's more radical undertaking.

The Show Must Not Go On

Excitement blanketed the town whenever Christiani Bros. Circus, well loved traveling companies offering performance oddities, pitched camp. Our posse never went for entertainment; we sent war parties, finding or creating trouble. It didn't matter which came first with annual barbarian invasions. Such crude businesses triggered confrontations with their unwashed laborers—"rowdies" or "roustabouts." These invaders marauded and insulted us every year. Hostile interactions with friends or young female relatives caused fighting, because we protected our turf. Violent clashes occurred since junior high whenever these spectacles descended on us. It launched seek-and-destroy missions. Coming together in self-defense within our ghetto, we welcomed fights as intense escapes from a sense of helplessness wrought by smothering in northern Jim Crow. Successful violence nourished a positive group identity. It cleansed our souls, feeding the brotherhood's bonds.

As we destroyed those Jockos, circus workers pitched tents in Brandywine field on the town's eastern border. This location was inside Coonville. Officials locating seedy entertainment within our community were an insult because our population lacked the power to prevent those forms of exploitation. Who profits from so locating this shady enterprise?

My sisters begged to see the show, so I bought passes before ushering them inside, intending to join them by secreting an entrance. My plans altered when a ticket-taker took both of theirs and refused to let them enter. Pat and Dupe emerged from the big top's entry, devastated and crying. After explaining that we presented two passes, I got their advanced-level racist dismissal (like, *Nigger; we fucked you, Nigger*). Mistakes mean nothing to those people because their mindset is exploiting suckers at every turn. His response touches on my desire for extreme vengeance, reaching a level that only the most treacherous of them understand. It had an elevated emotional level tied to blaming myself for everything wrong, affecting my family.

My best reasoning suggests it came from the psychological effects of being a sickly child and developed from a night of terror when Mom left me in Memorial Hospital to get my tonsils out. The surgery was because the doctors couldn't define what was wrong with me. Later, within my inability to control our world, I couldn't abide someone hurting Patsy or Dupe (Helen). Years before, I took the blame and accepted punishment for their misbehavior. If things get broken or misused, I'm the owner. Beatings were nothing compared to being present when my siblings got strapped. Faking crying, begging for mercy, and eliminating trauma from witnessing Patsy's or Dupe's punishment became easy. Going into the circus, too, I should have ensured their welfare. We walked home robbed of ticket money and denied "thrills and excitement under the big top." They cried every step of that long mile. When arriving back across town, set on exacting revenge, fellows approached reporting an altercation with circus toughs. We marshaled troops and discussed their presumptuous aggression. Before their last show closed, we attacked.

Several men sat around small fire pits, eating sandwiches and drinking coffee. In a brief skirmish, we fell upon them with fists, sticks, and baseball bats. After ensuring Genie punished a particular worker, we disappeared into "Coonville." Later, occupying Ralph Smith Moving Company's steps across from the colored Elks building, victory stories flowed with boastful descriptions. While engaged in storytelling, my planned decisive avenging action took shape. There would be no resting until delivering payback! Time passing couldn't dissipate or diminish determination.

I didn't head home after midnight. Instead, front pockets bulging with stolen train depot fuses (flares) I made my way to the circus. Since elementary school, train fuses in our arsenal and explosive caps were our guarded secret. My mission, stalking the camp alone, required resoluteness, repelling any possibility of turning away! I'd face up to ten years in prison, so this crime couldn't have witnesses. Evening dew descended and bathed the grounds in silence. No guards or others stirred. Although it was eerie not seeing people, there was no hesitation with proceeding. Flares landed on the main tent's canopy. The 1600-degree torches ate through the canvas, plunging into dry hay, covering the tent floor with flames. As I ran deeper into disassociation from arson, Goodwill Fire Company sirens blared. I slept peacefully that night!

Monday's news told another story about vandalism. I'm relieved at not burning people or animals, but that wasn't considered within ice-cold anger. Detectives were out of luck if they looked for the arsonist to show up and admire his work. It was delightful reading that fraternities committed another notable prank. Frat boys demolishing lawn jockeys before torching a nest of circus "deplorables" made for a busy weekend! Blacklisting WC added a gratifying bonus, enhancing my arson's impact. After word spread throughout roaming entertainment networks, Christiani Bros. representatives declared that the circus would never come back. Traveling sideshows have long memories if they get treated less than welcome by the small towns they exploit. Before daylight on Sunday, everything disappeared from Bolmer Street's site. Only charred bits of canvas lying on burned straw remained. On injustice balance sheets, things had evened. However, it wasn't my final rebellious act before exile by court order.

A final probation violation occurred just before busing to our state track meet with Jack (Williams). During the week, there was a series of school-year concluding fights with the Italians on campus. District 1's bus from Norristown was arriving at 1 PM. Our band engaged a Dago gang on the railroad tracks at noon. Assembling at Gay Street Bridge's tunnel recalled Bob Dungle's train-hopping accident. Train tracks cut through sloping hills, cradling freight cars. Knoll contours aided running starts and leaping onto ladders near passing car tops. That fateful day in 1948, an early lumbering steam engine chugged through the tunnel, filling it with smoke-laden vapor. We held our noses against choking on toxic fumes until the wind from speeding railcars sucked it away. Boxcars trundled by faster than usual since this one wasn't stopping at the small passenger loading platform just ahead. Yet, they slowed enough that daredevil jumps resulted in riding to Union Street crossing. Caboose attendants watched our foolish playing with expressionless faces.

Dungle jumped first, challenging everyone's bravery. He missed his chosen railcar's ladder, falling under the wheels. Bulging earth, fitting tight to cars, left no room for tumbling away from danger. Everything funneled inward. He lucked out, only losing the joy of his remaining childhood with his lower right leg taken off knee-high. It could have been worse. At ten years old, witnessing such trauma forever ended any attraction for trains. Stonewall and Henderson, our boy scouts, employed years of practicing with tourniquets.

Meanwhile, as the fastest, my getting to the rail station for help took only seconds at top speed. A fire station ambulance arrived in minutes. They loaded George with his cutoff leg beside him, and he lay in shock, too trau-matized to cry. Techniques for re-attaching limbs didn't exist. We couldn't look at Mrs. Dungle's face while telling her what had happened. She screamed and broke out, running to Chester County's emergency room. In our heads, screams resounded until both hospital doors closed. None of us visited or ever inquired about his recovery, with each witness feeling relieved it wasn't them. Afterward, he had trouble keeping up with his wooden prosthesis, receiving ridicule and little sympathy. George's hardened, irascible nature added another negative trait. It's a reason for daily taunting. These thoughts rose from 1948. We gathered in that place eight years later to cripple some Italian boys.

The possibility of missing the last battle if district transportation came early caused worrying, even though there was reason to fear I'd get injured or arrested. Losing out on running at State was an issue, but more pressing matters were at stake. Prevailing against an Italian gang was more critical. The actual fighting ended fast. Our opponents fled before injuries occurred. We underestimated them, not expecting they'd appear. The fray left me unmarked without throwing rocks or busting anyone's head. My boys kept me away from the immediate battlefront. Before hearing sirens, I'd escaped onto District 1's bus. No way had authorities figured I was connected! I sweated for a few minutes until hitting Pennsylvania's Turnpike heading west. I'm one name that didn't come under investigation. Once more, running delivered me from more entanglement in WC's criminal justice trap. After returning on Monday, administrators organized talks between our groups (Negroes and Italians). Settling this conflict went nowhere. Dago grievances concerned contact between our members and what they claimed were "their women."

Our factual dispute was racial and territorial, but surprisingly nothing in the discussions addressed racism. We didn't care because our thing was fighting every week. A truce resulted until classes ended.

Our remaining school calendar almost passed without another incident. But no one has a perfect vision of racial oppression's pervasiveness, insidiousness, and relentlessness. So, we fell into a graphic exposure to discrimination in front of our classmates during days of activities approaching graduation because they scheduled our class party at a nearby roller skating rink just across Pennsylvania's border in Delaware.

An advisory panel proposed this shindig capping off a banner year. The committee's choice required detailed arrangements between our planning team and the skating business's reps. Two hundred seventy graduates commit to attending. Our group's participation reaches 100%. That level of involvement resulted from meetings purposed to show togetherness and a positive connection with the school. Every Negro classmate belonged to our recreation center's youth organization, "Senior Pals." In 1956, our gang dominated club endeavors. That dynamic existed because of possibly finding racist arrangements at gatherings, threatening sensibilities or safety. Designated gang members scouted environments, evaluated conditions, and then decided on acceptability for participating. They'd counsel members to avoid problems or bring higher numbers to mount confrontations. Freddy, Stone-Jaw, Snake, Pal, Hindu, Genie, and I entered minutes after several student government members. Excitement at seeing us felt excessive, but it upset those handling admissions. Delaware maintained segregation, and businesses never accommodated mixed-race gatherings. This setup was deceptive because no physical Mason-Dixon Line separated Union ground from Confederate states. Compared to West Chester's more permissive northern version, Southern/Northern Border Jim Crow limits applying to our proposed graduation celebration escaped recognition by planners.

Student Reps (white) reacted, shaken to the core by unanticipated developments. Fragile white girls' tears gushed when Crackers turned us away. What an embarrassment! Our class had rented an entire night's skating operation, and everyone contributed! Now, two Jim Crow practitioners refused Negroes entry. Planners, lacking visceral feelings toward racism, didn't consider fundamental cultural differences affecting people of color. We had paid cash for humiliation and dehumanization. Our scouting corps stood firm after discussing this predicament. Our strategy was to physically confront discrimination, making systems momentarily correct themselves and each other.

With their massive power, our institutions must practice values taught about citizenship rights. They should force suspending exclusionary practices. West Chester officials had enough means to prevail, but was there enough will? Freddy left, picking up reinforcements. Hindu located nearby phone booths, calling reinforcements. We informed our reps of an impending altercation unless they suspended their ban on race-mixing. If they didn't relent, there would be no joyous "Class of 1956" evening! It was a promise! They wasted no time involving relevant authorities. Several carloads of members reinforced our commitment. Faculty advisors pulled everyone together within an hour, saying the rink was open. Such minor struggles and victory's brought no satisfaction in celebrating the passage from high school in this manner. Active resistance affirmed necessary organizing. It showed the difficulties of preparing for every injustice that further dehumanizes and destroys us. Monday, at school, Principal Wingert met with our leaders to apologize. He expressed appreciation there was no violence. Nothing got mentioned of other damages. Are we supposedly okay with racial discrimination by now? Was it something ignorable as inconvenient, another assault without lasting impact? Thought execution involved in such data processing is mind-boggling.

There was an erroneous assumption of no effects beyond specific moments! People don't consider harm when consequences have no outward physical manifestations. This time, it's unrealistic thinking by good-intentioned white people. We never studied, complained about, or defined long-range effects. They didn't do it either. These are frequent failures. On Graduating, Negro athletes made token appearances at several white parties.

We finished with bull-shit'n and jive'n at Smith's, our favorite hangout, where we enjoyed a great sense of belonging. What was my feeling? I'd done myself justice, fighting against forces of destruction that poisoned life. My next moves were to follow the unjust court by leaving town.

CHAPTER
SIX

Pursuing Dreams

Daily adaptation is the Iglóian environment's process.

Neal:

In two years running the Penn Relays at West Chester High, I watched this little guy (Jim Beatty) from Chapel Hill (UNC) out-kicking people. It impressed me, and his performances put UNC on my radar. After graduating, I checked out colleges and enrollment near Philadelphia, including Temple U, wondering what I wanted. I couldn't stay up north freezing!

The University of North Carolina's campus had promise. There were more Chappells in this state than anywhere else. Growing up, I heard little of Dad's origins or his folks. Like many young boys from broken families, I craved meaningful relationships on my father's side. That influenced attending UNC, although outward reasons were joining Beatty. Florida State (FSU) qualified as another workable location but required general medical check-ups. So, I grumbled while rejecting them. Surprising acceptances came from

Carolina and Georgia based on SAT scores. Although my final report cards were unimpressive, my SAT numbers ranked high because I understood testing techniques, although graduating 120th out of 214 isn't great. That ranking came from never studying or carrying books home. I wasn't interested in good grades during later public education. But testing, I recognized, was a gimmick! I hitched rides into Wilmington, Delaware, for an SAT exam, producing outstanding scores.

Well, if I'm gonna get educated somewhere, warmer climates below the Mason-Dixon Line looked better. Eligible locations should have field houses containing 220-yard indoor ovals. So, I surveyed universities, including Vanderbilt. No inquiries revealed they were academic. Records showing nothing but "C" classes prevented admission there, so indoor workout facilities didn't matter. Possibilities for FSU followed, expecting warmer temperatures. They had a current National Collegiate Athletic Association (NCAA) 440 champion. That created suitability, but they wanted their damn heart test results. It could have turned into problems. No matter, I selected UNC, which had a state-of-the-art enclosed setup. Also, they had Beatty from those Penn Relays years, where he beat everyone by finishing two miles. Dave Scurlock is an NCAA-ranking half-miler topping national charts before college. Having him made them more attractive. It didn't cost much, and Carolina accepted me without medical checks.

My feeble mind entertained thoughts of avoiding physicals and joining the track team. However, their program's requirements matched other institutions. They demanded an extensive physical. A heart condition check was supposedly avoided by not enrolling elsewhere. Hospital physicians naturally found blood pressure issues (hypertension or HBP). HBP is a Chappell family affliction; I'd managed the condition for years. High school physicals never caught the problem. Not drinking, smoking, or other unhealthy activities controls chronic hypertension. Once cleared, I met Dale Ranson (UNC's head coach), who welcomed me and asked about my needs. I could use free food, so he pulled out the nearest mess hall's directions!

I had money from managing Glick's stationery store for six months;

the accumulated funds covered the second term's tuition, from January to June. So, they granted admission. Mid-January, my merchant sailor brother headed for New Orleans, accompanying another seaman working on a cargo ship. Driving to Louisiana, Donald wanted to see Dad. We hadn't seen him since Pennsylvania courts banished him from the state and forbade contacting his children before their eighteenth birthdays. I didn't want any part of that and insisted on getting dropped at UNC's main dormitory before they looked for John. It was between semesters. As usual, the campus was empty during breaks.

I was wearing WC's sweater, only finding out later wearing non-UNC colors isn't acceptable. Everyone said Beatty was at Boston's Knights of Columbus Invitational. The first young man I saw advised everything was closed and then gave room directions. Whoever bunked there before hadn't moved out. After crashing on their bed, although someone else's clothes filled closets, I pondered; one hell of a setup! There I was, in the South, where I didn't know anyone. Right away, I found Keenan Arena. An indoor winter training site was the single feature I sought in choosing a school. Tracks were familiar territory. Upon entering, I bumped into Joe Friedberg, a sophomore from New York transferring from Baldwin Wallace, and Frank Sirianni, a Jersey boy. We became instant buddies. We were 'Yankees' locating spots. We had similar experiences, including the annual Philadelphia Convention Hall's high school events! Coach O'Shields and his Cheyney Wildcats began inviting me at eight years old. Those events left indelible impressions. I appreciated the indoor's electric atmosphere and its spectator closeness. Part of the attraction could have been different tactical demands for racing on banked short turns. Both newfound fellows shared these notions.

Once the outdoor season started, they saw me competing well. Bonds thickened with a win at North Carolina State. Before long, Mihály Iglói, Hungary's National Coach, moved here after Melbourne's Olympics, accompanied by László Tábori, his committed disciple. They refused to return home, escaping the 1956 revolution one step before Russia's invasion. Sports Illustrated supported their efforts to avoid Russian subjugation. During World

War II, Mihái spent time imprisoned in Siberia, so another arrest waited if he reentered Hungary. Russian forces know international athletic achievements become a patriotic motivation for continuing revolts. International athletic successes stimulated Hungarian nationalism, heightening popular resistance.

These Hungarians' resumes were unparalleled because 1955 was exceptional for this extraordinary middle-distance triumvirate. Sándor Iharos broke four world records, adding a ten-kilometer mark later. Tábori was the third person to go a mile under four minutes, equaling the 1500-meter record on September 6, 1955. István Rózsavölgyi held 1000, 1500, and 2000 meter marks. Their feats are history's most acclaimed breakthroughs by a nation's athletes. Their tremendous accomplishments came from Iglói's program. Often speaking in gripping broken English, his preparation rule insisted, "Every day hard training must make." We mimicked him as a way of showing extreme respect. We directed his signature expressions at each other, copying a Hungarian accent. Group playfulness further ingrained his dictum into our psyche. Brainwashing ourselves by repeating his work ethic brought positive results. Communicating by copying his style extended Hungarian achievement into our efforts. It influenced our desire to improve, and we perceived ourselves as connected alongside their esteemed triumvirate. We each pursued becoming another Iharos, Tábori, or Rózsavölgyi. That is how a simple transitive psychology of relationships took root.

A plea requesting aid went out when they left Australia to come here, and scuttlebutt claimed Sports Illustrated managers used their contacts. Interested parties searched out housing across America, and UNC owned motels for housing requiring no rent. Unbelievable, somebody chose UNC! When asked, Ranson said, "I think we are fortunate in having a fine group of boys in school at a point when a man of Iglói's expertise was available."

1957 Track Season

On April 5, Larry Karl, Chapel Hill's sportswriter, announced Iggle's arrival. An article asserted, "Mihály Iglói... will prove significant in the lives of a dozen Tar Heel runners." So, Ranson decided younger and lesser talented people should become his charges. Dale sent his untested troops, declaring, "Coach, I give you these boys." We watched Mihái, knowing little English, struggling with understanding this guy's southern drawl.

Our headman attempted to convey everything by affecting a Hungarian accent. This scenario, introducing his same group, repeating the exact words, warped by a crazy (southern) imitation of Mihái's speech, occurred daily. Ranson repeated his act until everyone understood. This whole thing was weird! You could only think comedy was unintended! If attempting to affect a Magyar accent wasn't so funny, it was embarrassing, comical, and failed communication! Coaches refused to release Scurlock, Beatty, or other seniors, but younger kids presented no risks. Freshmen landed under the world's best coach! Iggles said a few had the potential to achieve in a demanding program. After a short time, I was judged as a promising prospect, while Carolina coaches saw me as an outlier. I was different, with an independent mind, a carefree lifestyle, and an unappreciated taste for pulling pranks during practice. Placement under the Hungarians couldn't be luckier. I soon learned how stringent his requirements were! Tábori provided an invaluable conduit.

László translated two-way communications and taught while executing Iggles' directives. They had been serving at Honvéd Budapest Army Sports Club since 1950. As Mihái's right-hand man, leading and managing from inside executions, he modeled many descriptors, signifying changing pace, stride lengths, leg turnover rates, interval times, and rests. Basic workouts started with 20 min warm-ups, plus ten, fifteen, or twenty easy 100s, before repetitive sprints over various distances. Tábori practiced strict precision, steering us through our paces and leading each step.

Our group absorbed László's understanding, becoming increasingly comfortable executing demands. The program had detailed individual-ized requirements woven into it. Conditioning improved where variations were necessary for addressing individual potential while performing crucial aspects of programs within smaller groups. We did intervals, increasingly following orders ourselves. So, more demanding sets grew expectations. But what did we know besides obeying his commands and marveling as racing improved? Over time, we evolved into exercising independence and showing precision.

A few weeks of training passed before UNC's proven veterans joined the brilliant coach. Luck connecting with Jim made me become an Iglói follower, but he could not. Jimmy worked out separately from László but challenged him before long. Jim learned by observing, although not being directly instructed. Am I alone thinking Iggles should have been handling every distance man? This reasoning became undeniable when his sub-four miler won "The Carolina's Mile of the Century." I viewed their contest up close as a "rabbit" running a personal best. Unfortunately, the Hungarians were only here from January 1957 until major California summer competitions. Then, they moved to southern California, not intending to return. Their influence made me first among frosh 880 men. After the track season ended, I got their most valuable freshmen trophy.

Once exams wrapped up, we loaded Friedberg's Chevy, heading for Los Angeles. Rolling along Route 66 was enjoyable but uneventful. Curious, we veered off Route 66 onto Highway 93 over Boulder Dam (Hoover Dam), after Kingman, Arizona, into Las Vegas. After many hours of crossing the barren landscape since entering eastern Oklahoma, Nevada's desert oasis loomed ahead. When passing Lake Mead, surrounded by darkness, the distant lights were remarkable. Extensive neon displays, gaming varieties, entertainment, booze, and every imaginable form of excitement beckoned. It's my style of environment.

Iggles was without work in San Fernando Valley, refusing to handle us, and László had no races. When considering it, where was the return on investment for coaching novices? We did not know what they were creating. Our scene wasn't meeting expectations for finding a viable spot in Santa Monica. Within days, Friedberg contracted mononucleosis. It started as a severe sore throat, a fever over 103°, and swollen Cervical Lymph Glands. His condition turned alarming when severe abdominal pains accompanied a full-body rash. We stayed at Hotel St. Moritz, across from Warner Bros. Studio. A lady who managed the desk mixed potions of liquor with herbs to overcome his ailment. Her crazy formula came near to killing him! By then, his father was through attempting to fix health problems long distance from Manhattan and ordered him home. So LA friends sold his 55 Chevy convertible, and Joe flew. His dad offered to fly me, too. But hell, I wasn't giving up on the Coach. At 18, I kept the room by myself without contacts or funds! This weather's year-round possibilities were phenomenal. As a kid, the creature I morphed into in this environment was frightening. I'll never tell that story! Surviving Los Angeles is no simple task, especially if you're not seeking movie industry fame or fortune. You're suspect when not doing that.

Kitchen labor at Liberace's brother's restaurant, Dillon's Copper Skillet, on Sunset Boulevard, was a good gig. Washing dishes and busing tables proved desirable work. Dillon's faces Columbia Studios. Motion picture stars, comedians, etc., drank coffee while talking with employees. The most likable person around was Aldo Ray, a newcomer. He was a colossal movie personality. This actor told many hair-raising Navy Frogman war tales and stories from his stint as Crockett, California's Town Constable. But I was not cultivating work contacts or looking for acting jobs. I aimed to survive until Mihái started again. No restaurant owners or family were present. Overall, living arrangements were only "all right." During this period, distinct possibilities for several secure years in Chapel Hill remained a safety net. Tar Heel's staff kept in contact. They offered a full ride. So why refuse such an opportunity? On that note, I headed back to Carolina.

Stepping through the academy gates in January 1957 allowed no delay in getting into shape before the outdoor competition (March). I was unknown when first joining the Heels. Low status, however, didn't last. Under Iggles' tutelage, I rapidly improved. Personal bests soon surpassed an earlier 2:05.7 880. A 2:02.5 win against NCSU's frosh and a 2:03.6 followed, winning over Wake Forest. Personal bests improved again by a full second (2:01.5), beating South Carolina. When pacing Jim's Carolina Mile test against László, it dropped below 2 minutes (1:59.8). As everyone saw, these beginning achievements earned an Athletic Association Numeral Award and a grant-in-aid starting fall term.

UNIVERSITY OF NORTH CAROLINA
CHAPEL HILL, N. C.

DEPARTMENT OF
PHYSICAL EDUCATION AND ATHLETICS

28 August 1957

VIA: AIR MAIL

Mr. Neal Chappell
5715 Camerford Ave. #108
Hollywood, Cal.

Dear Neal:

I am counting strongly on you for track this year. You have a great future ahead of you at Carolina. I hope that you will not let anything interfere with your returning.

You should try to return to Chapel Hill by September 10th so that we can work out a satisfactory job for you at the Chi Psi for your meals. We will be able to provide you a room this year and I will do my best to help you with possibly a hundred dollar grant-in-aid. If your grades improve so that you have a C average at the end of a full year, you would be eligible to apply direct through the Student Aid Office for additional assistance.

Please let me hear from you again upon receipt of this letter and I will be looking forward to seeing you soon. You should be able to pick up a ride if you will begin checking immediately. There are always people coming from California across the eastern part of the U. S. A.

We had a note from Joe Friedberg and I am sorry that he has been ill. Apparently he is on the mend now and expects to be back this fall though he will not be able to do any running immediately.

With best wishes, I am

Sincerely yours,

Dale Ranson

Dale Ranson
Track Coach

DR/bsc

P.S. Where are Igloi & Tabori

Frat jobs and food halls went well. Meals were free, and extra dough made living comfortable. They hinted at scholarships because performances were more effective than those receiving grants. Acknowledging this possibility confirmed their positive appreciation and stimulated me to work harder for better results. Not only were coaches saying I was an asset, but Chancellor Aycock's faculty committee agreed! That provided adequate validation for a small-town kid!

Training hard while surviving Hollywood wasn't possible. I was returning early, and accepting UNC's offered aid until graduation made sense. Heady stuff for a Thornton, Pa, lad! Ranson's note showed Mihái expected me to reach 1:52 soon. His opinion erased disappointment from not generating LA connections, further boosting my interest in returning to UNC. Dale Ranson's efforts to dissolve any reluctance to come back proved successful. His communiqué made continuing at UNC reasonable since I couldn't train with the Hungarians. A tentative statement defining likely support came after Friedberg left. It identified available support, stipulating the academic status required when receiving aid. Their offer included one hundred dollars per month, for miscellaneous expenses.

Dale (Ranson) requested immediate responses. I felt lofty expectations motivated him. He suggested coming back post-haste. Careful language showed staying at UNC made sense. I realized we were talking about reliable University support. His program got unquestioned generous funding! Coach Ranson included a note asking for news of the Hungarians.

While expecting an official grant letter, I was among those earning E. J. Evans' freshmen award. Evans, Durham's mayor, had a son, a Tar Heel senior. He wasn't an athlete, though. Why did Durham's mayor create prestigious recognition for Chapel Hill athletes? It's an enigmatic award because Evans' lifelong residence was near Duke University, UNC's greatest rival. They must have been track and field devotees. A Big Four Blue Devil stadium 880 victory highlighted my season, influencing Evans' selections. A write-up by Red Hamer captured the two lap's essence:

> The most exciting race of the afternoon was the 880-yard run. About 100 yards from the finish, Carolina's Neal Chappell began to make his bid to overtake Duke's Tony Bazemore who had taken the lead about 100 yards earlier. Chappell took the lead right at the finish line and the two men finished so close together that the judges gave them the same time. 1:57.6. In response to a question of how it feels, Neal said "I'm sending this time to Zim (West Chester High School's Harold

I. Zimmerman). It should make him feel good about my growth. I owe a lot to him as my high school coach."

.... Before we get off the general subject of track we understand that Neal ..., 1956 West Chester High grad, has spun off a 4:40 mile with the North Carolina frosh team. Neal is already credited with doing the 880 several times in less than two minutes this season and it causes us to wonder if the Warriors wouldn't have had a state champion this season if the 17-year-old hadn't "skipped" a grade early in his schooling.

The Daily Local Newspaper's sports writer presented some essential experiences of my freshman year at UNC in my own words:

...the frosh track team ... went undefeated for the third time in the last four years. Since I last saw you I've been in three meets. First, we ran NC State under the lights. I had to run the two-mile that night, so we wouldn't be stale for our events when we met Duke. So I ran the thing in 10:21. It really hurt. I guess you use different muscles running two miles. (My specialty is the 880.) ... Next we met Duke over there. The feature was the mile run between Cary Weiseger, a Pittsburgh boy, and our Cowles Liipfert. Weiseger ran against '56 West Chester miler Jack Williams in the PIAA state championships. Liipfert was last year's North Carolina mile champ. So far this year Weiseger had done 4:22 and Liipfert 4:26. To spice it up they put yours truly in there as a pace-setter. I hit the 440 in 63 seconds and led until the 660. Then it was all theirs. Liipfert won in 4:21.4, breaking the incomparable Jim Beatty's frosh record. Since those two boys were too tired to run the 880 and since I loafed to a 4:40 third place mile, I gladly accepted the 880 bid. I won in 2:00.2, my fastest time in competition up to that time. This made Weiseger mad because we won the meet by one measly point and he figured he could have won the half (mile) and the meet for them. Nasty break, I say.

…. I have really benefitted from working with Iglói and doing the Hungarian workouts. These Hungarians are really great people.

I saw returning to Carolina as essential. Twenty-five hundred miles were driven in thirty-seven hours, guaranteeing to tax my body. Before becoming competitive enough, a short travel recovery period and surviving moderate intervals were necessary. Landing back on campus absent volumes of taxing Iglóian work after spring meets was not good preparation.

However, commitment to improving was such that there were no impact-ful breaks. Summer in Los Angeles doesn't deter being diligent in working on fitness. I never go over twenty-four hours sans intense exercise. When motor-ing distances, stopping afternoons for one-hour tempo runs are routine. College training and showering accommodations grace every stop. Locals welcomed capable visitors joining their sessions. Talented guests contributing by showing their ability was exciting. Using their resources never presented problems. When needed, eating cafeteria food or commandeering empty dormitory beds worked. When I arrived in August, the conditioning was better than after spring. It took a few days to tune my legs. Upon moving into Cobb Hall, an aid commitment appeared, stating a dollar figure of 25% more than expected.

THE UNIVERSITY OF NORTH CAROLINA

CHAPEL HILL

THE UNIVERSITY OF NORTH CAROLINA COMPRISES: THE UNIVERSITY IN CHAPEL HILL, STATE COLLEGE IN RALEIGH, AND THE WOMAN'S COLLEGE IN GREENSBORO

WILLIAM BRANTLEY AYCOCK, *Chancellor*

October 2, 1957

Mr. Neal Chappell   (Mailed to local address: 145 Cobb Dormitory)
Thornton
Pennsylvania

Dear Neal:

It is a pleasure to advise you that the Faculty Committee on Scholarships and Student Aid of the University of North Carolina has granted you an Athletic Award under the rules of the National Collegiate Athletic Association and the Atlantic Coast Conference for eight semesters beginning September, 1957.

The award covers $125.00 per semester for a total of $250.00 per year. . This award is granted by the University with the understanding that in accepting this award you agree to conduct yourself as a gentleman at all times; to do satisfactory work in your studies and to remain eligible for competition in athletics; to serve and promote to the best of your ability the best interests of the University and its institutions, including any University teams with which you may be affiliated; and to train and practice faithfully and conscientiously for the fullest development and employment of your talents.

During the term of this award you must not receive any additional aid except from those upon whom you are naturally or legally dependent. If injured while participating in athletics supervised by a member of the coaching staff, the award will be honored; and the medical expenses will be paid by the Athletic Department.

Please sign and return the enclosed form in the addressed envelope signifying your acceptance or rejection of this award under these conditions.

We shall be happy to have you as a member of our student body and wish to help you in every way possible in your efforts to prepare yourself for a successful career.

Sincerely yours,

W. B. Aycock
Chancellor

WBA:ghr

1957 Cross-Country Season

The preliminary outlook for UNC cross-country was great. Dale Ranson used a newspaper interview announcing: "Freshman Harriers Look Good." He touted main prospects—Worth Sweat, Bob Foxworth, John Boles, Bob Costello, and Harry Miller. My name wasn't among those impressing anyone. On the first outing at Mecklenburg, I surprised everyone by placing second.

Miller was eight seconds ahead. I outpaced five teammates. After that, Miller finished two slots ahead, leading us against North Carolina State University (NCSU, NSU, or NC State). We lost, with Worth Sweat and me finishing fifth and sixth, getting the same clocking. Our match against Wake Forest saw Miller finishing 1st (13:24), with Sweat 3rd and me 4th (13:31.5 and 13.51.5). Not being listed as a valuable first-timer was an oversight. In a triangular that included Duke, Miller finished 4th. I was 5th with Foxworth, Sweat, and Boles, capturing 9th, 10th, and 12th. The Big Four Championship between Duke, Wake Forest, NC State, and UNC had Miller 4th, again, with me 7th. Team-wise, we were behind Duke and NCSU. Since I was improving fast, suitable recognition would come.

Iglói's work helped through 1958. Since summer, I could keep suitable fitness without him, but progress slowed. An adaptive issue after x-country was maintaining acceptable form through Christmas into the New Year. For this, I ran Amateur Athletic Union (AAU) events while on vacation. I was behind Browning Ross and Ed Mather, Penn State's harriers' captain when finishing York, Pa.'s handicapped race. Ross won in York, dominated the Mid-Atlantic region, and was the most-known performer at two miles or more.

The opportunity to hang out and chat allowed absorbing Browning's ideas on average mileage, hills, the need for rest, light training, and diet. Everything got logged for use later. That was vital information from a perpetual regional AAU winner. I ran their Middle Atlantic Road Runners' cross-country race, covering 5.2 miles averaging a 5:15 per mile pace, and bagging it! It showed I continued performing well while on vacation and confirmed I'd continue improving at UNC, after Christmas. I planned to arrive early and use the field house oval. With everyone preparing for the 1957-1958 winter campaign, I intended to be among our best 880 runners. I wanted a relay spot for Philadelphia's Inquirer Games. There, my family could see me running on the big stage. Based on the Atlantic Coast Conference Winter Games results, the chances of going to Philly looked good. Our two-mile relay corps swept the top three places. We'd plug in Wayne Bishop, a miler, Howard Kahn, Dave

Scurlock, and me for a great relay.

UNC's survivability involves lots more than running acceptably on a year's aid. Like most college athletes, I needed more funds than meager stipends limited by NCAA rules. Other athletes got added cash from their families. Such funds never existed for me. I had small savings from six months' work before coming south. I picked up a book to improve my gambling skills, consistent with pursuing a liberal arts degree. It was titled *The Education of a Poker Player* and was on the market after I enrolled. They said Herbert Yardley, who wrote it, was a genius. Studied gamblers called it their best book on this business ever written! After digesting basic lessons that explained what to do, I followed his teachings, making good money playing Stud around Chapel Hill. From opportunities at Joe's fraternity, I figured that plying our trade campus-wide would access more money. Frats were the perfect starting place because members didn't worry about where they'd find their next dollar. Often, their parents were wealthy, ensuring their offspring wanted nothing. A few frat house assholes thought they were dominant players, but card-playing expertise existed only in their minds. They were big fish in small ponds. They were tiny fish; their waters were barrels!

Popularity, however, had its drawbacks. We moved operations from Cobb when hearing that UNC administrators weren't happy. Underground passages discovered beneath dorms became our secret five-card draw or seven-card stud location. Tunnels were there during the Civil War. Now they had bare light bulbs hanging overhead. Confederate Army tunnels were okay for brief spells, but officials discovered them several times. Each raid triggered an appearance before an Assistant Dean. At his meeting, Dean Stevens asked, "Son, if you love gambling so much, why don't you live in Las Vegas, where it's legal?"

1958 Track Season

1958's schedule opened with me finishing high against the varsity League (ACC) rivals. On March 25, we engaged NC State in Raleigh. I had my journal for guidance. Absent Iggles, efforts worked better than expected. His former presence lifted expectations, instilling lasting confidence. The Hungarians instigated our distance program's current productivity. Mihái's leaving triggered uncertainty about reaching top-level NCAA status and raised questions about achieving our potential. These were the primary considerations. When they left, they gave me pictures containing good luck notes. They penned native language comments. Their gesture confirmed I had connected beyond the norm in their eyes. I aimed to bring Táborian dedication by combining spiritual investment with Iglói's methods and pursuing full personal development and fulfillment. I saw commitment beyond college competition as a desirable path.

An absence of dedicated mates was an invisible issue, diminishing sharing work and bonding for mutual support. Teammate camaraderie didn't reach profound levels. No one voiced interest in going to such lengths to train or compete as I. Others only sought short-term scholarship benefits. No current mates ran more than demanded by scholarships. They weren't aiming at or beyond challenging the world's best. Most of all, none thought along spiritual lines! My efforts approached passing culturally dictated practical limits. For me, the purpose of running edged toward developing purity as a historical hominid value, along with accompanying physical, mental, social, and cultural accouterments of society extending from early human survival. I won't say I rose sufficiently in awareness, desiring more than typical utilitarian motivation by this point. Even though common student-athlete expectations promised concrete endings, such as lucrative professional careers, nothing standard qualified as a good end for me.

It's hard to consider performing for the success of university colors or seeking student admiration as building a love of running or realizing identity essentials. My quest for a higher purpose was in its infancy, and learning from Iglói constituted the most precise vision of the path forward. For enough moments, I pondered, finding erstwhile mythical levels of meaning. Sports undoubtedly helped me through difficulties as a confined Episcopal Farm School youth. Once moving to West Chester, I wanted to compete after high school, which required more education. Everything is a work in progress.

As luck had it, leading figures (Iglói, Tábori, and Beatty) modeled potential, anchoring my sense of self and improving my athletic performance. They never preached but led by example. Pursuing a meaningful life involved more than immediate gratification or people's approval.

Such understanding made 1958 a period of marking time. The motivation wasn't high going through moderate training. The significant meet occurred at home, dominated by Maryland's squad. They were ACC's championship favorites. Before then, we beat North Carolina State, Virginia, Wake Forest, and South Carolina U. Facing Terrapin half-milers, the battle centered on beating their Fleming. A winning 1:56.1 showed promise. Later performances improved, and we attained new heights with every outing. We were delighted with a 4 x 880 relay second place without Dave Scurlock, our star, at Gainesville. His ankle injury hadn't healed. Varsity events, relays, and x-country fulfilled obligations, but commitment sagged. Mihái's absence hung in my mind. Another missing boost was support from like-minded persons. Partners seeking more than college aide packages, logging miles for the sake of it, didn't exist. My desire to live among runners arranging their lives centered on the sport mounted. These are people Jim Grelle called "running Junkies."

The Way to San Jose

Far from the Coach's hands-on guidance, we used preparing indoors for 1959's outdoor season as motivation. It had been over a year since they set up camp in San Jose. Iglói has Santa Clara's Youth Village paying his expenses, while Lazlo becomes their janitor. From 1957 to 1958, I was in Carolina. Five months of 1959 were at Uncle Coty's. Undergraduate Chapel Hill judicial activities left me uneasy, triggering my fleeing from a developing storm involving fraternities and athletes stealing exams. I knew who was involved, but no investigators or government adjudicators could pull information from me. This case revolved around illegally possessing University office keys. Those owning the secret insisted clandestine building entry tools came into possession of an "athlete caretaker" during Charlie "Choo Choo" Justice's football reign. Each graduating class passed them to those remaining, known as "caretakers."

For incalculable reasons, I fell into knowing those inheriting the keys. Navigating that moral conduct legacy swamp, an undercover Honor Council worker made contact when hearing I could copy tests. That person's suspicious interest looked like a setup! Council members investigated activities violating their rules. They scrutinized issues around cheating, plus other quasi-criminal indiscretions. Through these shenanigans, Hertz was present, maintaining a keen memory:

> Yeah, what we were pretty much dealing with in terms of having the keys to some of the important buildings is a historical practice for athletes and some of the notably rogue fraternities on the UNC campus. When I first saw the magic keys, they were in the hands of a couple of football players. Ed Furn and Snuffy were the most likely "Caretakers" at the time. This is how athletes maintained access to tests prior to their being used in their classes. That's how they are able to get passing grades in their courses, stay eligible to participate in sports, and some eventually to graduate. For one final operation, I was a lookout guard about one building's length away from the Printing Operations Center that houses the exam printing office. The Center is a low slung brick and cement building that is highly secure. There are no windows that open to the outside and the front door is the only way in. The magic keys are absolutely necessary for entering the building. Once inside the main center, you need a skinny guy to climb through the transom into the test printing room. That's why the football guys needed some track guys in on the deal. As the lookout, and seeing campus security officers approaching from a distance, I ran to the printing office building with a warning that the campus fuzz was close. Neal was in the area with me as the group inside the building all escaped. I had my own information sources on campus and the next morning I was able to tell Neal that

security had his name and they were coming to Cobb dorm with a summons from the Honor Council. In a matter of minutes, I helped to push his car out of the student parking lot on to Country Club Road heading for south US Highway 501, as he hastily fled to Miami with only a duffle bag of running clothes.

No doubt, they sought to end our poker business. When closing in, anonymous snitches claimed they saw me climbing through transoms and entering office areas. (Would anyone with keys do that?) Before this questionable caper, investigations had gotten so nasty that leaving town made sense. Football and basketball players didn't want me hauled before Judiciary Committee hearings, fearing that incriminating information, including names, might come out.

Naturally, Joe represented and Hertz described proceedings:

It's called the 'Honor Council." The committee is made up of students who actually try fellow students in front of their court. The committee members are trying to build a reputation for themselves that they are to be feared and are much tougher than the damn city courts. They are trying Neal in absentia as the only one responsible for the illegal keys to the buildings and for stealing and selling tests. The bluster and bombast of the prosecution would have been comical if not for the possible serious outcome of the trial. The evidence, however, was circumstantial and largely contrived in the attempts of some relatives of student council members to entrap Neal. Joe, of course, presents a magnificent and successful defense. His argument completely destroys the prosecution's case and committee member efforts to use the trial to garner personal prestige for themselves among the student body. Joe is the one that comes away with a reputation as a more than capable lawyer.

There was no use worrying over UNC crime-fighting developments. What was important was I'd enjoyed a decent year! The outdoor season looked okay, but it was best to leave. I left, escaping to Unc's St. Petersburg digs. While tucked away, news arrived that Friedberg continued defeating Men's Honor Council prosecutors. His mission was to show dominance. Trials are not fun for me, but enjoyable from a safe distance! I'd bet on Joe.

Friedberg's saga showed conditions never change. If I was caught inside North Carolina, test stealing scandals and illegal entering offices would bury me. They'd prosecute their trumped-up legal charges. I understood gambling success got them pissed. A few Honor Council hotshots couldn't get over losing. They avoided catching name jocks or frat cheats. Who wants adverse effects hurting football player eligibility? Nobody sought that since methods for beating athletic eligibility rules emerged after WWII. Student-operated court processes gave Joe practice while studying criminal defense law. It didn't eliminate the hassle, not even when represented by a top-notch lawyer! The pressure became enough to go to Uncle Coty's.

After hanging around St. Petersburg, I decided to explore regional universities' track scenes. There were great workout possibilities besides cards. I was right about checking out Miami University (Hurricanes)! Coach Downs allowed me to direct practices there, knowing I performed at UNC. After seeing how I commanded training sessions, he didn't disguise wanting me to join, and partnering to execute workouts made establishing broader contacts easy. Lew Schoenberg became a valuable accomplice, lining up a frat house room with food. Comfortable Phi Epsilon Pi House living got enhanced by exercising Yardley-fed skills. Track staff gave added care, hoping I'd transfer. They had me racing, wearing their colors without enrolling. Against NCAA rules, I entered competitions, and no one questioned my university status. I beat Harvard, for example, when they visited during spring break.

Downs was friendly from there, wanting help to elevate his enterprise. There were recent attempts at making meets a big Miami U attraction. He proposed bringing track out from under an overwhelming shadow cast by football. Knowing my experience inside Iglói's program provoked hopes for learning methods through me. He offered to correspond and exchange ideas, but not steal techniques. NASA Cape Canaveral held an event that Lew (Schoenberg) and I attended in April. We didn't realize Tábori was part of an invitational commemorating the launching of Explorer 1, the first US satellite. Ron Delany, among other greats, took part. Wrapping up conversations, Tábori mentioned forming Santa Clara Valley Youth Village's Team (SCVYV).

It wasn't sure he was serious, but László encouraged me to join them. What good fortune! Florida's sequester brought renewed contact with the Hungarian duo! Their suggestion that we reconnect was what I craved! The subsequent steps were obvious! So, I called Sirianni at UNC, Frank was eager to leave. Miami's coach knew what was happening. Before parting, he said, "I would appreciate your sending detailed descriptions of Coach Iglói's schedules, with any insights about the Youth Village procedures, from a management angle." For showing integrity, he touted runners getting lucrative Camp Cabbossee summer counseling jobs outside Winthrop, Maine. It showed his quest for information describing San Jose operations wasn't for personal gain. He was suggesting mentoring young men together. They could become world-class runners, turning Miami U. into a Mecca. After thanking folks, Lew and I left Miami.

In Chapel Hill, Frank Sirianni challenged, "Let's drive to California now." Twenty-four hours later, my possessions filled his Ford because I was not returning. Driving non-stop wasn't different from the Los Angeles trek with Friedberg.

Surpassing disastrous health developments of earlier adventures, we had an accident after departing Lake Tahoe for San Jose. A young couple driving their new Mercury traveled Highway 50 at 90 mph, approaching Kyburz 30 minutes past Placerville. Narrow winding lanes cut through Sierra mountain forests, offering breathtaking views. Giant granite outcroppings, heavily wooded slopes descending into deep valleys, swift streams, and few human encroachment signs, except roads, awed us. This divider-less road proved dangerous at 40 mph! When passing, a car sideswiped us, plowing head-on into another westbound vehicle driven by an Alameda Naval Air Station officer. That multi-car wreck killed three.

We were the only ones surviving, even after getting hit first. Surviving unmarked was inexplicable. The accident required several hours to extract bodies from tangled wreckage. An article appeared in the May 3, 1959, San Francisco Chronicle Newspaper. This accident kissing death, while not worrisome, brought too much stress on Sirianni. After a few more troubles, he sold his damaged vehicle, fleeing to Jersey. Shoenberg decided he'd enter Portland Oregon's Reed College. At heart, Lou favored becoming a scholar instead of an Olympic 5000-meter champion.

Reed's liberal arts college emphasized undergraduate studies. World-renowned academic rigor had many graduates earning doctorates. Their culture emphasized imaginative thinking purposed toward dedicated citizen-ship participation. Considering his zest for learning, this was Lew's choice. His sedate passion for entering a magnificent academic environment was admirable. Reed's campus surrounded a nature preserve encompassing native plants and animal-filled wooded canyons, soothing one's soul. Everyone needs walking trails. Being solo suited me. I could join SCVYV, find room-mates to share expenses, and make surviving easy. This was a unique promise with an elite track club in a city featuring legal card rooms. Owners began backing me for bolstering action once I started playing. Being underage mattered less because superior talent was valuable. Establishments offered deals for working while underage! Once again, poker supplemented training and education. I planned to attend San Jose City College (SJCC or JC) and running was our job when Kenny arrived!

It was May 1959. At UNC, I felt my high school friend deserved a high-er-level opportunity but did not consider those matters significant when at Chapel Hill or elsewhere. Among my concerns was forming a solid rationale and encouraging Kenny to look ahead. At West Chester, we both had a love for running. It was a shame not finding out what his speed and endurance could do. That discovery required adequate coaching like Iggles transforming UNC novices. Not maximizing his potential by joining us was an injustice.

He could reap tangible benefits from SCVYV. That was one idea, but more profound thoughts arose from prior university successes. Given a greater understanding of the world, my feelings, and our place, I contemplated:

Kenny going home to slave at Schrom's (our super-rich classmate) is not right." He'd suffer in those sweatshops on west Gay St., where light bulbs hang by almost bare wires. There were frequent worker electrocutions! Mentioning escaping northern Jim Crow to face a western version wasn't a useful selling point. Hell, talented people have to get out of there!

Adding all this up, having him find his way to San Jose and seeing what happens seemed sensible. If the Youth Village team didn't suit him, riding a Greyhound home was the choice. One thing was for sure; there would be no problem passing classes at universities. We both could handle relationships with instructors and do coursework at any institution. He'd complete sixty Junior College units for free, regardless.

UNC's offer proved I could qualify for athletic scholarships. If we showed physical and academic talent, professional jobs would come after completing BA degrees. So our quest wasn't only running track. The practical aspects were straightforward. But explaining views and behavior to parties without exposure to our passion was strange. They couldn't fathom embracing such an unparalleled depth of athletic expression or its importance for self-identity, as in my case. Conversations informing Kenny emphasized education, creating a decent life after leaving restrictive eastern communities. "We ain't gitt'n nowhere stay'n there." Staying home guaranteed ongoing police surveillance. He'd face constant arrests without reasonable cause. That's how society keeps non submissive individuals restrained. It's doubtful that classmates expected we'd pursue college. They damn sure didn't think we'd find work requiring more than high school! Nothing would have happened if my brother Jack hadn't crashed his motorcycle, almost killing himself. I returned east, visiting JC on his deathbed. One day uptown, Kenny's mother was shopping. Our conversation triggered me contacting him again. Remarkably, those events occurred!

So, Jack's slow healing and my missing Mihái's (Iglói) workouts weren't the best. I wanted to work with the Air Force's Truax, Schul, and others. Through everything, I couldn't let Kenny get discharged (October 1960), reclaiming his Paoli platinum refinery job. He'd languish, breathing chemical cesspool fumes all day—dirty, depressing, and sucking life from him. There was nothing else available, ever. I knew living there would deny future prosperity. Jack's Nield Street house could prove convenient, but what careers would be possible but clerking, earning fifty cents an hour? Many people considered four dollars per day good money. I lived well, bussing restaurant dishes and shilling in California card rooms. And there were vegetable and fruit canneries. San Jose's least fortunate folks did hard cannery labor for reasonable pay. In my scheme, a month's work would allow drawing unemployment compensation off-season. It's easy surviving by taking night classes while collecting $25 a week. California provided greater possibilities than anywhere. There's no sense living elsewhere. I'd committed to intense workouts for 1959 and a long-range goal of making 1960 my best.

It's early May 1959 in San Jose with Frank. Typical 30 or 40-minute jogs precede ten, fifteen, or twenty 100s over grass. Neither he nor I ran for half a month. There weren't good workouts before that, and such a gentle jogging foundation couldn't prepare for what followed. Beginning after a week, Iggles jumped on us. Ten log entries portray his brutal demands toward making us world-class performers or breaking us. (Sirianni had a belly full, sending him home.)

By May 10, our conditioning advanced, warranting logging everything and noting conditions. It was a set procedure.

5/10/59 15 min jog—16 x 220 on infield barefoot, 110 jog between. Pace = "strong" on one and 'swing' on the next. 10 x 100 easy on grass

5/11/59 30 min jog—15 x 100 medium speed—5 x 220 at good swing,

5 x 220 good speed tempo and repeated twice with 110 jog between. 10 x 100 easy barefoot

5/12/59 15 min jog—15 x 100 medium speed—16 x 330, 3 at swing tempo and every 4th at speed tempo.150 jog between reps. 10 x 100 barefoot easy

5/13/59 30 min jog on grass

5/14/59 15 min jog—4 x 10 x 100's first 10 at swing tempo, next 10 at speed, swing, speed.

5/15/59 20 min jog—10 x 100 medium speed—20 x 220 with 5 easy, next 5 swing tempo, 110 jog between reps, 10 x 100 jog

5/16/59 20 min jog—10 x 100 easy- 4 x 660 medium swing tempo, 330 jog between reps-10 x 100 jog

5/17/59 20 min jog—10 x 100 easy speed—16 x 220 medium swing tempo, 110 jog between—10 x 100 all out. This feels like my best day yet as I was sick, blistered, chest pains, etc for the past 2 weeks.

5/18/59 20 min jog—10 x 100 easy, 6 x 100 all out

5/19/59 1/2 hour jog, didn't wear socks and feet blistered. Bad chest pains too. 10 laps on the area field.

5/20/59 1/2 hour jog, 7 laps..very sore feet

5/21/59 1/2 hour jog, 7 laps...10 x 100 easy barefoot on grass

5/22/59 1/2 hour jog, 7 laps...20 x 100 easy barefoot

5/23/59 1/2 hour jog, 7 laps...10 x 100 middle speed, 10 x 100 hard speed, 5 min jog, 10 x 100 middle speed

5/24/59 jog 3 big laps on grass..12 laps sprinting straights and jogging curves

5/25/59 1 hour easy jog..felt heavy, did 10 laps on the double field

5/26/59 15 min jog. 16 x 220's on infield barefoot good to hard swing tempo, 10x100 easy..felt good today

5/27/59 30 min jog- 15 x 100 middle speed- 5 good swing 220's and 5 good speed 220's repeated again, 110 jog between runs- 10x100 easy barefoot...felt bad today

5/28/59 15 min jog-15 x 100 middle speed-16 good swing 330's, every 4th was good speed, 150 jog intervals, 10x100 easy barefoot. Really wasted today

5/29/59 40 min jog blisters are down, callouses developing

5/30/59 nothing, went to modesto relays

5/31/59 30 min jog- right arch and Achilles tendon sore

6/1/59 15 min jog- 40 x 100, 10 good swing, next 10 good speed felt sick!

After surviving three weeks of pure agony, I was coming out strengthened and seeking more! It felt good to head for achievements, and there was no reason for self-doubt! Once again, life was on an even keel.

The outlook became more promising when Jim Beatty, whom I long admired, arrived. He started trailing behind Santa Clara's current group. He's out of shape. Noticing him struggling through warm-up routines, I dropped back, lending support. He once gasped, haltingly gulping air. "Chap, in less than a month, I'll be leading this menagerie." Such commitment and determination were characteristic. It's wise to key on him, marking progress. Steady improvement continued as hard workouts increased. Feelings grew toward reaching the top of the world. Then everything crashed!

6/1/59 20 min jog- 10x100, 20x220 5 easy speed, 5 good swing tempo, 110 jog between. 10x100 easy...felt very heavy

6/2/59 20 min jog- 10x100 easy- 4x660 middle speed, 330 jog between- still not feeling well

6/3/59 20 min jog- 10x100 easy- 16x220 middle swing tempo, 110 jog between, 10x100 all out, ran alone, best day yet!

6/4/59 30 min jog- felt good

6/5/59 20 min jog- 10x100 easy, 6x100 all out

6/6/59 nothing, coach not here

6/7/59 nothing,

6/8/59 nothing

6/9/59 20 min jog

6/10/59 3/4 mile jog, 12 more laps, jog the curves, all out straights- 10 min jog- felt good

6/11/59 jogged one mile, supposed to be 12x150 middle speed, and 12x60 all out, but ran 24x150 and then 10x100 all out. 100's hurt the legs

6/12/59 40 min easy running

6/13/59 supposed to be 40x100 10 easy, 10 hard speed, but only did 10 easy, 7 hard and felt out of it

6/14/59 rest day

I traveled home early after Jack's 1960 life-threatening motorcycle crash. Donald said, "If you want to see your brother alive, you'd better get back here." I arrived the following day! A stack of newspaper articles covering the seriousness of Jack's accident waited as preparation for my visiting Chester's hospital. Jack's condition was as precarious as it could get. Later, JC recalled his experience's metaphysical nature:

I remember an out-of-body experience while lying there in Chester Hospital. I vividly recall being outside of the hospital looking in. I had gone out through the window and it was cold outside. I looked back into the room and thought "it's too damn cold out here. I better get back in there." I got back into my old body again. That's how gone I was.

On entering intensive care, he was alert but not communicating. Upon seeing me, JC acted excited, making noises, signing, and gesturing. He languished for months before his brain's fog lifted. His senses came back after days of semi-consciousness. Spiritual feelings engulfed me, sitting there daily. It's where Mom brought me into this world. The greatest danger for patients is staph infections. Staphylococcus screwed up Jack's body worse than his motorcycle wreck. Later, JC recalled:

I had to have massive amounts of antibiotics. It probably set a record for humans. I understand that my case was discussed in one of the medical journals in 1960 for having received an extraordinary amount of antibiotics. I never saw the article, but I heard about it.

I watched him hanging on by a thread, which called for giving as much encouragement as possible for survival. On a foray into town, Kenny's mother walked past Woolworth's, and I wasn't sure she remembered me until we talked. News about him raising hell in Pensacola's Jim Crow environment was not good. There's too much trouble with local authorities, and military status keeps him off a Florida chain gang. She spoke openly about many arrests for fighting. Police had planned to lynch him by staging a deadly manhunt after his next violent act.

Out of shape after four years of military service, joining SCVYV and attending junior college was a life-saving path. I mulled this over plenty since becoming an Iglói disciple. There's a possibility for him thwarting west coast Jim Crow. My experiences brought recognition that ever-higher performance levels should take precedence over other pursuits. We are at our best when focused on workout goals while striving to improve as students. I knew it, but Kenny had no ideas along those lines. Down south, racists fomented difficulties, distract him every day. There were physical and soul-wrenching problems in surviving political, social, and economic tyranny's inhumanity enforced by Jim Crow's relentless oppression. He should have been racing nationally, not out drinking, fighting, or getting thrown in jail. With our partnering and Iggles' coaching, he'd get beyond that crippling destiny and into a better life. Junior colleges were cheap, and proven athletic ability guaranteed scholarships and finishing BA. Degrees. There's no prospering when slaving in east coast factories. Information from Mrs. Noel enabled me to contact him at Eglin Air Force Base outside Fort Walton Beach, Florida.

Kenny:

I did not know the extent that mindfulness regarding running had grown with Neal, fostering communication that changed my life. Neal drew me back into running and onward into college. From interacting with Charles Chapman years earlier, I understood that one's best only comes by achieving higher-level consciousness.

CHAPTER
SEVEN

Life and Times at Eglin Air Force Base

*The moment is everything for people trapped
in a state of hopelessness and helplessness.*

Kenny:

As a condition of release from juvenile detention, the court demanded military enlistment, and I left West Chester choosing the Air Force, and hoping I'd learn good-paying career skills before being discharged. Nothing worked out well. My eventual duty station was Eglin Air Force Base (AFB) in Florida, driving refueling trucks and managing motor pool petroleum supplies. This base operated like a bustling northwestern panhandle jungle city. Teams went out to kill poisonous snakes and scorpions every morning. As often found among people confined in rigid institutions, there were plenty of tough misfits. Lawbreakers, under court sentences, were plentiful. Enough assholes tried building reputations as "bad actors." Even though other individuals had bullying difficulties, none bothered me.

And there was Jimbo Nations, an ignorant hillbilly from Tennessee. Nations underwent October's basic training with me at Lackland, near San Antonio. Jimbo's mental capacity appeared questionable. A drill instructor, the same age as us, nicknamed him "Hot Nuts" for scratching his balls while standing in formations. Buster Brooks, next door at Eglin, severely beat him every payday when they'd drink until losing their senses while gambling. His busted lips beneath blackened eyes healed within ten days. Were there possibilities such battering would extend beyond victimizing Nations? Naturally, I enlisted with defensive skills and offensive measures ready.

Beating Hot Nuts went unchecked until Buster tried bullying Pickford Jones, who shipped from Tachikawa Airfield outside Tokyo. After hours of drunken dice games, Buster needed to kick some ass, choosing the new guy. Most didn't realize it, but Pickford had karate and jujitsu black belts. He also gave Kenpō private lessons. Pickford began throwing Brooks. Different flips, twisting and dislocating limbs, and slams against walls destroyed our barrack's exit. Brooks got somersaulted down our wing on his way through locked, heavy steel doors securing the corridor's exit. When the Air Police arrived, no witnesses stepped up. Floor-mates described everything. Building maintenance installed a new door right away. Hot Nuts had a reprieve when Buster never returned, and this kind of drama convinced me to maintain top physical condition.

To stay in shape while enjoying special privileges, I joined Eglin's boxing team, coached by Duke Snider, a classy lightweight. Daily training developed confidence in handling disputes. More than anything, drinking cheap booze occupied off-duty interest. Our imbibing until oblivious on weekends, creating fun times with fighting, became standard practice. The first years on base saw fifteen arrests, charged with disturbing the peace, and there were additional run-ins involving Pensacola (PC) swabbies.

Valparaiso Showdown

Our experience was from an earlier century, as an emerging era ends the old one. Country niggers remained broken people from slavery and failed reconstruction. They were small-minded, silly, and backward; that's our precise condition, too! We were alike, except government orders sent some of us. My being an airman trapped and suffering in the antebellum South resulted from bad choices. Would anyone with brains choose this? My lacking logical thinking triggered many times cursing decisions and caused repeated questioning showing natural stupidity. Yet, it never dawned on me that, although given some freedom of choice, we rarely behaved wisely—nothing registered along those lines. The importance of most activities available off military reservations qualified as negative or insignificant! GI's in towns sought petty pursuits without reasoned thought. They carried on dumb stuff like drunken arguments. The poorest sections of small towns housed niggers and beat-down stores and shops. Social gathering places mirrored movie sets depicting dirt poor settlers inhabiting false-front buildings. These semi-rural northwest Florida settlements were only missing hitching posts outside saloons featuring swinging shutter-style batwing doors. Fort Walton Beach, Niceville, Valparaiso, Crestview, DeFuniak Springs, Panama City, Milton, and other towns emphatically depicted Negro deprivation. The environment had a mid 1800s feel.

Entering one-horse hole-in-the-wall joints, attempting to escape self-imposed misery, constantly drained us. Hollow gut feelings accompanied forced acquiescence to mutually assumed total inferiority. I remember an occasion of seeing B.B. King in Panama City's lone joint and foolishly expecting reinvigorating hope in that unjust world. Prospects of listening and dancing to BB weren't stress-releasing enough to override angst generated from wanting better while being helpless when encountering prejudice. Such daily trials were not dismissible. Our longing for change stood as empty desires since no prospects existed, enhancing a depressing view of self-worth. Consistent deprivation stayed with frequent adjustments to the consciousness of place and time through volumes of liquor. It was a life of getting drunk and committing stupid acts, but only learning what happened when told by someone later.

Next came reveling in it all. Sadly, self-defeating practices have occurred week after week. Every juke joint struck me as borderline inhabitable one-room shacks with seedy bars displaying smudged glasses matching filthy, excrement-crusted toilets. Some nights went by sleeping in cars after puking your guts out. Local Negroes frequenting saloons reflected these places. Familiar patrons are broke-down—winos, derelicts, bums, skags, skanks, sluts, and whores. The number of servicemen marrying females frequenting these awful hangouts proved downright mystifying. Before long, husbands ship alone to Thule, Greenland's god-forsaken wilderness Strategic Air Command site 750 miles beyond the Arctic Circle. Threats of year-long tours of duty haunted us.

Banishment hovered as maximum punishment, enforcing Eglin's ways, including following racist norms under Jim Crow. Wives of those manning arctic outposts still functioned in joints as they did before GIs wed them. At a steady pace, airmen married ahead of shipping out while others returned from exile. Reclaiming spouses, they battled "Jodys," who lived with their wives during absences. These dysfunctional transactions kept repeating. We all saw, but those trapped were blind. If you tried advising or warning them, you had senseless fistfights! Mystifyingly, eastern city homeboys embraced these warped arrangements. Throughout my service, I hypothesized larger governmental schemes of mixing populations by sending troops drawn from the North to occupy the South, forging unions with civilians, plus vice versa vis-à-vis Southerners. Young recruits entering unreceptive environments might cause doing something bold or, most commonly, nonsensical.

Bobby Harrison staggered into our barrack's lobby after partying late in Valparaiso, Florida (Val-P). He displayed cut hands draped in torn clothing. Bobby was a self-styled pretty boy with a light complexion, straight hair, and a missing central incisor. He told his latest story with great relish. We eagerly crowded our lounge, listening to misadventures. Nothing's hurt with mighty embellishing or substantial lies. Typical conflicts were 100% because of Bobby's arrogant narcissistic judgment. Gatherings saw injuries, regardless of blame or responsibility. Anyhow, Harrison claimed he shuns aggressiveness. He was not to blame for getting sliced by "crabs!" (We characterized resident males as "sand crabs" because all they could do for sexual gratification was stick their dicks in the beach sand.) Most young women wanted servicemen. Plenty escaped their nightmarish, oppressive environment through marriage. A few befriended servicemen, securing survival needs (food, clothing, and shelter). (I met a girl who hid the fact that she was pregnant, tricking me into thinking her child was mine. Our connection flowed too well. So, being wary, I stayed away until this girl's pregnancy started showing. Reports were she inquired of my whereabouts.) Bobby's slanted tales followed his typical MO. His over-aggressiveness, especially when approaching women, defied logic. As strangers, why invade small-town bars alone? No basis existed for anyone, especially young men, to welcome him.

Non-southerners exploited harmful local conditions. There's little that local victims can do about overcoming opportunity and power imbalances. Issues boiled down to "us versus them." That's what determined our behavior. Talk about arrogant false togetherness; we are bullies seeking to punish young men resisting us exploiting their diminished lives! With Bobby Harris, Bill Davis, Nat James, and I set on delivering severe payback, this quartet lacked superficial knowledge of each other. The determining force was Bill, an unpredictable instigator, frequently courting death. A demonstration of the point was riding with him, speeding over country roads from Crestview after visiting a woman. Her husband had shot at him before. His Studebaker's bald left front tire blew, sending us into roadside trees, going 90 miles per hour. Visions of my teen years flashed while plunging further into the young forest, knocking down smaller trees and approaching larger ones. I saw Mom's sadness over my demise. That settled any doubts about this deranged Flint, Michigan motherfucker's dangerousness. Later, we learned Bill enlisted, fleeing Flint, Michigan on murder charges, when FBI agents cuffed and escorted him away.

We experienced an era where the moment is everything in our confusion of hopelessness, drowning in helplessness. We long for relevance in our eyes. Maybe victimhood is as much as slavery's descendants can expect from this political, social, and economic cesspool. Absent intentional self-misdirection, mainly through some form of debilitating intoxication, little solace exists. We reacted to Bobby's mishap, failing to see his victimization as manufactured by our needs. Rational thinking and mastering our lives may only be possible in worlds beyond current reach. Desperate, we tried and failed at contriving to be in that place. Outcomes coping here were often painful, realistic, sad, and comical. The primary skill mastered was us fooling us.

Imagine four young niggers riding their base shuttle to Valparaiso because nobody had a drivable car, invading a tiny settlement intending to avenge an injured comrade they didn't know. Our misguided quartet dressed wearing dark azure raincoats as the Air Force's only stylish garment. The shuttle stopped near Mississippi Road, a State Highway 397 Air Force bus pickup spot outside town. It's a mile walk through poor neighborhoods of shotgun houses to enter Negro businesses' one-block stretch. Rundown dwellings edged a double-wide dirt street abutting wooden sidewalks. Four strangers searched for someone that only one had seen before.

We hadn't considered the best hours to possibly catch the previous night's offenders. We had no idea if we could find our quarry, while avoiding attention. We nearly abandoned hunting when a likely pair stepped from between decrepit buildings. Once they recognized Bobby, they moved, confronting him. These young lions got another chance to finish an escaped wounded prey. Paces away, I read both sides' body language, intending severe damage. Maybe that is why neither saw Harrison wasn't alone. The pair advanced with resolute boldness, without wariness or caution. This stunning display only lasted a fraction of a second. Unaware of moving, somehow I landed front and center of the confrontation. Proceedings fell under my control. All figures but the short bully faded into the background. Businesses blended into gray backdrops, and companions posed along the fringes of my awareness. Images blurred.

One advanced, sliding his knife from wrinkled wool slacks. It was the weapon he used to cut Bobby. I warned him while he was pulling a switchblade, "When you come out of your pocket, you better come out good." The self-conscious language sounded like hokey lines from cheap Hollywood western white hat-wearing cowboys. Thoughts of righteous indignation accompanied smooth-toned speaking while I calmly drew a .32-caliber

German Luger from under my coat. As its chrome-plated barrel flashed, that bully froze before retreating, using awkward, unsynchronized cross-legged movements, backing toward Nanny Shelby's Kitchen. He said he wasn't being serious about his blade and hoped we could all forget everything. "I's doan meant no arm. Dis ah Bigg mus tak." With difficulty understanding the Pidgin dialect, words got deciphered by approximate sounds. Funny, when coming within arm's reach, aged Nanny Shelby started closing her restaurant, shutting him out. She knew this guy and witnessed him receiving a well-earned beating. I whipped the reflective barrel across his shaved head with Nanny's door closing. That first stroke ripped the scalp back to the front. He screamed, collapsing as his bald pate split, gushing blood from a gash, exposing seven inches of fresh skull bone. Another pistol swing creased the top, ripping down, almost removing his left ear. With this blow, he lost consciousness—plunging from his knees, face-planting into Mrs. Shelby's doorway so it couldn't close. They had to be real assholes if Nanny denied them mercy. This way, Bobby's dispute reached a favorable conclusion.

We retreated, backing away with guns drawn and fearing home support mustering against us. However, we left Val-P's dark town unchallenged. Our great dilemma remained: not having return transportation. We invested no thought and, thus, embraced gross stupidity. We were without transportation on an empty road, and hitchhiking was not an escape plan. Anyone wanting suspects could find us.

So, we're niggers from northern cities packing guns, colored Yankee vigilantes patrolling the Deep South, awaiting free transportation, worried about escaping arrests by Confederate sheriffs. Colored people weren't after us, just their sheriff. It took only seconds getting strung along Niceville highway before deputies pulled over, checking us. I stashed the .32 under a drainage pipe two hundred yards away. That's why I was out of sight when Bobby and Bill got questioned. Sheriffs carried them so Negro citizens could say they assaulted their sons. They excluded Nate while sitting on the northbound 397's bus stop bench. He appeared as traveling north, not with us. Sheriffs returned our compatriots minutes later. Witnesses told deputies those two didn't do it. Valparaiso's subjugated community showed appreciation that resident bullies got beat down. Native support defied our expectations. We relaxed, congratulated each other, and caught the next shuttle. Valparaiso's showdown story replayed thousands of times, and our status rose, becoming legendary "crazy" figures among barracks troops. We are not going to Valparaiso again, ever.

Of Folk Heroes

Before a period of growth, nonproductive acts filled 1957's off-duty hours. Positive changes developed after Charles Chapman entered the flight line refueling shack during the winter of 1957. Already, I had behaved foolishly in so many ways but survived. Amarillo, Texas's experiences (see Chapter Eight) augur innocent confusion when landing in Pensacola, thinking it has to be better. The segregated north's physical environment was centuries ahead of Fort Walton Beach. Forced acceptance of gross poverty and inequality defacing the world's largest Air Force Base's doorstep made hostile reactions inevitable. With flurries of violent self-destruction, I scrapped all innocence. Massive changes began when battling three sailors and a prostitute shivved me from behind. Talk about calls too near death!

I didn't know anyone when frequenting Pensacola (PC) that summer. An attempt on my life occurred early amid transitioning from languishing in Fort Walton Beach to finding a place in a bona fide city where Negroes enjoyed a section known as "The Blocks." Newton's Sugar Bowl, a Negro-owned soda fountain, occupied the northwest corner of Belmont and De Villers streets, drawing colored youth as their favorite socializing place. There, I began connecting with local characters, like Spider, and getting acquainted with the community surroundings. The primary activity became sharing gallons of Red Mountain or rotgut hard liquor. Our regular drinking spot was an alley across from the Savoy Club. On every occasion, collective imbibing welcomed all comers.

One time I was kidding with "Little Lois," who was walking to the Savoy Club. She was learning the business of whoring, I'd heard. She understudies

Big Lois, an old whore, weathered well beyond her years, with an ugly face, broken body, and uglier disposition. It wasn't clear whether her novice did tricks. I wasn't her customer, which made us more like friends. Three dudes approached as we talked at the inner edge of the cracked sidewalk. Their leader acted offended and faintly opposes friendly contact with Little Lois. I sensed an argument coming and moved onto the sidewalk from the Window Factory's recessed entrance. While exchanging insults, the anticipated violence drew spectators. Not that I favor fighting, but as many youngsters learn rushing head-strong toward manhood, there's no backing down.

From my viewpoint, sailors silly enough to become angry over talking to fledgling prostitutes aren't threatening. My mistaken assumption was he possessed enough courage to go one-on-one and didn't realize he practiced creating situations to gang up on lone individuals. The biggest coward's name was Lame. He used hidden companions against any sole adversary. "Coward" designation played out with subsequent events. This gutless sailor had two companions. Both were sneaking cowards. During our initial argument, this lead coward's lackeys stood back—never indicating it wouldn't be one against one. When Lame charged, his cowardly support jumped from behind. With no idea what put me down and not feeling any blows, but rolling over and rising twice, three assailants tried kicking me. What luck, with several feet stomping, numbers blocked each other! Quickly up again, realizing there were multiple opponents, everyone within range became a target, assuming those near me were enemies. Engaged in swirling combat, differentiating spectators was impossible. There wasn't space or time allowing me to identify friends, enemies, or spectators. Everything transpired too fast. Left hooks downed a coward, and following right crosses missed. Pivoting and delivering another left, a second sneaking henchman backed off. Instantly facing Lame alone, it shouldn't be puzzling; he rapidly retreated, but it was. The rest scampered off, too.

Suddenly, I'm exhausted as surrounding masses explode, scurrying full speed in every direction! There's a vague awareness of chaos under bright streetlights descending into darkness. Moments ago, the world buzzed with life, noisy color, and energy. Then, a crushing veil engulfed everything, as Chi force siphoned out, though struggling to keep my eyes open—remaining conscious! Sounding quite distant, people screamed, "He's bleeding! Somebody stabbed him!" Those words cut through fuzzy consciousness, loud and clear. It must be me, but I didn't feel any damage! It hit me as unbelievable that a senseless argument could become a death sentence. The Blocks went barren, sparsely populated with scattering ice-encased distant figures—observers stationed too remotely to be sickened by gruesome, bloody details.

Exiting a fuzzy gray-scale space-time compilation, where pools of fevered spectators once loudly frolicked, I stumbled—an isolated soul dazed from extreme physical exertion. Body chemicals plunging into my bloodstream (fight-or-flight responses) were buoying. Staggering, trailing blood, I was aware of struggling with remaining upright. Locomotion feels like tip-toeing up De Villers, then along Belmont's gutter. Instinctive attraction to lights mapped this course. With me approaching them, former engulfing crowds fell away, maintaining uniform safe distances. People reacted, performing rhythmic choreographed routines synchronized with my precarious stumbling balancing. If tripping forward, they retreated. Pausing and swaying left, they stopped, leaning right. When stumbling backward, they surged toward me.

In seconds, my quest changed from staying conscious, collecting myself, and regaining focus, to lying down, resting, and dying. Nineteen years didn't flash before me, although wondering, "What Mom might feel? What'll she say?" crept over me. As a consummate practical person, she may conclude it's mercifully reaching the end of a tortured life, extending since early childhood. Figures lining the horizon whispered unintelligible words marking stages of slumping in the gutter, managing progressive slowing motion. Then, the gentle final moments conclude with my left ear feeling the sharp coldness of rough curbstone. It seemed the end. The silence extended forever—lingering between living and dying—as two girls kneeled, coaxing me, "Get up! Get up!" Though barely grasping consciousness, voices pushed through my dulled senses. Struggling, I sat, and then was lifted to the curb. Familiar faces and voices were encouraging. Jeanne, a young girl, is among the nicest of those frequenting Newton's. We had pleasant talks. She spoke, almost whispering, "Someone stabbed you. Let's walk to my house for a ride to the hospital." The girls helped, pulling and supporting me, making it halfway to A Street. Jeanne's mother drove to Pensacola Naval Air Station's Emergency Room.

Doctors stitched neck wounds, three shoulder punctures, and another in the middle of my back. Blood oozed in small rhythmic spurts until sutured. Navy medics joked, weaving a dozen stitches while depicting penetrations as inches deep. "These are punctures. Someone used a sharpened spike!" one mused. The exactness of how events unfolded continued to be undetermined. Doctors suggested letting city authorities know what happened. That wasn't my way. Satisfaction required administering justice outside racist legal machinery. Probably, the swabbies weren't armed. Their hands were empty, using fists and tangled feet. Flashing metal would suggest differently, so no one brandished knives. Another person with viper tendencies must be involved. Such individuals have reptilian qualities; as such, they're degenerate enough to stab their mothers. Who did such despicable work?

After recovering, most fellows frequenting the Blocks suggested immediate vengeance. My thoughts were studying it longer was best. Making things worse with only small satisfaction is easy. The scum who did it walked free, enjoying themselves after their murderous attempt. They did it unprovoked, without giving killing or maiming another human a moment's concern. How miraculous, escaping immediate irreparable damage! This person deserved in-kind retaliation by any measure of society's interest in conserving human life. Associates felt justice was bludgeoning the stabber to death. Identifying my attacker caused even more wrestling with determining my fitting response. Acquaintances learned Big Lois did it. (By standing against high odds, I'd gained local followers.) I never saw her ugly visage there. She probably arrived late and carried out sheer viciousness. She often shared our cheap wine in a broken bottle-covered alley beside Abe's liquor store. Now, I visualized breaking empty jugs and disfiguring her toothless, scarred face. Cognitively connected as bottles passed, allowing each a swig, we knowingly eyed each other, silently acknowledging my obligation to take her life.

Deciding about revenge challenged intelligence and reasoning. It tested my growing understanding of relationships between basic humanity influenced by environmental exposure. A satisfactory outcome meeting all needs, plus just revenge, was definable. Ego, concern about my image, and the desire to show that nobody attempting to kill me would get away with it required action. Over time, a vision formed from analyzing what happened. Please don't mistake my ultimate requirement; desiring her demise reigns supreme. Analysis tells me anyone so devoid of conscience, so able to murder innocent strangers, couldn't last. They are long past deserving to remain alive! Others will dispatch that whore soon enough, so my needs are covered! Whenever sharing cheap libations, I hunted urges to kill her during such moments. Those were challenging battles of questioning rash thoughts. Processes included repeatedly visualizing her demise; leading to understanding others would do it. Waiting felt comfortable. That realization relieved me of reactionary forces (s) engulfing me when people attempted to end my life. Less than six months after telling friends she would die from violence, someone shot Big Lois multiple times. Her life ended, leaving Belmont Street's hovels and exiting the rear door of a squalid room. Hearing about her murder warranted an affirmative nodding shrug, dissolving any burdensome expectations. Authorities made it known that her executioner wasn't wanted. I was among those with motives.

They Call Him Blue.

Blue's a drink'n fool.
Blue's a danc'n fool.
Blue's a fight'n fool.
Blue's a love'n fool.
The street corner philosopher.
The most loyal friend.
Blue ain't noth'n but a fool

It's a remarkable twist when assaulting someone elevates them into an iconic figure. The brawl's story lives with "Blue" fending off multiple attackers until stabbed by additional people. Incredibly, he survived the ordeal! (They were talking about me, a.k.a. Blue!). With fighting so hard while wounded several times, the popularity of his heroic stand registered! Talk resounded through the community. A fearless stranger can simultaneously take on three sailors, and survive getting stabbed from behind. Salley, a friendly sailor from New Jersey, identified the initial assailants as Navy, now self-exiled.

Weeks later, everyone, including sailors, airmen, and other people frequenting the Blocks, greeted Blue as their friend—this person showing courage gained mass appreciation. Even civilians harboring hostility toward outsiders befriended him. Connecting with them brings a greater understanding of racial oppression affecting young civilians. He felt their helplessness, enduring overwhelming degradation maintained by full-blown Jim Crow. He sympathized with Negroes facing domination from the skewed competition with service members. A complex of inequities made young women inaccessible to native men. Navy and Air Force personnel's money, education, and world exposure raised them above regular citizens. Racist shackles dominated, inhibiting human growth. Local young men face impossible odds encountering invading Yankee brothers pursuing the community's single women, their most valuable resource. "Blue" had rare acceptance among residents. Folks realized something about him; as Robert Coles stated about those kinds of people, "Every day (they) try hard to become part of the community—to relinquish aspects of the very egoism the rest of us spend our lives, in various ways, trying to enhance."

Factors influencing his elevation included gaining dancing notoriety. Starting in junior high school, he sought recognition for dancing more than anyone. His performance of the newest northern urban steps contrasts with a usual shy, quiet, monastic introverted persona. It was his method of entering an expressive realm. They called him a "dancing fool." Steamy bouncing dance floors, R&B music, and crowd encouragement stimulated overcoming internal constraints underlying preferring withdrawing. He accessed center stage as a fighting "man of the people" and a dance innovator. Combat courage is a part of it. Being versed in literature, poetry, philosophy, history, and politics was a good addition. Dancing, however, expressed heroic presence, elevating the people's music and dance legacy and delivering a commanding impression. The "dancing fool" designation was because performing spoke, touching everyone. There are anthropological foundations and tribal roots involved with dancing being a cultural expression of people celebrating their continuing existence.

Once finding common ground, I joined with airmen seeking more satisfying lives than afforded by Southern norms. Sufficient connections formed, removing any vulnerability to youth that opposed GIs. Most Negroes accepting my nom de guerre meant more cooperation. It's a logical progression, garnering respect accompanying a heralded reputation. We called ourselves The Beatniks. After gaining relevance in the Negro quarter, energy pursued more lofty aims. Kerouac, Ginsberg, and Sartre became preferred readings. Dizzy Gillespie's be-bop music completes our identity ideas. Shared interests cemented our association, merging into a collective departing from norms characterizing conditioned passive response patterns and accepting hardcore racism plaguing Negroes.

We adopted a uniform, donning trench coats trimmed with chocolate-orange plaid corduroy pocket flaps, sleeve trim, and collars. The Beatniks held sway, gracing the Sugar Bowl. Many philosophical discussions welcomed all comers while holding forth. Frustration as soldiers defending our nation while encountering racial restrictions often boiled over. Excessive use of alcohol, drug abuse, and intra-group conflict were destructive self-expressions coming directly from segregation's rampant discrimination denying our humanity. Soon, our major planned activity became randomly assaulting white men. Violence was seriously misguided and sometimes comedic. For example, we invaded Main and A Street's striptease bar as our final set of outlandish acts. White airmen said that Saturdays, scantily clad white females stripped bare at midnight. That information produced an unparalleled opportunity to fuck with the joint's redneck patrons. We'd arrive around midnight and wait outside until strippers finished removing "G" strings before rushing in, viewing naked white females, and outraging patrons. When rednecks chased after us, we disappeared into the ghetto. Every time, chasing niggers proved impossible wearing cowboy boots and left us laughing in the mirage of our segregated sanctuary.

To stage an ultimate attack required an enhanced purpose. Our largest raiding party waited outside for angry crackers. They would rush into a significant battle. Activities included fighting whites elsewhere in Pensacola between the initial and crowning strip bar invasions. We attacked people every weekend. Two of us scouted the fringes of neighborhoods until finding victims. All of them were tough, fighting like hell. We individually took them on, surprised them with a few blows and escaped! It was akin to the Native Americans counting coup, the top of their graduated system of war honors. If asked why this behavior, I'd call it reacting to oppression! Rather than turning effects inward, embracing self-destruction using drugs, alcohol, and violence against each other, we lashed out, attacking perceived beneficiaries of systemic discrimination. Our pitiable mission sought to make us feel better while continuing to suffer under white supremacy. No telling if any white victims were racists.

We were attacking whites into summer's heat through the fall and winter. Early in 1959, law enforcement planned to end our assaults. PC had two Nigger cops covering Dark Town, dealing strictly with Negroes. One of them everybody labeled "Wyatt Earp," pulled up one spring evening uncharacteristically. He angled the squad car, opened the door, and walked over to us, leaning against the Sugar Bowl's store-front window. He said, "The folks downtown know you're responsible for attacking whites. They're waiting to stage a manhunt, killing you." He backed away, turned, slid into his car, and drove off slowly. We weren't supposed to get warned. There were snitches among Pensacola's oppressed, and we gained nothing by fighting random white men. That's a foolish way of opposing racism. Wyatt Earp's message ended any thoughts otherwise. Also, considerations of becoming underground figures had already filled discussions. Ceasing our attacks couldn't guarantee we wouldn't get lynched. Identification as Negroes is sufficient! It gave welcome relief to stop maintaining a rebel image.

Charles Chapman

While acting out the persona of "Blue," a significant figure entered when Charles Chapman appeared in 1958. There's nothing unusual about finding new arrivals occupying former vacant rooms. He was tall, maybe six foot four, and mulatto. From the beginning, he sought to dominate our building's eastern wing. His door stayed open as he sat there, Mozart's Eine Kleine Nachtmusik's volume turned high, amused while watching undisciplined fools passing. Patient and spiderish, he waited within his web. Soon, I was an unsuspecting dolt pulled into his web of influence. Classical music, familiar from high school studies, combined with acting mysterious, was the bait. Chapman showed off playing chess alone, between displays using math and geometry instruments.

Hundreds of issues warranted seeking his enlightened views. Our jobs included refueling jet planes, providing house furnace oil, and maintaining motor pool gasoline supplies. Chapman enlisted after several semesters at Oberlin College. He'd attended Officer's Training School (OTS) but chose to wash out when deciding against a military career. By custom, he got two years enlisted as a corporal to complete obligations. Upon arriving, Chapman imposed his will, influencing our flight line servicing center processes and, days later, corralled specific vital administrative functions. His slide rule served as the principal tool. Converting cylinder inches to gallons awed the entire crew. With his mechanical calculator, he performed intimidating demonstrations analyzing gas, oil, and jet fuel usage and costs. 3201 Wing Fuel Operations' messy flight line records got organized by week's end. Intellect and education enabled carving a niche. He set his work hours and selected tasks for applying math skills. The need to organize headquarters documents freed him from non-professional duties. Periodic government audits requiring detailed information moved him to higher-level audit preparations. Soon, Chapman joined Captain Messick's headquarters group and was assigned an office. Any idiot could see that refueling planes wasted his talent.

Further showing moxie, he secured special base housing for his mulatto wife overlooking Memorial Lake. Journeying to uncommon independence,

Chapman drew me close. After leaving the mess hall before his move into lakeside housing, he'd often yell, announcing he watched me, noting my potential. He often suggested playing chess, undoubtedly his way of testing my mental ability. I accepted his invitations and beat him by playing chess while listening to Baroque music. We discussed topics from philosophy to politics. My classical music knowledge impressed him, alongside reading literature classics and consistent chess wins. It surprised him. (I had read my brother's instruction book.) Observing Chapman's machinations, notably how he managed complex interactions and disarmed higher-ranking personnel, pointed my path forward. Controlling how others addressed him, he only received requests from operations officers, never getting orders. Common relationships were noticeably off-putting, with Dixie-bred sergeants not having secondary schooling. His intelligence gave him control of day-to-day activities and implicated accessible opportunities. I mail-ordered Keuffel & Esser's basic slide rule with an instruction book and mastered essential arithmetic functions after two weeks without needing help. It wasn't hard after watching Snake and Hindu (childhood friends) working theirs through school. Replicating Chapman's calculating gambit wasn't the aim. The general purpose was to show capabilities and create opportunities by forging qualitative separation above everyone else and showing the ability to manage numbers beyond basic levels. (After basic training, they already knew I graduated tops from fuel supply school.)

Before long, we exchanged views of society, with discussions channeling my thinking in new directions. Racism's saga, politics, economics, and our people's 400-year journey filled his preaching when exchanging ideas. His opinions of what this country owed Blacks struck me the most. (He identified as "Black," never Negro or colored.) First among issues comes our national practice of education and culture, ignoring or denying Blacks undergoing unspeakable subjugation throughout centuries. The larger society maintains an overwhelming web of constraints impeding substantive conversations about race. Political and educational responses, such as contemporary narrative presentations covering recent American developments, have been cursory. The rulers refuse to present American human enslavement's full depth and breadth. By being denied knowledge of African civilizations' validity hundreds of generations before the Atlantic slave trade, Blacks cannot grasp the totality of injustices or degradation thrust upon them, sustained over several centuries. Creditable accounting must start well before 1619's European-sponsored slavery. Without enough coverage, existing celebratory practices continue America's tradition of not permitting meaningful recognition. Blacks are owed an immeasurable debt from slavery. Original chattel and their descendants toiled, denied just compensation. Comprehensive factual accounts have been overdue but are needed most during any age! Considering ongoing total oppression, expecting survivors to sustain good psychological health, accessing only crumbs or refuse from their stories is unrealistic.

To paraphrase Chapman's discourse:

Social sciences, including anthropology, determined humans create memories, sustaining knowledge of their history and cultures because such vital elements were indispensable for survival and well-being. It has been essential for successful future individual and group viability. That was how people progressed. Populations held lacking definitive grasps of their past supporting organic culture amounts to being born unaware and alone. Results ensure missing foundations for a dignified existence and nothing forging progress. Rational functioning proceeds in jeopardy for any large body of associated humans, not knowing who or what they are in a rewarding sense. Owners refused slaves' life-affirming possibilities by renaming them and denying their progeny, sustaining their heritage embodied in original African names. Inherent in branding Africans as Negroes, they denied them the power to identify or define themselves. One question is why and how, with human sensibility, slavers continued conscious dehumanizing practices until military defeat. This continuing query has yet to find an adequate explanation (s). Overt methods proceeded for centuries, followed by another peonage era where former chattel continued laboring without just compensation. During this time, countless bodies and souls encountered irreparable degradation. Undeniable negative consequences remained. Later cursory acknowledgments avoid and deny owning extensive destruction visited upon victims. Infinite greater recognition is owed sufferers (past, present, and future) because of abject slavery. Few think complete and accurate presentations aren't essential. No commensurate effort compensates those robbed of land or labor. Martin Luther King, Malcolm X, and others insisted that, at the least, victims deserve the truth. Even more so, each person deserves the fullest extent of the substance of their personal and ancestral history. Everyone should get their labor's fruits.

Randall Robinson teaches,

...when the case is that people have been denied their worth and dignity throughout their existence, they are owed adequate repair. As much as Black people have needed mending, in equal measure, the nation has not pursued restoration. Not only has that not happened on even a minuscule warrantable scale, but there also hasn't even been an inkling of random conversation about it. As a society, no talk about such a historical debt or need exists. The pathological destruction, denial, and distortion of heritage that occurred to African slaves and natives have been incomparable in human history. We are talking about three centuries of stripping victims of their names, their culture, and fundamental sovereignty over their bodies, and their ability to survive under their own volition. During that period, any hint of exercising personal will in managing one's day-to-day existence was met with inhumane punishment, not the least of which was death and worse for families. All too often, they had their ears, tongues, genitals, or one or more limbs cut off. They were subjected

BROTHERS OF THE WIND

to every possible measure of wholesale sexual abuse for generations and generations. Such acts were considered by any semblance of authority to be acceptable behavior by the slavers. It was routine. The vast population of mixed blood offspring they are responsible for fostering constitutes evidence of the slavers' penchant for unfettered depravity. It has remained all but impossible to calculate the number of rapes that it took to produce such worldwide millions. Someone should try to do it! That amount of abuse can be sustained in a single society without the social order self-destructing, only if the abusers have total dominance of the entire population from the cradle to the grave. By most measures, these miscreants stand as the epitome of sexual predators and child molesters. As victims in the maelstrom of unspeakable abuse, our African forbearers got stripped of the knowledge of who they are. With their history erased and their memory suppressed, they were worked and driven, like animals, to death at an early age. Without pay or profit, they built the country. Many of the wealthy and business interests, although not directly connected with slavery, profited and got their wealth from institutions that were fed by slavery. The benefits of free labor broadly applied.

These views make up the most representative thoughts of Charles Chapman. His offerings were at the heart of my awakening, seeking a healthy self-identity while remaining in the war (military). Such was the growing foundation for comprehending essentia within reach. Jim Crow's dictates and plantation society remnants all show the correctness of Chapman's views. I carried this perspective for future use, clarifying what has lasting value.

His mentoring worked wonders, stimulating my becoming more analytical about everyday interactions, operations, and practices characteristic of southern culture influencing Eglin. Developing a reasoned view of hostile forces operating was vital for coping. My struggles became clearer while taking Psychology 1A and 1B offered by Florida State University (FSU) at Eglin's Base Education Center. FSU studies further enlightenment with lieutenants, captains, and spouses filling classes. Courses provide up-close opportunities for observing our bases' privileged personnel in neutral environments. I saw, heard, and compared others' performances to mine. Such educational formats instigate lessening apprehension and make a difference because living under oppression, like many Blacks, had repressed my potential. Add to that the holdover adverse effects of digesting the "other's" inherited advantages and behaving in ways acceptable to them outside the classroom. Traditional settings' constraints lower confidence and assertiveness among the least influential people.

Most adults attending FSU courses enjoyed officer status. They were our elites. Uniformed officer's presences beyond classrooms triggered apprehensive deference from enlisted personnel. Women were extensions of husbands, college-level schooling, and upper-middle-class upbringing. Entering satellite programs, I expected competitive disadvantages because whites had B.A. degrees or other higher education exposure. Most attendees had similar college experiences, making them familiar with these subjects. I started discerning that the intellectual capabilities of those present were images with little substance. None displayed the intellect assumed to be possessed by ruling-class students. The woefully limited ability of officers' wives was eye-opening! These folks had trouble grasping terms or definitions, understanding textbooks, communicating ideas, and testing. However, their questions, exposing issues of interest, identified that problem-riddled households predominated. Mainly, they came seeking help resolving personal or family problems. To a person, there were behavioral issues with wives, husbands, and children. These people enjoyed racial and military privileges yet became troubled, finding difficulty coping satisfactorily despite advantaged positions. I had grossly overestimated their abilities. Psychology courses showed officer classmates and wives weren't more intelligent or better suited for leading. It brought into focus a tremendous revelation. Socialization deliberately distorts unnatural arrangements, often leaving less capable, privileged individuals commanding. Racially dictated roles and relationships shepherd these types into occupying command roles. The inferior academic ability of enough students caused me to ponder. Supervised by noncommissioned personnel, with most not finishing secondary education, added more injustice. These were lessons for future situations. Their questionable academic aptitude rendered every exercise of their power a more severe gut punch. Lots of non-commissioned officers never went beyond primary grades. We complicate our path with difficulties from oppression.

As accumulating funds settled in as my most important goal, maximizing earnings didn't take long. Lucrative means emerged from having relatively higher intellectual ability than most enlistees. When Squadron leadership saw what I offered above other troops, my assignment changed to managing motor pool refueling operations. Servicing the base's automotive fleet opened an ongoing robust underground economy's door. Key personnel learned I controlled vehicle petroleum supplies. Tech Sergeant Titus, in charge of the motor pool, visited, proposing my use of any motor pool vehicle by providing free gasoline. Now, the unassigned vehicle inventory was available for me to exploit. The ability to rent transportation to others brought extra income. By week's end, a mess sergeant sought trading cases of T-Bone or rib-eye steaks. I realized I could get started in underground enterprises. Successful pilfering requires managing ledgers and ensuring supply losses don't exceed volume fluctuations caused by evaporation or temperature changes. Items, such as steaks, bring easy money from civilians and, if careful, provide reliable income, allowing accruing cash. Soon, side-money accumulated financing was sent home, while full pay, and more, went directly into savings.

Round Up the Usual Suspects

Flying aboard a C47 "Gooney Bird" from Fort Walton Beach to Andrews' Airfield outside Washington, D.C., took six hours. The bus to Amtrak added another hour. Including the train ride to Philadelphia and traveling by car to West Chester meant fourteen hours total. Arriving Friday around 9 p.m., Dupe, my sister, and brother-in-law Bill dropped me at Barnard Street. Exhaustion hit, so it was sack time after Tastykakes washed down with Amish Birch Beer. Mom awakened me early because friends phoned about a meeting. Getting dressed didn't take long.

Near uptown, patrol cars stopped, blocking the sidewalk. They collected my Pennsylvania driver's license and DOD card. Travel papers sat home, so any influence there couldn't happen. An impending national emergency must be the reason behind stopping me! An international crisis triggered leave cancelations! That wasn't the case, given the officers' attitudes. Positive possibilities evaporated while they cuffed my hands behind me. (Strange, but in last night's dream, Mom woke me saying police officers were downstairs wanting me uptown concerning robbing someone.) An authentic version of my dream proceeded. I was inside a patrol car, snatched by law enforcement, destined for jail. I had been on a tight travel schedule, the last 24 hours of my time accounted for. Air Force records show I was far from crimes that can't involve me. Thoroughly puzzled, I rode to headquarters. While seated there, several whites passed.

Soon, their clerk exited an office. She said a mugging victim fingered me as the perpetrator. Moments before, I sensed someone watching me. A balding man's ashen pudgy face sporting wire-rimmed glasses flashed when the door on my right cracked open. His visible features appeared terrified; seeing the entire image might scare me half to death. Something terrible grabbed him. The notion he'd identified me escaped my thinking, and earlier occurrences didn't connect at that instant. I encountered similar pale faces from behind jail bars in other places. More than once in Pensacola's city jail, someone bore witness, saying I robbed him at gunpoint. Such false witness qualified as equal ridiculousness because the base's guard logs showed me there during those robberies, not Pensacola or Pennsylvania. Officers ignored my train leaving D.C. when said robbery, 120 miles away, took place. Under racist rules, concrete facts of innocence won't keep you from getting arrested and being deemed guilty of crimes you couldn't possibly have committed. That was Black people's burden of encountering inherent racist irrationality. It surprised me, but top squadron brass understood this principle. That's why I was never punished related to actual or contrived transgressions. Unfortunately, the military refused to push against Jim Crow.

Using his most polite manner, an officer promised only to keep me three days pending charges. He tried sounding acceptable, functioning harmlessly, trying to explain his repressive imposition, as if being wrongfully jailed isn't a reason for feeling wronged. Cops needed time sorting through everything as if their actions occurred innocently, so they shouldn't get labeled as abusing authority if proven wrong. There goes this vacation! Would West Chester authorities come after me if I hadn't returned home? They'd ask my whereabouts, finding I'd been gone since 1956. Then they'd call Eglin to check. So far, it's summary imprisonment. Worst circumstances ever for spending one's leave!

Three days passed since getting body-snatched, with no ability to call anyone, and I'd define that as getting kidnapped. My parents discovered my fate when the jail cook spotted me. Their Black cook let my father know right away. Daddy came seeking why they arrested me. When told I'd serve more days as their stickup suspect, he left, set on freeing me. That escalated efforts to concoct more evidence than bogus eyewitnesses. I agreed to lie detector testing. Anything would beat stagnating there, but it won't worsen if testing suggests lying. This massive fashioning of guilt, deciding I robbed someone, was mind-blowing!

They'll keep pursuing confirming charges each time one avenue fails. We had to go to Philly. (I hadn't considered that small-town operations couldn't afford popular technology.) Those machinations were different, eating up part of three days arbitrarily taken away. Their pink-cheeked, newly uniformed rookie officer ushered me into a squad car parked outback. He acted nervous, insecure, and too green! Clip-boarded paperwork fumbled into the rear seat. He's an errand boy, I thought. We were going to Philly's polygraph testing facility. I consented, not thinking about what awaited or that, internationally, Philadelphia's police are renowned as peak hardcore policing practitioners. I could understand why this rookie turned so nervous. We entered policing's big leagues, and there was no measuring up! These were no-nonsense professionals. Hick officers received begrudged cooperation but no respect. Following an uneventful 25 miles cruising Route 3 (West Chester Pike), we parked and found P.D. offices topping William Penn Hall.

Two detectives waited, moving us along as if wanting this worthless business finished. Hicks wasted their time! Their largest room had tables of prepared polygraphs. The setup and pre-testing of one unit by establishing baseline readings proceeded. You'd think that under normal circumstances, professionals would explain the equipment's use, but there's little regard for hick uniformed escorts and niggers. There's disdain regarding most people's legal rights. An attendant attached testing components to my chest and fingers, and the blood pressure cuff choked my right bicep. They check heart rate and breathing patterns and detect fingertip sweat.

After answering questions, examiners observe reactions noting bodily functions showing dishonesty. My familiarity with lie detectors came from Popular Science Magazine articles. For example, Professor John J. Furedy says most detractors of employing polygraphs developed similar views, such as "The 'control' question test is a flight of fancy. It's used as a psychological rubber hose to induce confessions. Its foundation, based on false claims, fosters distrust while posing as their path to truth." I particularly appreciated FBI Agent Drew C. Richardson's explanation, "The Polygraph screening is unscientific, lacking theoretical testing or proof.. It lacks validity. Diagnostic value of this type of testing is that of astrology or tea-leaf reading." (FBI Agent Dr. Drew C. Richardson)

The examiner's expectations of consistent, accurate equipment results, claiming scientific certainty, threw me off the most. Unless detectives are better than professional actors, they were unaware that polygraphs lack reliability. His outlook suggested that only mentally disturbed individuals could defeat otherwise infallible machines. Maybe because of my mystery novel crime-fighting exposure, there's no expectation any device says innocent! Indeed, law enforcement would use every possibility of pronouncing me guilty. Despite mental underdevelopment, I saw their satisfaction validating their sense of superiority, fulfilling their supremacist mission. Any sign of lying allows dismissing contrary evidence and might scare confessing. Their purpose, rushing me into Philadelphia, was intimidation, not seeking proof of innocence. The rookie shepherding me is the only one intimidated. These hick West Chester lawmen appeared as transparent petty operators. What weak plans! Their claims that asking questions produces detectable false-hoods struck me as being farfetched. The utter dishonesty of their scheme was the actual criminal practice here. None of them cared that I couldn't have robbed anyone. They collectively perpetrated this farce as though honest servants of justice. They were despicable—the worst kinds of criminals. Authorities could only hold me for 72 hours. I'm assured of release when Daddy's lawyer showed up.

I envisioned a dimension of truth concerning lie detector validity. When involving matters of the human spirit, mechanical devices alone are so foreign that they can't fulfill presumed purposes. I considered this, especially the case for oppressors wielding technology-promoting environments of unbridled permissiveness for themselves. Under those conditions, electro-mechani-cal emotion measuring won't produce indisputably helpful evidence. How can such methods work within settings lacking fairness, mutual respect, and sincerity? When coercive efforts fail, authorities call subjects mentally deranged. It's their way of explaining modern engineering farces. How our experience unfolded amounts to treacherous officials attempting prosecu-tion by assuming the machines functioned correctly. They enlisted bogus validation from more vicious law enforcement agencies, markedly brainsick, idiotic, absurd, and purely authoritarian. That's where self-discovery entered. I found myself because it's an occasion of unparalleled insight into who I am.

Contrary to our justice system's bent and massively frustrating these persecutors, the worthless being emerging from warped socialization is not me! Their incredible frustration showed when a detective's spittle projec-tile-drenched pronouncement sprays my face during failed criminalizing efforts, "You're one sick nigger." This reaction emerged while they grew increasingly agitated as testing flopped. The ordeal featured plain-clothed officers huddled, whispering, and adding others to alter unwanted outcomes. Different devices kept getting tried as if earlier ones uncharacteristically malfunctioned. My wry smile was contemptuously displayed throughout these proceedings, struggling with their magical entrapment instruments.

As unflagging failures continued, naked hostile viciousness emerged. Philly detectives directed the usual vitriol, threatening us. My rookie nearly wet his pants when an especially gangster-type snarled, "Nigger, if'n u don't wipe dat smile offa youse face, I'm onna shove youse fuckin edd troo dat wall!" Such verbal extremes convinced me their plan could never deliver. They'd lost when their only recourse was making extreme physical threats.

My internal satisfaction grew large. I turned to my rookie, full on fear engulfing his ashen face, and asked, "Are you going to sit there letting them threaten me?" He all but shit his pants, frantically gesturing to stop talking when our plight warranted loud, panicked cursing. The city detective threatened, "Wha da hell yu tink e's gonna do? We'll fuckin make boate uh yu arseholes dis'rpeer, an dat'l be da fuckin end uh it!" Man, I thought, we are well over our heads in this shit! He spoke the absolute truth. These big-time motherfuckers don't play! Nobody fucks with Philly's enforcers! They're experts, handling problems employing their particular extra-legal practices. My cop, so frightened his body shook, and the holstered gun flapped like rhythmic hand claps, stood! He struggled to utter, his voice wavering, "LLLLes' jus ggggit da hell outa here!" We rose, leaving, running to avoid ending up on the Delaware River's bottom. Riding back and filling the air with the unrelenting scolding of my rookie for shrinking from protecting his prisoner and not standing against abuse was hilarious. He repeatedly begged, "Would you please shut up? You tried to get me killed! Both you and those fuckers are crazy!" Arriving where we started, complaining of racist treatment and not protecting their prisoner, I deliberately scolded the department using the third person. Entering the station, Daddy's lawyer had delivered a Writ of Habeas Corpus. They couldn't keep me from the sanctity of England's 1215 Magna Carta.

At last, Mom and Daddy got fully exposed to the paradigm of racism's "unjust casualty side" instead of an "aggressive deviant side" drawn of me as a teenager. An innocent victim's dimension always existed, but law enforcement hung tags of unwarranted deviance with provocation sufficiently submerged. Violent encounters with racists and brushes with law enforcement stemmed from unwarranted deliberate incorrigibility as a criminal individual, a gang-ster. Current events unquestionably exposed the relentless powers operating for our family's destruction, making them question former beliefs, thus showing justice has little importance. It revealed that claimed righteous sides were often illusions or deceptions, regardless of where you looked or what you thought you saw, invariably conforming to racist aims.

Cops embraced ill-appointed instruments of justice; readily pushing aside evidence confirming the impossibility of me committing crimes while traveling from 1000 miles away. Their dedication to injustice dismissed facts proving the impossibility of doing this specific holdup negated by official travel documents structured to military life. Officers refused to call Eglin Air Police, confirming robbing someone was impossible. Traditional guardians and operatives ignored proof of innocence and arbitrarily convicted coloreds. Such fundamental racial control dynamics prevailed. They're practicing injustice and openly abusing my family, who understood but cling to hope to find otherwise! Those beliefs are vital to pursuing daily Black civil practicality.

Misadventures during those specific days cleansed me of any remaining regrets of juvenile criminality. Unfolding events gave my father a different notion of former anti-social conduct that cleansed my conscience of frequent lies told under his roof. Daddy always accepted my lies, but Mom didn't. I felt spiritually freed, resulting from the bonding and acceptance of confirmation as a captive of racists. Being affected this way was a revelatory factor missing since the 1951 injustice fiasco, bringing police officers threatening Barnard Street. That's when five of us followed our usual path home, leaving junior high. Splitting our travel between mine and Snake's house, we meandered south along High Street, and I veered west on Barnard as they headed east.

This particular trek from school turned different. Vineman's Furrier, mid-block past Market, had a giant bear rug covering the floor. With jaws agape, the bear's gigantic head faced the plate-glass front. An unidentifi-able object filled its mouth. We stopped on Tuesday, pressing our mugs to the glass, guessing what had lodged between the bear's teeth. This silliness repeats over four days. From inside, behind curtains, a patrolman charged out on Friday. Without smearing our mugs on the glass, the chase went live! We didn't envision any harm by peering in stores and didn't run fast, never expecting to get detained. Considering our behavior as childish, we figured he was shooing us from the business! I trailed with a cased trombone and a load of books under both arms. He followed while yelling "stop!" When he gained ground crossing through traffic, his focus shifted to me. Lagging from carrying so much stuff, he expected to collar me. By increasing speed and leaving him standing still, it had to be upsetting. My lead extended enough to disappear before he reached the next corner. I went east to Matlack crossing Barnard, right on Matlack, and again at Union until Darlington, then north to Barnard.

My parents would of course find out. I'm the only kid outside of Philly who runs that fast while lugging books and a trombone. Two officers appeared during dinner. They said I didn't stop when ordered and threatened to arrest me for not obeying commands. Yeah, I think that's racist, authoritarian bullshit! Do I have to comply even if they are wrong or off base? They don't mention young niggers looking in store windows as forbidden. (This scenario intends to control Black boys outside their homes.) Not being catchable carrying a musical instrument and books made his chase embarrassing. I'm sure getting sucked into chasing me pissed him big time!

The problem was getting chased caused white supremacy enforcers to enter our only sanctuary. That could destroy any sense or hope of security. The greatest sins befalling colored families were activities bringing law enforcement to our residence—exposing the family to the racist whims of authorities. It's different if transgressions were decidedly political. That negated any recriminations or regrets. I took an extended lashing for the trombone incident. Physical punishment no longer hurt and couldn't affect my behavior one iota. By that age, fear and pain lost their meaning. Although foolishly endangering my family, suckering that cop into senselessly chasing me felt worth getting beaten. However, not a decade later, being home unintentionally brought the ultimate sin again. The following day, with my parents thinking it best, I flew out. Indeed, the cops hadn't finished! They'd come back on GP! Fifteen thousand feet above the lush, forbidden Delaware Valley, thoughts came that Daddy should tell them whenever I planned visits. But experience says they'd arrest me, anyway. That's the code under which we live.

While I'd hoped to locate Ernie Gardner, routine entanglement with law enforcement destroyed that possibility. The word about Ernie, my juvenile crime partner, was that he returned from incarceration warped, becoming part of West Chester's homeless wino population. That instant of sentencing guaranteed his psychological destruction, or worse. No chance that prison wouldn't utterly destroy him. I gave up on finding out. What could we say? Any mention of history revives those vastly different fates. Talking would make sense if he prospered. That prospect was not realistic, with systems raining prejudicial inordinate punishment on colored youth. This last hometown misadventure made returning to the unsavory environs of Eglin feel like entering a welcoming sanctuary. Unfortunately, that couldn't last. Virulent Jim Crow never countenanced that.

CHAPTER
EIGHT

Slavery circa 1958 and Beyond

*What standards of behavior are fair, just,
and equitable for the captives of racists?*

Kenny:

We stopped to piss before crossing the 3 Mile Bridge on US 98 from Gulf
Breeze, Florida, into Pensacola. It was hot and muggy, nearly raining
100-degree water. Jeff, Nat, Sally, and I joked while discussing plans for
getting drunk and raising hell. An Escambia County deputy sheriff pulled
up once our bladders emptied, and we stepped into our car. I was driving my
four-door straight-eight 1952 Packard. Its plush seats brought comfort when
riding over uneven two-lane Southern highways. Clippers floated, rising
before settling on a road's rippling contours. Car seats remind you of stuffed
furniture gracing richly appointed living rooms. The night was starting, and
now its promise evaporated under the glare of flashing red lights.

Maybe a gas station or convenience store got robbed, or both. Robbers were medium height and medium build Negroes. Everyone matches that description. We knew handcuffed niggers were as good as or better than any criminals remaining free in race-driven policing systems. Their car search came up empty. That there was no evidence of a crime didn't stop them from taking us into custody when simply calling Hurlburt Field's entrance post could prove we were fifty miles east during the robbery. We bullshitted with sentries exiting Field # 9 at 8:30 PM, 30 minutes before squad car lights blinded us. There was no chance of white deputies accepting our story. They weren't interested in contacting Hurlburt Field's guards. The cops had no interest in finding reasons to grant our release. There wasn't an opportunity to argue innocence because more deputies appeared and handcuffed us. An officer noticed four 20-liter Jerry cans of gasoline lowering the trunk but didn't perceive an issue. One officer questioned why we were carrying so much fuel. Thinking fast, I answered, "This car guzzles gas. An extra twenty gallons takes us round-trip to Mobile tonight." They knew it was a matter of life and death whenever Negroes stopped on roads after dark. Many highway businesses were Klan hangouts. It couldn't occur to them that I managed Eglin's gasoline supplies and practiced illegal use of government gas.

Since the alleged crime occurred in Pensacola, I thought we'd land there when arrested. Caged in two cars, we sped eastward through the cultivated countryside. Upon reaching US 90, signs pointed toward Milton, 26 miles east. We did not know if that was our ultimate destination. Our destination isn't ordinary. When arrested near this spot a month ago, they booked me into Pensacola's jail. Why was this different? Our best tactic was showing patience, especially when they hadn't pulled guns. They're taking us where Military Police (MPs) don't have ready access. Why is that needed, other than feeding their amusement? Are they exercising arbitrary judgment and costing four niggers sixty hours until MPs exercise custody? (I'd make that a favorite ploy if I were a racist cop.) Remote imprisonment opened up many evil possibilities. Deputies said nothing. The way ahead was unpredictable.

When chauffeuring Sgt. Benson, I had passed through Milton, touring

Florida's panhandle. "Ben" had "short-timer" status, six months from retiring after 25 years. Each week, we drove several hours exploring his chosen direction. He wanted my company with hundreds of men available and enjoyed booking a big rig, pulling 5000 gallons of premium. Traveling from morning until evening, we never feared running out of gas. It is different scenery on each outing, various highways, and small villages. Whenever Ben had the urge, we filled his super cool 1958 Chevy Impala, all black inside and out, heading wherever. Whitewall tires hid behind fender skirts. A yard-long ceramic panther crouched, filling his rear window, a long, sleek, shining black animal strikingly representing the car. Why Ben enjoyed rolling with me stays undefined. Our discussions were nonstop, covering literature, music, and history. Never delving into sexual matters, he was very effeminate, even prissy. Questions and conjecture reigned across our barracks concerning his effeminate manner. His Panther car's charisma, Ben's subdued personality, pending discharge status, never working, and big bucks lent sturdy legs supporting widespread speculation.

Often, we passed through Milton, seeking more interesting settlements with tourist attractions. Now, by racist designs, we were captives, heading toward an early Klan stronghold. Specifics of these rural areas' past or present racial atmosphere are unknown, and our procession blasted into the past as if through time portals. From reading on antebellum and post-civil war southern culture, visualizations dominated thinking. Visions of beatings, lynching, castrations, Negroes vanishing, hooded mobs burning crosses, and corrupt law enforcement with hanging judges dominated our thoughts. We struggled with making sense of this predicament—constructing hope that we'd survive. They never stated our destination, which could be anywhere, including execution or worse.

Continuous inhumane treatment of minorities haunted these parts. Road signs indicated locations, with none representing civilized destinations. These folk epitomize crackers, so any capture might end by being thrown into an alligator, rattlesnake, or water moccasin pit. Farm scenery flickered in and out of my vision while penned inside the rolling prison, trying to gauge this injustice. I fought off conjuring a condemned man's feelings on his last journey. Farms stretched along Route 90, sporting lush vegetables interwoven with ripening melons. Heat and stifling humidity oppressed, abundant rainfall made it so. With darkness approaching, oncoming vehicle lights struck our eyes—flashbulbs, snap-shooting pictures spaced by gaps between staggered headlights. Rows of vine-ripe melons faded as corn stalks cast bold green splashes before disappearing with the receding landscape. We slowed, passing Milton's village sign.

Streets were empty and quiet as if nobody lived there. Behind a ground-mounted sign reading "Milton City," its fired clay brick facade had gold-painted wood framing. Overall, looks didn't show purpose. Their jail appeared when they opened swinging red doors inset with ornately etched glass squares, behind which were steel cages. Three forward pens and three behind remained unoccupied early that Friday evening. We shuffled to individual cells, sitting, quiet, waiting. There was no discussion, as any open conversation would be used against us. Additionally, talking would unleash a real sense of danger. Though never captured together before, we understood the risk of being there. Thinking alike, this was another level of repressive degeneracy. We were captives until Air Police (AP) or Navy Shore Patrol (SP) arrived. Hopefully, they'd get us before something more awful happened.

No bail nor lawyers, and no court appearance exists for powerless niggers kidnapped by sheriffs! Once the cells clanged shut, who cared about broken laws? No charges got levied, so what was their objective other than conducting racist assaults on Niggers' freedom? MPs checked lockups from Mobile, Alabama to Panama City, Florida, on Monday mornings. When found, they'd arrange releases following long-standing informal practices. For us, these military and civilian law relationships were suspect. There were apparent agreements in play. So they stole three days of some nigger's freedom. Is it personal amusement, harassment, or terrorism?

We felt blanketed—smothered by helplessness. To escape these events would mean confinement on the base. Many before us endured similar victimizing, a stark reminder of second-class citizen status. There were no secure places, no civil rights protection, and no defense against racist whims. Weekend captivity was consistent with most problems we faced. There wasn't a remote expectation they'd treat us as citizens following the US Constitution and Bill of Rights. That was the view handed off by veterans. Unrealistic hope was prevalent in trusting that uniforms and government papers provided protection from routine murder by police. Those benefits weren't so visible or usual. Everyday interactions showed such wishes were folly. Of course, civilian niggers got no relief either.

But nothing was a more disheartening demonstration of our plight than an unexpected encounter when riding a shuttle from Pensacola Naval Air Station to Eglin (an Air Force mega-base) in freezing winter rain. Upon arriving at Field # 9, I boarded their Fort Walton Beach shuttle. The transport dropped us on Main Street outside the United Service Organization Club (USO). I knew President Franklin Roosevelt created the USO by combining elements of popular civil agencies. The Salvation Army, YMCA, YWCA, the National Catholic Services, the National Travelers Aid Association, and the National Jewish Welfare Board joined to improve emotional support for World War II GIs. While centers continued after WWII, southern locations admitted only white troops. There was no public shelter while waiting for main base buses. A "whites only" policy was the USO's awful reality. White airmen hurried off the bus and ran inside to stay dry. Hot coffee, chocolate, and cookies waited. We (Negroes) followed until USO personnel denied us entry. Left outside in pouring rain, we hunched over, soaking wet under GI non-water repellent raincoats. They wouldn't even allow huddling in the doorway. The only insult missing was APs forcing us to leave. Facts say regional norms dictated discrimination's acceptance by Armed Forces leadership. Government-issued foul weather gear looks nice but doesn't deliver human rights.

How was excluding us allowed when an organization embraced by the US Armed Forces served the world's most crucial airbase? The entire complement of Air Force units graced the reservation. TAC, SAC, Rescue, Transport, Missile, and R and D commands operated mission support sites within

Eglin's overall infrastructure. Local and national military leaders weren't interested in changing racist practices rotting the social fabric at Eglin's door. Realizations like these established another valuable place marker on my journey to enlightenment. It wasn't only a matter of southern USO practices. Every white airman welcomed their racial privilege, and our white brothers never refused racism's advantages or rejected discrimination's benefits. Above everything, I realized this top-to-bottom authority chain accepted and supported racist conditions.

Eglin employed a consortium of civilian workers in every area, especially in construction trades. Carpenters, plumbers, electricians, and others were full of rednecks. Rumors of Klan ties abounded. Essential advice on arriving in March 1957 centered on exercising extreme care when interacting with civilian workers. Rednecks could insult and abuse with impunity. Nothing changed regarding segregation or discrimination within this era, diminishing our lives. At the same time, command leaders declined to oppose Jim Crow; discussing the resulting injustice while spirited off to Milton made no sense. The MPs—the military—would likely arrange release before long. Those we served under never took action against pre-civil war and reconstruction culture keeping their Negroes in jail for being "other" (not white). The big lie about serving and preserving freedom, liberty, and equality couldn't be more visible. These hopeless conditions needed changing through organized struggle. Most of us lacked education, sophistication, and guidance and acted unproductive. Too often, pursuing worthless activities was a fundamental reality of daily life. Incarceration in Milton was an example of harsh reality encouraging more thoughtful, managed approaches to using our time.

Milton's lockup was filthy and not conducive to staying healthy, with toilets encrusted with accumulated human waste occupying corners of each cell. Stinking bed mats lay atop metal platforms. Each pallet's headspace butted against nauseating toilet bowls. Three cell walls had barred openings and no glass. Hot summer days followed by sweat-producing muggy nights made imprisonment miserable enough. Sleeping mats harbored countless fleas, chiggers, and lice. Desperate to escape biting insects, we removed infested bed pads, lying on bare pallets while feeding hoards of mosquitoes buzzing nonstop through glassless windows.

Internment grew alarming at daybreak. Sleep came because an old Negro occupied the next cell. This veteran of local confinement stood gripping his cell's bars, watching as we awakened. Short, dark-skinned, bow-legged, and draped in too-large faded blue overalls, he gave advice. Cautions focused on eating since he was familiar with these specific unhealthy accommodations. There were heartfelt pointers like "stik tu da grits n bred, n doan et da meat r stu." Poisonous food mattered less since we feared consuming offerings around such filth would make us sick. His words confirmed our assessment. He said, "De call'd me, Hawkins."

While talking, those red doors opened, and a sizeable pink-skinned man entered, wearing powder blue polyester slacks and an unbuttoned gray polyester shirt. Brown loafers had cream-patched tops. In the roasting morning, both pants and shirt had stains collecting sweat from high up his fat gut, pooling and framing his crotch and wetting his puffy back into his ass-crack. Sweat ran across his chest, causing his breasts to stand out like a woman's. Both eyebrows and temples flowed narrow sweat streams, outpacing mopping with his soiled handkerchief. That flushed, soft, reddish, pudgy face looked 40. This cracker's obvious climate-induced suffering brought Kipling's warning ("… even the greatest fools obey…") for those with common sense not to venture outside at noon. ("…only mad dogs and Englishmen go out in the midday sun…") I thought, "He's not suited for this climate."

"Does anybody want jail time reduced by working in my fields?" was his question. Before finishing, Hawkins jumped up, rushed forward, and cursed that contemporary slaver with each step.

Pulling against cell bars, Hawkins called the modern-day Legree everything imaginable. "Dirta mu fuka, dirta cock sucka, stinkin arse ol, blood suck'n bast'rd, fuk'in peck-a-wood, dirta rot'n cracka," he delivered such contempt as we never heard. The plantation boss fired back, "youse black gol dam nigger, youse lucky ah cain't git inna dere cause'n a'll beat da liv'n ell outa ya. A'll knock da tar off'n youse arse."

Hawkins went berserk, climbing the crossbars, screaming, "Op'n da gol dam cell doe," genuinely pleading to kick Legree's ass. His rage was flabbergasting! We were convinced he was dead serious, and it was scary! Either Hawkins didn't care, or he was there enough to understand the sheriffs wouldn't open the cells. The slave driver exited in a huff after we declined CONVICT LABOR, and our defender quieted. Jeff, Salley, Nat, and I were speechless! It was hilarious and terrifying! I'm surprised Milton's sheriff didn't put chains on that nigger and lease him out.

Witnessing an old Negro's reaction taught me something valuable. We'd never seen locals resist! As things quieted, Hawkins' proud defiance remained for us to contemplate. We saw too much fear and submissiveness around these parts and couldn't venture beyond ghetto boundaries without heightened wariness. Hawkins felt satisfied and continued mumbling, saying what he'd do to slave masters. Our encounter demonstrated that Negro enslavement would continue for foreseeable years.

The existing "misdemeanor convict leasing practices" in 1958 were 20th-century slavery. What inhumane behavior! By sheriffs working their prisoners, farmers accessed free labor. Those doing unpaid fieldwork sought to escape horrible jail conditions. Most hoped to avoid chain gangs. What were the exact arrangements and prices? It was good fortune that attempted enslavement was the worst of these crackers' inhumanity!

Air Police found us on Sunday but wouldn't take custody until Monday. They looked for us since Jeff had weekend duty. His superiors declared him "Absent Without Leave" (AWOL) when he did not report. That triggered APs to check customary regional jailing points. Otherwise, there would have been no Monday rescue. Once in their custody, they refused to let me retrieve the Packard. We had no choice but to report to our units. Punishment was standard when missing assignments, even if you were innocent of crimes. It was an add-on when living under racist domination. I hit upon a method short-circuiting their desire to administer disciplining at every turn, using simple evasive maneuvers. Major Boyd, Commander of Headquarters Squadron Section, was intelligent and reasonable. He appreciated someone questioning and testing norms.

I'd say he liked me. So, meeting him first after a violation was fortunate. Master Sergeant Patrick, on the other hand, only cared about adding hardship. Whenever arrested for disturbing the peace, I reported to Major Boyd, not Sergeant Patrick. It was unplanned. While waiting inside squadron headquarters, Commander Boyd entered and asked what I wanted. After hearing my story, he ordered forgetting the incident and returning to work. Sergeant Patrick corralled me later. When he assigns extra duty, I tell him, "The Major said, 'Forget what happened and go to work.'" His face turns red while barking, "God damn it, next time, you see me first." Once his boss said no punishment; there was no messing with me. After that, I saw Major Boyd by accident before Sarge when any trouble occurred. Deftness in avoiding Sergeant Patrick caused poor performance reviews, resulting in classification as "not qualified for promotion and re-enlistment." More incidents occurred, but Sarge could never exercise his wrath.

Meanwhile, since attending university extension classes, seeds of interest in further education grew within me as a path after discharge. A multiplier of potential developed when a friend became the barboy at Eglin's junior officer's club. Jimmy Wilson was a hustler and recruited me, arguing three nights each week brought more funds than our monthly pay. Ten hours equals an airmen's monthly stipend, earning eight dollars an hour. Part-time jobs allowed me to send my entire allotment home! Extra cash accumulated fast for schooling later.

Working beside him on weekends, it wasn't long before I covered typical slow weeknights alone. Busy weekends, we both worked. Bartenders proved to be good people. They helped with learning job duties and made operations run smoothly. Opportunities to watch commissioned personnel's drinking behavior were enlightening. Invariably, some young officer became disrespectful. Among eye-opening experiences, many wives showed out. Our charge was not to let drunks upset us. They cautioned against allowing disrespect to trigger anger or open responses. On rare occasions, someone treated us like dirt. Most often, this got others compensating with praise and generous tips.

One night, Jimmy caught several attacks from a particular officer. This guy was the biggest asshole among regular patrons. He yelled, cursed, and demeaned Wilson. My partner acted unmoved while taking abuse, although he was also an extraordinarily "rotten," vindictive person. He, too, is a real bastard. Jimmy got pissed but held it inside. A weird thing was nobody paid me any attention.

When the bully ordered pizza, Jimmy taught me his psychological defense technique, administering revenge. Before applying commercial tomato sauce, I watched him shape the thawed pizza dough and rub it inside garbage cans. Each can's greasy inner wall had the remains of sticky rotting food waste. With putrid slop ooze smeared on that crust, he blessed his "special order" by harking and spitting into its layer of tomato sauce before topping it with cheese. I could only imagine how those pizzas affected people's stomachs. Repeat offender specials included wiping his asshole with dough before adding garbage can froth and spit-infused sauce. Observing his counter moves to disrespect erased concern over verbal attacks by customers. After witnessing Jimmy's defense, ill-treatment could never bother me. Over two years, there was one instance of me doctoring pizza.

We never saw Negro captains or lieutenants patronize the club. Common sense said the atmosphere wasn't acceptable. The cowboy orientation and country music weren't what Negroes enjoyed. Also, drinking liquor doesn't stimulate productive inter-ethnic relationships. An L-shaped hut fit 20 tables fronting a polished hardwood dance floor occupying its longest side. The hut short stem, extending right, accommodated closet-sized kitchen rooms—storing ice, preparing food, and washing dishes. Live entertainment elevated late Fridays and Saturdays when crowds got drunk enough to dance. Funny that music never matched dancer's movements. We had favorites whose lack of rhythm was entertaining. Another curiosity was there were no personnel above the captain's rank. Regulars were lieutenants and captains. Neither Majors nor Colonels mingled. No customers were people we saw on the job. Eglin's top echelon officer's Bayview Club, outside Ft. Walton Beach, was classier. Upper-level ranks socialized there. Jimmy and I helped whenever foreign dignitaries visited.

We had serving jackets over dress uniforms to pour Champaign. Tips were less than from heavy drinkers. It was a more respectful clientele—no cause warranted doctoring food. Job earnings accumulated fast; a week passed before I sent Mom extra funds. I realized the essential goal of saving sufficient college funds from multiple sources. I felt hopeful about getting discharged and pursuing higher education. Even with fresh insight and vision, completing that final year and avoiding disastrous contact with racist justice (injustice) was jeopardized several times. I tried hard to steer clear of confrontations. Regardless, shit happened!

1. On June 18, 1959, I was arrested in Pensacola, Florida for disturbing the peace—released to the Shore Patrol
2. On November 29, 1959, I was arrested in Pensacola, Florida for disturbing the peace and fighting—fined $20.00
3. On May 21, 1960, arrested in Pensacola, Florida for disturbing the peace; threatening with a ball bat—released for time served
4. On July 10, 1960, I was arrested in Pensacola, Florida for disturbing the peace and fighting—withheld sentence

One saving grace was the military's permanently assigned attorneys attended court and settled any claims without my having to appear.

1959 and 1960 arrests constituted gross carelessness as I approached my October 1, 1960, discharge. Problems kept happening while keeping a low profile. Although being cautious in avoiding public exposure, I still got arrested. Military protections saved me. I never encountered discerning right and wrong, innocence and guilt within justice systems, or contacts with authorities. The unpredictability of treatment meant choices relied on luck panning out. Physical and psychological survivals were tenuous interdependent prospects. They are becoming more prescient as I'm closer to leaving Pensacola and the Air Force.

COMING TO CALIFORNIA

Nobody says it, but California is the Promised Land for running.

Kenny:

Neal is a white high school friend more dedicated to running than I; he visited our hometown in the summer of 1960. I hadn't comprehended our life-changing connection coming into play. With no consideration of possibilities after graduating, we shared a consuming interest in track and an appreciation of friends, mates, West Chester staff, and our broader community. I, at one point, had to use their connection to escape incarceration for committing violent acts. I squandered social capital from sports achievements to nullify behavioral mistakes while lacking non-athletic opportunities. For both of us, our sport was a saving grace. Neal asked for news of me when seeing my mother shopping uptown.

After four years of service, my post-high school job cooking ore and extracting platinum at Malvern's J. Bishop & Co Platinum Works represented a secure future of hard labor. Mom told Neal there weren't other plans, and attending college went unmentioned. He wrote, "Don't return to West Chester; come to San Jose and join Santa Clara Youth Village's track team. We can attend community college for two years, tuition-free. We can earn track scholarships to a university and get bachelor's degrees!" His correspondence included basic conditioning instructions before reaching San Jose. Letters said the training was under Mihály Iglói, former Hungarian National Coach, at the University of North Carolina (UNC). He reconnected with Iglói and his world-leading runners, such as Jim Beatty and László Tábori. I heard of Tábori and knew Beatty was UNC's outstanding distance runner. Tábori, one of Hungary's three world record-breaking runners, had finished 4th at the 1956 Melbourne Olympics. Neal insisted on a new direction with possibilities for doing rewarding professional work. That beats platinum refinery labor—wasting my youth cooking raw ore in nitric acid vats. A normal future comprised returning to Bishops, marrying my teen sweetheart, having six children (she did that), and a limited existence. My brother Gerald came home from the Navy and his education quests went well using the GI Bill. His plan worked while no liberating ideas or opportunities awaited me since the GI Bill was ending.

Desperate to get immersed in serious exercise before 1958, I joined our base's boxing team, training three hours daily. Fighting, I used superior endurance and being faster to out-point opponents. In two crucial bouts, excellent conditioning didn't help. Leg speed and endurance made outlasting opponents my strategy, which served well until 1958's Florida State Amateur Championship. Fighting at West Palm Beach Air Force Base, I battered the defending state champion until hit with six deliberate low blows in round 3. Combating dirty tactics is difficult. The referee halted action, cautioning about fouling on each occasion before Coach Snyder threw in the towel after a seventh low punch. When laid out, the doctor pushed both testicles from my stomach back into my scrotum. I stayed there, holding them from retreating up the inguinal canal. At the Air Force World's (Andrews Air Base), months later, I fought the reigning champion, a lefty. I never saw his punch flooring me within a minute, falling cross-legged and causing a sprained ankle. How shocking, finding I was floored with no idea how! I felt no impact before trying to stand. Then I thought, "That guy punched so hard, its force traveled through my body and broke my left ankle." Later, we figured that Duke Snyder didn't put out the resin box, coating the bottom of my shoes and supplying traction. Boxing shoes, without resin, cause fighters to slip on canvas rings, like walking on ice. Balance, defense, and attacking were impossible without traction. His first experience of coaching in a World Championship flustered Duke. He wasn't attentive to small details. After taking a mandatory eight-count, the referee ended it. Frank Davis repeated his Air Force and inter-service 154-lb championships. Later, after becoming Research and Development Command's Light-Middle Weight Champion, our boxing program dissolved when "Duke" transferred to Germany. That ended the incentive for maintaining fighting shape. I tried workouts using Neal's instructions, encountering incredible physical difficulty. Even though attempting programs, completing them was beyond my capability. I didn't do well relying on hand-written instructions.

His workouts showed my non-existant understanding of world-class training. Each workout's volume appeared to exceed human ability.

After my discharge, I said goodbye to Mary and left, walking out of sight on Cervantes Street (Mobile Highway or US 90). There, I started hitchhiking in the late afternoon. Why postpone my life-changing journey? I needed to diminish the local hold with distance, and getting picked up and carried miles away before dark would do the trick, so there's no turning back. Thumbing across eight states was an uncertain, dangerous undertaking, especially when five were authoritarian white supremacist-ruled territories. There is a heightened risk around bumming rides alone through Florida, Alabama, Mississippi, Louisiana, and Texas. Those were racism's heartland of absolute oppression through Jim Crow law and Klan violence. Hitching after nightfall could become harrowing since there were inevitable waiting periods on isolated roads through territories with histories of murderous violence against Blacks. There is Emmett Till's 1955 lynching, and there were more after that. I avoided Mississippi's Pearl River County, where a recently publicized lynching occurred. Authorities arrested Mack Charles Parker for raping a pregnant white woman on April 24, 1959. Before standing trial, an angry mob dragged him from the "safety" of Pearl River Courthouse. They beat and shot him. His mutilated body surfaced in river shallows near Poplarville, Mississippi. News Journal newspaper ran the story for a solid week. Parker's murder triggered a "personal emergency alert" among Eglin Negroes lasting six months. This current undertaking (no pun intended) came with great apprehension. I could have traveled by Greyhound but never swallowed the mandatory sitting in Negro sections of buses. Early lifts carried me beyond Florida's panhandle and deep into Louisiana.

Frequent drivers were affable white guys. Conversations were easy and friendly. I thumbed on a lonely stretch crossing Louisiana's numerous swamps the first night. This quest was chancing death in so many ways! Visions of a murderous history got stimulated by distant bloodhounds baying at 3:00 a.m. There was possibility of being lynched and given a watery roadside grave. Emmett Till's murder became fresh. His specter appeared, floating across the blacktop above the swamp fog. Chains and a cotton gin fan draped over him by murdering racists shined like new, reflecting distant galaxy lights. I realized I could disappear forever. I didn't mind dying. That's an ever-present consideration facing Black males, understood before puberty. But I reject passively dying in racists' hands.

Circumstances turned favorable when a Black school teacher drove west from Baton Rouge and headed to Shreveport near 4 a.m. Sustained conversation staved off sleep until arriving at his home around 7 a.m. He went straight home, wanting me to meet his wife and children. While eating eggs, bacon, and grits, they contacted friends and arranged transportation to Dallas. Their church secretary had business with their sister congregation each week. What a fortunate coincidence! Those church people were terrific! We drove two miles and met Antioch Baptist Church's representative heading to north Texas. My friendly church rep found another church member bound for Amarillo, Texas. This driver provided lunch before leaving Dallas. I looked forward with anticipation because Amarillo was familiar and straddled Route 66, the nation's most popularly acclaimed highway.

I'm now shedding Blue, the aggressive street-fighting character, with deliberate intent. Leaving Pensacola meant seeking an environment where such characters have no place. Traveling through Amarillo and a forgettable past was a perfect point for letting Blue go. If future environments required a unique presence, those qualities, and purposes must appear in San Jose, California.

Return to Amarillo

I was familiar with Amarillo after spending several months attending tech school and learning fuel supply operations during the winter of 1956 - 57. Those ten weeks were an assortment of accomplishments and tragedies. What an awful environment where nothing natural or manufactured was attractive! Mornings, part of Oklahoma blows in on a dirt-filled wind storm. It blows back out as the sun sets, leaving soil covering everything. While cleaning dust nonstop, we breathed and ate it. Barracks built of overlapping wooden slats during World War II couldn't block dust-filled icy winds swooping through loose boards. Dirt coating inside windowsills soon blankets every flat surface. 5 a.m. reveille assemblies have frigid blasts carving our ranks' new asses, standing at attention during morning roll-call before dismissal and racing into warm chow halls. Morning experiences repeat when mail-call assembles and sundown retreat sounds. Escaping cutting winds was our most satisfying daily occurrence.

Nearby Negro settlements were the picture of abject poverty. Negroes lived with broken windows or rotted frames. Wood on houses' sides decayed, and weathered paint sun bleached into odd colors. Many structures were coated and held together with compositions of mud! Every home needed massive repairs. We passed by settlements on our way to playing basketball at Warford recreation center. Physical competitions rarely were free of confrontations, and there were frequent issues when particular guys dominated the courts. Landing positions with established teams was challenging, and contests featured regular verbal combat, threats, and near-fights. I went there with Refueling School mates from New Jersey, one Black, and one Caucasian. Their matching Jersey accents, from different colored faces, were strange. Labatch was slender with an accurate soft mid-range jump shot. He flashed terrible rotten teeth with an ugly smile, claiming to be Russian. And wiry little Turner, showed professional skill handling the ball and sinks shots from downtown. With them, I defended, running full-court presses.

One evening we were dominating, holding sway turn after turn. Three white boys came on, claiming our evening's final. Sizing up opponents was expected, and they swaggered. Others there knew these late arrivals. There was an expectation they'd win, claiming honors. Competitive attitudes filled Warford gym. I judged two of them. Coded artwork colored a tough guy's buffed arms. His tattoos sent a macho hombre message. Trouble comes with his brand of play! The other person was big and mild-tempered. They always ruled their games. Right away, we're controlling and serving a royal spanking. Turner was impossible against tattoo guy trying everything to defend against him.

Not much worked to tamp down their inflammatory trash-talking. The white boy employed hard fouling and couldn't slow Turner. Contact soon became explosive. Before ending, open punching ensued. My teammate took a terrible pounding! When downed, the bully jumped on, karate chopping like hell. His attack was strange. Why do that? Man, I felt awful! Turner's face swelled as if his head got shoved inside a beehive. Maybe that's karate chop's purpose? That inked-up guy had the trouble he wanted. Turner's battering hurt more, considering it was fair. Turner lost himself after that. Playing basketball paused. I blamed myself for not controlling, fighting, and not ensuring an even outcome or favoring Turner.

After his beating, conditions weren't satisfactory in my book, either. The event weighed on me, and I couldn't shake those images. Turner lay there, bleeding from his nose and mouth. Huge knots of swollen flesh balloon his face after each chop. No mental effort could dismiss those scenes. The images wouldn't go away. My conscience and regret drove me to the recreation center around closing, stalking tattoo boy. Three homeboys tagged along in case followers accompanied him. Sometimes the bully roamed accompanied by girls, while on other occasions, it was his boys, or mixed. That puzzled me; you wouldn't think his type attracted friends. Maybe they were only followers.

His tattoos penetrated my thoughts. I felt an immediate general distrust of him. For sure, bullshit is coming! An initial appraisal was he sought ego boosts by fucking-up smaller or weaker people.

For an extended period, the guy disappeared, and fruitless pursuit tired my homeboys, but I wasn't quitting! Before my early teen years, I learned from Gerald that hunting and trapping require patience more than anything. I stood outside, cold, shivering, and waiting. It was personal and I knew what I had to do. I couldn't say whether the shivering was from icy winds or an anxiousness to balance the score. I watched him, happy, going his way, enjoying life with his cronies. That was before cornering him between the rec center buildings. Intent on righteous payback, I kicked his ass like he did Turner. When down on his back, I stomped his nose and mouth. Swelling, matching Turner's head, grew knots over blackened eyes and both sides of his face. When he begged for mercy, I left him bleeding underneath a stilted building.

Heavy brig (jail) time would result if I were busted doing such damage. I always took chances, but situations gave me no choice! It's consistently part of my story. Labatch and I resumed playing, expecting Tattoo's boys to want me! Turner never joined us and never recovered his mental confidence. Vengeance meant nothing to Turner and everything to me. Payback couldn't fix him psychologically. I might have learned from his broken spirit but didn't grasp any enlightening insights. Deep-seated values come from childhood, requiring responses. Until then, conflict didn't end. Attitudes developed growing up in Coonville's protective embrace and functioned like ancient codes of honor. Sensitivities became ingrained and necessitated a mental struggle not to act foolish.

In tech school during Christmas of 1956, I chose to remain on base over flying home. These months were the first winter holidays away from home. Staying was advancing my independence toward growing up and gaining inner strength. I was sacrificing emotional comfort with my family by going through Christmas on night Kitchen Police (KP) duty. I spent my breaks studying Texas skies, standing under winter's crisp, sparkling night canopy behind the mess hall. While considering we shared distant stars, I raised deep feelings, missing family. On Saturday, four of us took the base bus into Amarillo. All former West Chester classmates remained, so we knew each other well. They'd checked Nigger-town before and thought it was okay. From inside the shuttle, we could tell life there was awful. Call it a colonized people's village! Negro enclaves hold lesser beings, the opposite of colonizer strongholds and the bright-lit communities of whites. We paid two bucks and entered the broken-down Negro bar/dance hall. Once plastered with small light-reflecting mirrors, their disco ball turned under crumbling ceiling plaster. Dozens of reflectors were missing. Even so, there was little chance any mirror-clad decorations could brighten such a battered edifice.

Few young women frequented this hangout. Hard living broke them. It etched hard lines into faces and abused bodies. Amarillo is their wasteland.

Coloreds' living conditions appeared worse than anything I'd ever seen or heard described. Such poverty was an assault on fundamental human values. I was experiencing firsthand their degrading existence. As darkness fell, someone suggested hiring a prostitute. Two homeboys got their idea by talking to a resident. It wasn't me, as I had never had sexual relations. Oh, I'd had girlfriends, but none of them were ready. My perception of self-worth depended on running successes, while others around me sought sexual conquests. I had little energy for relationships with girls. That night, a local approached us, asking if we wanted to buy some pussy. Clarence and Harry answered, "Yeah." We discussed our situation, decided that staying together was better security, and piled into his car. At the destination, he parked between rows of two-story shacks and disappeared.

Meanwhile, we discussed escaping by running south if robbers came. Our contact returned alone. The eleven dollars cost was two bucks each and one for him. We entered a tiny kitchen with a single-burner stove and no refrigerator. An old light-skinned man sat beside that stove, warmed by its small oven. One bedroom was through an opening draped with soiled, tattered curtains. A man, a woman, and a kindergarten-age boy descended steps from above. The little boy waited on the stairs, looking us over. His stare settled on me more than anyone. Maybe any child would sense that I knew it wasn't right! This dwelling is their home, not your everyday cathouse, and these folks weren't professionals! The husband mumbled, requesting the money. "Y'all gots da ten dolla's," he said, subdued, and turned toward the old man. "Far up da watta fo dem boyz kin warsh dem sef."

Grandpa went out back and returned carrying a chipped enamel-coated pan of water. He put it on their single gas burner, heating it for washing before and after our dirty business. We chatted while I sat without critical thoughts. I could only grasp the occasional word: "Onlyist dawta, n' 2 chil'un." He's her father. I didn't sense anyone else had doubts, but questions rose in me from shame. There was her husband accepting payment from strangers for sex with his wife, and thank god he disappeared with the $10. The woman's father helped strangers having intercourse with his daughter, providing boiling water and towels for cleaning.

No situations are more off-kilter than children watching strange men enter their mother's bedroom. Finally, there's the husband's friend who sold his friend's wife. I see every aspect of these actions and words as signs of doing wrong. Nobody mentioned it, if others had terrible feelings. What an unforgivable low! I'd never felt that small and must never again. While realizing how wrong it was, I bowed to group expectations. Prostitution like that, I recognized, was the most desperate survival attempt. With our most significant commercial holidays approaching, these folks desperately need economic resources. If this was their subsistence means, conditions shouldn't prevail in any society, causing families and individuals to destroy themselves to exist. Who willingly serves countries supporting such hardship?

There would be no dismissing this as justifiable transactions arranged by their agent. I acted, feeling nothing before, during, or after. She lay on the covers, fully dressed other than her underwear. We each dropped our pants around our ankles, climbing on and off after seconds. It was my first sex. How senseless are first times like this? What despicable behavior! As the person committing this shameful act, I had the disturbing awareness that uncovered potential thoughtlessness and self-centeredness in crippling measures. Seeing the depth to which I had sunk, more thoughtful considerations raised the necessity of changing my internal makeup. Such costly lessons must convert into building a wiser essential being. Instances of contact with wrongfulness of that magnitude made standing up and voicing objections a moral imperative and implanted in me a refusal to take part! Ideas or behavior hinting at being so misguided can't involve me unless raising staunch objections. Having humane standards won't prevent acting stupid or making mistakes, but it demands no second-guessing and ensuring there are no regrets. That's the vital turning point. Achieving such consciousness might land me in difficult positions but wouldn't bring something worse—internal conflict and self-blaming.

I had no thoughts of revisiting Amarillo while stationed there. Release from guilt stemming from disgraceful behavior came when flying over

Amarillo on an airliner to Pensacola. From altitude, surveying what appeared to be a peaceful, unthreatening cityscape allowed me erasing the mental grip of failure and feel a relieved conscience. The happy ending was graduating as the top Refueling School student. They allowed their leading graduate to select their next duty station from worldwide positions. If I had known what awaited me in a rat hole called Fort Walton Beach, I'd have accepted three years in Japan. I chose Eglin because it is the nearest to home since Dover AFB (Delaware) wasn't available.

Three years later, I traveled through Amarillo again, hitchhiking, to California. My transportation from Dallas dropped me past the city's edge around midnight. The spot was great for catching rides with westward-bound drivers on Route 66, although looming threats existed inside country-western-themed drinking spots behind me. It made little sense to move with businesses providing bright street lamps. The immediate concern was that, at 2:00 a.m., bars emptied passels of drunken cowboys that might threaten me. My fears proved unfounded as no hassles occurred. Businesses closed, but nobody paid any notice. Heightened concern was much ado about nothing; thankfully, no cowboys said anything. Everything went silent after the bars closed. Around 3:00 a.m., a big rig stopped. His destination was LA, but he needed sleep. We rolled along historic Interstate 40 through the early hours, the only vehicle out there. We struggled staying alert, and I was supposed to keep him awake. That failed when we both fell asleep. The teamster awakened me after scraping guardrails on a steep mountain curve, and after that, our remaining scared held us until reaching Tucumcari's trucker's stop. Breakfast was on him. Praise the lord, New Mexico wasn't secessionist or Jim Crow! Here forward, relaxing and consuming food alongside whites was okay!

Since my truck driver still needed sleep, my best option was continuing ASAP. If I got stranded later, he could do a second rescue. Our plight got resolved before finishing breakfast. The trucker canvassed restaurant customers and found someone delivering cars to LA who welcomed company. This traveler, eating alone, was taking a car to Santa Monica. We dropped off a sedan in Albuquerque and picked up a station wagon. Then, it was

"California, here I come!"

After Tucumcari, things were uneventful; we passed miles exchanging stories. Landscape flew by; we changed drivers at two-hour intervals through the night. Joe bought lunch, dinner, and breakfast. Before noon on Wednesday, we pulled over to the San Bernardino Freeway's junction crossing US 101. The next big rig rolling up the ramp onto 101 signaled to jump on without stopping. He was en route to San Francisco and going through San Jose. Cruising in a semi-trailer from Los Angeles was relaxing and enlightening.

No more wondering about getting to San Jose before being killed, injured, or arrested. Until then, I hadn't envisioned California's landscape or highways. The unfolding scenery was consuming. Coastal hills around Santa Barbara and lettuce fields through Salinas impressed me. Active oil wells scattered near Paso Robles and eucalyptus rows shielding miles of vegetables before and after reaching Salinas were most intriguing. Those trees were not native, from my limited knowledge, and I wondered about their presence. Oil pumping rigs mimicking gigantic grasshoppers indicated California's wonders and the state's welcome promise. Early October's glorious weather was satisfying. We lowered the side windows and were buffeted by warm air rushing through the cabin. I reflected on driving Air Force tanker trucks, and now this! There was a moment when I drifted into visualizing the satisfaction of living here until death. Immediate impressions already leaned in that direction. Once passing through San Juan Bautista's hills, orchards lined 101 stretching across all horizon points. Then, an hour later, this undulating sea of fruit trees, changing into its fall color palette of leaves, broke off at San Jose's city limit sign.

Thousands of orchards, defining the Santa Clara Valley, surrounded San Jose, featuring climate and soil amenable for agriculture. Arable land abounded, so many independent farmers had successful operations. With so much fruit growing, vistas showed continuous orchards end-to-end. I imagined the limitless raised carpet of blossoms when they all flowered in the spring. Six hours passed until I was dropped outside Greyhound's San

Pedro Street depot. San Jose was a medium-sized city. At first impression, it felt like back home in perfect weather. It was bigger than West Chester but had a small-town atmosphere owing to immersion in farming and produce canning cultures. It made an idyllic setting, and life felt less troubled. I could tell racism was less prevalent than in WC—not as crippling or debilitating. Better yet, it wasn't the Deep South. I thought to myself, "If developments allow, I'll stay here the rest of my life." It was Wednesday evening, October 5, 1960. After only three days of traveling, I proceeded unshackled from virulent Jim Crow.

CHAPTER
NINE

Road Rats

The Answer: "A rat's travelling bag is always packed."
The Question: How did Neal get his belongings
together and escape from Carolina so fast? (Conkle)

Kenny:

I relaxed for a moment in San Jose's Greyhound depot. Next came locating San Jose State's (SJS) 7th Street athletic complex. There, I'd find information pinpointing Neal's whereabouts. People knew SJS for sprinting. *Sports Illustrated* featured Ray Norton and Bobby Poynter as the world's best sprinters in June 1959. That happened before I learned that my friend had connections there. Young men exercising knew him and did not know if he would return from a trip. I faced a quandary.

Being homeless was not good. I got through the first night dozing on bus depot benches and in the all-night San Jose Theater. Neither was legal, restful, or satisfactory. Local police hassle everyone and required possessing tickets for departing buses. Movie ushers awakened people by nudging shoulders! Thursday and Friday night, I climbed into Spartan Stadium after eating. Sleeping on bleachers worked. The typical crisp chill after sundown helped with resting, but required I wear every piece of clothing.

My daily routine became observing athletes' training. Processes and aims running different repeated yards, plus various intensity levels, remained unsolvable puzzles. I didn't have enough exposure to put an understanding together. My Bulova's hand, counting seconds, approximated times for yardage but showed little regarding their fitness. The best feature was locker facilities providing showers and toilets. I was considering what might come if I stayed until Sunday. Hitchhiking across the country alone in one direction was plenty. With ticket money burning holes in my pocket, my choices were either waiting, or riding a Greyhound home. Such weighty decisions stalled in my mind. It took so much effort getting here; it made no sense to retreat to West Chester and quite possibly give up a once-in-a-lifetime opportunity.

I relaxed, leaning back on wooden bleachers late Saturday as dusk's coolness descended. While considering departing after another day, Neal came in, searching for me. His confident swagger seemed like waltzing past successive clusters of runners hailing each while exchanging humorous comments. Indeed, everyone knew him! Personality-wise, little had changed since graduating. He asked, "How long were you here?" I made light of being homeless since Wednesday. Sleeping in Spartan Stadium was a minor sacrifice for our future, not worth mentioning. He muttered stories about crashing at Jack Marden's mountain cabin. While Iggles' elite group toured Europe's track circuit, he searched for gambling jobs around Tahoe. There were opportunities for high-altitude runs before everyone returned. The first business now was finding housing! Our meager funds presented a dilemma. We needed rent, a security deposit, and eighty dollars in Air Force severance pay was nothing. Survival called for extra resourcefulness.

Neal:

In my "51" Chevy, we checked apartment buildings on 4th at William, picked an empty flat hidden from their manager's residence, and climbed through an unlocked window. After fourteen days, the Ann Darling apartment's super-intendent caught us. He was a graduate student and forgave our intruding. An automatic decision while rent-free was making sure Kenny didn't appear to be living there. That strategy countered housing segregation. He entered and left, feigning visiting. Whenever we moved, we would hide him while I rented and present him as visiting until owners or property supervisors dropped their concern. This strategy proved successful after being refused when seeking apartments. Assorted white friends role-played as roommates.

Kenny:

Jim Crow housing presented critical systemic barriers to becoming a Youth Village track club member. We strove to be regular citizens, integrated, and satisfactory. Being comfortable away from track work was crucial. I could waste no time achieving the college standards set by Iglói. That was our biggest hurdle. Our common understanding was that everybody can't prosper under Coach Iglói. Adapting wasn't that easy. With past European achievements, his charges were renowned for toughness. László Tábori led as our model. Neal, of course, had performance-based connections with the Hungarians after being with them at UNC. As an unheralded newcomer, without running for over four years, I needed to show talent ASAP. Naturally, folks only reluctantly accepted new arrivals.

The few residents looking like me lived south of campus. When we jogged along 6th Street each day, a couple of mulatto families watched. Everybody was friendly enough, but two welcoming girls were young high schoolers. Their exotic beauty drew teen hard-heads waiting outside their houses. They acted curious, waving and speaking, but they appeared amused by our odd penchant for jogging everywhere. Day after day, week after week, they saw us only dressed in sweatsuits. It must have been strange. For me, even superficial contact provided satisfaction. The social atmosphere was such that any Black people opening up helped against feeling alone without familial connections. Seeing Goldie and Jeanne, with suitors pursuing teenage courtships, struck me as hilarious. Flirting with us teased those suitors. Daily interactions generated helpful comfort.

Neal:

Little space existed for anything other than hard training. Our most incredible good fortune was drawing California state unemployment compensation. Collecting $25.00 unemployment per week brought enough to survive. The standard monthly rent was $100.00, and the remaining stipend bought food and gas and paid utility bills. We did well scrounging more resources and capitalized on unemployment eligibility rules by claiming job hunting while attending night school.

I don't know if many cities matched San Jose, with overall environmental conditions conducive to running. This region had everything for growing food year-round; as health-sensitive runners we welcomed that potential. On wintery days, pantyhose or long Johns kept our legs warm during jogs between high-stress intervals. Year-round low-temperature nights were great for deep sleep, an essential affecting recovery from extreme exercise. Few flying or biting insects made an added welcome feature. Sometimes, fire ants punished anybody who stretched out on the ant-infested ground. Our surroundings made an ideal runner's environment. The general climate was a blessing, with so much produce growing everywhere. Neighborhood fruit trees, nuts, and gardens abounded, creating free food supplies.

English walnuts lined roads. Back east, they sold in markets for Thanksgiving and Christmas. San Jose's streets rumbled with constant streams of trucks delivering harvests to Senter Road and San Carlos Street canneries from nearby farms or as distant as Bakersfield. Local breezes filled with fragrances from processing produce, baby food, Lifesavers candy, Juicy Fruit chewing gum, and more—only in San Jose, "The Valley of Hearts Delight!" Cannery jobs during summers reestablished unemployment income eligibility, starting after seasonal work ended. When they closed after summer production, unemployment compensation got reinstated until canning began just before school was out. What an accommodating state feature!

San Jose State's clay oval became our focus for existing. When not working out or resting, we concentrated on mental preparation for executing Iglói's design. SJS's facilities were bare-bones; their athletes and assistants groomed adobe surfaces. Spectator bleachers ran along 7th Street. Pennsylvania tracks only used cinders; we hadn't seen firm clay surfaces. They were hard-packed—more productive than cinders. "SCURVY," the nickname for Santa Clara Valley Youth Village's (SCVYV) team, practiced after college athletes finished. Contact with them was limited. Sometimes they stayed, watching our segments. Most considered us crazy, suffering so much. I imagine they wished to see if anyone broke.

Conditions improved when we found additional roommates, reducing per capita expenses. The first person added was Gil Renneckar, aka Hertz. Our friendship was tight ever since he played college basketball. Three Pennsylvanians in a San Jose apartment were unusual; connections engendered matching worldviews. When quizzed on origins, Hertz related:

I was raised in McKean County, located in the middle of nowhere at the very top of the center of Pennsylvania. The towns of Bradford, Smethport and Port Allegany housed my early relatives with mostly Hamlin, Redfield and Gillett surnames. Phyllis Gillett is my mother. She married Laird Renneckar, my father, of Massillon, Ohio. My great grandfather Byron Hamlin was Pennsylvania's first State Senator from our district. He also was a prominent lawyer and owned the McKean & Buffalo Railroad. All of this is to say that I come from respectable stock and have a reasonably standard upbringing.

My big event of memory is the flood of 1942 when I was 5 years old. As a child, it was exciting when the water was running through our house not far from the Allegany River. I had to be rescued and carried next door by our neighbor wearing hip hugger wading boots.

I watched in great anguish as our dog was swept away by the waters rushing three feet above the flood line.

I spend the first two years of high school at Admiral Farragut Academy, a Naval Academy Prep school in Pine Beach, New Jersey, with an appointment to the U.S. Naval Academy. The appointment was later rescinded when it is discovered that I'm color blind. With that, I transferred out of Admiral Farragut Academy and graduated from Port Allegany Union High School in 1955.

By high school graduation time, I had basketball scholarship offers from several schools. My family also had connections at the University of North Carolina. In particular, my mother is friends with Maurice Julian, who is also known as the Dean of Franklin Street in Chapel Hill. In my teens, we spent time in Chapel Hill and frequently visited the Julians. I even swam in the Jr. Olympics for the Chapel Hill Swim Club. The Julians have the main haberdashery store on Franklin Street. Alex, Maurice's son, was known for his "Colors by Alex" clothing design. So at college selection time, with the Julian connection extending to the basketball department, I discounted my offers from Alfred Tech and Temple University, and elected to go to UNC. From there, with two years of college completed and my military reserve duty with the Pennsylvania National Guard out of the way, it was time to visit the West where Neal invited Buck (my childhood friend) and me to join him and find work in the canneries for the summer of 1961. So here we all are, Road Rats, looking to make our fortunes with the developing opportunities in the sixties out West.

He desired to explore new territory, and California offered tremendous opportunities, plus life was simple. Before arriving, Kenny heard our UNC stories, including athletes possessing printing office keys for copying academic tests and other misadventures and historic achievements by frosh basketball players.

Kenny:

An often discussed Carolina basketball tale hinged on our roomie Hertz's phenomenal 1957 foul shot. Neal and him were bull-headed, non-stop talkers, constantly interrupting one another. Gil interfered in telling their "Famous Free Throw" story, insisting on doing it himself.

I came to UNC in 1957 to play basketball. That was a pretty heady time because the school's effort to build a consistently national championship caliber team was poised to bring the desired results. This year's varsity team was touted to be the best in Carolina's history. Our freshman team, of which I was a member, had the potential to become as talented as the varsity. Every year, the frosh team got a chance to show their potential in the annual Freshman/Varsity Blue vs. White game. Our year was no different with the exception that expectations for the frosh to perform well were higher than usual. The ebb and flow of the Blue vs. White game in 1957 was living up to expectations for both sides. Well, there I was sitting on the Carolina Freshman team bench having just been substituted out of the game. The clock was winding down inside the last minute and the National Championship caliber varsity had a one point lead. Next, a fifth foul is called on Mike Steppe, our high school All American guard. Our coach, James Ambrose "Buck" Freeman, called for me to take Mike's spot. "Buck" likes referring to me as the "McKean County, PA., all-star." It was a dig at me and also a sign of affection. He said "You, McKean all-star, git in there." Off I went to help bring the ball up the court. On the second pass from John Crotty, I moved the ball to the right side at the top of the key looking to hit Dick Kepley with a pass. That's when Tommy

Kearns, Carolina's varsity All-American guard, fouled me while attempting to steal the ball. Now I, Frederick Gillette Renneckar, nick-named by Lee Shaffer as Hertz, (as in Rent a Car) must go to the free throw line for the potential game winning points! It's not the kind of situation that I would actively seek out all the time! It's a one and one free throw situation and we are one point behind the varsity. If I make the first shot, I get to take a second one. The first shot swishes. Going through the net it sounds like a whip cracking! The next free throw is a high pressure shot to possibly win the game! The varsity coach calls a time out. They want me to over-think the situation, get nervous, and freeze at the line on the second shot. I ask "Buck" if I can alter my second shot using a bank technique as I had done in high school to win an important game. He replies, "Use what's most comfortable for you." I stand at the foul line taking a deep breath as the packed arena falls silent. Next, the second free throw travels on a high arc to lightly touch the top of the "shooter's square" painted on the backboard. It deflects down through the basket and gently ripples the net. It's unorthodox and it's history because the varsity misses their final shot. It's the first time that a freshman team beats their own varsity team that is expected to win the national championship. My personal thoughts are completely drowned out by the noise of the crowd. I'm not immediately sure that I had done the right thing! It takes a while to be convinced, but my freshman teammates, the varsity players, and all the coaches see it as a beneficial outcome. The future looks brighter for everyone.

Neal:

1957's NCAA Basketball title, when UNC, riding on Lenny Rosenbluth's shoulders, beat Wilt Chamberlain's Kansas University in triple-overtime in Kansas City, created fantastic stories across Tar Heel land and the nation. While remembering championships, nobody ever tired of Hertz's 1957 Blue vs. White game foul shot. 1957's varsity went 32 - 0 for NCAA games, so their only loss occurred against their frosh. It's an event that doesn't get old. That Championship's impact made me realize UNC's complete sports investment. Interest in Tar Heel sports extended throughout North Carolina, and I learned campus jocks had advantages wherever they went.

After adding Gil, another roommate would complete our household's foursome. We hunted for candidates, stumbling onto an excellent one. During an early morning whimsical foray, Hertz entered a nearby apartment, rifling through dresser drawers. This resident worked nights for the Southern Pacific Railroad, sleeping days. He awakened, seeing Hertz searching through his belongings. Thuntz's first assumption was a burglar! Tom Huntsman was our newest addition. He's tagged "Thuntz," who described encountering an intruder: "The big ugly fucker said, 'Relax, I'm Hertz. I live next door, and I'm looking for cigarettes.' Thus began a wonderful friendship with an eclectic bunch of intelligent rats."

He'd seen it all. The 82nd Airborne paratrooper was not afraid to take chances. Thuntz entered our world, prepared to follow "Rat" life. He summed up his path:

Some of the early years were spent in Santa Monica, Ca. My family moved several times. Once living near Ventura, on a Sunday morning when I was 5, our radio announced that all vehicles were to avoid highway 101 near Carpentaria. Of course this alert drew tens of thousands to the Carpentaria beach in front of the Union Oil refinery. Sitting offshore about 600 yards out was a Japanese Submarine shooting at the refinery with its deck gun. For about 6 hours the sub shot over the heads of more than 100,000 people. Finally a US Coast Guard ship arrived from Long Beach and chased the sub away. After it's all over, the radio pleads with people to deny it ever happened and to never speak of it. In the 1970's the sub commander wrote a book about the incident. He was a Petroleum Engineering graduate of UCLA and had gone to the refinery for a job. He was told "This refinery will never hire a Jap." When his sub was recalled to Japan, he used all of his ammunition to damage the refinery.

A few years later we moved to Arizona where Dad and some buddies were drilling for oil. We had no electricity, a hand pump for water, an outdoor toilet, and I went to a one room school. All 8 grades are covered in one room, and there are never more than 17 students in total. There is one other boy in my 8th grade class and he was drafted into the army out of the class. In those days, a kid could be 17 or 18 years old and stay until the end of 8th grade in a public school. That arrangement wasn't unusual. Some days I rode my horse to school. In the 7 years we lived in Wittman, it rained 3 times.

In mid 1945, at about 4 in the morning, I'm in our one-seat outhouse, with a flashlight in hand. The sky suddenly turned a brilliant white. It's bright enough to read the Sears catalog we use for toilet paper. Dad came running out of the house demanding to know "What have you done?" Sometime later we learn it was the first "A" bomb test in New Mexico.

At 13 years I went from an 8 student school to a 1200 student high school in Madera, California. Much like Neal, I skipped several grades due to my reading ability. We lived on a small farm and I still had horses. Because of living on a farm, I got a car driving license at 14. I worked weekends in a grocery store or in the fields, picking cotton, cutting grapes, or driving tractors. I paid $25 for my first car, a 1932 Ford 3 window with a rumble seat. Of course, as a new kid in the school, I hung out with the wrong crowd. Somehow, I survived even though my buddy ended up doing 3 life sentences in Folsom or Vacaville. Athletics helped me through it all. I define myself as a rinky dink football player, a decent boxer, and a fair 880 yard runner.

At 17, I entered Fresno State University, again as a rinky dink football player and a so-so boxer.

At 18, I enlisted to be a paratrooper. It was fun, but I was not into long term commitments. I was a rigger/loadmaster. The Suez War ended while we were flying to fight the Brits or someone to save Israel. In 1957, I was with a few companies of troopers that spent some time training in Laos. When we were replaced and went back to Fort Campbell, President Ike was on national TV saying "We have no US soldiers in Laos!" This began my distrust of the US Government.

During the time training with the group of runners in San Jose, I never attained the 1:56 done in a high school relay. That's when I decided to focus on education. My eyes and my vision of the future turned toward a MBA degree from Stanford University.

Kenny:

Meanwhile, everything necessary got done for settling into the college neighborhood. There was little comfort in facing racist constructs, often disrupting days, threatening well-being, and producing negative encounters. I'm Black, so prevailing institutions (political, economic, social) opposed my presence, health, and welfare. Battling was constant. Neal (whose physical characteristics allowed using multiple racial/ethnic identities), Gil and Thuntz could draw on functionality unavailable to me. We all understood prejudice, using people's biases to our benefit when possible. I don't know if my housemates had extensive concerns over the extra efforts required. I assumed they stayed unfazed by the bigoted encounters. Hertz, Thuntz, and I did military stints, shaping our preparedness to handle most confrontations. Our traditional veteran brotherhood set in with Neal captaining operations. Vital to overall survival, he got paid by downtown poker saloons to shill.

I recognized limits for them and didn't expect they would mirror my racial consciousness. Neal would do anything for me, as I would for him. We had enough sensitivity to each other's frailties to manage them 100%. I had no interest in being anything other than a person of color. General interplay with other college Negroes was crucial, although some avoided recognizing our "so-called race." That outlook fostered an unsatisfactory proposition. While not wanting or having any say, I favored my white friends traveling their paths as I traveled mine. We committed to exploiting good and bad for our benefit. Tactics included me triggering racial animus by attending white gatherings, creating distractions. By current measures, national reporters judged SJS #1 party school. Coed parties offered fertile ground for collecting essential household goods, sustaining our rat enterprise. Upon entering any white party, boys gathered, muttering concerns about me.

Most guys wanted to enforce racial association boundaries, while girls had no problem chatting. There were polite conversations until white boys took offense. Whenever sitting beside girls, talk focused on school life. Parties played current musical hits, including Chubby Checker's "The Twist" and Ben E. King's Drifters' "Save the Last Dance for Me." Music could be Negro, but oddly, colored people weren't acceptable guests. While tension mounted among males toward expelling me, women grew perturbed, trying to arrest the increasing hostility. These disturbances allowed the "rats" to pilfer refrigerators, cupboards, and bathrooms.

While I retreated, my partners hit kitchens, secreting away provisions under their coats. My mission was sustaining the disruptions and avoiding getting beaten until my cohorts completed their tasks. Our "wasting" occurred on weekends, supporting food, dry goods stocks, toothpaste, soap, toilet paper, and cleaning materials. Rats labeled foraging operations "wasting." It ensured our survival and we proceeded like locusts descending upon fields, wiping out crops. It wasn't confronting racism but exploiting it. The intent was to use cultural weaknesses for profiting without confronting prejudice, exploitation, and racism. Whenever we found hostility too lacking, my accomplices provoked animosity toward me. If opportunities arose, expropriating funds supported paying our utilities. As an issue of honor (among thieves), we never stole jewelry or personal valuables. Even though observing some limitations, moral judgments didn't move me, nor did arguments decrying our wrongdoing. Given America's prevailing culture, there was no avoiding racist minefields. Rats' principles—survive by any means—held.

Hertz's job provided other essential supplies such as towels, fresh linen, blankets, soap, and toilet paper. His De Anza Hotel security position allowed accessing hotel supplies. When cleaning workers complained, "We don't have any clean sheets," he responded, "You need sheets? You open this closet and use the bedding serving 300 rooms. Just take what you need." Biweekly, Hertz returned soiled linen and brought fresh replacements. Yeah, it's rationalization that we were using giant exploitative corporations' resources. It was not what our children should do. Here's his view:

> … most people never go anywhere away from where they are secure and comfortable or do anything but the most conventional, safe, secure, and non-risky activities. They rarely, if ever, venture into the unknown world on their own. These experiences were totally educational for me. Voyaging across country and surviving in all of these different places without established support systems was not normal. It was the kind of stuff people wanted to hear about from me. They wanted to vicariously experience it when I go back home and talked to old friends that never left the relatively secure environs of our youth. They had no real stomach for the challenges and difficulties we embraced by venturing out into the world without basic support and safe havens. People back home wanted to hear about how I took chances, and what it took in guts, ingenuity, and bold thinking to survive and prosper. To me it is a rare form of education for life and developing the best understanding of self. I had traveled a lot when I was little. We came out to Palm Springs looking to relocate at one point. We stayed awhile, eventually moving to Lake Tahoe. I met Bob Hope when I was thirteen. I was born in Palo Alto.

Neal:

Gil's childhood friend, Norman Gregg (AKA ole Buck), joined us. Norm's arrival added a former sailor. So, we had Army (Hertz), Navy (Buck), Airborne (Thuntz), and Air Force (Kenny). Service connections boosted forming bonds from similar trials under military discipline. Interaction unfolded, pitting "us against settled Californians." There is no forgetting escaping disaster at Carmel's Highlands Inn, an eye-opening blunder. It taught me to be aware of far-reaching dangers when revisiting difficulties in personal histories before applying good, thoughtful judgment.

Festivities were underway in this exclusive celebratory setting as four intruders entered. A Naval Officer from Monterrey's Naval Language School was marrying in an elaborate ceremony. Officers attended, wearing formal dress uniforms resplendent with sheathed gleaming chrome swords and gold epaulets on dress whites. Officers escorted female companions wearing fancy gowns. Our foursome invaded the elite reception in assorted blue jeans, khaki pants, and pullover shirts.

Attendees paid no attention, with everyone considering us guests. No one, neither the bride, groom, nor other family members, noticed us. We sat through regal pageantry, enjoying an elaborate meal and drinking expensive champagne. Too many toasts rang for the honored couple while Norm got drunk with others! Our sailor partner grew angry enough to fight. Buck served over three years classed E1 (Seaman), always hating commissioned officers. After consuming more sparkling wine, Buck's angry, negative view was becoming problematic. He got pissed, cursing his less-than-satisfying service career. Ole Buck projected responsibility for past difficulties on officers facing him. I never expected him to erupt by grabbing and French kissing the bride while cupping her flat ass in his enormous hands. Fighting erupted, and we were forced to battle our way out. Officers attacked each other, which was a puzzling development!

Carmel Highlands Inn sits off Highway 1, against eastside hills. Kenny analyzed our dash to avoid sheriffs:

We were riding down the narrow road in a V.W. Beetle. If sheriffs caught us, which would require little effort on such a narrow, isolated road, they'd have three whites and a Black in a Beetle. We were who they wanted. The two in the front were over 6'3". We in the back were over 6'1". It was the only way to squeeze inside the car. There was a tremendous sense of relief when we reached Monterrey and a populated city's anonymity.

The perspective for actions embraced for surviving in San Jose traveled from its Baldwin-Wallace College origins, located a whistle and a holler off Ohio's Turnpike in Berea, Ohio. There, the "Rat" orientated campus life was born. In the beginning, Joe Friedberg observed, "Tony Conkle experienced and transported that lifestyle and instigated and fed our emerging ratting acts." Joe became friends with me during our first UNC semester. He explained how "ratting" began:

If anyone is to blame for its emergence and propagation beyond BW, it has to be Tony Conkle. Conk was on the football team at Baldwin Wallace with a bunch of Korean War Vets who were the personification of the word Rat. Moondog Milby, Paul Shockeye, Al Smith and various others fit the mold. All of them were past their prime as athletes and were just putting in time. Shockeye worked for Capitol Airlines at the Cleveland Airport. He customarily stole the first class meals that remained on the planes and brought them to the dorm. That was the nature of Conk's peer group. Rats always tune-in to and really take advantage of the existence of such ignoble excesses in the social, economic, and cultural fabric for the purposes of their survival and prosperity. I tried out for football at 118 pounds and met Conk, but, at that time, we had nothing to say to each other. I was totally depressed about my selection of Baldwin Wallace as a school and became a kind of social outcast. I was the only Jew on campus and this is a Methodist-related college. It was really lonely for me. I was sitting by myself at a campus function and Conkle ended up sitting near me. I knew who he was and knew he competed in the Decathlon on a national level against Jim Brown. I knew Jim from high school and the New York Pioneer Club, which we both competed for. I was Jim's ride to the city for track meets. These two guys were really big-time athletes! A small college like Baldwin Wallace is a strange place for Conkle to be. Harrison Dillard, an Olympic sprinter and hurdler may be the only great athlete to attend BW until Conkle arrived.

Tony was the consummate athlete with a long list of accomplishments. He had an illustrious high school career with many notable performances during and after:

- Won the Ohio High School State Meet in the Shot Put in 1952 and 1953
- Set the Ohio High School State Meet record with a toss of 54' 9".
- Placed 2nd in the State Meet Discus, 2nd in the 100 and 3rd in the 220
- In 1961, Conkle threw the Shot 58' 3-1/2", a NAIA Small College record.
- He ran the 100 yd. Dash in 9.7 and the 120 Hurdles in 14.9.
- In club competition, he threw the 16 pound shot put 59' 3".
- As a 66 yr. old power-lifter, he set four National and four World records including a 501 pound squat.
- In 2005, Tony was inducted into The Ohio Association Of Track And Cross Country Coaches Hall Of Fame.

Conk and I hit it off for some reason. I think he liked me because I seemed to hate everybody. I entered the intramural wrestling tournament at my weight class and won it. Winning led to me being recruited to the wrestling team. That gave me all the opportunity I needed to be mean and nasty, and did little for my social grace and acceptance. Conk was probably drawn to me because I was a nasty little bastard and had no friends. We got very friendly when track season started because we both despise the coaching staff. We really bonded when I drove my car with four or five guys in it to the Quantico Relays and I valeted for Conk in the Decathlon. We invaded the Mary Washington College campus together and lost count in making at least twenty unsuccessful attempts to pick up coeds. That's the first time I remember hearing the term when Conk said 'I guess these southern girls don't go for us rats.' That's the term that the guys on the football team used for themselves.

As we traveled around together over the next several months, we embraced referring to ourselves that way. For instance, a rat always has a swim suit handy and a rat can always borrow his fellow rat's toothbrush if he loses his. Wherever we went, the way of the rats went with us. It got further elucidated when I took Conk home to Great Neck and he disqualified just about all of my high school buddies from ever attaining ratdom. They just always dressed too well! When I met Neal at North Carolina in the winter of 1956-1957, he was immediately able to diagnose me as a New York Jew and I immediately diagnosed him as made for Ratdom. I explained the genesis of it as attached to Conk. Neal and I bonded immediately and were virtually never apart for the next few years. But that is another story.

Local colleges started in September, before Kenny's October arrival. Entering then made no sense; thus, enrollment couldn't happen until February. (He'd applied for an early discharge to attend fall classes, and requests got rejected for discipline problems, including an extensive misdemeanor record documenting trouble in Pensacola.) The time from his release until spring track season focused on gaining conditioning to deliver performances warranting scholarships. So, three-quarters of a year remained for earning full rides. It started loosely defined with not knowing how well he could run. I learned what performance range brought grants when walking on at North Carolina, earning my scholarship. By locking on me, offers would come by matching my advance toward prior proven ability (UNC) and beyond. He ran 440s and 880s.

Good mile performances were within range for us both. I coupled my 880 preference with the 440. Kenny needed strength and endurance to support his natural speed. The same program maximized my pace and exploited leg speed and endurance. Eighty percent of training was preparing for the 880. The remaining workload covered differences between specialties. "Iggles' method" suited us.

Kenny:

In every aspect, Coach's plan was challenging beyond belief. Hampered by my lack of world-class preparation, I struggled even to keep up with less capable participants. Jogging warm-up segments bordered on being too strenuous. Each day, over several weeks, 15-minute jogs followed by "easy" 110-yard strides took everything. My difficulties began when veterans led the collective. They gradually build toward 80% maximum effort, always doing 2.5 miles or more. Members facetiously labeled this jogging. So-called jogs ended up becoming involuntary tempo runs. I was exhausted before hard intervals started. Next, spikes replaced flats, completing this warm-up phase by doing strides. They termed that first set of 10 "easy" or "easy speed." On these, I tried conserving energy because, afterward, intervals got more demanding with elevated pacing. Specified intervals covered seven miles until arriving at the final 110s employing varying speeds.

Often, completion felt near when only hitting the requirements' midpoints (110s, 150s, 220s, 440s, 880s, and 1320s combinations). I held on, hoping my sprinter's speed would enable me to stay with my mates while suffering and urging myself to hang with it! This torture continued until near breaking. Just when I verged on failing, Coach assigned something light. When struggling through gut-busting parts, it appeared he wasn't watching, but at the right moment, Iggles pulled us back from self-destruction. He had an intimate awareness of 30 people developing daily, so he employed the right volumes and intensity levels, to realize an individual's potential.

After a month of acclimating, I progressed, meeting challenges and coming into my own. Watching elite performers, they relished major work-out segments verging on self-destruction. It was clear; above all else, they loved running. That goes for me, although in no position (or condition) to make it show. After all, I alone hitchhiked across the country, traversing lynching territory, seeking to become an integral part of this magnificent movement. Now, I was building toward my cardiovascular tipping point, where lower-intensity repeats gradually become manageable. It hit people at different times because teammates continued struggling after training for long periods. The gap before thriving closed for me each day. My advance required dispatching doubt while embracing the pain necessary for success. I sensed superior leg speed quickens improvement for brief spells, balancing with better-conditioned teammates. I reached levels allowing dialing back exertion while matching veterans. That relief signaled a transformation from dreading approaching days to relishing growing satisfaction brought by adequate performances.

Faster progress came with my partner reducing difficulty by pulling me through intervals. Drafting on him makes it more tolerable, and improvement by becoming more comfortable following him was good! My way forward hinged on sharing leading rounds, ensuring steady advancement. Leading means advancing toward my potential and seeing that transforming continues apace. Now there was no reason to worry about or doubt attaining goals. Hopes for future achievement grew into learning that I have what it takes to represent SCURVY. Once reaching that stage I am accepted by established members and identified by interested observers as "one of Iglói's runners." An SJS athlete approached, declaring, "You're one of Iglói's men!" I realized opportunities were no longer uncertain! Qualifying for athletic scholarships was a realistic prospect, and getting there progressed just fine.

Neal:

Outsiders considered surviving under Iglói was exceptional because daily exertions far exceed their tolerance. Those aren't our concerns because Kenny and I observed that if those joining SCURVY did not become true believers, they couldn't survive. Since rejoining Iggles, I'd seen people leave because requirements were too stressful, even for proven talents. Two touted high school youngsters from Palo Alto visited, testing their metal and fitting that description. One boy quit after three sessions. His partner lasted until Saturday. Excellent university distance men tried but never stayed. It was more than most expected. Mihái's programs defied analysis. Sufficient benefits didn't come unless one believed in the Hungarian's leadership and welcomed his demands. Our coach wasn't always visible while executing commands. After sequences, he emerged, instructing what to do from there. Later, when home, we spent time assessing and reassessing execution, including the effort's impact and conditions under which achievement took place. The growth process bred fierce loyalty.

Beatty said Iggles documented everyone's workouts. We never saw him writing. Nothing was communicated while we execute orders unless doing all-outs. He'd yell, "Drive! Drive! Drive!" ensuring that each interval received maximum exertion. We ran no day's design twice or knew what demands followed. Even when completing (we thought) more than enough for one day, Coach made us warm down, then repeat earlier steps, concluding by jogging barefoot 100s. Sessions ended by gathering in groups for stretching. Members circled, exchanging notes, complaining about enduring pain. Quiet moments afforded time to commiserate with comrades who prepared for longer races (over one mile). Others were Wolfgang, Magee, and Tom Brown; 18-year-old Charles Grant rode Greyhound buses from San Antonio. This kid stuttered worse than anyone I ever encountered. His stuttering vanished under Iglói's influence. Amazing how such an affliction disappeared! What Charles went through probably triggered mental changes, overcoming more than physical challenges!

But he wasn't the single unique personality. Among SCURVY's distance coterie was "Gritville, U.S.A.," (a Tennessee hillbilly kid), Joe Szurcik, European Junior Cross-Country Champion, Ray Shnore, Latvian 5K and 10K National Champion, Jerry Laird, and "Little Joe." None could tolerate high-intensity sped-up stuff. We did not envy their volumes of moderate repeats, building extreme endurance for racing more than a mile. Once, I asked them about their work. They had ten miles warming up on road routes, then a 40 or 60 x 440 track workout. That volume left me wondering if they ever lost count! In the remaining group, we contributed our respective capabilities to help elite performers (Beatty, Tábori, Schul, and Grelle) progress with championship preparations.

Kenny and I created affectionate terms for punishing assignments (our view). "The Hungarian Hades" became our favorite descriptor since "only Magyar's design and administer such prolonged daily cruelty. After all, their ancestral roots are Transylvanian! Just check László (Tábori); many years enduring incomparable pain etched into his face!" Another label depicting Iglói's torture was "Muerte por Los Magyars" (death by the Magyars (Hungarians)). We used our romantic Spanish version when our suffering corps' collective spirit needed more poetic expressions than usual.

Below is my December 5th through 11th, 1960 journal, after Kenny joined. Entries document fourteen weeks of 440/880 training before entering collegiate races.

Workouts for the week of December 5 to 11, 1960	
Monday- 15 min jog (2.5 miles) warm-up + 15 x 100 mid speed + 4 x 660 at hard speed with 330 jog between + 10 x 100, 1 easy, one all out	Cloudy—no wind—cold—track smooth
Tuesday- 15 min jog (2.5 miles) warm-up + 10 x 100 mid speed on grass with little jog turnaround interval + 4 x 150 x 3 sets with lap jog between sets, first 2 at good speed and 2nd two at good swing + 10 x 100 shake-up with usual turnaround jog interval	Cloudy—no wind—cold (40's)—track smooth
Wednesday- 15 min jog (2.5 mile) warm-up + 10 x 100 mid speed with usual interval + 1 x 660 good speed with 330 jog + 3 x 330 with 220 jog between at good speed repeated 3 times with lap jog between sets + 15 min jog (2 miles) warm-down	Partial cloudy— slight south wind—cold temp—track soft
Thursday- 50 min jog (7.5 miles) on grass + 10 x 100 mid speed	Cloudy—no wind—cooler temp - track soft—a welcome rest day
Friday- 15 min jog (2.5 miles) warm-up + 15 x 100 2 easy, one good speed + 10 x 220 at 'hard' speed with 110 jog + 10 x 100 shake-up	Cloudy– no wind— cold - track good
Saturday- 30 min jog (5 miles) with 6 x 150 'build-ups' built into the jog	Cloudy– no wind— cold — track good— must be getting all of the crap out of our legs

Sunday- 20 min jog (3 miles) warm up +15 x 100, 2 mid speed, one good swing with usual interval + 4 x 660 good speed with 330 jog between-lap jog + 3 x 330 mid speed with 110 jog + 4 x 150, 2 good speed, 2 good swing with 50 yd jog + 10 x 100 shake-up	Partial cloudy— slight wind— cold - track soft—now we resume the punishment

NOTE: Doing the workouts with exactness requires an understanding of how Iglói's terms converted elapsed time for a distance, stride length, and turnover rate. The shorthand for these is "speed" and "tempo."

Notations display complex requirements. Increments in each sequence came from the Coach's formulations as performances progressed. An ability to recall details for each individual astonished us. We asked him for past log corrections if log entry accuracy was uncertain, and the experience was mystifying. When reviewing accounts, our physical ability's depth proved more significant than ever imagined for demonstrating resiliency.

ESCAPAR DE LA PRISIÓN DE JUAREZ

Neal:

With Christmas coming, we decided to go home in Kenny's 1956 Volvo bought from Thuntz. Our choice was traveling south down to Pensacola, visiting Mary, sleeping at Eglin Field, and seeing Friedberg in Chapel Hill before arriving home (West Chester and Thornton). We traded off driving until exhausted. Roadside stops were short periods, pushing on as soon as feeling capable. Our first break after leaving San Jose was Las Cruces, New Mexico, an 1100-mile stretch. Late at night, we crashed on empty State University dorm beds. Security rousted us after sunrise for trespassing. Once entering El Paso, Kenny suggested touring Juarez, Mexico. It might be nice to pick up souvenir presents for relatives back east. He wanted hand-carved chess pieces for his brother. We descended onto Avenida Juarez after parking state-side to walk over the Rio Grande via Santa Fe Bridge and found a taxicab to see the city.

That taxi launched a ride into serious trouble because it wasn't long before we entered an isolated neighborhood. The streets looked threatening. Water splashed over the 1953 Dodge on muddy roads. Views through rusted flooring flashed water-soaked ground passing beneath us. Conditions felt possible for getting robbed or worse. Proven instincts triggered such thoughts. When ordering our driver to go back, he demanded $20. Our $5 counteroffer more than covered five minutes of riding, but he threatened we must pay or face arrest. When speaking, it sounded like "Si us. se pone asi; o me paga $20 o le llevo a la policía y les digo qué me querian vender drogas. Esto les va a traer muchos problemas." After haggling, he acted as though accepting terms. Our last $8.00 offer elicited gestures of agreement. But wait! Perhaps continued bargaining got mistaken for no deal because before we realized it, we pulled over at a makeshift jail on an unlighted corner deep in the barrio's bowels. There, he had us arrested as drug dealers by guards carrying M1 rifles. They wore Mexican army uniforms. Maybe dress makes no matter in policing such a violent, drug-infested place. These developments were unreal! Our cell was an empty house's living room having no bars or window glass! An eight-foot diameter hole in the roof further exposed the place to the frigid outdoors! We gazed at stars while pacing, skirting an ice-glazed pool covering the floor's sagging center. Ahead loomed a supreme test! Escaping meant nothing without transportation. We'd find opportunities tomorrow when taken to their central lockup. Walking in circles all night staved off freezing.

Dressed in lightweight sweat suits left us unprepared for being outside in December temperatures! We ignored the freezing drunken prisoner dissolved into a southwest corner after being shoved there near 1 a.m., reeking of tequila-saturated urine. At sunrise, six unfortunate souls arrived crouched in a barred cage over-wrapped in chicken wire atop an unmarked rattling flatbed truck. Such was their way of collecting criminals from random sites, riding through neighborhoods in open-air cages, and gathering more captives, arriving at Juarez's prison frozen stiff. I had visions portraying Les Misérables' scenes in real life. This mirrored classic transportation to the guillotine! Now our survival test began! Jail was a previous French fortress with parapets spaced around its top built by Maximilian. This citadel occupied an entire block, encapsulating its storied history. That unsavory past was evident from the fortified location's expanse, construction, and its outer wall's impenetrable look. Juarez's notoriety for violent lawlessness started when the early settlement arose. Over time, an endless parade of imprisoned subjects created its reputation for harsh conditions. Those living within achieved an unrivaled brutal law enforcement reputation emerging from lawless frontier conditions. Juarez's history didn't bode well for ill-prepared American youths. Fellow prisoners formed dual lines of hundreds, stumbling along outer walls before disappearing through 8-inch thick steel doors. They built those gates to menace captives; with walls showing the way in, suggesting there was no way out. The construction made sure no one knew what went on inside once those gates closed. We stopped and paused after each advance. Guards forbid talking or looking behind. Two hundred downtrodden peons stretched single-file ahead.

Early arrival placed us midway among captives before business opened. One broken, toothless soul behind us whispered, "Son las Ocho de la mañana." (It's 8 a.m.) 500 more steps placed everyone under closed captivity. Only the guards spoke, herding everyone through solid polished steel gates. Sunrise reflecting off east-facing doors blinded us. Polished arrays of massive, half tennis ball-sized rounded rivet heads secured door panels. "Permanezcan en una cola recta y sigan moviéndose." ("Stay in a straight line - keep moving!") This sorry column proceeded along a hallway into a big room on the right. On stepping inside, one happy, chattering, fellow stood behind his tall lectern beside a waxed table blocking another room's entrance. He wrote names while collecting unfinished liquor and drugs possessed by prisoners. Our clerk placed confiscated articles on that large table with a flourish, speaking and joking, giving every individual a belly laugh as if they were friends

Kenny:

This prison stood, casting an air of foreboding, as shadowy and threatening as France's 16th century Bastille. Unfortunates ahead stumbled through a dark doorway leading down into a dungeon behind the booking clerk's station. Operating efficiency was apparent. Stairs descended, disappearing into the blackness. Momentarily focusing, girding myself for challenges if gangs or specific characters dominated catacomb culture, I knew conditions might require fighting to the death and violently securing safe space. Prisoners were 100% victims of society and combined self-destructive responses. Their sad countenance of dirty, ragged half-starved human beings attested to their complete demise. No aggressive personalities here! Prisoners shuffled heads down, and backs bowed. These spirits broke, but they had numbers! My partner's preparedness for these circumstances was no mystery. I'd never seen him shrink from any challenge or threatening situation. I'm confident he'd stand up to any threats. When our turn, the clerk wanted our names. Sounding curious, he asked for reasons for being there. "¿Como se llama? ¿Qué hace usted aquí? ¿Por qué está usted aquí?" We dredged up some high school Spanish, giving our names and living in California, "Nuestros nombres son Neal Chappell y Ken Noel. Somos norteamericanos de California." Neal spoke, "El conductor del taxi trató de cobrarnos demasiado. No quisimos pagar tanto. El queria $20 y sólo le queríamos pagar $5." ("The taxi driver charged too much, demanding $20. We offered $5, not expecting topping $10.")

Delighted surprise illuminated the clerk's face. He spoke with great animatión, "Salgan de la cola y siéntense aquí cerca de mí. Quiero practicar hablar inglés y Uds. dos pueden tratar de hablar español." We only got part of his words spoken too fast, "aquí a mí" and "hablar' ingles," yet understood wanting company to practice English. Our reading of this unfolding scenario proved correct as he proceeded to translate. Now, he had subjects for practicing English. He mentioned teaching us Spanish. Once seated, he asked if we wanted whiskey or tequila, pointing at columns of bottles - or some marijuana, gesturing toward piles of contraband. "¿Uds. quieren beber o fumar algo mientras se sientan?" We declined together, "no gracias," and sat on beautiful antique chairs against the wall. Until booking finished, we'd avoid the dungeon. Logging remaining prisoners requires 2 to 3 hours. Language lesson's ended as conversation advanced in English, exchanging life stories. Ignacio Velasco, a tall balding man, is thirty and grew up attending schools in Hermosillo before moving to Juarez. He continued studying 'Inglés' and grasped every opportunity to practice. We explained our trip to El Paso and getting taken into custody. Presenting ourselves as college students and world-class track athletes impressed him. He dreamed of continuing education for a university degree. Ignacio turned out to be a cool guy who took to us. He desired to be hip, as evidenced by focusing on American slang, never realizing already being very cool. Ignacio was sharp and witty - knowledgeable about life and the larger world. He's someone we would befriend anywhere or under most circumstances. His manner, performing duties, starkly contrasted to the seriousness of the occasion enveloped in the repressive confining character of prison. He's imprisoned as much as unfortunate souls proceeding to confinement deep underground—eagerness in bonding connected firmly to longing to be free. Under different conditions, Ignacio would have success in prestigious jobs, pursuing more lucrative, intellectually rewarding endeavors. Making us understand his aspirations extended beyond current circumstances meant a lot. Alas, a wife and three children rendered going elsewhere imprudent. Family pictures confirmed his devotion. Justification for holding on to significant employment was unnecessary. Hours passed plotting our way out and, thereby, rising above those walls, gave him an escape! We were more than grateful for having him. Ignacio was also interested in track and aware Mexico City bid to host 1968's Olympics. The three of us talked much about that. Upon ending prisoner processing at 11:30, he decided we should stay with him to plan for our freedom. All of us needed to eat, so our friendly clerk used cash piled on the table and sent a trustee to buy food. He enlisted us to help verify currency counts before stuffing a small wall safe. Contraband got stacked on shelves in an eight-foot-tall mahogany cabinet's floor-to-ceiling locking sections.

Ideas solidified while eating tortillas, beans, and peppers. The food itself, comforted. Complete control over funds and contraband collected each day indicated his thoughts regarding our plight had standing. Ignacio scheduled an audience with "El Señor," ruling the entire operation. Neal and I should "remain silent and humble while I do the talking." "When El Señor speaks to you in English, you must only answer "yes Señor or no Señor." Any detailed explanations depended on Ignacio's interpretation. Between 3:30 p.m. and 5 p.m., El Señor has time and only shows after siesta. Waiting and reviewing the plan, Ignacio became anxious. "The Señor is a sportsman greatly appreciating skilled athletes. Your track accomplishments are impressive and prove you can't be dealing drugs." Ignacio had confidence his help, and our athletic ability would bring freedom.

Neal:

Kenny and I felt this was our system opening conjured while shivering overnight in that holding pen under December's Moon, reflecting on an ice-covered floor. Ignacio, serving as an advocate, embodied the saving grace sought while riding caged through Juarez surrounded by urine-soaked, drunken, drugged-out folks. Ignacio found us, as we did him, connecting in doing something impossible: engineering an escape from Mexico without paying. Now, meeting "El Señor's" approval remained. Meanwhile, there was great uncertainty about whether the head prison administrator was coming. Ignacio cautioned, "El Señor takes off at will." Today, he appeared at 4:30 p.m., only staying an hour. Ignacio saw him for fifteen minutes, explaining our plight. We entered at 5:00, bowing silently before sitting on ornately carved chairs. These were extraordinary furnishings brought from Spain. With his gold and diamond ring-encrusted left hand, El Señor directed proceedings with pudgy-fingered gestures. Rings covering each digit flashed spectacular lights. Several had two. Ignacio remained standing. When introduced, we stayed silent. Then, he argued why our misfortune was true. I looked for any reaction in El Señor's smooth, chubby face. He was big (6' 4" and over 275 pounds), a very light-skinned blue-eyed aristocratic man. During this audience, there were three questions. Accent free, he queried, "Do you drink alcohol?" "Do you use tobacco?" We responded, "No, Señor." We answered, "Yes, Señor," when asked, "Do you go to college?" "He wants to see your hands," Ignacio interpreted. Soft fingers handled ours, gliding, touching our palms. It startled us; an aristocrat touched us. There were no drugs or tobacco stains; our hands felt smooth, not calloused by menial labor. Then, swiveling his oversized exquisite leather chair and addressing Ignacio, he said "Ellos están Libres." Those words were understandable. Ignacio's confirming translation lifted an enormous weight. "You are free to leave this prison." Our "Gracias" was enough.

With Ignacio's map of directions to the border, it was out the steel doors at a racing tempo. To be polite, we accepted an invitation to visit upon returning west. That stop wouldn't happen. It's incredible; when we crossed back over the border, our car sat untouched after twenty-four hours. Thuntz's Volvo sped beyond El Paso onto Interstate 10, penetrating Texas' emptiness.

After clearing metropolitan confines, our discussion reviewed the unlikely events in Juarez. No matter how complicated matters appeared, we never doubted we would escape harm. (That says something about our character.) Only we had no idea how it might unfold—escaping from prison in Mexico without paying defies history! Perhaps our memory of high school Spanish class helped. Juarez pulled on our entire spectrum of language and character. Extracurricular Spanish club member socializing paid off. If this equated to a final examination, no classmates could have passed!

Wrangling your way and escaping any Mexican jail is impossible when speaking any language. A significant discovery was we had inner strength and resiliency in facing an impending disaster that could have ended by losing more than freedom. In my judgment, we proceeded, unfazed. It became a personal character-building close call, avoiding major disaster. An actual benefit emerged from our harrowing mishap.

(Later, back with Iggles' Los Angeles Track Club team, another 1A classification draft notice got delivered, earmarked for sending me to fight in Vietnam. I strategized on managing my draft status, feeling my hereditary blood pressure issues guaranteed unsuitability. In addition, confessing imprisonment in Juarez might help them judge me unfit to serve. When questioned during pre-induction interviews, draft officials learned Mexican authorities jailed me in 1960. An updated Selective Service Card arrived, conferring 1Y status. For whatever reason, physical or moral, classification rendered me undesirable! That night, we celebrated an immeasurable victory. Our border adventure turned out worth every minute! Though scary, it was an unqualified rat accomplishment!)

Once clearing Juarez, we pushed beyond Texas through other Gulf Coast states to Florida and stopped in Pensacola before driving fifty miles to Eglin. Knowing Kenny, several fellows arranged for us to sleep in an empty barracks room and eat with troops in the chow hall before leaving for Tar Heel country after breakfast. Friends at UNC, after my sophomore term, provided meals and beds. Friedberg's roommate, for example, partied late, so Joe told Kenny to take that bed. Therefore, knowing Joe would manage any issues, he slept well until waking for breakfast. While downing eggs and pancakes, Joe recounted handling his roomie:

He came in after partying and exclaimed, 'Joe! There's a Negro sleeping in my bed!' I told him Kenny was a professional boxer here from California. I said, 'You'd better leave and not wake him up cause he'll kick your ass.' He went down the hall and found an empty spot.

An issue arose upon entering Lenoir Dining Hall. Grumbling surfaced among several dozen youngsters already eating. It fell to Joe, who welcomed challenges, to convince those at breakfast that his Negro friend should eat, although Carolina schools practiced segregation. Only Negro cooks, or kitchen help, entered dining facilities. None slept in campus dorms or ate with whites. Frat types required talking down from fears of dining while Negroes were eating, too. Regular students were more than satisfied minding their business. Both visits integrated UNC's housing and cafeterias during December 1960.

Negroes serving breakfast acted pleased and amused that Kenny enjoyed their cooking. I'm sure everyone understood Friedberg opposed segregation, and he stayed ready to challenge Jim Crow at every turn. Retracing steps back to California meant sleeping in Friedberg's dorm, eating meals unquestioned, and integrating campus facilities. Our next break was Eglin, arriving for a weekend playing profitable poker. What an ideal place for meals, then crashing after earning some G.I. dollars!

Meanwhile, Kenny stayed in Pensacola, using a garage unit behind Mary's grandmother's home. Without fearing racial impropriety, we slept in Mrs. Shelby's detached furnished space before leaving for California. It was a quiet stay, enjoying the room Mary and her friends called "The Club House." Potential issues with local authorities mattered little, but Mrs. Shelby acted wary. Customs forbade behaving as equals anywhere. Everyone expected trouble if the cops knew. Indeed, no regular whites cared. It was a relief exiting B Street onto Highway 90.

Kenny:

Return travel panned out uneventfully compared to events on the way to North Carolina. We retraced our trip, pushing beyond El Paso, stopping in Las Cruces to sleep in an empty New Mexico State University dorm room. This time, security didn't come. One night's rest was refreshing enough to last until San Jose, only making refueling stops. It felt like going home! That much had changed since October!

Neal:

Back in San Jose for the New Year (1961), and regretting lost conditioning crossing the U.S., Mihái was unhappy about our interrupted progress traveling over Christmas. I can't say if Beatty or someone else mentioned it. Leaving, suspended training, but being independent spirits, means exercising such liberties. Arguing that among distance men, superior leg speed allows breaking rules; free spirit came from our swifter legs and caused pranks! Our favorite was increasing the pace more than acceptable, disrupting repeats while leading SCURVY's superstars. After staying on pace, we'd increase the tempo, ushering them through blistering reps when least expected, stressing the group. László always complained, damning our tricks and going ballistic. He'd scream, curse, jogging into more intervals. Being subjects of László's ire, delivered in mixed native and English expletives with their Magyar nyelv accent, was priceless. Kurti and fiai, a szukák (son of a bitch and you sons of bitches), are valued words! These episodes occurred spontaneously, not premeditated. Sucking less speedy people into going at their top-end through challenging stretches was good fun; knowing when to strike was instinctive. Iggles never did more than laugh. There were big laughs when documents came in mid-January announcing UNC Cross-Country honors for 1957. Why now, with involvement so long ago? After being chased out by law enforcement and receiving positive recognition while moral turpitude charges waited, I was mystified. Joe (Friedberg) couldn't stop laughing when he heard.

CHAPTER
TEN

San Jose City College 1961

"Education is an important element in the struggle for human rights. It is the passport to the future, for tomorrow belongs to those who prepare for it today." —Malcolm X.

Kenny:

My first enrollment at San Jose's junior college (SJCC) was in the spring of 1961. Jim Litchen coached the track team, so Neal called him inquiring about joining. He explained our commitment to the Santa Clara Valley Youth Village and Iglói. We chose races we'd run. We planned to train with the Youth Village while competing in various Junior College (JC) Championships. Otherwise, I represented City College when it fits SCURVY's schedule.

Northern California JC Relays were 1961's first consequential championships. We arrived unknown, having not performed in league meets. Of debut selections, we picked the sprint medley and mile relay (4 x 440). We each anchored one. Although prepared by *Iglói*, we didn't consult with him about what to run. On the medley, my 440 started a mix of sprints and middle distance that most coaches consider insignificant.

I used minimum effort, handing off with a healthy lead. Two 220s followed, concluding with an 880. Teams don't use their best personnel, so our winning passed unnoticed. Jim Litchen expected this win, knowing the teams' best half-milers weren't at Neal's level. We gave it no thought as he anchored with two easy laps while saving energy before the meet's biggest test (4 x 440). Since we held back, we considered our sprint medley respectable and not worth bragging about. Friendly staff from geographically close institutions asked Litchen our stories, and Jim kept it low-key on our histories.

Litchen understood that Iglói made us better than he'd seen. He was a gentle guy who had not encountered bossing track much; his primary interests were trout fishing and preserving federal parks. Litchen was retiring after this season; he owned a rustic cabin near Lassen Volcanic National Park. Conversations with him focused on trout fishing. We never discussed running as an art and science. While crossing the infield, he mentioned we aroused significant interest with other staff. Plans for dealing with us would have to wait until later. We thought it obvious; using an effortless style of executing kept our actual ability under wraps. It saved legs until the four-lap final, which teams hungered to win. Notable "hot shots" got promoted; Sequoias College (COS) tops the rankings. We relished being unknown.

San Joaquin Valley newspapers trumpeted COS predictably dominating contests. Publications gave explicit declarations stating their superiority. Modesto was inside their territory and disadvantaged everyone else for coverage. Sequoias' vaunted 4 x 100, 4 x 220, and one-mile relay anchor-men got media praise. Early 100s, 220s, and 440s put them on top statewide. They had a quarter-miler, below 48 seconds, which dominated media coverage. That primed their squad's laying claim as northern California's best. We'd love to surprise them. An unlikely victory would be super sweet, given preseason predictions. Throughout the day, orange and blue-clad athletes racked up wins. They wore overconfidence upon thrusting chests, parading with each conquest. Neal and I relaxed on the infield grass, enjoying the mustering orange and blue peacocks. Beating favored teams clips their wings, bringing them back to earth. In major track meets, 4 x 440 titles always delivered more satisfaction than other contests.

Mile relays meant so much that winning was celebrated as if scoring million-dollar jackpots! This event established bragging rights between rivals regardless of the outcomes of other events. Since our foursome had never run together, how we'd perform was uncertain. Chu Chu Fikes and Dave Steeb ran legs before us. Those two stayed near the leaders, and made pulling off an upset seem possible. Deficits were within three strides; something Neal could wholly erase.

Litchen had let us dictate race details. We huddled, laying out plans. Our roles went beyond "captains;" we functioned as coaches. In plain language, "Chooch" and Dave couldn't get behind by over 10 yards. We emphasized the need to be faster through the baton-exchange zone. That's where lost ground could get recovered through tactics. Steeb took the stick early, reducing Chooch's run by five yards. The same tactic applied on Steeb's exchange, making him cover less than a lap. Our strategy was to build momentum throughout by positioning faster individuals at each stage.

Chu Chu, leading off, handed to Dave, and Neal aimed to recover deficits after receiving from Steeb. Rival foursome's third positions were not within seconds of him. He often overtook teams, sometimes coming from last into first. Customary line-ups started with someone who could finish leading. Coaches preferred staying in front and ending fast. Usually, their slowest member came right before the anchor position. Many times that worked, depending on personnel quality, but not always. Since high school, we had used the "building momentum" strategy. Consistent with momentum theory, adherents start their slowest guy and advance through stages with people getting faster. Such an arrangement makes slower members fight harder if they're trailing. This scenario unfolded as envisioned. Chu Chu and Dave Steeb fell behind but maintained adequate contact.

Neal:

I responded immediately, moving past three places and forcing a path through. That is normal during heated contests, bringing no problems as an expert with elbows and arms! There was greater freedom on the backstretch because four runners ahead settled a stride apart. My speed increased to a very-hard swing tempo, and I passed into second place. Still comfortable, I eased beside the last guy with 100 left. Kenny motioned me to stay and not change lanes; it was unnecessary. With me ahead, he stepped deeper into the zone, taking Lane 1. Our exchange went from my left to his right hand. We were aflame with an unlikely victory possible. I watched him burst out fast, then slow, while trailing anchors fought each other. It was a relief when he maintained pace, keeping pursuers at bay on the back side straight. There wasn't much chance of getting taken in the last curve. We were leading on to the home stretch; I went out to see if he needed to move over if anyone tried passing.

Meanwhile, infield occupants rushed the sideline, and bleacher spectators crushed onto outer lanes, cheering the grand finish in a wave. After their loss, heated protests between COS's managers and NorCal officials claimed I fouled them, and Litchen considered protests warranted dismissal. So, Jim was happier than ever. Chu Chu's and Steeb's delight was extreme within our collected team. Other school representatives offered animated congratulations. Everybody enjoys defeating big shots.

The bus ride home became an hour-long celebration. Kenny and I declined to feel too enthused over these initial successes. This meet was our maiden outing, things were only starting! In one fell swoop, we emerged as bona fide forces deserving respect among California JCs. Unimagined success made it easier to call shots. Most beneficial was SJCC supplying our equipment.

Kenny:

Matching at quarter-miles, I watched Neal with high expectations, relief, and encouragement, as he lifted his knees and passed COS 50 yards before reaching me. Quality exchanges make victory more possible, and everyone claimed tight spaces. He came side by side with Sequoias and eased past. So, I inched forward three steps, cutting my distance. With more strength, added yards didn't impact him. For sure, it shortened the remaining effort by several yards. Maintaining momentum beyond a lap would present no problem. His facial expression was a key indicator, becoming more discernable with every full-leg reach. It contrasted with COS's third guy's grimacing mask of pain. My partner's serene look was familiar. When moving well and prevailing, he had an effortless style, relaxed facial muscles, pursed lips, and half-closed eyes.

I moved inside (lane 1), drawing determination from him. His effort lasted until I pulled the hollow cylinder from his grip. These moves put rival anchors behind me. Securing the baton away from anyone approaching from outside, I shifted it to my left hand while speeding up, deterring immediate challenges. In Iggles' lexicon, this phase was "very-hard speed." "Very-hard" defines the effort exerted. "Speed tempo" defines running form, including leg turnover rate. It means using shorter, quicker steps.

Chasers slowed behind, in order to avoid extra distance, negotiating Lane 2. I reduced my "Very-hard speed" to "hard swing," throttling back. Here, stride lengthened while turnover lowered. Then we sped up together as a single mind, maintaining matching strides, holding him on my hip. I'm hearing and feeling him working harder than I.

Nobody survives severe speed increases so far from finishing. Attempted passes now feed into our strategy. Throttling up when entering the last curve discouraged challenges while keeping him in Lane 2 and forcing covering 3.4 added yards. Midway through the bend, I relaxed, conserving energy; I converted from longer to shorter strides. This opponent had sustained higher turnover, staying positioned to challenge when exiting the turn. I felt his decline. Self-checking said there was enough within me, holding the current rate.

Unless the opposition was feigning tiredness, first place loomed ten clicks away, coming fast with each forceful exhale. I shifted beyond "very hard" to "all-out," pulling onto the straight; I never saw opponents again. That was surprising! Why didn't anyone battle over the final 100? Where was he? Neal's work enabled an improbable upset and turned everyone's anticipation into amazement. We had immediate success in launching college careers through Iggles' design. Customary hugs with teammates preceded warm-downs and reviewing experiences. Seven miles of gut-wrenching intervals waited upon arriving home at twilight.

Neither world-class training nor competitive ability changed the everyday disposition of the urban survivalists (Rats). Under SJCC's banner, statewide travel opportunities offered expanded possibilities for wasting. Wherever we visited, resources got exploited. Instead of riding SJCC's bus to May's West Coast Relays, we drove. City College provided rooms at Fresno's namesake Hotel. After racing Friday and Saturday night, we attended celebratory bashes. When leaving town around 2 a.m. on Sunday, Dave Steeb appeared. He took us to their underground liquor cellar catacomb beneath the hotel. Our eyes adjusted to dark rooms full of popular alcoholic beverages. Neal and Steeb waited as I drove from the parking lot to the street. After loading our gear, we hauled whiskey, scotch, and champagne cases, stuffing the car. Spirits were Jack Daniels, Cutty Sark, and Johnny Walker. With everything quiet, several nervous trips carting boxes of each brand filled our vehicle. Security or employees weren't around. We left with more booze than anyone could exhaust over future college years. When partying after that, stolen alcohol traveled with us. Now and then, bottles got sold, raising pocket money. The car stayed loaded with beverages, ready when supplies lagged. (It's not odd that Neal pulled a fifth of JD from his trunk when Hertz met him at Lake Mead in 1965. That bottle dated to 1961's Fresno cache.)

How stupid was that liquor heist? What would have happened if we were caught? Stealing alcohol, as severe criminal behavior, never gained traction, deterring us. Circumstances dictated that obeying laws, racist or class-based structural restrictions and their effects limiting opportunity didn't make antisocial behavior unfavorable or promote following rules as a proven value. It isn't straightforward. We bucked prevailing conditions at every turn unless more favorable opportunities ensued. Stealing booze isn't good! We thought rising above burglarizing is what counts. Guilt over pursuing survival by any means doesn't occur. We trade such commodities garnering necessities.

Neal:

In many respects, Iglói was an absolute genius. He memorized each of his thirty or more devotees program's details. Mihái recalled daily requirements and could identify each set's distance, quantity, and pace. He gave designated speeds when asked for goals before races, including forms covering each phase and race times within tenths of seconds. We tried deciphering some intricacies of his method. There were volume, intensity, and patterned day-by-day, week-to-week, month-to-month, and season-to-season requirements. We hungered to know the impending daily demands. With Coach, that never happened. Only warm-up jogs repeated within daily programs.

15-minute warm-up jogs went no slower than 6:30 miles. After that, only Iggles understood what yardage, forms, and paces followed. The method of this madness was indecipherable! It became apparent; he doesn't allow comfort by knowing demands before approaching execution moments. This practice instilled a determination to cope with adverse circumstances arising during or outside competition. That was how we saw it. Conditioning's essence not only featured sprinting over varying yards but demanded managing increasing stress levels, approaching breaking your will, and not knowing what follows forced us to develop physical toughness, mental resilience, and adapting. Upon completing rests after each set, Iggles gave quantity, distances, and tempos, marking subsequent intervals. They weren't predictable. Each runner processed accepted orders while launching into additional repeats, holding nothing back.

After dinner, we logged that day's requirements. This documentation gave no clues toward predictability. Specifics on ability came when Coach conveyed executing races. His charges never stepped to the line, wondering or doubting readiness. Kenny continued skepticism about predicting times. Misgivings vanished when qualifying for 1961's California's State Championship. Instructions were "ju vil roon zi 440 een 47.7." Without conscious thought, he ran 47.5. Neither of us considered doing well that soon after joining SCVYV. That ranked him the nation's second-leading freshman. His quarter-mile was the Jaguar's all-time best, and he placed 6th at the JC Championship as the only freshman in the final!

We were undefeated in regular-season competitions, running 880s, miles, and 440s—a 1:53.1 Northern California Championship 880 set records. I advanced into the JC final, doing 1:52.1 and placing third at Modesto. Our 4 X 440 team qualified but finished last. Officials ruined our placing when our lane stagger assignment got reduced in error. Our leadoff man ran 5-yards more than everyone else. That season we succeeded, breaking San Jose City College quarter-mile, half-mile, and 4 X 4 records. Modesto's result beat earlier SJCC and Northern California marks. Placing was enough for getting noticed in San Jose's newspaper. Performances rated full scholarships at any university. There was one problem. The last thing we wanted was leaving Mihái!

Kenny:

With school ending, my struggles connecting with Negro students continued. It was relative isolation without ready access to self-affirming relationships. Satisfying basic human contact needs in a racist environment was essential, which required establishing supportive connections with other colored folks. My roommates' needs got addressed by interacting with the broader population; they attended parties and engaged with coeds and others. Regular student interactions, unlike mine, comprised more than spending Saturday nights "wasting" (pilfering or plundering). It took longer for me. A meager social life wasn't troublesome in the short term because time investment, energy, rest and recovery, practice volume, and intensity made interest in other activities an unlikely reach. But, as months passed, desiring more relevant life-affirming interaction became a conscious wish.

Since October's thumbing to San Jose, I'd made sporadic attempts at establishing relationships in an existing Negro youth network. A prohibitive informal stratification discouraged contact with those there. Common barriers among colored people were familiar, especially those attending college. They subverted themselves, pursuing elitist recognition. My first patterned exclusion exposure came weeks after arriving. On a stroll near San Jose State (SJS), three coeds walked in the opposite direction. I waved, saying, "Hi." Upon crossing the street to introduce myself, the boldest one said: "Oh, we thought you were someone else!" They turned away, laughing. That joke was on me! Not having familiarity with them made me unsuitable for an amiable meeting, drawing responses prompting feelings of rejection and puzzlement. Through talking with younger JC Negroes, typical Negro student social patterns became apparent. Acceptance qualifications were: well-groomed, fashionable women, star football players, light-skinned men and women, those at SJS as opposed to City College and those from local middle-class families. Stratification played out in several ways as defined by questions governing supportive contacts:

- Who is acceptable for engaging in conversations?
- Who is admissible to social gatherings like parties?
- Who is worthy as a dance partner?
- Who is fine as close friends?
- Who are acceptable suitors?

Exceptions to standards granting recognition existed. Since SJCC's minority-dominated basketball squad was California championship-caliber, it gave Big Sims, its star, status equaling SJS football players. His extraordinary charm and captivating personality helped and enhanced his super athlete status. Unbeknownst to Neal and me, our basketball team followed track performances. We found that out when interacting with them on spring semester jobs that school administrators generated. The first instance stood out because of our skills in milking additional benefits by turning an hourly low-wage job into a profitable enterprise. At the winter classical music concert benefiting Jaguar sports, other athletes watched amazed as we capitalized using the "wasting" modus operandi. We sold tickets begged from attendees (with extras) before spiriting away unsold Champagne stocks over the fairground's fence to sell later.

My barren social landscape improved at June's annual picnic in Alum Rock Park. It was the paramount gathering of Negro college and city youth. Folks attended from Oakland, Richmond, and Vallejo. Upon entering, nothing had changed with Negro stratification. People affected airs of sophistication. Many gatherers sipped Champagne from fancy glassware or nursed expensive drinks such as rare cognac over ice. Not knowing anyone, I wandered around drinking Thunderbird wine couched in a brown paper bag. No doubt that beverage choice, plus its presentation, stood at odds with this crowd! My penchant for independent thinking made acceptance difficult. However, there's no changing or adopting a pretentious image. While strolling among the assemblage, questions sounded from under a small maple tree. "What you got in that bag?" This long, thin dude was relaxed. It was Big Sims, SJCC's star hoopster, and this was our first social meeting. I pulled the tall green bottle halfway out of its contoured paper bag, revealing Thunderbird's label. There was no need for me to speak. "Gimme a taste!" he said.

In street culture, such requests contain meaning far beyond desiring swigs of fermented grape juice. It said, "I'm like you, not one of these people fronting! Further, we should enjoy friendship and trust by sharing a libation of the streets, even courting other's distaste by drinking from the bottle." He welcomed relief from phoniness and pretentiousness typifying picnic behavior. Two dudes imbibing cheap wine from a cloaked bottle were true antitheses. We found each other. The impact of connecting was that his stature gave me instant acceptance within the entire populous. That development was unexpected but confirmed I needed social relationships. This meeting released me from nine semi-isolated months. Conversation while sharing cheap vino indicated he wanted to connect after observing our deft exploitation at SJCC's music concert. Big Sims, with other ballplayers, attended our competitions. Until now, we had no awareness of any appreciation other than teammates and the Jaguar newspaper's sports editor. While there weren't significant changes socially, I stopped feeling like an outsider. New awareness erased insecurity, allowing progress as a college environment actor.

LOS ANGELES TRACK CLUB

Neal:

Terrible news came after working out with Tom Brown all summer. Mihái returned from a productive European tour intending to set up an LA site with his elite performers. They created the Los Angeles Track Club (LATC) with increased financing and jobs. SCVYV's administration ended its senior programs. We had to decide on taking scholarships or rejoining Mihái. Club changes brought strong motivation for moving on to other endeavors. I elected to play poker in Tahoe. It was summer when SCVYV's top group went overseas, but I wasn't at the foreign tours level. Hertz's access to jobs was a reason for relocating to South Lake. His interests changed fast since he joined Pennsylvania's National Guard the prior November. Spring of 1961, he got discharged and left UNC, escaping shenanigans around cheating on tests, including possessing test printing office keys. San Jose's cannery work stimulated his wish to play professional basketball. He didn't tell the relocation story then, only later:

> I was taking off for a tryout with the Pittsburgh Wrens basketball team. When I left California driving to Pittsburgh, Pa, I only made it as far as the Milk Farm in Dixon, California. I was stranded there when a tire blew out. The rim was twisted and turned, and there was no money to fix it. A local mechanic set the cost of repairs at $65. Well, all I had was enough to get me to Pittsburgh without any glitches. That was enough to eat, sleep and buy gas, which isn't that much money. So, I stayed at the Milk Farm for two weeks after the people at the restaurant said I could work as a soda jerk in the bar. There was free food and a place to sleep. They put me in the bunkhouse with the farm hands and other workers. This was good money,

including my tips. In two weeks, I had $150 and that's fine. From there, I headed up to Lake Tahoe with the intent of continuing on to Pennsylvania soon. I stopped in Tahoe to visit some friends from UNC working at Harvey's Wagon Wheel Casino for the summer. Ronnie Cabot and a couple of girls were there. They recognized me and immediately got me into taking a security guard position. They simply told the security supervisor that I should go to work. Meanwhile, I'm thinking 'do I really want to do this?' They sold me with tales about all the stars and celebrities that come. Actually, the basketball opportunity with the Wrens had passed because there was a timeline for me to show up. I was supposed to be there within two weeks after leaving San Jose. Two weeks at the Milk Farm killed that possibility. I had no way to contact the Wrens' coaches or let anyone know of my problems getting to the tryout. So, that was that.

Tahoe seemed like a good place for me. I note this period because Wayne Newton was working there as a teenager. It was my job to take him around and keep him on the legal side of things. So, no getting drunk or carousing. He wasn't exactly cooperative, but I got to know him pretty well. We formed a friendship that will last. Then I went on a long trip back east with Neal. We drove to Mexico and picked up somebody. That part was very mysterious to me. We drove on to Chapel Hill, North Carolina, then immediately turned around and headed back to Tahoe. It was about a five-day trip with driving all the time. When we got back to Tahoe, they had filled my job at the Wagon Wheel. They said I had to wait for an opening. With that, I went over to the North Shore because they were hiring at the Cal Neva Lodge. The guy took me on right away. He said, "Yeah, we need someone right now." I took my 44 caliber long pistol that was on loan from the Wagon Wheel. (I didn't have to return the pistol until later.) You have to have two things: your pistol, for which you have to show evidence of training and experience, and a certificate of approval from the county. It is all military type stuff. We were deputized by the county. My inclination was to see how things went at the Cal Neva. Well, it was a fascinating summer filled with meeting all kinds of stars like Juliet Prowse and Ann Margaret. Ann Margaret was under age and required special attention to keep all of her activities in compliance with the law. She was another one who didn't want to listen to her security. I had to be a little forceful with her and even wrote up a report documenting her behavior. It's funny because the next day Sinatra stops by to talk. He says, "Skipper, I don't want my singing friends being harassed." The problem was not me. It was what the law allows. At 19 years old, you can't hang around a bar for more than twenty minutes when there is drinking. Frank, of course, didn't care about any rules or restrictions on what he wanted to do and who he wanted to do it with. Because of his mafia connections and the mafia money in the casinos, Frank didn't accept that laws and conventions applied to him. We soon got past all of that hassle and conflict of interest and on to a more cooperative footing. Later, Frank sent me a letter of congratulations when I graduated from Tri State University in Angola, Indiana. The letter said he was happy I took his advice and returned to school. Calling me "Skipper" in his letter was special because Frank's use of it comes from his relationship with the Kennedys and the fact that JFK was in charge of PT109. He also referred to Peter Lawford and some others in the circle as Skipper, too. Incidentally, Neal has been doing quite well here at South Lake Tahoe with me. When Iggles moved to Los Angeles, Neal left San Jose and came to Tahoe to live with me. I got him into Bill's card room working as a poker shill—essentially performing as an accomplice of the gambling house and acting as an enthusiastic customer enticing others to play as much as possible. He really enjoyed this type of work, so he committed to staying on in Tahoe. One day, Kenny showed up and they took off heading for Los Angeles to rejoin Iglói and his group of runners with the LA

Track Club. Guess I should've expected that. I knew it was going to be a long time before Neal and I would connect this closely again. Later, I saw Neal after he moved to Vegas on one of my travels back to Pennsylvania. One time, I was transporting a car for AAA. I had been out there on a job interview after graduating from Tri State. Del Monte flew me to LA with the expectation that I would accept the job offer. They gave me a one-way ticket. I was using the AAA car delivery opportunity as a cheap way to get back to Mansfield, Ohio. I picked up the car in LA. Some woman wanted it delivered for her son with some of his belongings in the back. Even though I have to go to where they want the car delivered, it's worth it. Cleveland was the destination and they paid $100 plus gas. I can easily get from Cleveland to Mansfield where there was a job I wanted. I decided to go through Las Vegas to get together with Neal one last time and see what he's into. He had a number of things going and couldn't connect that night. For some strange reason, we decided to meet in the morning in a parking lot at Lake Mead. We sat talking in the car most of the day. We ate sandwiches and eventually shared a bottle of Jack Daniels pulled from the trunk of Neal's car. Neal is not a big drinker, but JD is Neal's liquor of choice. The sun was long gone over the horizon when we decided to leave.

Kenny:

I mulled over Dubby Holt's full scholarship at Idaho State University, arranged by Tom Smith, who succeeded Litchen. The vision was to find university housing and marry Mary, my longtime girlfriend from Pensacola. Plans progressed—accepting an offer in late September. En route to Idaho, I paused at Hertz's Tahoe apartment with Neal. Since mountain weather dropped to freezing, he leaned toward joining Iggles. On Saturday, I drove east on Interstate 80 with all my possessions. When reaching Battle Mountain in Nevada's desolation, I stopped and walked behind the car to piss. Gusting freezing north winds cut through my clothing, chilling my ass to the bone.

That portended Idaho's winter conditions. On climbing back inside the car's warmth, quick frozen ideas thawed, deciding the next moves. After fifteen minutes of sitting and thinking, the Volvo turned west on 80, back to South Lake Tahoe, and I abandoned Pocatello. Hertz's empty couch was available in Tahoe until we determined future steps.

Neal:

After discussing my taking Nevada University's (Reno) full scholarship, Kenny and I rolled out my Chevy on the 450-mile trek to rejoin Coach Iglói's group. They moved earlier, becoming the LATC. We were back on a mission that felt right, and our first stop became Burbank, right before LA! Gene Zubrinsky ("Z"), an SJS friend, lived there with his parents. Z held world records in jumping heights over his head. A 7 ft high jumper, we knew him well enough to request a bed and food. Their hospitality enabled us to find an LA area apartment.

Two weeks with Z's parents became an unexpected adventure because they were quite a pair. His father possessed immeasurable patience, endless generosity, and understanding. In real life, he was an intelligent man often portrayed in theatrical productions as an unheralded, unfulfilled hero. In an instant, Kenny drew to Z's father as he did his own. They possessed a similar caring temperament. Z's mother was the sweetest, but she was on him 110%. We knew, though tolerating our presence, she remained wary. Our vagabond lifestyle triggered concern. The possibilities of influencing her only child to continue errant behavior were ever-present. Her son created sufficient anxiety without our help.

Aware of being burdensome, we tried limiting our dependence on Zubrinsky's family and hurried to find an apartment to sustain our ability to return if needed. Z's father was happy to lend support, and, with justified reservations, his mother agreed.

Near Coast Highway, off Pico Boulevard in Santa Monica, we found a converted garage with single beds, a small kitchen, a refrigerator, and a two-burner stove. Toilets and showers filled a garage next door. We shared facilities with Sam, an alienated amateur philosopher who wanted to escape this "mad-mad world." He acted depressed; missing his children strained his mental stability after losing everything through nasty divorce proceedings. Neither ancient nor modern philosophy could release him from suffering those losses. Sam talked about Socrates and Bertrand Russell, mixed with Freudian analysis, trying to practice on us. We weren't interested, owing to running as intensely as we did, but he contributed by taking us to Wilhelm's two-story house. Wilhelm, a huge retired German chef, had vast knowledge covering philosophy, history, classical music, and Olympic sports. He wanted elevated conversation while cooking five-star cuisine.

Regular Sunday afternoons featured classical music, discussing experiences with Iglói, and recounting Saturday competitions. In particular, he understood dedication to running, knew all about the Hungarians' achievements, and "got it" regarding sacrifices. Many people judged us as crazy or bums. After hearty dinners, we were sent home with containers of leftovers. We felt Wilhelm's gourmet cooking and Marilyn Conkle's (Tony's goddess wife) delicious pasta dinners guaranteed our survival. Other than people's generosity, innovative scrounging to meet needs was normal. Staple meals came each week from Campbell's Tomato Soup, Velveeta Cheese, and Sunbeam Bread coupons in Santa Monica's Newspaper (Outlook). Each month, Chicken Pie coupons provide special treats. Night after night, our staple diet was tomato soup with grilled cheese sandwiches.

We found taking hundred-count newspaper bundles deposited on Pico Boulevard at Lincoln most efficient. They dropped papers off at 4:30 a.m. on Thursdays. (We clipped free grocery offers before replacing stacks by 5:00 a.m.) Armed with coupons, we hit multiple stores daily, stocking up on freebies! Our alley garage apartment wasn't much, but with scavenged food, we fashioned independence. After three days, we settled enough to join Iggles' group. Life stabilized sufficiently for focusing on running while continuing formal education at Santa Monica City College. Zubrinsky arrived, enabling us to move into a house on Pier Avenue. He left home soon after we set up there, delighted at being independent. As he tells it:

Soon after our two or three-week stay in Burbank, the three of us relocated to Santa Monica, where we lived for a year and did some training at the local high school. When I came, they moved from the garage apartment into a house. Ken and I affiliated with the Southern California Striders, then the premier West Coast track club, and through the influence of Striders javelin thrower Dr. Steve Seymour, plant physician at Continental Can Company's facility in East Los Angeles, we gained employment there. (This was before there was a Santa Monica Freeway, and most of our commute across Los Angeles was on surface streets.) My job was in quality control, where I sampled metal can bodies from the production lines and tested their seams and interior spray coverage. Ken was relegated to the basement, where, using an implement with about a dozen pegs at the end of it, he transferred cans (as they came down a chute from the floor above with one end already affixed) into large boxes destined for the facilities that would fill them and apply the tops; it was a repetitive, mind-numbing activity. Ken and I never discussed it, but I have always felt that racial considerations got me the better job. In any case, it was during our time in Santa Monica that Ken became the dear friend that he remains to this day.

Meanwhile, a significant threat hung over me as West Chester's Draft Board served notice with the Vietnam War underway. My dissent started from day one. Objecting to unwise government actions goes with that, and no U.S. involvement made sense. A look at our history tells it. They are not sacrificing me!

Kenny:
LATC's band established their base at southwest Los Angeles' Rancho La Cienega Park. Team composition carried over from SCURVY, with lead characters unchanged except adding Bobby Seaman. We resumed supporting roles. Our program, however, became different, with volumes of long intervals

(from 440s to miles) with less intensity, building strength through winter. We experienced immediate improvement, which surprised us. I marveled at our growing strength. Fitness couldn't go better. We began understanding processes and how our stars could do so well. Beatty, for example, was peaking to break Ron Delany's indoor mile record. Now, we didn't doubt the success of Mihái's project. Beatty and others were more than ready. Those with him, like Grelle and Dave Martin, had equal abilities. However, they would sacrifice by carrying Beatty to a new indoor mile standard in less than four minutes.

Jim Grelle, one of Bowerman's greats from Oregon, joined us in San Jose. His Procter & Gamble sales representative position benefited our collective. He brought endless soap and personal hygiene products. Neal and I, carrying elites through swift pieces, felt important. We continued that role upon arriving at Rancho. We were proverbial rabbits during essential high-speed parts. When Beatty went under four minutes at the Los Angeles Sports Arena, we were as proud as anyone. Great satisfaction came from helping world-contending teammates succeed. That's when I saw inevitably competing at that level soon. 1962's track season promised to tell the tale. I was on course to become the first African American to break four minutes in the mile. (Before the Youth Village team moved to LA from San Jose, Neal and I traded the lead on a mass 1320 time trial. We took Beatty, Grelle, Tabori and the others thru at 2:56 in flats and eased off to finish the mile in 4:06.)

As workouts progressed, talk circulated of needing a 400/440 man at Grelle's alma mater. LATC financiers seemed keen on contributing to Oregon claiming 1963's NCAA title. A 47.5 as a freshman, finishing 6th in California's J.C. Championships, made me our Club administration's choice to help Oregon. There was value in going there besides earning a degree because Bowerman's program included practices from Iglói. There was a symbiotic relationship. I was returning to Iggles whenever out of school. Hesitation brought hostility from Los Angeles Track Club's executive powers. Upon declining to seek a spot in Eugene, dismissing me didn't take long.

The problem was they promised my services to Oregon. Officials talked with Coach daily, more often than usual. One had glasses, distinguishing them. The guy eyeing me graduated from OU. For not going, Track Club founders acted angry! They wanted me gone! From my perspective, giving up self-determination and bowing to the wishes of these presumptuous white men wasn't worth it. Planning my future without knowing or agreeing struck me as bosses exercising white privilege. While leaving constituted sacrificing an international track career, I didn't think twice. LATC officers promised use of my talent displayed arrogance and condescension. They discussed me as if I was not there. The bespectacled man led, behaving as if they owned me, wanting me to know it and feel powerless—a slave at auction. Mihái said nothing. If he had suggested it, I'd have gone straight away. Neither Beatty nor Grelle nor anyone else mentioned it. If either had asked me, I would have gone. No official Oregon communication arrived. That could have gotten me there. The way scheming played out showed others were also wary of LATC administrator machinations. While figuring those controlling attempts as abusing power, I never expected to encounter an authoritarian mentality with a civilian non-profit organization. There was nothing like that with Father Schmidt's Santa Clara Valley Youth Village. LATC management experiences became well-taught lessons in self-respect. I elected freedom, moving forward toward becoming as much as I could be on my own. That meant continuing alone using what Iglói, my Zen master of running, taught. Financiers dismissing me from the LATC came and expelled Neal. These guys judged runners according to their wishes. Since arriving, they labeled Neal borderline desirable, even though he was Mihái's first American disciple. He committed his running life to Hungarian hands before anyone else. Judgments against him ignored that fact. Rather than seeking employment, his income came from poker. Los Angeles County had many card rooms. So, as survival worked in San Jose, gambling supported our minimalist lifestyle devoted to workouts. His occupation was legal and not frowned upon here. In LA, card rooms were abundant, and considered an acceptable profession (we thought) for earning an income.

We heard via Beatty and Grelle that gambling's legality wasn't acceptable enough for self-righteous type club officials. Star members said club officers considered playing poker professionally a problem, not me. "Owners" included me because of our super-tight relationship. Sure, I'd leave, even if what they sought was getting him out. That goes without saying. The reasons behind expulsions weren't honest. LATC controllers manufactured an unacceptable moral character with someone shunning regular employment. How dismissal applied to me, a school bus driver, was puzzling unless one recognized club financiers' questionable purposes. They founded the club for selfish reasons. While presenting themselves as noble sportsmen, benevolence, as far as we could tell, skewed toward benefiting them personally. Looking at each, they could never become outstanding athletes. Their successes in establishing profitable businesses left them wanting relationships with accomplished trackmen. They craved vicarious associations with athletic successes by LATC troops. Power managing a notable Club enabled palming off themselves to news organizations as "sports aficionados." Next we know, these men make broadcast television commentary when LATC stalwarts compete. Months after dismissal and before returning to San Jose, Coach Iglói sat with me during LA's Coliseum Relays. We relaxed, talking, and the coach asked at length about training. I pulled logs out of my shoe bag, fashioned from tenure under him. When parting, he handed me a business card and said he wanted me to return to training under him. By then, Pasadena A.A.'s management supported us. Knowing we were outcasts, someone advised us to call Pasadena's "Twin Winton's." The brothers were recruiting and enlarging their team. Prosperous businesses yielded money to support Pasadena's club matching the Southern California Striders. Don and Ross Winton deserve credit for reinvigorating my enthusiasm. Wrongful dismissal from the LATC created disillusionment; however, Pasadena's support encouraged me to continue. 880s (1:50's) on Pasadena teams were good at the Mount Sac Relays and Coliseum meet. Mihái saw I had remained committed and complimented me on successfully conditioning myself. That meant an awful lot, bolstering my appreciation for him. Although valuing his compliments, understanding, and offer, I wouldn't return after being cast out. The future, competing under Pasadena's banner while completing an AA Degree, was set. Then, I'd take a 4-year scholarship.

MIHALY IGLOI

COACH - LOS ANGELES TRACK CLUB

3904 SANTA ROSALIA DRIVE

AXMINSTER 3-6572   LOS ANGELES 8, CALIFORNIA

Another reason Santa Monica stood out was I left there after nine months without making a single new friend! I attributed that to the need to display more income. The norm seemed to be Black people acting high-classed with expensive clothes and automobiles. Those props weren't how I defined self-worth or gained anyone else's value. For someone as poor as me, this place could never become friendly. San Jose, a large city with a small-town atmosphere, felt more accommodating. Above everything, Iglói's ultimate gift was teaching about training. Coaching myself and others at a high level was possible with his workouts. Mihái's teaching was there to draw upon moving forward like any possessed knowledge.

608 Briggs. Street.
Harrisburg Penna.

Helen.
Just a few lines to let grandie know that I saw
the man about the taxe. And he said If It was
like I stated the lawyer I was right about you did
not have to paid on the house but you would have
to paid taxes on the car. But he said you should
go and see them up at the court house and
find out just what taxs you would have to paid.
And If It was only on the car of cause you
would have to paid that but If they insist
upon you paying taxes on the house then she
should get her lawyer to go up there If
her. Now that is all I could find out about that.
I am sending you the money for you. I am
sending It alway. And you can do what you
see fit to do with It. I hope you are feeling well
and hope Jery and the rest of the family are well
will see you on friday. I am alright and it
is very cold up here. I saw Martin. If you are
go to the hospital before I come home and If it is
a boy? It Kenneth it is a nice name dont you.
think so. I close with love and kiss Jerry for
me and tell him to be a good bay
                              I remain
                              Mollie.

How Kenny got his name from his father.

Dory Miller

Kenny in ElksBand

Daddy leads unit in Elks Parade

CERTIFICATE of PROMOTION

This certifies that _Kenneth Noel_

has been promoted

from the _9th_ year to the _10th_ year

of the _Junior_ DEPARTMENT

of the _St Paul's Bapts SS_ School at _West Chester Pa_

October 5th 1947 _Mrs C. Knight_

D. G. Carkin _Rev J. C Clark_

10 year indoctrination

The African

Lawn Nigger
(wikicommons)

Mr Harold. E.
Zimmerman

COATES AND AVON

Three Marks Shattered In Annual County Meet

Pierson Leaps 6:03 ½ For Class A Record; Javelin And Discus Standards Set In B

Three records fell — one in Class A and two in Class B — and one standard was matched as Coatesville High and Avon-Grove High emerged Saturday afternoon on West Chester High Athletic Field as champions of the 24th annual competition for Chesmont League and Chester county high school track and field honors.

Neither the Red Raiders of Coach Walt Funk nor the trackmen from the rose growing area of southern Chester county had a breeze to title rating.

Coatesville, which shared the Class A or Chesmont crown with West Chester High in 1955 and won it outright in five consecutive prior years, got its stiffest competition from Pottstown Saturday. The Trojans, in fact, outscored the Coates in firsts, 5 to 4, but could not match the overall balance of the Raiders.

Coates Total 50

To win Coach Funk's lads rolled up a total of 50 points. Pottstown finished with 42½ and West Chester, limited to three firsts, collected 29. Conestoga, Phoenixville and Downingtown finished in order.

Avon-Grove, in Class B, won five events and accounted for the two new records in that division. Kennett Square and Oxford each tabbed four firsts. Nabbing their fourth straight Class B championship, the Avon-Grove athletes amassed 51 points. Kennett checked in with 46 and Oxford with 42. Unionville, returning to track competition this spring after a lapse of several years, gained only three points.

Good High Jumping

The new Class A record was set by Art Pierson, six-foot-four Coatesville high jumper, when he soared 6 ft. 3 ½ in. to beat his own mark of 6 ft. even, set last spring. Not only Pierson but the boys who finished second and

CLOSEST FINISH of the 24th annual track and field meet for Chesmont League and Chester county high school athletes is shown in middle photo with Jim Baxter, left, of Coatesville High and Neal Chappelle breasting the tape in a 2:05.7 880-yard run. Their time was identical but the finish judges gave Baxter the win on grounds that their eyes told them his body was first to touch the cord.

On the left, Don Endy, individual is shown safely ahead on his way in low hurdles. He also won the 1_ jump to power Pottstown High in team title.

Championship Summaries

CLASS A

120-High Hurdles—1. Don Endy, Pottstown; 2. Jack Williams, West Chester; 3. Bob Van Horn, Phoenixville; 4. Ron Puhl, Pottstown. 0:15.3.

100—1. Ken Noel, West Chester; 2. Dick Poff, Coatesville; 3. John Barber, Pottstown; 4. Richard Jackson, Coatesville. 0:10.4.

Mile—1. Jack Williams West Chester; 2. Gordon Egolf, Coatesville; 3. Jim Beitz, Conestoga; 4. Chas. Frank, Conestoga. 4:44.5.

440—1. Noel, West Chester; 2. Warner Blair, Conestoga; 3. Dave Thomas, Pottstown; 4. Erwin Rubincam, Downingtown. 0:52.1.

180-Low Hurdles — 1. Endy, Pottstown; 2. Van Horn, Phoenixville; 3. Puhl, Pottstown; 4. Jacks, Coatesville. 0:21.4.

880—1. Jim Baxter, Coatesville; 2. Neal Chappelle, West Chester; 3. Elmer Tredwell, Coatesville; 4. Juck Eachus, Phoenixville. 2:05.7.

220—1. Barber, Pottstown; 2. Poff, Coatesville; 3. Puhl, Pottstown; 4. Rubincam, Downingtown. 0:23.6.

Mile Relay—1. Conestoga (Dave Flood, Ken Talbot, Jim White, Warner Blair); 2. Coatesville; 3. Pottstown; 4. Downingtown. 3:43.

880—Novice Relay — Phoenix-

50; Pottstown, 42½; West Chester, 29; Conestoga, 18½; Phoenixville, 13; Downingtown, 4.

CLASS B

100—1. Vaughn Morgan, Avon-Grove; 2. Viscount Nelson, Oxford; 3. Francis Taylor, Kennett; 4. Ed. Lee, Oxford. 0:10.4.

Mile—1. Mike D'Orazio, Kennett; 2. Bill Reiter, Kennett; 3. John Clendenin, Oxford; 4. Rod Nixon, Oxford. 5:01.4.

440—1. Richard Kellett, Oxford; 2. Charles White, Avon-Grove; 3. Bill Gates, of Kennett Square; 4. Dennis Rose, Unionville. 0:55.7.

180 Low Hurdles — Nelson Oxford; 2. Louis Lee, Avon-Grove; 3. Bill Draper, Oxford. 4. Cliff Losee, Kennett. 0:22.8. (Equalled record set by Willard McKim, Avon-Grove, in 1954).

880—D'Orazio, Kennett; 2. Ron Thompson, Avon-Grove; 3. Stan Jones, Oxford; 4. Jim Christie, of Kennett. 2:12.6.

220—1. Morgan, Avon-Grove; 2. Taylor, Kennett Square; 3. Lee, Oxford; 4. Linwood Martin, of Kennett. 0:23.9.

Mile—1. Kennett (Mike Weinmayr, Wick Peacock, Bill Gates, Chas. Bernard); 2. Avon-Grove; 3. Oxford. 3:49.4.

Lower Merion Sets Hurdle Record
In Sweeping 6 of 10 Relay Events

Team Winner

Lower Merion High School's track athletes swept six of the ten events and set one record as they played host to the suburban schools in their annual relay carnival yesterday on the General H. H. (Hap) Arnold Memorial Field at Church road and Montgomery pike in Ardmore.

The Ardmore athletes set the only new standard in the 480-yard shuttle hurdle relay. They hung up victories in the 440, mile, half mile, shot put and broad jump relays.

Beat Coatesville's Mark

The record breaking team in the shuttle relay included Don Jackson, Hugh Barr, Dave Satinsky and George Hearn. They negotiated the obstacles in 56 seconds flat to shatter the former mark of 57 seconds made by Coatesville in 1932. The Coatesville team was Mac Harvey, Cliff Reeves, Jim Lipp and Rod Percy.

Hearn and Jackson were members of two other Lower Merion relay quartets. Jackson competed on the 440 and mile teams. Hearn carried the stick in the 440 and half-mile tests. Tom Anderson, Nicky Stuart and Bob McNeill were also members of two Lower Merion relay winners.

Samango, Simon Victors

Al Samango and Bill Simon took the shot put with a combined distance of 92 feet, 9 inches, with Walt Reed and Tom Royster taking the broad jump honors by putting together 40 feet, 6½ inches on their leaps.

The other relay winners were Upper Darby in the medley, West Chester in the two mile and Norristown in the pole vault. Abington and Springfield (Delco) tied for first in the high jump.

West Chester's Neal Chappell turns the job over to Jack Williams for anchor leg of two mile relay race yesterday at the Lower Merion High School Carnival at Ardmore. Williams took care of things in fine shape, winning the event. West Chester won in 8:51.2.

Senior Jack Williams, shown above anchoring West Chester High to victory in the two-mile relay at Downingtown Friday ahead of the Whippets' Dave Attilio), again ran the gun lap and the Warriors romped to victory in the two mile relay event in Saturday's 10th renewal of the Lower Merion Relays at Ardmore.

Williams and his running mates—Ken Noel, Bob Harris and Neal Chappelle—were clocked at 8:51, breaking the West Chester record of 8:52.9, set at Downingtown the day before. The previous mark was 8:53.2, chalked up by Noel, Don Falini, Williams and Norm Bell in 1955.

Lower Merion Team Breaks Mark
In Low Shuttle Hurdles Relays

Setting a record in the 473-yard shuttle low hurdle relay, Lower Merion High School dominated the 10th edition of its annual relay carnival, gaining six triumphs in 10 events.

George Hearn, Don (Dusky) Jackson, Hugh Barr and Dave Satinsky comprised the team that set the meet's lone record of 56 seconds as a strong backstretch wind hampered the runners.

The mark clipped a full second from the 1932 Coatesville record.

Hearn and Jackson combined with Nicky Stuart and Tom Anderson to carry the major load for the Aces in gaining four relay triumphs. Each ran on three teams and each took the anchor position in victories of 9:48.4, 440: 3:36, mile, and 1:34.4, 880. Bob McNeill was added to the mile and 880 combinations. Jackson anchored the 440, Stuart the mile and Anderson the 880.

West Chester won the two-mile with Jack Williams running anchor after a lead had been compiled by Ken Noel, Bob Harris and Neal Chappelle. The time was 8:51.2.

Upper Darby, District cross country champions, strode away with the distance medley with Art Saxten, John Bahm, Art Polanchuck and Dick Harris behind.

Neal robbed of 880 Championship
(Daily Local News)

Mihály IGLÓI 1957

Neal at UNC

Chappel Winner In Cross Country

Neal Chappel, West Chester, won the cross country race of 5.2 miles sponsored by the Middle Atlantic Road Runners Club Sunday in Woodbury.

Chappel led all the way and was clocked in 27 minutes and 18 seconds. Several hundred yards behind him in second place was Joe Stefanowicz, Ridley Park, in 27.58.

Pete League, Pleasantville, N. J., was third; Bob Chambers, Philadelphia, fourth; Harry Berkowitz, Camden, fifth, and Larry Delaney, Cheltenham High School physics teacher, sixth.

Order of finish:
1—Neal Chappel, West Chester —— 27.18
2—Joe Stefanowicz, Phila. —— 27.58
3—Pete League, Pleasantville —— 28.21
4—Bob Chambers, Phila. —— 28.28
5—Harry Berkowitz, Camden —— 28.42
6—Larry Delaney, Pennsauken —— 28.55
7—Bruce Williams, West Chester — 30.05
8—Leon Dreher, Phila. —— 30.21
9—Robert Fuhrman, Phila. —— 30.51
10—Frank Kelly, Phila. —— 31.11

Winter Break training

CAROLINA SWEEP—Carolina's Howard Kahn, Neal Chappell and Dave Scurlock, left to right above, achieved a sweep in 880-yard run trials at the Indoor Games yesterday, each placing first in his heat. (Staff Photo by Tom Inman).

UNC 1, 2, 3

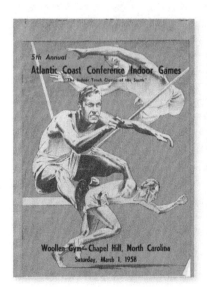

ACC Indoor Games

5th Annual
Atlantic Coast Conference Indoor Games
"The Indoor Track Classic of the South"
Woollen Gym—Chapel Hill, North Carolina
Saturday, March 1, 1958

14th
ANNUAL
PHILADELPHIA
INQUIRER
GAMES
JANUARY 24
1958
CONVENTION
HALL
Souvenir Magazine 50¢
SPONSORED BY THE PHILADELPHIA INQUIRER CHARITIES, INC.

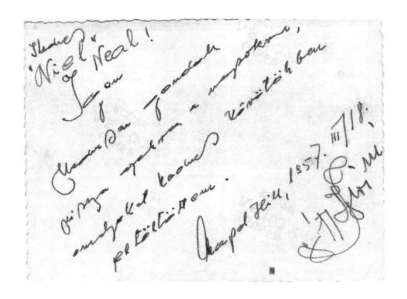

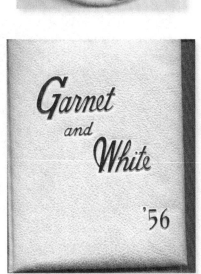

University of North Carolina Athletic Association

1960

This is to Certify that

Neal Ralph Chappell

is entitled to this Numeral Award for his excellent and faithful work on the

1957 *Track* Team.

University of North Carolina Athletic Council

C. P. Erickson
Director of Athletics

Oliver K. Cornwell
Chairman

Joseph T. Hilton
Coach

University of North Carolina Athletic Association

1961

This is to Certify that

Neal Ralph Chappell

is entitled to this Numeral Award for his excellent and faithful work on the

1957 *Cross Country* Team.

University of North Carolina Athletic Council

Chas. P. Erickson
Director of Athletics

Oliver K. Cornwell
Chairman

Dale Ranson
Coach

JIM BEATTY ANCHORS TEAM TO NEW AMERICAN RECORD
Youth Village runner laps Ken Noel at conclusion of four-mile relay race

Pasadena AA

Neal's 8K National Championship

1964 NCAA

OPHR Principals

'Slim' Makes a Good Living
Playing Poker in Las Vega

LAS VEGAS — The man walks into the card room of the Dunes Hotel and quickly sizes up the action.

His dress is casual; neat but not pretentious. He doesn't have the telltale wrinkles of most tourists' trousers and his manner indicates he isn't in a hurry.

The time is a little after midnight, just about the time he goes to work. He has no set hours. But when he works, he might be at his job for 36 hours straight. Tonight, the action is small and he simply watches the players and the cards.

Gamblers in this town know him as Slim and they have a great respect for his ability. Slim, in his mid-30s, is a professional gambler. His only game is poker and is one of the best in this part of the country at it.

A testimonial to his ability as a card player is his longevity in Las Vegas. He's been here more than 10 years and his yearly earnings are comparable to that of a successful New York stockbroker.

Slim's earning power is in direct correlation to the tourist delusion that he can go to Vegas and leave as a winner.

...winners never leave

Vegas," says Slim, "because when you win there is no reason to leave."

Slim is a part of a small but select group of men in this country who approach gambling strictly in business terms. They know the odds, they know owther men's weaknesses, and they possess the prime ingredient of a professional gambler — discipline.

"There is no great mystery to making a living at poker," says Slim. "Basically, everyone will get the same hot and cold run of cards over a year's period. The secret is discipline — knowing when you're cold and having the ability to walk away from the table no matter how lucky you feel or how much money is on the table."

Slim has won and lost small fortunes at card tables in Las Vegas. His success lies in the fact the has won more than he's lost.

"My goal," he says, "is to make sure that you and everyone else in the game are in my pots and to make sure that I'm never in your pots."

Translated, that means smart poker, not getting drawn into a $50,000 pot when you're sitting back with

a low pair or three o kind, and then getting bu when the luy on your r beats you with a full ho kings over jacks.

Slim has studied all f of gambling with the cl thoroughness of a mathe cian. He knows the od every casino game in ence. For him, the game of chance that c played successfully is p

"The best odds of al casino games is craps Slim. "If you score first roll, it's time to But no one ever doe there on, it's all dowr all in the house's favc

Slim has one theo casino gamblers wl house doesn't like That is — everyor limit on their losse one sets a limit on nings.

Slim says anyone will give you two b for passage of Nev casino gambling r this November.

"And as soon as their doors," he the trace of a sm poker face, "ever the country will take off the hous be one of the first.

U.S. Track & Field and Cross Country Coaches Association

1964 All-Americans College Outdoor Track & Field

Event	Gender	Last Name	First Name	School
100 Yard Dash				
	Men			
		Bryant	Marv	California State University, Fresno
		Newman	Darel	California State University, Fresno
		Workman	Sam	California State University, Fresno
		Stebbins	Richard	Grambling State University
220 Yard Dash				
	Men			
		Workman	Sam	California State University, Fresno
		Hayes	Robert	Florida A&M University
		Stebbins	Richard	Grambling State University
		Roberts	Ed	North Carolina Central University
440 Yard Dash				
	Men			
		Alverson	Constantine	Central State University
		Owens	Donald	Grambling State University
		Davis	Brian	Lamar University
		Hawthorne	Nate	Mount Union College
880 Yard Run				
	Men			
		LeBlanc	Joe	Lamar University
		Fox	Jim	Mount Union College
		Noel	Kenneth	Texas Southern University
		Schneider	Ed	Truman State University
Mile				
	Men			
		Schipper	Bill	California State University, Chico
		Crowley	Bill	Long Beach State University
		Riley	Gavin	San Diego State University

Cross Country Championship

Carlsbad 5K

Victory at Valley Forge

National 10K Champions—Joe, Bob, Neal and Kenny

Neal leads a tour at Tahoe
(The Tahoe Tribune)

Three World Records include 4x1500, and 4x1600 Relays:
Ken Noel, Gene Antonides.

NAACP
California Hawaii
STATE CONFERENCE

Rick L. Callender, Esq.
President

Reverend Jethroe Moore II
1st Vice President

Alyssa Smith
2nd Vice President

Naomi Rainey Pierson
3rd Vice President

LaJuana Bivens
Secretary/State Director

Ida M. Johnson
Assistant Secretary

Olivia Verrett
2nd Assistant Secretary

Carolyn Veal-Hunter
Treasurer

Satia Austin
Area Director - Southeast

Darrell Goode
Area Director - Southwest

Delois Richards
Area Director - Coastal

Dave Smith
Area Director - North

Regina Smith
Area Director - Central

Freddye Davis
Area Director - West

Alice A. Huffman, PhD
President Emeritus

April 19, 2023

Dr. Kenneth Noel

RE: California Hawaii State Conference of the NAACP 11th Annual Legacy Hall of Fame Ceremony

Dear Dr. Noel:

Greetings on behalf of the California Hawaii State Conference of the NAACP. Congratulations! We would like to induct you into our Legacy Hall of Fame. Our 11th Annual Legacy Hall of Fame Ceremony will be held Saturday, June 24, 2023, at the Sheraton Grand Hotel located at 1230 J St. Sacramento, CA 95814. This annual event allows us to honor outstanding community leaders who have fought tirelessly to advance civil rights. We would like to honor your work with the Olympic Project for Human Rights. Dr. Harry Edwards, Tommie Smith and John Carlos will also be inducted during this ceremony.

We will celebrate and express our gratitude for you and your legacy's impact on making California and Hawaii a better place for all. We will also bring together NAACP members, corporate partners, supporters, and future leaders of the Youth & College Division.

The event schedule is as follows:
5:30pm - 6:30pm VIP/Sponsor Reception with Honorees in the Carr Room
6:30pm - 9:00pm Legacy Hall of Fame Awards Dinner in the Magnolia Room

In regards to your accommodations, we will provide Black Car transportation to and from the event (if needed), hotel accommodations for two nights at the event hotel and reimbursement not to exceed $200.00 per day during your stay in Sacramento.

Thank you for your sacrifice in the fight against racism in the United States. You continue to be a source of pride and inspiration for the community, the California State Conference of the NAACP, and those we serve.

We also send this letter as an electronic agreement confirming your acceptance and attendance to your Legacy Hall of Fame celebration in addition to the terms of what the CA/HI NAACP will provide for you. We ask that you sign this document electronically by April 21, 2023.

Brothers of the Wind

CHAPTER
ELEVEN

Back to San Jose and Forward

*The forces of liberation are served even
if a message of liberation, freedom and
humanity touches only one person.*

Kenny:

My relationship with Thomas and Joyce Brown made returning to San Jose from Los Angeles easy in 1962. I met them when joining Santa Clara Valley Youth Village's team. Thomas was my hero as a high school senior who became my teammate four years later. In 1956, Neal touted a fantastic race for California's high school 880 Championship. It involved Tom Brown in the most significant High School half-mile to that date. Jerry Siebert from Willets won, running 1:53.8. Tom, from Merced, finished fourth. He equaled the time of the third-place finisher. Half-miles under two minutes were unknown elsewhere before then. We thought such teenage performances were impossible. East Coast teens had yet to approach those times. Neal's and my bests were 2:05. George Wright, a noted author, teacher, and track analyst, says:

> Many people still consider 1956's meet the greatest ever. There have been several outstanding State Meets. Yet, I understand the lasting importance of the 1956 meet was that the competition across the schedule represented a breakthrough in talent, execution, and depth. We should see Tom Brown as part of raising the talent level in high school track and field for the future.

Landing in San Jose, plus becoming Tom's friend, felt incredible. We connected with Tom on and off the track. He and Joyce had three children, with their fourth planned. Everyone welcomed me as part of their family. You could describe them as the salt of the earth! Their roots were Arkansan carried forward by settling on the San Joaquin Valley's rural lands. Coming to California resulted from the great migration leaving the 1930s mid-western Dust Bowl. Their core values focused on family, work, shared hardship, and perseverance. They were our population's best folks! When returning to San Jose, their tiny apartment had scant space. I slept in the upper right kid's room bunk. While Thomas earned starvation wages as a Weld Grinder at Food Machinery Company, unemployment checks were my income. We were destitute, surviving off simple provisions. We struggled to pay rent and survive on a low nutrition diet of oatmeal, beans, and rice. Pilfered from nearby farms, we added produce. Our diet included more than enough corn and cabbage, plucked from neighbor fields, often cooked with pork fat. Tom and I hunted squirrels inhabiting the east foothills forests, bagging wild meat to bolster stews, recalling poor folks' country living. Every penny of my government check went to rent and food costs. Too often, there wasn't enough.

We did quality intervals and races through the summer, competing in Stanford's All-Comers events. A dollar allowed doing multiple 880s or back-to-back miles, getting our buck's worth. Our practice was dominating each heat, taking turns finishing first. There was fun stuff, such as two-man teams racing for an hour, alternating 440s. You rested while your mate ran. If you or your partner went faster, that left less rest between turns. Those made excellent preparation going into 1962's Junior College cross-country season. Endurance building is the focus, knowing that matching Tom was excellent training. We trained by employing Mihái's program from our notebooks, recording his instructions. Training with Tom supported my decision to return to San Jose. LA was friendless.

In July, a janitor's job opened at American Can Company on Third near Keyes Street. They gave me the graveyard shift, paying time-and-a-half. Its major drawback was work cramped my social life, and partying was out. Other issues were odd exercise schedules and sleeping during daylight, making aggressive fitness improvement difficult. Full-time laborers' work conditions lowered the quality of racing at Stanford's All-Comers meets and easing off lost little considering how low-level competition was. In one instance, peak conditioning could have made an August afternoon more consequential. That was when Peter Snell, Olympic 800-meter Champion and world record holder, surprised everyone by joining us at Angell Field (Stanford). Weeks after, an article covering Snell's revered New Zealand mentor, Arthur Lydiard, titled "Coachly Wisdom," by Roy Benson, described Snell's generous engagement:

I learned that the New Zealand Olympians were coming to one of our All-comers meets. They would be stretching their legs against us ham and eggers in our dinky local meet as a break during the long plane trip to Europe to race in the big-time, summer circuit. I seem to recall about 30 of us half milers, mostly high school kids, lining up for that race. It was our chance to tell everyone that we had run against the Olympic champion. Well, I wound up running the race of my life as I came in forth "only" 6 seconds behind Snell. My time was a PR of 1:57. However, much to my embarrassment, Snell made up all the time on me over the last 180 yards. In fact, his kick was so powerful and fast that it almost left the timers too amazed to stop their watches on him. The only reason I was able to still be with Snell and two other leaders at such a late stage of the race was because of Kenny Noel's race strategy.

Kenny is a quarter-miler from San Jose City College who can run 440 yards in the low 47-sec range. He figured that his best chance to beat the Olympic champ was to grab the lead right at the start, slow the pace way down and save himself for a big kick where his quarter miler's speed would off-set the half miler's endurance. Well, he did just that. We came thru the first ¼ mile lap in 58 sec. For Snell, who had set a new world record of 1:46.3 in Rome, this must have felt like, not a jog, but a walk. But it was a perfect pace for me. Things started to pick up the next 220 yards as we came thru the 660 yard split in 1:25. Forty yards later, Snell showed Noel something astonishing: distance runners can develop a sprinter's level of leg speed by training at 100 miles per week. Snell literally left Noel in the dust of Stanford's crushed granite and dirt track when he shifted down into first gear and took off.

Participation involving Snell was special. Racing with him boosted our insignificant venue and highlighted my fragmented career. Schemes, surprising this legendary champion, were no way to treat our esteemed guest.

Fall 1962

Tom Smith (Smitty) took over San Jose City's (SJCC) program after Jim Litchen retired following our 1961 successes. After recounting my history, he accepted I might not join practices but would have availability for Golden Gate Conference (GGC) contests. Having known of me, he saw little wrong.

Night classes were always my thing. That schedule allowed exercising during any waking period, affording necessary study time. Our cross country bunch had potential before my arrival, and I boosted them as solid GGC and Northern California (NorCal) title contenders. Prospects prompted this newspaper article from The City College Times:

JAG HARRIERS BEGIN DRILLS

San Jose City College cross-country coach Tom Smith is whipping his Jaguars into shape for the upcoming Golden Gate Conference season.

The Jags open at home against College of San Mateo Saturday, Oct. 6.

Smith is working with a promising squad that includes lettermen Ron Nelson and Bob Ingram, plus former star Ken Noel, who has re-entered SJCC. Nelson is the school's record holder in the two mile-run (9:45.9) while Noel has turned in a record 47.6 quarter 1:52 half and 4:20 mile.

Among the outstanding freshman are Ron Pennington (Buchser), Ray Medina (Andrew Hill), Jim Sullivan (Camden), Jim Hamner and Dave Temoin (Lincoln), and Gordon Vredenburg (Hilo Hawaii).

(SJCC Times article)

San Mateo (CSM) and San Francisco (SFCC) were league contenders. This undertaking was seven years after competing beyond one mile at West Chester High School. I desired more certainty in my ability to perform over varying terrain. Indeed, superior speed can be decisive when running longer, less demanding races. My strategy was sticking close enough to win by sprinting, but only if someone threatened our team's victory. Otherwise, teammates' winning made everyone more competitive. Not knowing SJCC's personnel or practicing with them makes forming expectations impossible. An early outing against CSM on the Reed-Hillview golf course was ideal. San Mateo's Bulldogs saw themselves as tops. What my teammates thought of me joining without prior contact remained unstated. These guys competed against each other during high school enough to understand individual capabilities. As a stranger, that was my preferred way of starting our relationship. Landing on the scene and surprising everyone suited me.

Smitty had confidence, anticipating success with his instructions on tackling CSM. They bested CCSF, so defeating San Mateo boded well for going against San Francisco. My name wasn't listed because I hadn't gone against San Jose State's frosh.

SAN MATEO MEET INSTRUCTIONS

1. The start is important, get into position early and then settle down.

2. Keep well up in the pack—don't lag. A good team is one that runs together

3. Make your move early. Don't finish with too much. We have run pace quarters and halves, you should know "what your pace is" by this time. Pass quickly, then settle down to pace again. Passing quickly demoralizes an opponent,

4. The mile marks will be plus or minus a few yards, so don't be mislead by the time. I will tell you whether to pick it up or slow down.

5. Take each man one at a time. Remember the bad guys are from San Mateo. We don't want Hamner worrying about Temoin, or Sullivan about Nelson. Worry about San Mateo.

6. Cross country meets are won down the middle. San Mateo beat San Francisco State 24 to 35. They did it by taking 2, 4, 5, 6, 7 and 9. We are going to have to split them up down the middle

7. The tail-enders are going to have to take up the slack. Every man that can pull up tight will help the team. We have a strong first five. We need at least 7. We want a full effort. This is the best team in this school's history talent-wise. We can go all the way. Remember, you can't win them all unless you win the first one.

8. On the basis of last weeks meet with San Jose State this is the order; (we beat them by the way, if you eliminate the Upper classmen, 27-28).

SAN JOSE	SAN MATEO
1. Nelson	1. Jim Huff
2. Vredenburg	2. Larry Peterson
3. Sullivan	3. Sam Rutland
4. Pennington	4. Dave Kamrar
5. Prewitt	5. Frank Porella
6. Valenzuela	6. Clint Miller
7. Hamner	7. Mario Torres

Remember—In the Golden Gate Conference, we have a dual meet Champion and a conference champ. Every meet from now on is very important. Work in the classroom is very, very important. We don't want to have anyone come up ineligible because of grades. Please go to class and get the job done. **BEAT SAN MATEO!**

We excelled at running together and maintaining contact throughout courses, drawing strength from each other and pulling weaker mates into improving. One of our leaders garnered 1st with every dual meet. We finished as undefeated regular champions, bagging five wins.

1962 GOLDEN GATE CONFERENCE CROSS COUNTRY RESULTS

Oct 4th & 5th	San Jose	16	Oct. 25th & 26th	San Mateo	16
	San Mateo	42		Foothill	44
	San Francisco	15		Oakland	27
	Oakland	46		Diablo Valley	28
	Foothill	20		San Jose	22
	Diablo Valley	42		San Francisco	33
Oct 11th & 12th	San Francisco	16	Nov. 1st & 2nd	Foothill	15
	Diablo Valley	42		Oakland	48
	San Mateo	15		San Jose	19
	Oakland	46		Diablo Valley	40
	San Jose	20		San Mateo San	25
	Foothill	42		Francisco	30

Oct. 18th & 19th	San Mateo	21		San Jose City College	5–0
	Diablo Valley	36		College of San Mateo	4–1
	San Francisco	20		San Francisco City College	3–2
	Foothill	42			
				Foothill College	3–2
	San Jose	15			
	Oakland	49		Oakland City College	1–4
				Diablo Valley College	0–5

Since 1961, San Jose's growing Negro student population had recognized my intelligence, reliability, courageousness, and experience, including willingly helping others encountering various problems. Friendships grew within our small collective, including students, jocks, and civilians who got counseled when troubled. Young folks calling me "Dad" or "Father" became an honor. Those labels suggested I was older, wiser, and supportive, but willing to offer criticism if warranted. None used my given name. Later events arising during 1962 gave justification for being so named.

SJCC's basketball program recruited excellent players from the east coast. Most were from Baltimore or Washington, DC. Recruiters implied they had or might get scholarships but didn't promise. There was no J.C. financial aid! Once being stuck here, the only choice was to make things work. There was no money for going home, plus it was too late to enter college elsewhere. San Jose's minority athletes had only themselves as support. Most slept on pallets, floors, or wherever they found space. Living on starvation diets meant begging or stealing food at every opportunity. Disingenuous J.C. representatives readily forced new arrivals into packed housing, meager incomes from working part-time, G.I. Bill checks, or finding girlfriends with funds.

Added burdens, accommodating uninvited guests, exacerbated our tenuous existence. Since arriving, I'd observed valuing Negro athletes limited to their respective sports. Such pigeonholing feels degrading. We (Negroes), sitting around talking, voiced distress over feeling disrespected by white students. These difficult conditions drove me to organize ballplayers and protest. Their coach responded with promises aimed toward staunching rebellion. He presented himself as their helping friend, even when something less occurred. San Jose City's environment, City College student-athletes of colors' personal experiences, including failed promises, dubious communication, and opportunistic inaction by coaches, caused complaints. Responsibility for creating rebellion rested with the basketball coaching staff. Confrontation around players' conditions was probable.

It was raining two days before our perfect cross-country season ended. We took the GGC before the upcoming Northern California Championship near Sacramento (Rocklin). Thursday's workout honed conditioning by jogging indoors, avoiding the rain—or possibly getting sick. Coach Roget came when ready for practice, issued gruff orders directing me to leave. Team members were practicing shooting only days after they rebelled.

In jest, Big Steep (Clarence White) predicted trouble when Roget appeared. Players had experienced that he was capable of significant volatility, and seeing me pissed him off. These coaches acted dictatorial when controlling their gyms. He became hostile when I asked permission to run more laps, getting in my face and screaming, "Get out!" Reflexively, I stood unmoved, face-to-face. Physical threats didn't work, so he called for campus security.

It was amazing how fast they processed expulsion orders. I entered English 1A at 7 p.m., Mr. Burroughs said I must leave. "You're expelled." Burroughs was sympathetic, recognizing institutional racism. He offered to represent me. Though surprising, dismissal didn't prove distressing. Why hadn't uniformed security come? The feeling was odd. Dread of lost opportunity or self-destructing education goals never arose. Shouldn't being expelled be devastating? This development became another obstacle because of oppression! How curious—they acted without a formal hearing. Aren't summary dismissals from educational institutions reserved for criminal acts? Open conflict may not have served best for helping the struggling recruits, yet justifiable. It wasn't my business, but part of our constant struggle to claim humanity. Sleep coming easy signals righteousness.

With NorCal's Cross Country Championships coming in 39 hours, it was a good bet that sensibility would restore my eligibility. They'd never throw away guaranteed conference titles over disobedience when no crime was involved. The following day, Smitty waited, understanding there were valid reasons behind insubordination besides any specifics. Smitty made no judgments, recognizing conditions. He requested tabling resistance and apologizing, securing readmission per V.P. Goldberg's demand. We went to Roget's office, where I mouthed an apology. He called Goldberg, who decreed reinstatement. I'd guess they never did paperwork putting my process into records.

Such sports entities were always corrupt and complicit in exploiting athletes of color. My expulsion could impact basketball because Smitty, teaching PE, could retaliate. East Coast ball players relied on teacher benevolence to maintain eligibility. Acceptable grades depended on instructors overlooking educational shortcomings. We knew which players struggled without college-level academic ability. Familiarity showed that only two could do independent work. Most could only pass courses if granted alternative ways to reach standards. Coach Smith wouldn't hurt innocent young men because of my situation. As the leader of their harrier team, my calculation figured our upcoming state contest balanced or tipped resolution toward my remaining eligible. Coaches' expelling each other's bread-and-butter athletes wasn't sensible, knowing their football and basketball operations exploit minorities. Everyone saw this, although none ever admitted it. Roget interrupted, speaking. To his credit, he stipulated apologizing wasn't me expressing genuine sentiments. I thanked him for conceding that much.

Later practices showed learning from our tête-à-tête by improving treatment for players during his remaining SJCC career. This posture carried into his UC Berkeley position after 1968. While I was pursuing doctoral studies and an active Third World Liberation Front (FLTW) membership, he came under criticism from Black students. At FLTW's hearing, my testimony gave a positive view of his recent efforts in helping athletes.

SJCC's reinstatement was a curious procedure requiring an audience with Vice President Goldberg. After I delivered my faux apology, VP Goldberg summoned me. It was amusing that he acted like we were resolving life-and-death matters, which confirmed they recognized they were exploiting Negroes. The meaningless apology and the disciplinary talk were farcical games. Afterward, none admitted to the ballplayers' poor conditions or offered changes to rectify the exploitation. We played games skirting moral issues. Goldberg studied records, opened a folder, and turned pages. He said, "Your entrance scores are excellent." (I didn't understand that because I had never seen test scores or talked to anyone.) "You should do much better in your classes than your grades show." He continued, "You should get A's but you're only getting C's." I responded, "I don't get that. I thought C's was doing well. I was supposed to be satisfied making C's."

It wasn't comfortable when he said I was intelligent, stating my failure to understand straightforward goals for every student as getting the highest grades possible. Funny, positive changes came from being expelled, and thoughts elevating personal outlooks cascaded upon exiting his office. The future looked demonstrably brighter once I stepped outside, due to experiencing greater consciousness and revising perspectives. From that point, my goals increased to improve academics, as well as sports.

My larger goal became excelling in every aspect of the student-athlete role. Immediate results emerged from developing analytical skills guided by Mr. Burroughs. English 1B explored novels by Mark Twain, Hemingway, and more. My insights and interpretations for analyzing their writings received praise. My mission reset toward becoming every bit a scholar as an athlete, including steering peers to recognize classroom involvement along with sports. When they read sports stories and wanted conversation discussing track meets, I injected ideas related to classes. However, escaping sports' importance was impossible, and there was no denying it is an integral part of student identity or campus life. We achieved our goal by taking NorCal's JC Cross-Country title on November 16 (1962), led by my placing second after making a wrong turn.

SJCC TIMES NOVEMBER 16, 1962

Jags Capture Harrier Title

ROCKLIN—San Jose City College captured its second Northern California Junior College Cross Country Championships in history Saturday against a 14-team field at Sierra College here.

Coach Tom Smith's Jag runners placed four men in the top ten finishers over the three-mile course.

The scores: SJCC 44, City College of San Francisco 50, Foothill 99, San Mateo 122, Fresno C.C. 143, Sacramento C.C. 161, College of Sequoia 185, Sierra 210, American River 241, Reedley 244, Oakland 252, Diablo Valley 274, and Vallejo 293.

The top 10 individual times: Don Cofield, Sierra, 16:08; Ken Noel, 16:16; Ozzie Norris, CCSF, 16:17; Garlon Prewitt, SJCC, 16:18; Charles Oakley, Foothill, 16:21; Gene Plotkin, CCSF, 16:24; Ron Pennington, SJCC, 16:25; Jose Valle, CCSF, 16:26; Ron Nelson, SJCC, 16:27; and Lane Carlton, Fresno, 16:28.

Spring 1963

While soaring from November's success, 1963 half-mile expectations took shape. The goals were simple: win NorCal and State 880s. An article by the City College Times sports editor heralded my campaign's start, printing a flattering story.

I tailored everything toward improving my 880 times. A way of enhancing workouts is not tapering but training through dual meets, electing to run multiple events (mile, a half mile, and 4 x 440 anchor), but only fast enough to win. These plans worked because there was no problem taking NorCal—qualifying for States. On the other hand, combined income steadily declined, barely surviving with the Browns. (After Christmas, we relied on eating oatmeal and cabbage through May. Coach Smith staged school Turkey Trots guaranteeing my winning large birds for the winter holidays.) Vegetables continued flowing from surrounding farms after dark; sometimes, there was fatback or bacon fat as seasoning.

Thursday, March 7, 1963   CITY COLLEGE TIMES—5

Noel Leads Jaguar Spikers in Opener

San Jose City College's track and field team opened their 1963 season last Friday against Fresno City College and Hartnell Junior College of Salinas. The Fresno squad proved to be the superior of the three competing squads as they won the triangular meet held on the Jaguar oval. CC was second in the meet garnering 49 points compared to the winners' 66 and to last place Hartnell's 37.

Tomorrow the Jags travel to Stanford where they will tackle the tough Stanford freshman team along with Reedley Junior College. The first event will begin at 4 o'clock and promises to be an exciting triangular meet.

Fresno put together a 1-2-3 finish in both the hurdle events to capture the team victory. This team from Fresno is regarded by Northern California coaches as one of the strongest track and field powerhouses in Northern California, while Hartnell hails from the Coast Conference.

Almost as always, the ever incomparable Ken Noel put on an outstanding show, as he was a double winner in the mile and 880 events. Noel ran the mile in 4:26 and then turned in a 1:56.8 half

mile. This isn't Ken's best time by far but was enough to outdistance his opponents.

Coach Tom Smith's harriers lacked depth in the majority of field events and proved harmful in their bid for the triangular meet win. However sophomore Al Sequeria of the Jags was another double winner for the meet. Al, the school record holder for the broad jump, won the broad jump event with a jump of 21½ feet. Teammates Ken Neilsen and Steve Jensen placed third and fourth respectively in the broad jump. Sequeria also won the high jump with a leap of 5 feet 10 inches.

Sophomore Ron Nelson was the winner of the two mile event with

a time of 10:03. Jag Jim Sullivan placed third in this event while another teammate, Gordon Vredenberg captured the fourth position.

Other Jags placing in their events were John Corina, third in the 100 and fourth in the 220, Obra Ricks third in the shotput, Jim Puckett placed fourth in the pole vault while Ray Medina finished third in the 440 yard dash.

Coach Smith's team is out to improve the field events, which are lacking much depth for tomorrow's meet at Stanford. The distance events led by Noel and Nelson seem to be in fine condition with more hurdlers and sprinters needed in these events.

Ken Noel

Jaguars

BIG 158 POUND
6' AND SPEEDY

SAN JOSE

HE SAYS BIG FEET COVER MORE GROUND

BEST TIME | EVENT
9:36.4 | 2 MILE
4:20.6 | 1 MILE
1:52.0 | 880
:47.6 | 440

FAST AS THE WIND

My food supply needed to be adequate for challenging training or racing, concluding in June. If Smitty knew, he and Mildred, his wife, would provide daily sustenance. However, I was hesitant to eat better than my family, preferring to live through the same hardships as they. Undernourished by May, the strategy was to arrive early for Modesto's Meet and eat plenty before Saturday's final on their unlimited meal pass. Friday night, I overate and filled up on Saturday's breakfast and lunch. That's when Smitty confirmed his suspicion that there weren't enough meat and potatoes at home. My not requesting help disappointed him, but he understood why. Nutritional deficits don't recover by spending twenty-four hours guzzling protein and carbohydrates. There was hope for only minor improvement by racing time. On a deficient diet, winning would be difficult, but capturing second was easy. Fifty-six seconds is an ideal first lap, but my usual finishing kick proved weak. Still, runner-up placing attracted scholarship offers. I realized the goal motivating running track after four years of military service; earning four-year scholarship choices. A concluding achievement was the Northern California College Coaches Organization voting me "Runner of the Year."

Texas Southern University (TSU) captured my interest among the track programs under consideration. Choosing this Negro HBCU to gain from my academic and athletic ability was a decision motivated by our burgeoning civil rights movement. A job raising airfare to Houston, plus cash for incidentals, was next. San Jose's big industry was seasonal produce canning, and those jobs were perfect for summer cash and securing future unemployment compensation because they mainly hired temporary workers.

Summer 1963

San Jose's summer jobs were plentiful, enabling workers to receive twenty-six weeks of unemployment checks after factory operations concluded. Cannery contacts got me jobs. While taking classes, work at Duffy-Mott continued full-time. Work dumping pears on conveyors for sorting qualified as hard labor. Boxes weighed 80 lbs; average shifts required lifting 200 boxes. After eight hours, Del Monte was a short walk for a half shift as a janitor. SJCC night classes went from 7 to 9 p.m. This schedule allowed no time, energy, or commitment to training.

My summer geography and biology courses brought another brush with SJCC's Vice President (Goldberg). Special processing requirements arose, complicating my getting into Dan Epstein's Introductory Geography course. Epstein insisted on interviewing me. For his introduction, he was discouraging. He claimed this was the most challenging course offered anywhere. Biology qualified as arduous, too. He estimated that my passing these subjects together was impossible. It was an odd judgment, but he'd grant acceptance if Mr. Goldberg (V.P.) approved. Goldberg answered his call with me standing there. Epstein acted as though I couldn't hear their conversation. When my name came up, Goldberg remarked, offering loud cautioning. "That card? He might be trouble, but you can allow him in." I'd bet they were social friends discussing everything that happened last November in real time, including circumstances around my gym confrontation with Coach Roget. It's weird when professors interview potential students and get their V.P.'s approval for entering classes. Epstein talked, explaining his curriculum's extreme demands on the first day. Such warnings caused people to drop out. After another session, it was puzzling why he promoted so much fear. Class requirements proved reasonable, even though I was working twelve-hour days. My grades for both courses were A-. Epstein expressed pride, never granting higher grades. I was unmoved.

After school and working, my plan for September 1963, attending TSU on a full scholarship, changed. I continued at SJCC, completing an AA Degree while running cross-country. That reset made sense because TSU didn't have fall competitions. Another SJCC harrier tour builds a base carrying through spring down south. At least one race, as long as two miles, is probable in the spring. SJCC lost one 1962 teammate (Ron Nelson). My return meant likely repeating our 1962 accomplishment. Hedging bets on whether Negro Universities fit seemed wise. By waiting until January 1964 making my start, track emersion carried sustained focus throughout the semester.

Fall 1963

1963's cross-country title pursuit would be different from last year. Summer training went lacking after track season ended. Two jobs while carrying six units, left no time. It'll take months to get into racing shape. Although I lacked conditioning, our having everyone here except Nelson favored our repeating. A return, as GGC Champions, and defending our NorCal crown, provided another quest: finishing undefeated again. Nothing could beat holding our final J.C. race in spiritually uplifting Sequoia Park. Coach Smith's National Park Service associations probably enabled running there. SJCC's administrators funded our night's lodging near the park entrance. We arrived Thursday, November 14, before Friday's event, exploring the course among majestic redwood forests, relaxing while absorbing Sequoia Park's soothing atmosphere. Early the following day, we began expressing our competitive juices in the chilly mountain air. This location is the ultimate distance runner's setting. It would be impossible to surpass racing so deep within nature's realm.

We were fortunate to stage our most significant contest in this iconic national park. That opportunity promised a complete experience. Afterward, we regretted leaving and reentering the technological intensity of urbanizing Santa Clara County, once known as "the Valley of Hearts Delight." This NorCal differed from 1962's collective mindset. With great confidence, our approach had a worker's sense of purpose. No question marks arose since we were here repeating. Sequoia was neutral ground, so there's no particular home favorite after last year's winner. Altitude adds difficulty, but we each face equal disadvantages, if any exist. SJCC's investment paid off. Our repeat was extra special because rivals gunned for us. Time after time, we heard predictions it couldn't happen again.

The afterglow continued, but shattered days later. Many say that adults never forget where they were when Kennedy got shot. When parked facing SJCC's gymnasium at 10:30 Friday, November 22, 1963, a Government Emergency Announcement overrode "The Five Satins" on my 1948 Plymouth's permanent soul channel. "We interrupt this broadcast for a news bulletin. An assailant shot and seriously wounded President Kennedy just after his motorcade left central Dallas."

Disaster blew anticipating a beautiful day out of consciousness, causing momentary paralysis. My moving became possible because Buddy Frazier, a D.C. ballplayer, tapped on my window, asking, "You heard the news?" So, count me among those remembering their precise whereabouts in those moments. That tragedy converted positive visions for our nation into questionable concerns. Adjusting hopes, desires, and outlooks is necessary for pursuing goals and aspirations. Assassinations this monumental threaten society's stability, crushing the pursuit of social change. Paths forward could only be more complicated than if Kennedy lived. They loosed sinister forces that might be impossible to corral. Coach Smith's solution diminished our trauma. We did 10 miles deep within San Antonio Park, sorting things out, displacing anxiety from unprecedented adverse political developments, and restoring our team's mental normality. Thankfully, long runs generate potent soul-healing psychological and physical processes. Soon after school wrapped in December, I flew to Houston and Texas Southern University.

Texas Southern

Texas Southern's Tigers, under Coach Bakerson, were renowned for world-ranked sprint relays. On my January Continental Airlines flight, no thoughts surfaced, pointing away from moving to traitorous Texas—slaveholding, segregationist, racist territory. By 1964, many outward signs of oppression were fading. Unchanged virulent bigoted minds were plentiful, but negative encounters diminished. There was no reason customers should expect encountering businesses employees displaying aggressive racial prejudice in airports, bus depots, or similar locations. Who thinks interstate market employers abide employees publicly insulting Negroes day after day. Boy was that wrong! On venturing downtown, well before my dorm bed was assigned, I walked into a racist attack by allowing self-endangering naïveté. An incident at the Greyhound Station, picking up luggage shipped from San Jose, signaled significant vulnerability. No one thinks racism ended, but this assault surprised me. Forty-eight hours after arriving by air, Gerald Pratt, TSU's world-ranked pole-vaulter and team co-captain, and Coach Bakerson took me to get my trunk at Greyhound.

Virulent racism surfaced while standing before the baggage desk. The clerk deigned to serve us. Their countertop dial phone started ringing at length. This guy froze while three Negroes look on; the ringer sound lasts an uncomfortable spell. Finally, this cracker spoke, "If ya'll people step back, ah kin answer it." We moved, puzzled over what problem existed. The three of us watched him lift the handset, wiping its mouthpiece on his shirt. Our presence, too close, contaminated his phone with the filth of our existence. I exploded! "You motherfucker," and stepped toward him. Coach Bakerson grabbed me, saying, "Come on, Ken, don't cause any trouble." (Was it me making trouble?) Pratt locked his arm at my elbow, pulling me. We sat in the car until Stan returned carrying my military foot locker.

We rode silenced by racists, with me puzzled that our coach had no comment or counsel. No talk suggested adjustments for actions from crackers. If racists attack, but victims don't react, do offenses achieve relevance, lose relevance, or both? I rationalized solace, a short-term decline in conditions maximizing positive possibilities—one semester's single privation moment. Pratt, transplanted from LA, knew the feeling and didn't need to talk about it. That Greyhound station incident launched steps toward me leaving after June's exams. Such episodes dissolved my presumed noble intentions for attending HBCUs. My argument (with myself) was that intelligent athletes choosing such institutions were noble acts—doing so benefited Negro institutions, other students, and the Negro people. When establishing Student Nonviolent Coordinating Committee's (SNCC) campus chapter, we dropped using "Negro," calling ourselves Black. Immediate difficulties indicated any more developments guaranteed to throw cold water on any noble intentions. What made sense was staying within University boundaries, except when traveling for meets. We were on the road every Thursday until Sunday. Days passed safely when preoccupied with competition demands. With Professor Charles Bullock's requirements, frequent travel caused interesting classmate dynamics.

Professor Bullock's Sociology and Social Science courses were the toughest found anywhere. Countless people suggested avoiding Bullock. Against roommates', teammates', and the Coach's warnings, his subjects dominated my schedule. Nobody took those classes over other choices. The popular word was top grades are scarce. He said his grading allowed a single "A" per class each semester, and everyone deemed taking both impractical.

Bullock's requirements created an exciting dynamic. He dictated forming study groups requiring supporting each other. Because of weekly travel, group partners updated me after trips during Sunday afternoon meetings. Support circles reviewed material I missed while away. Students helping me boosted everyone's grades. Class teams served well in mastering coursework because my comrades benefited by extra effort elevating their learning while making me successful. Class leaders presented times and material review locations when I exited the Tiger, and classmates rendered aid without getting put out. This process's importance grew as I competed tooth and nail with a coed sitting front row in Social Psychology and an African stationed beside me in Sociology. We fought hard to be first. It's well enough, ending runner-up in both groups. (I'm the only student pursuing A's who missed Bullock's lectures for school travel. Bullock never factored that into his grading.) My regular absences increased the inherent difficulty, but colleagues' sharing made up the lecture attendance deficit. Connections with Professor Bullock and his groups increased academic interest, so it was a period for testing myself by doing focused library studying, and Social Science became my degree major. We spent many hours riding buses, trains, and airplanes, doing homework in hotels, writing papers, and reading textbooks. Collective experiences were unexpected but outstanding!

Rigorous athletic and academic schedules emerged. Fifteen minutes of jogging at 6:30 a.m. started my weekly work. European history came at 10 a.m., polishing off mornings. Lunch after 11:00 preceded naps. Bullock's times went from 1:00 to 4:00 Tuesdays and Thursdays. History and English were on Mondays and Wednesdays. Two hours doing intervals ended days on campus. Intervals, beginning after warming up, finished by jogging a mile.

Speed work came from Santa Clara Youth Village notebooks. Alterations were unnecessary with my detailed journal. Cruise-paced miles, after 10 x 110, added mileage-increasing strength and endurance needed for racing the two-mile and mile in the Southwest Athletic Conference (SWAC) Championships. After practice, there was a quick shower and supper before going to the library from 7:00 until it closed. No trouble sleeping!

TSU disappointed me. Conditions were less than satisfactory when seeking voluntary improvement under Jim Crow. Their plantation administrative mentality's "submissive Sambo" actions were disheartening. Administrators went overboard when enforcing paternalistic policies as paranoia reigned everywhere, fearing instant budget cuts by Texas' white supremacist legislatures. That reasoning made the place an education-oriented plantation. Students received administrative discipline if seen holding hands in public. Our Dean of Students crept around, catching youngsters kissing in buildings' dark corners, behind trees, or in bushes after sundown. I never envisioned such an Uncle Tom presence. The general population showed great ignorance and backwardness. Most people frequenting the library were socializing. There, Dean Wilson didn't hassle fledgling lovers. Several times, he complained to Stan, threatening my expulsion for wearing baseball caps when indoors. That specific problem got solved by Stan's assistants handling any official business.

The administration's juvenile nature was sufficient reason for resisting paternalistic conventions. After military duty's discipline, wearing caps became unconscious. Throughout the ongoing kerfuffle, observing Dean Wilson's gay mannerisms felt uncomfortable in face to face meetings. He appeared delighted when exaggerating effeminate gestures in front of me. After closing his office door, his projecting pleasure from our confrontations raised uneasiness. How does that promote buying the dictate that removing hats indoors indispensably demonstrates respecting an institution? Administrators, it seems, fashioned such constraints intent on bolstering controls. So much focus on doffing hats entering buildings is paternalism demanding absolute obedience. Wilson's dorm speech clarified this: "My controls are essential for our survival and advancement as individuals and as a people." Serious negative views on covering my head escaped me. It felt like he was fucking with me for personal reasons, striking me as perverted!

General literacy, including knowledge of world events, proved low in classroom discussions. Many coeds were beauties until they began speaking. Uninformed conversation subtracts from good looks. Numbers of Texas men were insecure, making them hostile against non-Texans. They were domineering toward women in demeaning ways. A despicable practice was using pet names and ranking females by skin tone. Those identified as "bananas" were considered prized. Each star athlete had at least one "banana." Texas females got harassed if they were too friendly toward males from other states. Fellow Californians endured threats for approaching Texas women. This behavior was extreme intra-group oppressive shit!

I'll tell a story showing how twisted life could be.

Years before I arrived, one of the best California high school runners came to the University, fell for and married a prominent Texas girl. Resentment of this pair had no measurable limit across the campus. Envy and jealousy extended into what was previously her circle of friends. That's not to mention the hate, resentment, and jealousy of the male Texas Klan niggers. They geared their system toward punishing and eventually destroying those rising above the petty, ego-driven "crabs in a bucket" existence. No one should be happy, contented, or prosperous outside of their domination as learned, mirroring slave masters.

What her so-called brothers and sisters eventually did was unspeakably sinister and destructive. While her spouse was traveling for track representing the University, she went to a student party with her friends. There, her girlfriends conspired to get her sufficiently drunk, in the name of friendship and sisterhood, so as to be physically helpless. Her friends then left the party without her. The resulting confluence of conspiracy created and enabled a situation for her to get gang-raped with no degenerates held accountable, only the victims—an innocent married couple. They cast the wife, in particular, as an immoral disgrace, and the husband would never know respect for having been married to her.

They saddled them with such opprobrium that their marriage could never last. But that, in its entirety, is where such countenanced rotten fabric of social relationships leads. These are the worst conditions a community can bring upon itself. These were deliberate treacherous acts assignable beyond the individuals involved. Such social effects remain active for a lifetime.

The event got recounted far and wide, so the nation's track and field ranks knew, and it was common knowledge across California. If I had considered that couple's experience, I'd have gone elsewhere.

Willy Warren, TSU's star football player and a sure bet for playing professional ball, claimed "big man on campus" status. He, protected by massive linemen, projected intimidating force. They took whatever they wanted. Football gangsters entered the dining hall late. Ignoring preformed lines, they stepped past everyone under Willy's command as I stood talking with other students, my first time seeing them at dinner. We had inched inside the outer doors when the gang entered, strolling by us. What a crass act! It's astonishing, considering how important maintaining the democratic social fabric is within an educational institution! Such actions defied expectations for sharing campus food resources. They violated the principles of turns relating to our social contract. Nobody exists above that!

Why young folks don't reject incivility en masse, so transgressors act sensible, boggles the mind. Veterans experiencing this had no answers. That set off thinking; those wanting not waiting turns can move by bullying. The assemblage thinks my grabbing a tray and walking by the bullies getting dinner is insane. Silence descends. I learned the gathering couldn't believe their eyes. My response was to highlight the bullies' incivility so they'd stop. People warned me about repercussions from being so insolent! My studious roommate and others advised avoiding going outside alone. Not that opposing bullies isn't dangerous, but my behavior tells gangsters that others have a similar or greater capacity for hurting people. Actual hard-nosed actors don't care! Growing up as a gang member before surviving military service, my point of view was that any repercussions unleash total war. There's little at stake for me, while gridiron thugs had careers they could lose. With serious disputes, career-threatening injuries are possible. Professional sports careers depend on health, while legitimate students' prospects come from classroom achievement. A track scholarship is simply an affordable way to pursue degrees, but unnecessary. My policy required retaliating 24/7 and answering any moves against me. Fuck calling the police! That isn't how I roll! It comes down to catching enemies sleeping or shitting. I'd damage knees—destroying professional ball careers. Greg said that gangsters dismissed me as "one crazy nigger." They understand "crazy niggers" are unpredictable. Here, it's probable that the stakes were too high. We didn't have direct contact outside the dining hall. They never approached me.

My Lanier Hall residents portrayed campus diversity. Greg and the other sophomore occupying bunks across the room were a wealthy playboy and a stereotypical nerd. Josiah, the graduate student below me, was gay. We got along undisturbed by our differences. There were no problems sharing time. Greg, a rich guy with an exquisite pearl-blue 1956 Chevy convertible, served as track manager, performing various administrative duties, including answering mail and maintaining uniforms. Sunday, before Drake University's Relays, Greg, seeking company while working in the coach's office, invited me along on leaving the cafeteria. That's an opportunity where calling West Chester or San Jose friends is free. At Stan's desk, reading his mail while calling home did me good. Curiosity drove reading open letters like one from Bob Ehrhart, Drake Relays' director. His message thanked Stan for accepting their invitation to bring his squad to Des Moines and showed per diem allotted covering 22 athletes, including a check ($1320).

Drakes check divided by our numbers contrasted with amounts distributed on similar trips, identifying more money than ever distributed. Calculations showed that if we received the intended sums, we could eat well while easing our overall economic burden. After recording Drake's sum, Stan's mail was arranged to look undisturbed. Later, I'd verify if he skims or makes honest distributions. It's crucial because we lack money for off-campus activities or eating other than cafeteria food.

We flew into Des Moines Thursday because Drake had us competing Friday and Saturday. The scenery busing into town was disappointing because I expected better conditions than the depressed slums seen riding through neighborhoods to the hotel. I never pictured Iowa Negroes living in abject poverty.

Our hotel was nothing special, with its large foyer mitigating cold winds entering their lobby. Team captains assigned rooms and ordered putting our bags away. Coach's briefing would occur within forty-five minutes. He clarified eating schedules, evening activities, and nighttime restrictions. Coach Bakerson spoke on Per Diem amounts. "The meet's in dire financial straits and has a tight budget. That means it's tight on us, too!" (Words came to mind: "This motherfucker thinks nobody knows what's going on!") After that proviso, he handed out ten bucks for Thursday's lunch and dinner. Friday, twelve dollars covered three meals. Saturday's allotment matched Friday's. Stan's distribution totaled thirty-four dollars. Our amount should have been sixty bucks. What breakfast costs two bucks—oatmeal and coffee? That's less than needed nutrition levels. Sixty was beyond sufficient. Forty does it, allowing pocketing twenty. I decided to demand my twenty-six dollars back at school.

Several of us went to see "America, America," a historical film. I tried discouraging freshmen from going because the film's length extended past curfew. The movie portrayed events dominated by Russia, which fed into my Russian History studies covering early twentieth-century conflict impacting Asia Minor. The story covered Armenian struggles to escape from the holocaust under Turkish rule by coming here. If the film had material for writing a paper, I'd watch until the end. When curfew came, the suggestion that others obey team rules fell on deaf ears. Young guys refused to listen. After the movie, we returned together. T. J., a captain, met us. As the oldest, they singled me out as the leading rule-breaker and ordered me to see Stan. T. J. remarked that major transgressions required punishment. I traversed the dungeon hall expanse, recalling tenement passages smelling like piss. When told, I stepped into Stan's room after tapping. That no witnesses were present was good because our conversation might turn ugly. He stopped processing more Invitational papers and, looking dismayed, said, "Ken, I'm very disappointed in you." (The exact words were what I envisioned. It was as if there couldn't be anything original with communication in these circumstances.) I preferred a question like, "Ken, is there a problem that I don't know about?" Instead, Stan explained,

"Because you are older, I looked for you to be a better example for the younger guys. I'm holding you responsible for everyone missing curfew. As a result, I'm going to have to punish you. What do you have to say for yourself?"

My response was simple:

"I'm not accepting any punishment. What I did was educational, and I don't accept responsibility for the young guys because I told them to leave on time. I've trained myself over the years and have maintained a personal schedule for eating and sleeping. I don't need a curfew because the way that I've done things has been successful. Not only has it been successful for me, but it is also successful for Carter (Bruce) and Hunt (George) because I am the one who trains them. They are following my workouts under my direction—not yours. I won't accept your punishment, and I want the rest of my money!"

The shock of disbelief triggered fear-driven guilty deflation. Stan's mouth shaped speech but no sound. His puffy lips, between piggish jowls, flapped as if talking but uttered no sound. He stared as if an unknown and threatening stranger confronted his behavior. The collapsed feigned coach-athlete relationship's phony rules and roles embarrassed us over a silent moment. It's an emotion-laden reality where trump cards appear in a friendly poker game, totally by surprise. He blinked, squinted, and then tried speaking. Words prepared as lies got abandoned on seeing my face's firm dismissal. Then he switched, trying to justify trickery, failed ethics, and exploitation. His reasons flow like a con artist failing rehabilitation, hoping victims are stupid, believing them.

"I only use the money (your money) to help others and help the team by supporting some of the guys that aren't in school. They will be in school and on the team when we need them. There are several guys living in the church near the campus that will join the team when they are admitted to school and they need this help. When someone gets hurt and can't compete, we can bring one of these guys in to help us. That's what I take the money to do."

"You didn't ask me if that's what I wanted to do with my money," I responded.

"I don't care what you do with other people's money! I want my money. I want my money every time! I won't break curfew again, but I want my money now and in the future."

From an envelope, he counted bills. His head wagged side to side while handing over my portion. Punishment talk evaporated. That can't happen! What was he thinking? How could he imagine my accepting such bull shit? Doesn't my history show?

Once setting my demand, we never talked about money or secret troops awaiting deployment. The California boys heard my story but may have reached their own travel funds' distribution understanding. It wasn't likely that any raised questions because they were only there running. Dependent athletes accepted conditions when having no other options.

After airing personal positions, restating responsibilities, and demanding honest per diem shares, my efforts zeroed in on running and studying. Major relay invitationals were coming, including Laredo, Kansas, Texas, Oklahoma, Pelican, and SWAC. Competition openers included Mexico City and Nuevo Laredo trips. A multi-team gathering in Mexico City competing against several Mexican Universities was among their preparations for staging the 1968 Olympics. We arrived on Friday for Saturday and Sunday competitions. That evening was for touring the capital and tasting urban Mexican culture. Representatives urged going everywhere together, so twenty Negroes ventured forth. Some Texas boys proposed finding the red-light district and procuring bargain-priced prostitutes. By all appearances, buying pussy was their normal behavior. Hotel Revolucion's front desk provided directions. Zona Rosa's brothel street, featuring undressed women gesturing, was close— maybe six blocks beyond our hotel. Five Texans entered one house, stepping past prostitutes sitting outside and ogling others occupying open windows. On the Texans' heels, several neighborhood men entered. In an instant, our teammates burst out at full speed. We reacted, sprinting toward the Plaza de Revolution. Quick looks behind glimpsed a shouting mob hot on our trail. They lost contact fast, pursuing trained runners. We disappeared long before reaching safety. Winded and safe inside our hotel, whore house escapees described what occurred. Jesus Villelongo, our Puerto Rican quarter-miler, interpreted:

Todos somos hombres de negocio. (We are all businessmen [pimps].) No podemos dejar estos negros cojan nuestras putas y arruinen su bichos y nuestros negocio." (We can't let these Negritos fuck our whores and ruin their pussies and our business.) Debemos demostrar a estos negros y putas quien sean los jefes. (We must show these Niggers and whores who is the boss.)" Their objection was the

Niggers' penises were too big and would ruin the sources of their income. They pulled knives to make their point clear. That's when the Texas boys bolted out of the house, and we all took off running down the street. Somehow, word went around the red light district, and a mob was already coming down the sidewalk when the Texas boys broke out of the house.

We spent the evening resting.

The next day's National Stadium action proved notable. Saturday, it was 1500 meters for me, followed by Sunday's 800, plus a 4 x 400 leg. Not knowing what to expect when competing at 7000 feet, metric miles had no appeal at any altitude. I sacrificed and ran the longer race to represent my school and country. Our hosts deserved more entertainment besides sprinting. TSU's weakest performers were far superior to Mexico's competitors. I trailed for 1400 meters before kicking and finishing ahead of four Mexican competitors, and immediately found a shaded bench, donning my sweat suit. Soon after lounging in coolness cast by an equipment storage building, a ton of bricks landed on me. That's how exhaustion caused oxygen debt above 2000 feet feels. O2 amounts in the air were lower than I'd ever experienced, creating feelings like suffocating until sufficiently restoring blood oxygen. Then, I realized my dilemma was mild hypoxemia, a short-term high-altitude exertion effect. After observing my distress, Hunt and Carter grew scared as hell. Although distances of 800 or less don't produce a noticeable impact, teammates were afraid of pushing hard. Sunday, after winning an easy 800, my 4 x 400 leg beat most of our 400 guys. After those races, there was no deprivation, even over 7,000 feet where the Sierra Madre Occidental Mountains extend into Sierra Madre Oriental's mountain ranges. Most team members leave Mexico with an understanding of needing specific preparation for low-oxygen environment competitions.

On Wednesday, our next engagement took us to Kansas University, traveling by rail. A relaxed Lawrence, Kansas trip soon became memorable when our train, roaring across Oklahoma going 70 mph, slowed fast, stopping midway between nowhere. Moments before braking, we hit thick dust clouds. Outside my window, a white-walled Buick wheel bounced alongside our Pullman car, going in the same direction. What an odd vast empty plains sight! Curiosity rose, and I wondered why we no longer sped onward until word passed that the train hit a car. We would be there for a while, and our conductor suggested remaining onboard. He warned against viewing the gruesome accident, but warnings become invitations for witnessing the carnage. Once stepping from the sixth car behind our engines, we saw mashed car parts protruding from under our diesel engines. I hoped the car stopped and was empty before getting slammed, but this driver's luck ran out! His collision reduced a powder blue 1959 Buick convertible to mid-thigh-high thickness. The driver's seat rested in the rear, with someone's remains. He posed, both hands gripping his detached steering wheel as if continuing cruising along the open road with his face sheared off at the ears. The rest of his head remained attached to his neck. Shoulder-length stringy blond hair splayed over the backrest. Against advice, Carter, a teenager, took a look. Later, amid deep sleep, his nightmare screams awakened Kansas U's entire dormitory.

A vital conversation with Bob Schul in Kansas raised future performance quality. America's top 5000-meter runner, National Champion, and record holder (1963) was a SCURVY and LATC teammate. In California, we trained together under Iglói in 1961 and 1962. Bob hailed me after our distance medley. While reminiscing, I complained of getting stuck on low 1:50+ 880s. After describing workouts, Bob suggested adding morning "easy" runs before afternoon work. As expected, after ten days, times dropped below 1:50. At TSU's Relays, our annual showcase, my best mile (4:16) lowered to 4:08, anchoring the long medley. James McClatchy, Lamar Tech's Scotland National Champion, dropped a 3:56, overcoming a significant deficit and beating me by ten yards.

4:08 indicates an ability to sustain increasing faster races over the remaining competitions. Now, welcoming each session, increasing work, and confidently improving, I longed for a 4 x 440 spot. Once Stan took over, Texas

Southern's sprint relay teams achieved worldwide recognition. 1964's 4 x 440 comprised three sub 46.5-second members and another under 46 flat. Our reserves are 46.7 or slower. They designated my role as distance events, beginning with the 880s. Regular duties allowed no opportunity for challenging 440 specialists.

Our B Team's Mexico City race caught me doing 46.5. That displayed my ability to match current alternates, but it didn't bring a pecking order position. Before our year ended, another chance surfaced when our program hosted 1964's SWAC conference meet at Houston University's Cougar Stadium. The two-mile starting competition was on Friday night, and the mile is Saturday afternoon. Saturday's 880 belonged to Hunt and Carter, my teammates. They were shoe-ins for finishing 1st and 2nd. I was leery of doing more than a mile unless there's endurance training, long intervals, or racing that far. Cross-country happened months ago, so I'm hoping competitors go slow, forsaking testing endurance. While drafting behind Grambling's and Southern U's distance specialists, halfway into the fifth circuit, my right hamstring cramped and felt like a pulled muscle. It's the only race I ever quit. We were losing points from the start, which was a reason for concern.

Stan expressed great displeasure, but his irritation meant nothing because risking season-ending injury completing a once-a-year 2-mile race is beyond the pale. He wanted championship trophy points and never protected athletes' health. From personal observation, he ruined sprinters, insisting they compete while injured. Bill Cowings, a phenomenal California sprinter, became a victim of Stan's abuse. Distances are my responsibility (shades of Major Adams) because others aren't capable. After cramping, treatment is for enabling completing Saturday's mile. Times near 4:18 can win. Greg's massage helped me recover enough to follow Southern and Grambling runners until the last curve. Slow pacing made serious effort unnecessary. My 4:16 win required no sprinting.

Observing the overblown importance generated by SWAC members wanting league titles was eye-opening. Entities on member campuses went overboard. Was I alone in thinking world-class times were more critical than conference victories? George and Bruce, my mentees, finished tops in the 880, and teammates earned predicted placing for other contests. Our march toward another League crown advanced despite my quitting the two-mile. We matched Grambling point for point until the last event. Either Grambling or TSU would capture the title by winning the 4 x 440. Only Charles White, Herb Stevens, and Wesley Blackmon committed to running it.

Other teammates, begging off, gave questionable excuses. These Niggers chickened out! We're home, facing a single event determining SWAC's winner. Informal 4 x 440 bragging rights are at stake, as well. Fear of failing was a probable explanation! I had never seen this many cowards together! TSU's entire self-declared "badass" sprinter corps chickened out! Vaunted 100-yard supermen faked injuries or disappeared! Their M.O. claimed courage but hinged on faked toughness! Either they feared responsibility for determining victory or defeat or feared the quarter mile's physical demands. Hunt and Carter refused after dominating their contest. Although welcoming 4 x 440 opportunities, my mouth stayed shut while our coach decided. He approached with dismay written on his face, coloring his words. "Ken, you're all we have!" There was no reason for anyone to expect an excellent result. Grambling, learning of inserting TSU's distance runner, changed their order, shaping their strategy to exploit me. They waited to see where I was placed (second leg, as my call), then moved Donald Owens, their anchorman, to destroy me. Charles White was guaranteed to pass in front. Grambling expected Owens to erase any deficit, blowing by and creating an insurmountable lead. My strategy was relinquishing the lead but going all-out down the back stretch to home. I intended to be fast through the baton-passing zone, sending our third man (sub 46.0) off to a good start. That was how our drama unfolded. After Charles handed off well ahead, Owens flew by, opening a 5-yard gap midway into the curve. I can only lose a little early and still enable winning. Besides that, Stan planted near the 220 mark, screaming at us to increase our effort. (I never considered he'd be there! He figured it unlikely I'd do the job. Maybe his screams could be decisive! He was desperate!) I lost 10 yards and needed to recover part. Every ounce of energy went into the final 300, through the curve, onto the home stretch, keeping Owens from increasing his lead and regaining steps by being strong and making the baton exchange. Herb Stevens, our phenomenal freshman, was less than four strides behind. Herb led, bursting out of the first turn. He exploded, pulling away, handing off to Wesley Blackmon 15 yards ahead. We finished having logged the world's fastest relay time, capturing the SWAC. Grambling's coach gave me their story. He approached, exclaiming, "Ken, you beat us!" He said their strategy failed when I kept closer to Owens than they thought possible.

What a soul-satisfying undertaking! Getting underestimated, being disrespected, being considered weak and exploitable, and defying expectations by beating overconfident detractors before our crowd brought satisfaction beyond measure. While I'll note that no other teams came into the picture, if I was so weak, Herb deserves full credit, dropping a 45.1. What a fantastic sight! Such a dramatic conclusion sent a festive atmosphere sweeping TSU until the semester's end. Our SWAC victory's last contest reigned as the dorm, classroom, and future gatherings' major topic. Stan had no comment. We continued to travel for invitational meets until school ended. Things were going great as performances improved, and we made April's national list.

NATIONS TOP TRACK MARKS BY APRIL 1964

880 (1.54.1)—1:48.5, Siebert, (SCYV), 1:48.7, Underwood, Oregon St), (1:49.1, Crothers, (Canada), 1:49.2, Van Asten,

Oregon), 1:49.3, n- Hessell, Unattached), Hunt, (Tex Southern).

Frosh), Sugden, (Ohio U.), Carroll, (Villanova), 1:49.8, Noel,

(Texas So. Frosh), 1:49.9, n-Wilson, (Okla. Baptist), 1:50.2

While nearing the season's end, results dipped below 1:49.0. Olympic Trials qualifying was possible, although I still needed to reach my training regimen's maximizing potential. On my steady march through logs, it was weeks before honing for international-level performances. There's an eagerness to engage in signature interval sets, clocking peak times over the waning semester. Steady hard work brought gut-wrenching sessions. By May, ever higher demanding intervals were proving digestible, including creating the ability to add more. Soon, Thursdays comprised maximum speed work, with recoveries descending toward zero. Anticipation grows by performing increased stressful work without destroying my body. That was preparation drawn from the past! Beatty (Jim) or other top Iglói troops described the most intense sequences as telltale for defining when they were ready to test themselves against world competition. Most considered shorter repeats, all-out 150s, and 100s, vital. They said, "You know you're ready because workouts feel like flying with ease."

Thursday, May 14, 1964 - 15 min jog (2.5 miles) warm-up + 10 x 110 easy speed + 5 x 110 hard speed. 10 x 220 all-out with a 50-yard jog between (with a 50-yard jog, as soon as you slow to jogging speed it's time to start the next all-out 220 interval) + 2 laps jog. 10 x 220 all-out with 50 jog between + 2 laps jog. 10 x 110 alternating 1 easy speed and 1 middle speed. Temp is 80 degrees and no wind. Next meet SWAC Championship.

Before making the 1964 Olympic Team, there were more obstacles than usual. A debilitating trek to Sioux Falls, South Dakota, and the National Association of Intercollegiate Athletics (NAIA) Championships loomed ahead. They were self-proclaimed "Experts in the business of small college athletics." Texas Southern pledged NAIA loyalty, no matter what. Their tight connection puzzled me. Complicated Trials paths presented conflicting schedules making my task impossible. It is complex, with several overlapping avenues. There were successive levels of NCAA championships after

Sioux Falls' NAIA meet. The Amateur Athletic Union (AAU) nationals come one week before the U. S. trials. We had four torturous days riding the "Tiger" to South Dakota, feeling more debilitation returning after competing. Throughout spring, surviving our bus trips presented challenges.

Maroon and white paint revamped the "Tiger," a converted city transit vehicle. That's all! Original hard molded plastic city bus seats lined the interior sides. The original, thin, cushioned padded bench remained across the rear. So much riding battered the life out of us. It's a wonder there were any decent performances. Trips to Nuevo Laredo, Mexico, and Baton Rouge, Louisiana, each requiring over 5 hours, were nearly crippling. TSU's "Tiger" gave no mercy. Travel to South Dakota and competing cost us six peak training days round-trip, not to mention imparting tremendous body stress. Because of legal liability, school policy wouldn't allow going directly to Fresno's NCAAs. We couldn't fly out or continue to Fresno from there. This year was my last opportunity to seek an Olympic berth. A win at the NCAA's College Division event offered my best chance for the Olympic trials but required missing the NAIA. Gerald Pratt (over 17 ft pole-vaulter), Curtis Crumb (a 7 ft high-jumper), Bill Cowings (a 9.3 100-yard sprinter), and Jasper Faison (a 13.4 hurdler), also Californians, joined me, departing early. Everyone preferred competing in Fresno.

After completing exams, we loaded a station wagon Pratt was transporting to Los Angeles. Then we rolled west on Interstate 10. Curtis' relative met him in LA, dropping me in San Jose on their way to Oakland on Monday. Friday, Crumb gave me a ride to Fresno, where Lamar Tech's Joe Leblanc and I tied as 880 champions. It only came out well because Neal, my running partner from high school, JC, and Iggles' teams, arrived at Fresno's Ratcliffe stadium as we hit the turn with 220 left. I was trailing the pack, boxed in; with little track left for corrections.

HAYES, NEWMAN WIN AT FRESNO

Fresno (UPI)—Rapid Robert Hayes of Florida A & M coasted to a fast 20.5 clocking in the 220-yard dash of the NCAA college division track and field meet, Saturday night as his competition failed to push him to what could have been a world record.

Hayes said he hopes to better the 20.2 pending and 20.3 world marks of Henry Carr of Arizona State, was in front all the way as he won with an eased-up finish.

Darel Newman of Fresno State also made a cake-walk out of the 100-yard dash as he won with ease in a 9.3—although half of the four official timers had him in 9.2.

There was less than a two-mile-an-hour wind for both races on the fast crushed brick Ratcliffe Stadium track.

The top six finishers in each event qualified for next week's overall NCAA championships if they also have better that meet's rigid entry standards. It, in turn, is a qualifying meet for the U.S. Olympic trials.

880-yard run—1, tie between Joe Leblanc, Lamar Tech, and Kenneth Noel, Texas Southern, 1:54.3.
3. Jim Fox, Mt Union, 1:54.5,
4. Ed Schneider, NE Missouri, 1:55.8.
5. Paul Richardson, Sacramento State, 1:56.2.
6. Jerry Reich, Pepperdine, 1:56.4.

220-yard dash—1. Robert Hayes, Florida A.M., 20.5,
2. Richard Stebbins, Grambling. 20.9,
3. Edwin Roberts, North Carolina College,, 21.0,

4. Sam Workman, Fresno, 21.1,

5. Vernus Ragsdale, Grambling, 21.4,

6. Gary Curtis, Cal Poly (SLO), 21.6

440-yard hurdles1. Andrew McCray, North Carolina College, 51.3,

2. Roy Burlson, Peperdine, 51.5,

3. James Hackett, American U., 53.1,

4. Doug Johnson, Chico State, 53.3, 5. Jon Dana, Cal Poly (SLO), 53.5,

6. Larry Godfrey, San Diego State, 55.0.

Neal screamed to break out. "Drive! Drive!" He used Mihái's command, demanding that I give everything! Neal didn't speak Hungarian, but his directives copied their accent, becoming as if our coach was present, triggering responses. The "Drive" command response had become ingrained, so high gear kicked in, closing on the leader's shoulder. It was Joe LeBlanc, and finishing came up fractions too fast when I inched past him! Officials, based on hand timing, declared us tied. People like Long Beach State's Bill Crowley, sitting across from the judges, insisted I prevailed! They even protested! Sunday's Fresno Bee sports page photo questioned their "tie" decision, picturing me breaking the tape.

My mistake was leaving the decision to outdated judging. So, my tying wasn't taking matters away from the judges. They flipped a coin, allowing me to pocket the gold medal. Joe's copy would come by mail. NCAA and Pacific AAU Championship victories motivated Pasadena A.A. to pay expenses to Rutgers, New Jersey, for the National AAU. It was great meeting Pasadena's "Twin" Winton's again. They were wealthy entrepreneurs who generously promoted various sports and supported national-level performers by providing expense money.

Meanwhile, I worked operating American Can Company palletizing machines after learning those skills while I was an LA Track Club member (1961 and 1962). On leaving Houston, I intended to enroll in San Jose State's

(SJS) early summer term, but transferring ASAP was denied after TSU refused to release my transcript. Records got held for skipping the NAIA, and I expected Stan's vindictive lashing out. We discussed transcript issues on a charter flight to San Diego. "TSU prevented me from registering for summer classes, and I'll go elsewhere unless my transcripts get released." Flying back from San Diego's AAU preliminary, Stan informed me that TSU sent the transcripts, and I attended SJS's August session, never revealing that I had decided to leave TSU.

So, west coast clubs collaborated, chartering flights to New Jersey (AAUs) beginning the following week. AAUs served as a tune-up before selecting National Teams. Once plans settled at Rutgers, AAU and U.S. Olympic Committee representatives decided that high participant numbers required reducing fields. USOC staff rejected having more than the semifinals for track events. The AAU final's plans changed, using them as preliminaries and quarterfinals. Olympic Trials become semifinals or finals, depending on the numbers surviving early competitions while achieving Olympic standards. From the start, altered conditions hurt. Now, AAU Championships stood as the way to the Trials. Others may handle matters better, but unexpected developments required responses beyond my capacity. I needed more resources or connections for addressing sudden changes, and I banked on responding well in heats.

Time before our moment of truth became a complex, blurred, haphazard preparation, with poor nutrition and insufficient rest. Any competitive conditioning built from earlier training diminished. Hopefully, our workouts just before traveling east remained usable. Drawing lane six in heat four worked. Morgan Groth was favored to win and pulled lane five. When he passed me, I'd follow, adopting his pace. Once beyond our one-turn stagger, we'd bunch going into the turn. Within one hundred yards, someone tripped, throwing us off stride and planting Groth's face, digging a swath of cinders gouged by spiked feet. I never regained balance or lost yardage after jumping over him. My place in the heat couldn't advance.

Once Groth fell, officials' negated his failure, providing a finals spot. Sam Bell, his Oregon State University coach, headed our team. Later, Bud

Winter from SJS explained, "They disqualified you for fouling Morgan Groth. Morgan got reinstated, advancing to the Trials." It wasn't disturbing that politics took precedence over race results. In doing poorly, being a scape-goat to move our best performers into chances at Tokyo didn't matter. What remained was following Tokyo's results. Groth sustained an injury, finish-ing his preliminary sixth. (Four decades later, conversing with New York University's Jimmy Brown while attending 2007's Penn Relays, he acknowl-edged they disqualified him over fouling Groth, too. Oddly, USOC repre-sentatives disqualified two Blacks for a single (supposed) foul.)

A favored politically connected runner advancing showed my limitations trying to operate unsupported at the National level. Competitive running continued financing my B.A. degree after transferring to SJS. Training and competing, fulfilling track obligations and studies were it. San Jose State's Grant-in-Aid replaced Texas Southern's.

CHAPTER
TWELVE

Viva Las Vegas

The Explorer, the Trapper, the Pathfinder, the Gold Miner, the Pioneer, the Gunslinger, and the Gambler were expressions of dominant cultural themes extending from discovery and creativity as the driving forces of progress in this nation's history. Those going forth into the land seeking adventure, fame, and fortune relying on their individual initiative continue to express our national spirit and the human spirit.

Kenny:

Neal's formative years found him taken with the Martino family's zest for poker. With later superior gambling skills and a penchant for risky pursuits, his establishing a successful enterprises in Las Vegas is no surprise. Poker roots took hold when Neal's mother married Harvey Martino.

Neal:

Two stepbrothers and sisters increased our family when mom remarried. Three properties were under construction for his children within each other's sight. Mom and I moved into Martino's original homestead as soon as they wed. Later, he rented that out after building a large brick home for Mom. He completed constructing the last two places, of the four occupying eight acres. Two boys and one girl each got a dwelling. The youngest daughter took their first house, where Charlie (Ennis), a long-time local carpenter, rented downstairs rooms. Harvey's boys had kids early, so cousins by marriage lived close. His sons were older, joining their plumbing business. Family members liked group gatherings. They loved relatives competing at tabletop games. These were essential connections. My interest in playing with cards emerged earlier while living in an impoverished Chester, Pennsylvania enclave.

I was six when Chester constructed a recreation center near our tenement where we lived sans our father. Officials toured our neighborhood, asking kids what activities we sought. During World War II, most little boys wanted toy airplanes, guns, or other war toys. When asked, I said, "I want those cards with dogs on them." Who knows from where that idea rose? That response suggests that interests emerged from previous life or infancy exposures. From nowhere, I'm doing magic, entertaining rec center kids. They loved it! Attention spurred learning more complicated sleights-of-hand. Before Mom joined them, Harvey's clan enjoyed five-card stud at frequent gatherings. A well-maintained, unique rectangular oak table dominated our recreation room. Pre-shuffled decks waited. When past bedtime, they caught me lurking halfway upstairs, absorbing everything.

My exposure to poker increased while lingering behind people, watching. When older, I admired Buddy, their oldest boy with crewcut red hair. Red-tinged stubble covering his pale face and grew toward a full beard. While talking or cracking jokes, he dialed into betting's flow and made calls mixed with passes. Enormous hands drawing cards buried them deep within. A calm expression behind gigantic paws deterred discerning patterns with his cards. He waited, smiling; nobody saw this but me. Then, with a flourish, he spread his winning cards over the green cloth. My eventual game style, fashioned along with other interests, used Buddy as a role model. His card manipulations required hand strength. It could be a plumber's characteristic. That realization started a quest for manual dexterity, becoming an expert at manipulating objects and performing magic tricks. It's easy when you are young! Soon, relatives enjoyed observing sleight-of-hand maneuvers. It began with making items disappear and picking selections from shuffled decks. I checked out library books, teaching illusions, and mysterious presentations. Audiences always liked mind-reading tricks, picking cards by suit color, mostly finding their choices buried within the deck. There were ten or more amusing deceptions. Magic performances laid the foundations for future work handling cards.

Hanging out at Coty's Market (Unc's) in Goshen taught me more. His friends loved poker after extensive European combat during World War II. I watched, thoughtfully mimicking them. They spent whole days enjoying stories recalled from the war-front, drinking and gambling away each other's pay. Their war tales were fantastic! However, nothing similar happened with my brothers and me from our father. No wagering took place during six years at Episcopal Farm School. Inmates had no funds, so we did silly games like "Hearts," not having things worth exchanging. Moral conduct codes didn't allow betting. Imagine the extreme consequences if gamblers would have been caught by Episcopalian authorities. They were "dedicated most to the moral development of wayward boys." Transgressions would've triggered character-changing beatings, for sure!

Once settled in West Chester High, I accepted invitations from Jewish classmates, joining Snyd Snyder's game nights. Poker culture thrived under the radar with Snyd's brethren at our school, with regular play providing easy money. Occasional travel to Downingtown's VFW meant joining Irish players from time to time. Also, there were Sons of Italy's games at Nicola Hall. Cagianno's Italian Deli Smoke Shop, bordering Dago town, supported five or seven-card stud games. Monthly Sons of Italy klatches were consistent moneymakers. Cops ignored these illegal activities, as well. Frequenting

Knights of Columbus' basement poker set up on Market Street grew normal. Fridays, after dark, I grabbed an empty seat.

When cops dropped by, they greeted everybody by name before leaving. Volunteer Fire Companies, Good Will, and Fame Volunteer Fire No. 3 hosted action every week. Law enforcement never cautioned volunteer firefighters about any form of wagering. They'd never arrest firefighters, so we carried on with it, with me enjoying winning tons. Then we started using Jack's (my brother, JC's) place. He arranged dates, so Pete Dalamas's Georgetown University preppies arrived from Jersey. Upper-class preppies wore tuxedos for attending Philadelphia's "mainline" formal events. Pete was a Hungarian that escaped one step ahead of the invading Russians and landed in Malvern, Pa, in 1956. He finished preparing for college there, attending Malvern Prep, where his dad held a position. Suburban Philadelphia's elite prep institutions functioned as pathways into expensive private universities. Pete's contacts reached from Malvern to Georgetown and a network of Eastern universities. (His friendship is my gateway to a vast culture of poker-philes integral to the quality of life on enumerable college campuses. Pete popularized games at Jack's across the network of schools. Based on his elite society connections, he was the person who told me to vote for Nixon so we could play poker on the White House lawn with Vice President Henry Cabot Lodge's nephews!)

Opportunities to take the elite's funds were the best. Upper-class contacts, including the Biddle's youngsters, were valuable for entrée into novice pools with overconfident, self-absorbed marks. After Philly parties, they often lost modest sums at JC's place. Singer, Okewer, Snyd, Shapira, and "Little JoJo," uptown boys, attended Jack's. Whenever she entered Shur's shoe mart, JoJo Sr. bugged mom about her youngest boy snatching JoJo, Jr's allowance, as if it was her fault! (For sure, poor people like us bought shoes there. Nowhere else existed for credit. Who complains about that?) Finding excellent games maintained by various civic or business organizations was no problem. Once seated and buying chips, they assumed I was a member's kid.

With preppie connections, we held sessions at Biddle's Exton Cross Roads estate. Augustus Peabody Biddle, III, and Henry Cabot Lodge Biddle were prominent participants, with their wealth's roots extending from Mayflower's Plymouth Rock landing. From pre-1776 associations, we entertained notions of holding forth inside Nixon's White House. You can't tap into American historical legacy more than gambling with those guys! Sessions that included top politicians' nephews elevated a refugee from a wayward boy's home was how I saw it!

Accessing those American Revolution legacy estates was great! Holding forth there, eating refined lunches, imbibing exotic drinks with classy servants tending to our needs felt special. (Sometimes, Kenny's mother cleaned those mansions. That's a surprising connection!) These teenagers had unlimited funds and were unconcerned when throwing away paltry sums. No stated arrogance accompanied inherited upper-class wealth. Their learned casual indifference fostered relaxed attitudes concerning daily activities. That contrasted with my tenuous existence. I opted for caution around them—a tad uncomfortable suppressing eagerness while depleting their substantial allowances. That which meant nothing to them was everything to me. Seeing imperious privilege's offspring's behavior, attitudes, and expectations, and they're assuming lesser class insignificance, proved eye-opening. It was invaluable character-building exposure. In high school, I encountered privileged mindsets everywhere, and they attempted to mask them. Managing those associations promised to gain social benefits.

Interacting with rich kids from the eleventh grade forward prepared me to handle poker at the University of North Carolina (UNC). Student permissiveness toward our university's underground wagering culture played right into my growing interests. Fraternities were fertile ground for lucrative engagement, readily offering opportunities for improving my cash flow. As a gaming hub, Pi Lambda Phi, a Jewish fraternity, held weekly poker nights. Its convenient longstanding locations offered steady earnings. Because of my success with different Philadelphia college frats, UNC's privileged students were familiar. Such familiarity proved helpful everywhere on campus. I took up where leaving off in West Chester, building a money source. When fashioning a gambling enterprise at college, I envisioned establishing a niche in Vegas' wide-open cultural landscape.

What Happens in Tahoe and in Vegas

Upon arriving in San Jose and seeking card games at colleges, San Jose State (SJS)) fraternities offered a ready-made resource for survival. SJS had national recognition as the world's #1 1960 party school. Campus abounded with dudes claiming respect as expert gamblers. Every frat had resident poker champions. It signaled that they were egoistic amateurs: "easy pick'ns." General professional views labeled them suckers. Pots were never large but were a snap. There were possibilities for more challenging card work downtown because California's rooms were legal! An added benefit was customers shared information for locating private games yielding quick returns. Though underage, establishments supported going "CAL," where bosses placed me at tables using house cash. We equally shared wins, and losing cost nothing. As their youngest ever doing it, I wasn't of age to enter these buildings. My underage status didn't faze them. Advanced skills, enough to beat customers, overrode concerns. Owners wanted games to keep going when participant numbers might drop otherwise. Many operations had this resource, labeled "shills," in Nevada, giving visitors more satisfaction. Owners cared less about legal age issues, which benefitted me.

One 1960s owner said, "Kid, we need you to go to Lake Tahoe and learn to shoot craps, but not the usual dice." There was something you did, throwing five dice using a rubber cup, a scam. He wanted me wised up on that. Jack Marden, a SCVYV teammate whose wealthy parents aided our group, owned cabins beside the lake, so I lived cost-free. So, there I was, looking for Gino's bookmaker when he entered Harrah's. By that time, my barstool seat had started hurting. It was 4 a.m., July 3, 1960, and I yelled, "Hey, White Owl," as he crossed the floor. I stood up, offering greetings as he was finding me a job. He was small and thin; face half-hidden beneath cascading white hair. His nose seemed too big for a tiny person. He squinted, focusing while walking up close. "Geno sent me here looking for work. Everything's closed!

Nobody's here early." White Owl said. "Come on, kid." We climbed to the second level, and strolling toward the back, he shouted, "Hey, Vinny!"

A response came, "That you, White Owl? Come down here! I'm inside the office!"

White Owl walked straight to Vinny, saying, "I want you to meet a friend." It hit me…Hm…that's interesting. San Jose Gino's last name ends with a vowel, as does this fellow's. Vinny manages Harrah's, but he is not a Harrah. He's very gentle and kind but has a Crime Family business manager's look. The conversation ceased while he phoned every section. He left messages with each (dice, blackjack, slots, etc.) to call him as soon as there was an opening. At 7:00 a.m., as I'd been up all night, his phone rang when the one-armed bandit crew called. He answered, "Oh, you do? What time? 4:00? Yeah, ok." He turned, "Son, do you have a white shirt with black pants?"

"Yes, sir," I responded.

He asked, "Can you be here at 4 p.m.?"

"Yes, sir," I repeated. Now, I'd support myself while learning bar dice intricacies. As a fellow worker, getting acquainted with folks operating Harrah's setups came naturally. They explained details, such as the game favoring the casino. Within weeks, the information Gino wanted from me got collected. Stuff learned needed to be simpler for bringing in so little as a resource. Gino saw that with our discussion. Here's an interpretation:

The goal of the game is to get the highest score in three shakes or less. To start the game, you must roll a "one," called an "ace." An ace is also considered wild. Ideally, you want five "sixes," the highest possible roll, which is known as "56" (five "sixes," see?). A loss is a "horse on you" or "horse on me," depending on the case. A tie to be decided by a third-round is "a horse a piece. (Punch)

Their generosity extended support later for Tahoe and Vegas. Whenever I worked in Tahoe, old-timers controlled everything. They handled dealing until summer when college students took over. Old heads' teaching had tremendous value. There were three raises, then a promotion to "Key-man." They gave me slot machine keys for servicing them. Fixing slots added manipulating machines to my burgeoning skills. During an early Tahoe stint, I was employed by the joints, maneuvering for promotions to secure higher-paid positions. Harrah's experience showed it wasn't so much what you know, although that helps. More critical was who you knew. Parents of a Las Vegas High School runner under my wing got me into the Fremont Hotel, a prime location. They provided work on the floor. Later, there was the Hialeah Race and Sports Book, whose owner was the brother of Cal Neva's executive director, so I knew the right people. The Fremont, though, had no Race and Sports Book. Another kid's dad managing the Dunes opened access to freebies there. Their comped meals and show tickets made life damn comfortable.

Valuable contacts always continued during the old days. Education administrators trusted me with chaperoning seniors' Disneyland trips. Runners petitioned the administration because they thought I was cool and would tolerate partying. By doing them services, parents showed more appreciation! A manager helping in Tahoe took a position managing the Vegas' Sahara. We visited often. These occasions were entrées into working casinos. Even with jobs plentiful, my being independent meant more. I forged ahead alone after LATC bosses messed over Kenny and me in 1962. Uncle Coty (Unc) landed in Vegas, making moving there easy. Since I loved running and lived

Local Harriers

All interested trackmen, not including those planning to take part in scholastic competition next month, who are interested in "working out," are invited to do so daily.

That's the word from Neal Chappell who is sparking a movement for the eventual organization of a track and field club for southern Nevada. Informal toil is currently in progress at Butcher Field daily at 8:30 a.m. and 4:30 p.m.

Chappell, an 880 man, ran for San Jose City College, North Carolina, Santa Clara Youth Village and the Los Angeles Track Club.

near a track, training was automatic daily. My outgoing personality set in motion, helping school distance runners. There was no avoiding involvement with youthful talent eager to listen. Full of advice after years under Hungarian guidance, volunteer coaching gave me access to school facilities. Experiences under Mihály Iglói and national-level performances afforded an entrée to join as an esteemed contributor within our community. Richard "Dick" Truman, Las Vegas High School's track coach, had a passion for coaching that matched my love of running, so we formed a potent pair. He recognized six years with Iglói had exceptional value. Mentoring kids and racing Thanksgiving and Christmas Turkey trots justified hard training. Before long, connected relationships, conversations, and casual competitions spurred Las Vegas Track Club's (LVTC) creation with other enthusiasts. From its start, the LVTC became a volunteer, non-profit organization embracing walking, jogging, and running as lifetime activities having physical and mental health benefits. Motivation for forming an exercise-oriented cooperative extended from prior club memberships.

In concert with training young boys, I sought to elevate jogging and running to the city's favored health activity. The LVTC shaped its distinctive participatory interest by encouraging our citizenry to exercise, raising funds by staging fun runs, supporting education programs and charities, and offering college scholarships. We, even more so, promoted our youth pursuing fitness. It stands among our most contributive work. From the beginning, we held club events when nothing else got scheduled on weekends. Saturday LVTC runs were for everyone. Opportunity existed regardless of ability if anyone wanted workout partners on weekdays. Parental associations resulted from mentoring our school's boys. A few parents managed significant casinos or small businesses. These connections provided desirable employment, including operating outside licensed settings.

Living the Vegas Life

I considered beating well-healed joints more rewarding. As an independent, returns are good while not missing workouts. Interested parties portrayed this desert city as accommodating outlaws and mobsters from the '50s into the '60s. While such characterizations didn't define me, similitude exists. Considering our local community's structure, there were opportunities for living as an unrestricted, unaffiliated gambler. My thinking sought outlaw-natured enterprise without engendering outright lawlessness or organized crime involvement. The idea was to generate significant earnings while not becoming beholden to mobsters or breaking the law. I have thrived for decades since embracing Herbert Yardley's book. Testing and proving theories from *The Education of a Poker Player* took innumerable encounters to know stud poker intricacies better than most. A concrete realization was sound practices should prevail at tables. To compete at such elevated levels that winning occurs when scammers try their tricks was significant. My penchant for defining success as "Legal Theft" amuses friends. An essential disposition was benefiting from a distance runner's sober existence while living on gambling.

I got accustomed to coming out on top in every locale, but high school and college were low-budget events, and San Jose ventures required more consistent success. Still, in Tahoe, there were other means of surviving. It was more recreational exploring and toe-testing the water, not likely getting more than one foot wet. Of utmost importance was growing more adept at applying Yardley's methods. Internalizing his preferences had to increase so that prescriptions got used without thinking. This level of command was essential if I expected to achieve a formidable presence. As Yardley described it, challenges for success are more than gathering rubes courting luck. Settings were vibrant, colorful enterprises where people acted out various human dramas that threatened our ability to stay focused.

Yardley's insight identifies that being disturbed by life's dances swirling inside or outside establishments makes professional execution more difficult. Constantly flowing characters, ranging from cheerful to depressed, could distract anyone, and that was the last thing desired if staying above usual chaos. I was stepping into the klieg light's glare as an actor, blind unless conjuring filters for managing pressures of any moment's intensity. How do I know when I'm ready for big-league action is a pressing question? Summers in Tahoe meant little for Las Vegas' success.

My debut launched after balking three times, aborting forays when those seated voiced objections about new people joining. The Fremont is where it started. After that, breaks never ended as favorable circumstances continued. I stayed on top, had the patience to make the best of it, and moved forward with earning a living beyond the Fremont. Many private engagements were small potatoes, as were lesser locations downtown. More promising tourist interactions were on the Strip. So, the Stardust (The Dust) came next as the Sahara didn't have tables. "The Dust" fell under Chicago's mob. Bosses gambled, too. However, they were not good, which turned into an excellent spot.

Soon, I'm knee-deep working the improved Sahara's plush tables sitting behind shoulder-wide slot machine rows. We had a comfortable glassed-in 30 feet by 30 feet space. The newly carpeted poker area contrasted with 100% traveled areas covering entrances. There were no windows or curtains shielding customers against curious slot addict armies. Contests settings featured shaded inset lights contrasting against succeeding sections. Their walls featured painted wood trimming around desert theme murals produced by local artists. Ten lengthy oval surfaces covered by green cloth each had eight chairs. House personnel didn't scrutinize traffic, so dealers controlled curious visitors, keeping a relaxed ambiance undisturbed by spectators.

When into enough pro turns but looking inexperienced, others lock on interpreting success as sheer luck or guessing correctly. That suits me fine! Once settled in Las Vegas, nightly traveling between locations and observing action soon came across as haunting joints. While doing menial Tahoe jobs, I didn't fully commit, not approaching attempting to survive on poker. Afterward, in Vegas, it's going all out toward achieving prosperity, with beginner's forays into various locales provoking great caution and focusing on breaking even, not losing. Raises and passes, calls and folds angled at staying afloat, and calming aggravated rookie nervousness. Sometimes anxiousness changed into being flat-out scared! Overcoming that was numero uno. Keeping pace falters when searching one's memory for responses. There were questions about poor-quality hands, not to mention the interplay of folds, raises, and calls.

By surviving, you grow more relaxed and competitive. Exceptional runners' stamina helps, but not enough for becoming "poker fit." It requires more time to reach sufficient longevity for producing a viable enterprise by holding fast and staying conservative! To travel along this path engenders developing and honing a solid, grounded research-based philosophical perspective from understanding theories of probability and statistics. It is called Bayes' Theorem within Yardley's thoughts. Someone unexpectedly helped me along because a college friend lent me *The Education of a Poker Player*, and I began studying what the game was about back then. It is not about luck but calculation, memory, patience, and skill in reckoning the odds and percentages. Above all is observation: the ability to recognize and interpret the small fidgets, quirks, and hesitations, the voice's faint changes in timbre, which indicate people's tension or confidence.

At UNC, I read Yardley through twice; first doubtful that anyone could play the game so conservatively. I stood appalled by my previous naïveté and optimism, shunning an objective basis. Then I went to subsequent games and tried applying what I learned. For two years at colleges after that, I played 'by the book'—that is, by Yardley, whom I re-read solemnly and ritually each week before games. And for two years, with a couple of minor and very mild exceptions, I did not lose. It was, in retrospect, a good, profitable time. Now my bank manager smiles at me whenever we meet and asks no questions—or rather, he stopped asking questions—and the reviews I wrote weekly began to seem more pointless than ever. They became merely a way of filling in the days before sitting at the poker table at eight o'clock on Friday evenings. Why bother at all when it is this easy to make a modest living? But mercifully, before I had time to follow that train of thought through to its end, calls came, as they sometimes did in those days, to another university or private location, and by the time I returned, the first group had scattered. The games I advanced toward were altogether subtler and sterner. Everybody knew of "the book," and some had read it.

Poker, let me say again, is not about luck; it is about winning and the disciplines necessary for this: abilities like calculation, patience, insight, deception, and ruthlessness. It embodies, in short, all the elements of Social Darwinism—the doctrine of the survival of the socially and economically fittest—the reality behind the American dream. As Walter Matthau said in an early movie, "Poker exemplifies the worst aspects of capitalism that have made our country great. In other words, the American dream—purveyed in political and advertising rhetoric—is the bluff by which Americans are persuaded to accept the altogether harsher, less forgiving realities of the lives most of them lead." The ideas, as mentioned elsewhere, go back in history, generating such motivational forces as "Manifest Destiny" and Calvinist ethics.

Poker by My Numbers

The classical game Yardley advocated is not only conservative but also profoundly pessimistic. He says, "I do not believe in luck, only in the immutable law of averages." In his style of poker, there is no room for play in any of the frivolous senses of the word, and frivolity is too expensive. He advises, "Assume the worst, believe no one, and make your move only when you are certain that you are either unbeatable or have, at worst, excellent odds in your favor." Yardley's is an iron-clad system when playing against weak players that need help understanding the odds or the endless finesses possible.

I was wrong for a long time, of course, and it was at the time I began to realize it that I first read Yardley. Read: "You should study your weaknesses and those of your opponents. Keep a poker face. Keep silent. Don't gripe when you lose a hand or gloat over a winning one." Above all, "A card player should learn that once the money is in the pot, it isn't his and should not influence judgments." Instead, you should say, "Do the odds favor my playing regardless of the money I already contributed?" What applied so cogently to money in a poker pot applied equally to the feelings I had invested in any prior disastrous personal affairs: "Do the odds favor my playing regardless of what I have already contributed?" With such a mindset cemented in thought, vision, and behavior, striking it rich and living to tell about it becomes possible in Nevada.

The trying part of the story was that my survival and initial success occurred during a train of Eastern mob influences featuring the likes of

Giancana, Spilotro, and others. I was able to up my income over the years by using different strategies and playing private and casino poker games with mob-connected associates. Since the 1950s, Vegas was a mob-declared open city for them to pursue their interest while suspending historical inter-city conflicts. One result was a surge in constructing casinos that, over time, brought the Sands, Dunes, Riviera, Tropicana, and Stardust. The biggest problem came in 1971 when Tony the Ant' Spilotro was sent from Chicago to collect money skimmed from casinos. He got involved in all sorts of other scams, which brought FBI heat to the organization as he tried to control everything in Vegas. At first, Tony took over loan-sharking and other street rackets from Marshall Caifano, one of the 11 original Nevada Black Book members. He monitored Frank "Lefty" Rosenthal, in charge of skimming at the Stardust and Fremont casinos. The money went directly to bosses in Chicago, Kansas City, Milwaukee, and Cleveland, unbeknownst to state regulators.

Spilotro, and a coterie of henchmen, executed criminal activities from various shops and stores on or near the Strip, including Circus Circus' gift shop, until law enforcement drove him out. His notorious burglary ring was called the "Hole in the Wall Gang" from drilling holes through the walls of the buildings they robbed. For years, Spilotro stayed out of prison in Las Vegas and Chicago with the help of Oscar Goodman, a criminal defense lawyer. He kept The Ant from being convicted for years by deftly defeating prosecutors. (If you haven't put it together before this, Oscar's successes defending some of the leading organized crime figures in Las Vegas paved his way to be its mayor from 1999 to 2011. His wife, Carolyn, followed him into the office. We elected her in 2011, and she remains until today.) It took until 1981 and an undercover burglary sting at Bertha's gift shop on West Sahara Avenue to break up the gang when at least one member, Frank Cullotta, cooperated, fearing for his own life. That signaled the end for Tony (Spilotro) and his brother Michael in a way that crime families regularly used.

Since I wasn't a part of Tony's gang as a resident independent operator, he had me barred from all the excellent poker games where I beat casino big shots daily. In those days, small pots provided adequate support, with rent from $100 to $200 monthly for the Vegas Strip proximity spaces. Occasional wins bringing thousands go a long way! Under California practices, dealer buttons pass from person to person—everyone dealt. So, cheating shenanigans were more prevalent. After California, understanding bottom dealing protected against scammers everywhere, but only a little-underhanded stuff happens when facing Nevada's mob-influenced controls. Well before 1986, to let the growing heat on me subside, I went to Minneapolis, where Joe, my college roomie, was a defense attorney and had connections with poker games. (Minnesota's state legislature exempts private "social gambling,"—making it possible to hold private poker games in your home, as long as there is no rake and nobody ends with more than $200.) A Minneapolis newscast reported a farmer found the Ant in a cornfield in Indiana. At dinner, Joe said, "I guess a lot of people won't be sorry to hear this." (I thought, "Returning to Vegas could be safe for me, now.")

I admit to having limited acquaintances with resident mobsters. There were occasions for professional contact with them or working in small capacities. That is not unusual during close interaction because neighborhoods are tight-knit. Gangsters influencing Vegas' formative years presented themselves as ordinary citizens. As otherwise illegal operations grew into regular businesses, significant operators became local community pillars, securing the status that such probity implied. They took part as neighbors, friends, or compatriots operating unencumbered and forming vibrant economy-building entertainment venues, creating extraordinary value. As committed citizens grasping the importance of supporting hospitality enterprises delivering prosperity, city managers functioned without gangster or criminal influence. Entertainment moguls, and underlings, lived in our neighborhoods. Regular citizens bump into them or family members everywhere. They do what everyone does. People shop for groceries and fill their cars at neighborhood self-service gas stations. They enjoy corner restaurants' food. Children attend schools, and families sit through church services at preferred institutions. These were exciting additions, building Vegas' social fabric. Having them infused extra spice into Vegas' savory sauce, making hospitality accommodations' growth boom. If only I had a recorder rolling! I'd own that interesting theater!

Organized crime benefited Nevada tourist centers and increased state taxes. Their educational contributions and help with public facilities were common knowledge. Commensurate rising prosperity for the economy, hospitality, bar, and restaurant employees under regimes satisfied most people. Part of the wealth accumulated from nonconforming practices, for example, not reporting earnings such as gratuities. Most citizens didn't care. If they desired, owners claimed undocumented gratuities. From experience, that was unusual, and the upshot was more opportunities or more significant rewards (as Gil, my roommate, often observed when working security).

Much of the skimmed casino money went directly to the early Teamster Union via mafia runners. Of course, the casino money was being carried back east to the eastern teamster's mob guys. That is why they never caused any real trouble in Nevada. The rumor in those days was that there was an agreement among all the different area mob bosses that they do nothing to cause problems in Nevada which would cost them money.

Accommodation between hospitality and entertainment industry groups left independent operators space for enterprises. Unencumbered cash flows increased prosperity and lowered peripheral goods and services costs. Affected meals and alcoholic beverage costs benefited us. Daily expenses were affordable, while food costs stayed damn near free. Two-dollar breakfasts everywhere were more grub than any person wanted. For a graveyard shift server at the El Cortez Hotel & Casino, 99 cents provided ham, bacon, sausage, eggs, toast, and coffee! How could we beat that? Hertz explained our pursuits as practical: "Is it any wonder that our college graduations got delayed?" Joining the culture, we searched Tahoe and Vegas for more lucrative purposes, capitalizing on the early golden days.

A lot happened across Nevada that twenty-somethings like Gil and me profited from pursuing. Scam-wise, plenty of shady activities found us nearly involved more than desirable. We, however, understood the need to avoid being tainted or consumed by most of it. Gil had to be up close for some activities; after all, he was Frank Sinatra's bodyguard. Sinatra called Hertz "Skipper." He served during the Vegas' gangster era's height when Frank associated with Sam Giancana. Giancana, whom Sinatra called "Johnny Holiday" or "Mister X," got listed in Nevada's Black Book, thus had no right staying there. Hertz's principal responsibility evolved into keeping tourists, including random guests, away from Sinatra's gang in public. Sinatra's group never wanted physical contact with patrons, particularly inside his Cal Neva Tahoe resort. They were funny that way! Hertz witnessed rat pack daily shenanigans. He had the distinction of getting summoned to Marilyn Monroe's cottage when she "mixed up her pills," and he phoned the medical emergency squad. Gil voiced skepticism toward the claim of "accidentally mixed medications." Being saved when attempting suicide was more like it! She hung around the joint that afternoon, looking wasted. With no daytime action, we were alone, with her looking terrible, even sick in the head! So, I didn't cut into her! That night, Gil told a sad tale describing her condition. Monroe "overexposed" herself at her Brentwood, CA, home less than a week later. Authorities declared Marilyn's death "acute barbiturate poisoning." Most people in the know expressed saddened relief. They found great solace; it didn't happen anywhere near Nevada.

Sinatra felt much aggrieved over his close friend's unfortunate mishap. He befriended and appreciated "Skipper," treating him as an older brother would. This most recent event provoked his insisting that Gil (Skipper) finish school. He ordered, "Start you a real-life away from gangsters and feds, without this fucking bullshit." Sinatra's stern advice struck home. Hertz returned to Angola, Indiana's Tri-State University, completing his degree. I started operating in the Dunes, with St. Louis and Midwest mobs in control.

The Nevada Black Book identified people barred from casinos. Sinatra got called before their Gaming Commission, and Harry Reid acted as Commissioner before his eventual election to the US Senate and becoming Majority Leader. They demanded Frank explain Mafia relationships, especially involving Sam Giancana. Harry and I knew each other as LVTC members, as he was a boxer, ran marathons, and lived near me. His boxing connection gets described as a love affair. I saw the phenomenon through our training and my activities supporting his political ambitions. We were the same age, and that enhanced our friendship. We had lived through the trials and tribulations of the same world events under similar poverty conditions. Reasons and subjects for discussions were unlimited. So, we often trained together, especially on his way to doing marathons, and I served in his campaign fund-raising events managed by the LVTC folks. He pulled off acting like an adoring fan while aggressively questioning Sinatra. Knowing Harry, as did I, locals laughed off so much sound and fury when he did it, building his political future! The principals skirted Nevada's restrictions by using cottages behind Frank's places, where he, Marilyn Monroe, Peter Lawford, Sammy Davis Jr., Dean Martin, et al. indulged themselves. Their activities made Tahoe and Sin City more exciting.

Not plying my trade or doing miles over golf courses or mountain trails meant frequenting clubs watching Peter Lawford, Victor Borge, Pat Kennedy (Lawford's wife), "Johnny Holiday," and more. They preferred shooting craps. Either ironic or comical, Bobby Kennedy palled around with the group and tried catching the Hialeah Sports Book, where I worked on my way to graduating from UNLV. Bobby was trying to trap the owner into giving out sports betting info over the phone, which was illegal across state lines so that he could shut their doors. Yet all the Kennedy relatives were hanging out with the Hialeah owner's brother and Sam Giancana, etc., all shooting craps and partying together. It's a weird dynamic with the Race Book's owner's brother at the Cal-Neva, where Sinatra's Kennedy-connected friends cavort! It seemed strange, so the best thing to do was keep your mouth shut!!

While exploiting these haunts, I wondered, if you ratted out someone, who in the hell protects you. Cosa Nostra members enjoyed rubbing elbows with politicians looking out for us. What could save you if you caught someone out of line and reported it? Everybody's on their side but you. It could put you in a bad spot! By staying consumed with training for racing, entering unpleasant situations was unlikely. It helped, not only being here for earnings but finishing college. After making so much money, studying again was challenging. But UNLV was handy at no cost. The Rebels' cross-country and track programs started with my enrollment, so it turned out perfect. That made adopting a student role a cinch.

Poker scamming took different forms. Although cheater's methods appeared unlikely to succeed, a few did. Using devious techniques happened more than imagined. Collusion qualified as the most used scheme. In colluding, crooks create several plans. "Soft play" is where actors don't bet or raise if hurting partners. Signaling is another frequent cheater tactic employed in several ways. Hand or finger gestures were usual. Practices include knaves arranging chips communicating tactical meanings. Others were shysters losing to partners (dumping) or raising, then re-raising each other (whip-sawing), trapping unsuspecting players between them. I also learned to pull from the bottom and stack decks. Remember, my history began with sleight-of-hand tricks entertaining the Chappell-Martino family back in the day. It is wise to know slickster moves for combating them. When others know their scams, crooks find cheating difficult.

Most free-lancing happened in the early morning when discordant mixtures of gamblers and music diminished. That is when air-purifying equipment eliminated daily tobacco smoke, and live entertainment went home. Reduced one-armed bandit patronage produced sporadic rings from machines. Non-professionals carrying past 3 a.m. plunge deeper into being damaged by long hours of gambling. They aggravate burdens by excessive eating, drinking, smoking, and lacking exercise. Pros, including me, look to profit from weakened marks. Exploitable turns come, like boiling desert days or freezing nights, and professionals roam joints surveying. If timing exploiting advantages gets off kilter, rewarding discernment could diminish, lowering living standards. So maintaining contact sources is essential.

Part of the practice is rooting out private suites where the action is uncomplicated. They offer more comfort, surpassing crowded floors and escaping watchful eyes that bring control by the "big boys." Preferred dress is like an amateur, appearing an average young novice. Casual attire was light-colored slacks, collared pastel shirts, lightweight sweaters, and loafers. Dressing in that style becomes a tactic adopted while getting established. There were instinctive gimmicks that may not be teachable. There's no telling how many improvement keys existed. Success depends on staying in line and remaining in line when someone else does better. Many opponents needed to develop better self-restraint. People were blowing up after bad beats. They descended into swamps, attempting to win with undesirable draws. Experiences, solid psychological makeup, and ingrained patience prevented falling into self-defeating traps. Among innate abilities was noting others' tendencies. This insight brought a sense of what to do as games unfolded. Timing's essential when checking play, seeing who wasn't cutting it, and identifying who is leaving. Early, while growing astute working in Vegas and elsewhere, observation points out many folks overestimating their own ability, sinking over their heads. Most should have larger bankrolls before joining. *The Education of a Poker Player* requires deciding up front how much one could blow, then quitting before reaching preset limits. Patented rules applied regardless of how wonderful the play looked, if not catching hands meeting studied standards. If winners reversed trends, losses could only reach 1/3 of upsides before leaving. "Money Management" requirements propelled accomplished skilled hands beyond daily grinders. Most participants never embraced crafted financial control methods. Without restraints, this leads players to continue past rational bankrolls. Crucial knowledge from studying Yardley says experts must have personalized business strategies. From that precept, some rules reject pursuing luck and favor preserving or protecting earnings. Non-destructive outcomes follow dismissing unreasoned luck as a practical tool. Essential for rational approaches were calculating odds, observing play, deciphering opponent's traits, and cultivating your memory. Financial management methods got reinforced by conversations with an old-timer challenging awareness for controlling earnings. Excuses for failing at that were, "I keep count, but am building my bankroll." He answered, "With no accurate records, you might kid yourself, dropping more than is wise. Precise accounting helps." After that, I kept detailed records. The sight of crazy amateurs blowing it when losing is a wake-up every time. Professionals laugh at undeterred losers. They are reminders not to act that way! If mentoring rookies, I'd preach money accounting, timing, patience, gaining more experience, and an excellent education before entering. I'd recommend adequate research before jumping into a hot competition.

Learning frequent opponents' ways challenges most people. When one recognizes faces, the question arises of whether familiarity suffices in supporting mastery in the trenches. Everyone has common or unique characteristics. Pinpointing strengths and weaknesses helps, especially when dealing with those not observable. Grasping mannerisms, such as different habits handling chips and if deals were workable or poor, is valuable. When facing varying immediate possibilities, people being talkative means something. Are there visible reactions when receiving straights, flushes, or four-of-a-kind? What tendencies manifested when they were prevailing or losing? Does body language or speech tip off prospects for claiming pots? Knowing how different folk play allowed understanding them, and having perception brings control. Aptitude for reading faces had to extend beyond familiar personalities, reaching unknown figures. Hallmarks enabled identifying better-than-average or weak performers. Such insights were essential when deciding on entering and staying. Games needed mediocre participants to make them worthwhile. Once started, prevailing required relying on data, and odds must hold promise for sticking with hands. Following probabilities for wins is fundamental for making outings more productive during any period. There were occasions of resisting the temptation to dismiss "doing it by the book." Failure to reject unreliable urges most often means losses. True professionals refuse to interpret triumphs as caused by lady luck smiling. Things don't occur because of predestination.

Building toward my most lucrative takes, extreme discipline adhering to Yardley's views and world-class runner's stamina dominated my senses. They were a saving grace; final scores suffice for carrying a Spartan lifestyle through the remaining days. Not working could move me out of the profession, but there was no replacing training high schoolers and the LVTC.

A Tale of Two Slims

Among my strategies was presenting a persona inclining preferential treatment by managers and employees. I wanted them to give me special access to games falling within reasonable boundaries as worth the effort. Establishment representatives granted me respect, with such regard manifested in being known as "Slim" across gaming circles. The full designation was "Las Vegas Slim." This moniker put me in a select group. Most Tahoe casino people use "Tahoe Slim." No surprise that Vegas' characterizations carried into that picturesque mountain setting. Amarillo Slim, a revered personality, predated my derivative identification. His notoriety was outside of taking the World Series of Poker (WSOP). He's a decent supporter, schooling friends on underhanded practices at our industry's fringes. Amarillo's nickname relates to his 170 pounds on a six-foot four-inch frame hailing from Amarillo, Texas. My moniker refers to a comparable physique at six feet two, 160 pounds, operating between Las Vegas and South Lake Tahoe. (Slim has since passed, so we'll miss his "old road gambler" tales.) That mystique influenced Hold' em's becoming the world's preeminent game. Before him, the established hustlers chose it for beating suckers. We did not embrace it nationwide, but since weaker players could do well enough, it stimulated growth. Top echelons playing different versions, such as draw or Razz, dominate 70% of Nevada's games. Amarillo Slim told me: "Nowadays, you win 58% of the time, which is great." Hold 'em allows suckers better fortune and gives houses more rake and profit. Benefits come with increased public participation.

The entire industry elevated following WSOP's popularity. Chris Moneymaker, a past winner, never did a "live" competition before entering. He perfected skills online before capturing a $30 internet "buy-in," which paid him $10,000 and entry into WSOP's finals. He took the damn tournament! Amazing! This popularized outcome accelerated Hold' em's attraction for internet kids. They morphed into junkies, and the average age of ten WSOP finalists a while ago stood at 26.5 and continues dropping!! How ridiculous!

Establishments were grabbing everybody's stakes with their fees! It goes round and round. Joints rake in these pots, and after 8 hours of reasonable limit Hold 'em, the damn cash fills house boxes! You only get two cards starting; why not give us just one? It's ridiculous! But yes, we started Nevada's first Hi/Lo 7 Card Stud, as they had no favored variations. After no time, everyone played them!

As Las Vegas Slim and Tahoe Slim, I affected traits that created a unique and familiar character. Deliberate sizing up participant quality when entering rooms constitutes a tactical display. (I played the Dunes most.) Dress is neat but not pretentious, observers noted. People romanticized Vegas character stuff, which spawned various news and magazine articles. While not courting recognition, it flattered me, although touted magazine and news descriptions bordered on embarrassment. One writer (a fan) penned:

His clothes are described as "not having the telltale wrinkles of a tourist." He projects the ideal manner of not being in a hurry. He usually appears after the clock strikes midnight. He works late into the morning, sleeps late, and is not committed to a specific set of hours.

Remarks on maintaining late nights were correct. Those hours were no big deal, and how I've grown while reserving a couple of hours for daily workouts! The narration continued:

Since he trains every day at the local high school or at UNLV, he's a well-known personality at each campus. There are enough nights when he doesn't play poker at all. Sometimes, the available games are too small. They are just not worth his time.

I spent extra time studying others' styles, figuring out when various actors might sit with me, contesting significant games. Another writer wanted more history and explanation of specific principles. His takeaway, covering style, was:

He has unparalleled discipline in continually courting an advantage. Observing and knowing the other players adds up to that. You can't be Las Vegas Slim and do it any other way. He always performs at the highest level. To him, it's all just part of being the consummate professional at poker. The moniker (Slim) applies as a sign of respect for his table ability. In his domain, it is clear that none are better. He arrived here in 1962, after bailing out of the University of North Caroline in 1958 and stints with prominent running clubs in San Jose, California, and Los Angeles, to pursue his chosen business. He's thrived at the tables until retiring after 30-odd years. It took from 1962 until 1966 to rise to the top ranks of poker professionals. That kind of longevity for success indicates his achieved ability at an unparalleled level. Undoubtedly, his earnings have been like a stockbroker's on Wall Street over the years. With unconscious intent, he drives to achieve such a level of income. The insight behind his success at the tables is an observation that the boon of Las Vegas is attracting amateur gamblers because of the novice's notion that, despite all appearances to the contrary, the industry operates on fair play. Therefore, their skill level, as indicated by their hometown successes against other amateurs, is sufficient for success on the big stages in the great city of neon lights. Indeed, that is not the view of the professionals. There are no readily accessible stats stating that they can't win. Such information, of course, is a settled construct in the gambling industry. It's part of Slim's internalized knowledge concerning the prevailing standards for what happens in the casinos and card rooms. Business practice is for people to leave the Strip and its environs with less money than they brought and, at the same time, feel good about it. That is Slim's purpose and intent. He put it succinctly in a conversation when he said, 'The winners never leave because there is no reason to leave when you win.' From the onset of his career, Slim has approached playing poker as a business enterprise. He is widely respected as one of the few players renowned for bringing a professional approach to every aspect of his activity on the poker tables. It also applies to his life away from the tables for anything that might adversely affect his play. For him, the key is the discipline in all things. This effort includes pursuing a lifestyle emphasizing health with exercising, nutrition, and improving physical and mental endurance to the max and adequate rest through a high level of discipline in all areas. He is perpetually ready for long grueling games, possibly lasting for days.

Through protracted study, extended time practicing, and discipline, intelligence at stud poker reduced uncertainty. My points on experience repeat over and over. Aspiring gamesters see Slim's success as challenging and mysterious, creating a steady bankroll. They didn't get it. Over long periods, everyone receives good and bad hands. Any year, dealing ranges from hot to medium, or some are cold. A key when managing random flowing good fortune was conservative restraint. Recognizing weak draws, then bowing out is a safe bet. Pot size or feeling lucky doesn't matter. Substantial wisdom and courage develop until thinking nothing of leaving deceptive temptation. When asked, quipping,

> My major strategy is to draw everyone into my winning pots and avoid being in theirs. I act smart and opt-out of big money pots when I'm going to lose. I don't want to be caught with thousands of dollars on the line when all I have is a pair or three of a kind when the next guy has a full house.

I studied every casino game, including respective percentages for patrons ending profitably. Skill only applies to poker, and my style is reacting smarter and faster and never sticking with marginal big-risk situations. Yardley preaches moving away from temptation. "Beware of ignoring applying known probabilities. Don't overstay when doing well."

Other activities weren't me, but shooting craps had the most potential. However, if I score on an opening dice roll, that is the time to quit. While nobody does that, continuing to extend favors the house. Internalized odds take shape within each game, with the best possibility available in the opening cast when shooting craps. The chances of winning diminish with each turn. Your choices were tossing again or quitting. If ahead, stop. From there, people's prospects are likely to decline. The essential move that dominant winners make is withdrawing at the right time! If that grows widespread, joints might run into trouble meeting bottom lines. My maxims repertoire holds that a primary strength is minimizing losses. The better one is that with not losing, there are more significant positives for winning. These are practices for professionals sustaining consistent overall wins and increasing gains. You don't seek wins being necessary to offset losing.

They set New Jersey's Atlantic City referendum for November. A previous vote (1974) went against it. Interested parties predicted their subsequent election passing. Nevada pros, including me, planned to arrive on time. The poll looked as favoring us. They'd approve the first legal American casinos outside Nevada. We reserved suites at Resorts Atlantic City. Opening Atlantic City's (AC) casinos, every prognosticator expected a Nevada shark's shiver. For houses, blackjack was their most popular choice. Most experienced places, though, changed pay-offs. They injected more decks, refusing new entries midway through packs. With such game-controlling moves, craps had the lowest probabilities against rollers. Independent betting insists that AC's operations needed to be more experienced in handling nuanced challenges. We aimed to take part, making history. They expected a host of Nevada's finest descending on Atlantic City. Published articles predicted that happening, and some writers mentioned my name. Various media guaranteed Vegas Slim's invading gang was coming.

I often wonder about the root motivation for embracing poker. My interest started from my childhood history playing cards, leading to amateurish high school and college wagering success. Plenty of people, however, did small competitions without committing long term. Relative numbers staying at low stakes are not worth measuring. Fortunately, marks were not competitive through my teenage years, including patrons at UNC. Students needed to be aware and not accept myths of being natural-born gamesmen. Most have inherited privilege and no experience working or struggling for survival. Parental dollars raining on them were usual. They considered it as intended for their indulgence. I wouldn't leave outcomes to luck. Such play prevailed before grasping statistical concepts, such as "the law of averages," when fair play had no place. There is no room for losing, even if winning required scamming. It took no machinating with opponents' exaggerated sense of prowess.

Compared to rich guys encountered, experiences instilled enough wisdom to quit while profiting. I was leaving while not provoking a "quitter while ahead" label that satisfied everyone. Know-how at that stage didn't qualify juvenile games as having a profound life-shaping purpose, and Yardley's guiding wisdom sealed that. There's a philosophical component exerting influence. "Education" steered toward realizing growing emersion as a skilled operator and finding prosperity following some of American society's cultural underpinnings. My thinking developed into seeing how much poker manifested America's pioneer spirit of seeking a prosperous frontier life. That ethos embodies the willingness to risk everything behind Las Vegas' creation. I shied from commitments disconnected from either the tables or running. A mentality existed for Wild West gamblers and gunfighters back in the day. Most had an internal makeup of ungrounded spirits, beginning as youths. A few acquaintances thought I had a similar core. There is no sense arguing against being a modern-day saloon-haunting gunfighter or a frontier explorer constantly searching out environments that ease childhood alienation's disconnectedness. That's why distance runs served me well, spiritually supporting experiencing the greater meaning of human existence. "Distance running has an element of meditation that readily becomes a spiritual practice and connects with journeys of faith."

If there was a transformative lesson in embracing Yardley's view, holding steadfast to not continuing without superior hands was it. His discipline eliminated pursuing wins when indicators weren't favorable, with an oath's power—a religious-like proclamation—with severe penalties (losses) if deviating. As a "true believer," I pursued poker's beautiful interplay, which Yardley gives the game. Artistry manifests when approaching being a complete player and achieving higher-skilled execution.

There were similar factors mirroring elite runners' commitment and focus on pursuing world championship competitions. There's no substitute for controlling contests by knowing competitors better than they know themselves. Because running is the essence of my being—my psychological anchor—everything essential becomes "lifestyle." That part approximates a religious meditative way of life.

Hard workouts made my fundamentals of living different, influencing human connections, mainly focusing on nighttime relationships. An important person was Bob, a freshly minted partner. When opportunities arose, we sallied forth, and both of us thrived. Our relationship prompted Linda and me to welcome him to stay with us. And yet, we were dissimilar in a fundamental way. We diverged on associating with prominent Vegas mob figures, but agreed on becoming experts at detecting slickster team shenanigans. We educated friends to avoid or defeat cheaters. Our studied practices were tools for preventing wins by conspirators and protecting our earnings. Thwarting knaves felt comfortable, confirming my love for competing as an individual. Bob, though, has never been for going against organized cheaters. He practiced total avoidance when any were present. Opportunities for defeating scammers were welcome to me.

There is no denying Bob's gains steering clear of cheaters. I also enjoyed individual success, including heightened competition against tricksters. Teams never were that good! Abundant individual sharks were posing more danger. Experiencing slicks "holding out" cards, marking them, or colluding with dealers happened. So, opposing sharks weren't only competing against teams.

Avoiding troublesome people frequenting favorite spots was an issue. Characters such as Pittsburgh George were mainstays. We couldn't ignore Sammy Fahra, a swarthy-complexioned Lebanese American. Sammy's clean-cut dapper dress belied his reputation for employing abusive language one hundred percent of the time as an accomplished player. Then there was "Nigger Nate" Lanette. He developed a reputation after biting off a dealer's ear. After a mob dispute, FBI agents questioned Nate concerning gangster Arnold Rothstein's death. Entertaining stories and defining dangerous characters' idiosyncrasies graced local publications such as "Gentleman Jack" Newton's writings. Bob had contacts that worried me. On demand, he repeated gangster idiosyncrasies in our circle. They remain fascinating no matter how often told. His comments give a telling picture:

I was only 22 years old and just moved in with Neal and Linda. I was out playing cards all night and I'm losing about $1500. We're playing a game called Razz which is 7 card stud lowball. It's about 7 a.m. and I end up playing against this older man who is very crude. We're both losing. We play about another hour and I'm ahead of him by about $400. Then, a woman joins us to play. After about 2 hours, I had gotten even and a little winners. I was very tired and I told them I had to go and get some rest, so I quit. Later that day, I told Neal the story and, after I described what the woman looked like with her light brown hair and nicely shaped body for her age, he tells me that the woman's name is Sandy. She's the girlfriend of Pittsburgh George, an old mobster!

Then Neal says the man I prematurely bailed out of the game on was Shoeshine Nick Simpson, another mobster not affiliated with any group in Las Vegas. He was his own crude ruthless gangster! Neal then tells me that he is surprised that this guy didn't pull out a gun and blow my head off right there for quitting on him. He, among other things, was notorious for hurting people that quit games while he was losing. I was told later that Shoeshine Nick has more money than any other mob guy. "He has trainloads of money," Neal said. I, however, seriously doubt that he had more money than Sammy

Fahra! Nevertheless, Shoeshine Nick was so crude and dangerous that he'd sit in a poker game and sit in one of the corner seats next to the dealer and if he lost a hand he'd unzip his pants under the table and PISS on the dealer's leg. And, nobody ever said anything! He had recently done the same thing to an unsuspecting dice dealer. That's how dangerous this guy was! Among other things, he had a card room near Palm Springs and had the go-ahead from the big boys to do whatever he could get away with in Vegas. It wasn't good to cross him. After my episode with Nick, he took a liking to me. We talked every time he saw me. He always wanted to take part of my action when I played, but I insisted on playing my own money. He respected my feelings and never pushed the issue. So, you can actually get close to some of these guys if you don't actively avoid them and carry yourself in the right way. I lived in Las Vegas for about a year and nobody was very friendly with the mob people. Suddenly, like in the next day, everything changed and they were friendly and accepting of me. I think, in my case, it took these people that one year to completely check me out and figure I was okay. In another sense, however, having a high level of acceptance among the Vegas gangsters also has its drawbacks. While living in Las Vegas, I kept a two-bedroom apartment at a complex called Woodlake in San Mateo, California. I flew there every month to spend a weekend with my two elementary school-age nephews. I have a roommate at the place in San Mateo. One time, out of the blue, he calls me in Las Vegas to casually tell me that two FBI agents, with badges and guns on display, knocked on the front door looking for me. It's a secure apartment complex with a security system for getting inside. That, of course, didn't stop them. They knocked on my front door and asked to talk to me. My roommate said he'd have me call them when he saw me. On my next trip to San Mateo, I called them and asked them to come see me. It's obvious, when we played cards in the Stardust hotel, the card room is next to a bar lounge that people could see through. We all know that FBI agents try to hide behind the building's support columns to watch people. For sure some agents saw me always talking to mob guys and whoever else they are watching. The agents visiting me in San Mateo asked a lot of questions about the people I knew in Las Vegas. I told them about meeting most of the Vegas characters about two years before and becoming friendly. I didn't consider any of them as close or intimate friends. The agents left with no useful information and I never saw them again. It's as simple as that! I've only told this story to maybe one other person.

Bob continued:

Poker really changed in the early 70's when no limit Texas Hold 'em started attracting major interest in Vegas. Neal didn't make the change as completely as I did. Up to a point, we are playing a lot of draw poker where you bet only twice. With Hold 'em, you bet four times. This is more interesting to me because it's a thinking man's game. It means playing strategically. The game got established all over Texas before coming to Las Vegas in the late sixties. With Texas Hold 'em comes the designation of aces as the highest cards in the deck of cards and not the lowest, as is the case with RAZZ. Aces are low in Razz where the best hand is Ace, Deuce, Trey, Four, and Five. (Seven Card Stud, played for low only). Neal and I do a lot of work in the Circus-Circus and actually dealt the first 7 card HI-Lo Split games, as it's called, in the state of Nevada. It eventually became more popular than most other games for a while. This was a point where we worked with some teams. Now, that may sound like we were scamming the games, after saying that we didn't cheat. With the teams, however, we trained people on how to play. We sponsored some of them to some extent and took a piece of them financially, but they weren't thieves. Split pot games and other games like "8 or Better" became very popular and promised to continue as such. In the earliest days of Hold 'em, I liked playing at the Golden Nugget, a casino in downtown Las Vegas. The Nugget's poker room was a throwback to the gambling joints of the old west. The place harkened back to the days of sawdust covered saloon floors with strategically placed spittoons. Its location and atmosphere didn't lend themselves to attracting high-rollers. I benefit from that because I didn't need big money to play and learn my new game of passion. I'm aware that those seeking to play Hold 'em for big money are pursuing a better setting where they can hold forth in a more upscale style. At the very end of the 60's, opportunities to play for higher stakes open on the Vegas strip at the Dunes. It was a much more prominent location that attracts inexperienced players with sizable bank rolls. The Hold 'em pro's immediately do very well here. I had to take my time and work my way up to that level.

As young guys, we are eager to make connections and to learn as much as possible. Surprisingly, some of the most dangerous and ruthless people in Vegas saw us in the right way. Some of the mob guys we knew, and I could talk with freely, were Yale Cohen, Phil Zalute, Jimmy Casella, Al Benedict, Fred Ferris, Joe Bernstein, Myer London, and Pat Callahan. Yale used to like to sit behind me and watch the game. I knew him the best and he was very very high in the mob. There were a lot of others over the years, but I can't remember all the names. Most of these guys respected us because we were good players—more than good enough to make a living from poker. Neal and I were so well accepted on the Vegas gambling scene that the floor men from the card rooms called us if the right kind of game was starting. World class poker skills make it possible to develop and access insider advantages and enhance ones success at the tables.

In reality, Neal wasn't one to get all that close to people. He was always preoccupied with running and didn't readily socialize away from the track. Neal knew all these people, but they didn't consider him an accessible person. So, he was never that close to where he could just sit and talk to the mobsters.

In many ways, we were defined best as "crossroad" gamblers. This is particularly in terms of exercising strict discipline with living an otherwise healthy lifestyle and being disciplined about predominately entering games we knew we could win. However, unlike true crossroads gamblers, our searches for games were generally limited to the Las Vegas area, Lake Tahoe, and Reno, Nevada. None of the customary years of traveling from city to city and to far off places for the thrill of the game was appealing to us. Although we traveled and gambled in Canada, Mexico, the Caribbean Islands, Rhodesia, and South Africa, that's not the life that either of us wanted to live. Neal said, "It's impossible to travel extensively, make a living playing poker, and keep up with my running schedule." This realization hit home particularly when Neal had to escape to Canada for several months when some of his associates in several different gambling and non-gambling businesses faced federal indictment for a variety of transgressions. The one good thing was that outside of the U.S., poker was very available and without issues with the mob as in Vegas. During this period, Neal was called "Tahoe Slim." Such monikers were not chosen by the subject individuals, they were earned by performing notably on the gambler's playing fields. One particular issue had to do with a deal for a small casino that turned into considerable trouble with the federal authorities. (A regrettable outcome of the confluence of difficulties with our casino deal was that three of our group spent 18 months at a detention facility in Boron, California after the dust settled from that investigation.) As sometimes is the case, good fortune often came from the bad. It turns out that one of the cellmates there had a son working for people with ideas and the ability to remake the Las Vegas downtown.

As a result of his jail stint, our guy got in on and benefited from the revival of Vegas' downtown. For some, as one opportunity closes, others seem to open. The ex-governor of Nevada, Bob Miller, wrote a book about growing up here with a mob-connected father (Ross Miller) telling a hell of a story. We worked in the joint that his dad 'owned' called the Circus-Circus back in those days and benefited from those kinds of contacts.

For both of us, the ability to play well came easy. We don't know if that means we are born gamblers, but we both became infatuated with playing poker very early in our lives. Some people were said to have within them an instinct for gambling. We also sensed, from the beginning, that winning with the highest possible level of consistency was never strictly a matter of chance. Being a skilled player also meant mastering all the ways for gaining an advantage over other players. One of the key skills is recognizing the tricks and ploys that opposing players are trying to use to their advantage. We are really knowledgeable and expert about doing that. Neal was particularly adept at spotting teams working together in games for their mutual benefit. He easily identified teams operating in games and communicating among themselves.

A couple of things happened in the 70's that are extremely important to me. We were into it at a level where we played everyday. I played everyday when I was in town. I, however, left Las Vegas every month or two for long breaks. Neal stayed in town playing relentlessly. Hold 'em wasn't so big at first, so its arrival had little impact. We were aware of its possibilities because we recognized that there were many "wanna be professionals" looking for a highly attractive opportunity to live an "old west saloon style" gambling fantasy. Neal and I sensed that Hold 'em was going to influence people of all stripes and abilities to play because they wanted to think they were like

some of the current popular world-class gamblers. We were aware
that the new game in town didn't mean more games for us because
we were playing Lowball. It was apparent early on that Hold 'em
was getting bigger and had the potential to surpass the attraction of
Lowball in no time. It ws rapidly becoming a game of the past. We,
like everybody else, had a limit in terms of the types of games that
we were comfortable with. The growing attraction of people to the
new game eventually had an effect on our ability to make a living
because it had a higher degree of difficulty. Neal, in particular, didn't
have as many games to play in as there were in the past. We were
already seeing that more addicted players were playing more Hold
'em just to get their daily fix. It's like they'd found the highest level
gambling drug. We, in contrast to the poker addicts, only played
for the money. That is why we saw Gamblers Anonymous, which
was founded in Los Angeles in 1957, being advertised so much in
Las Vegas. You never saw Gamblers Anonymous so heavily advertised until Hold 'em started being promoted so widely. The Vegas
gambling promoters were successful in making many more people
want to play. They were using all the available advertising avenues
and starting to sponsor special events that attracted large audiences
and increasing numbers of low skilled and unskilled players. Neal
was not so interested, but I was!

CHAPTER
THIRTEEN

For the Health of It

Western medicine is an instrument of institutional control. It upholds the will of the dominant authority.

Neal:

For kicks and selling nutritional aids, I paid attention to people moving to Vegas to escape various allergies. Regenerative food curiosity elevated once entering the business. Advocates assembled several herb combinations to strengthen immune systems, helping combat allergic reactions. I constantly tried concoctions on potential users, landing many as long-term patrons. People stricken with unspecified ailments looked for commodities providing relief or cures. It was easy selling stuff, but I was searching for solutions for their conditions. Troublesome cases are what I was after. That's how Howard Bowie, a giant at over 6'4", became a project. He claimed to be affected by everything. Our efforts helped prove his claim. An unlimited number of substances and materials caused him adverse reactions. He labeled himself a "universal allergic."

Researchers often diagnosed that disease as "mast cell activation syndrome."
He couldn't go inside dwellings containing anything besides wood, metal,
glass, or leather. He went so far as to string a clothesline between his house and
mailbox. Mail hanging got reeled into the home. He couldn't be around anyone.
While Las Vegas houses loads of afflicted characters, a municipality near
Kingman, Arizona, contained an entire population. Also, there's an enclave in
British Columbia, Canada, filled with highly allergic individuals. After trying
some favorite supplements on Howard, I enlisted my naturopathic doctor to
investigate. "Doc" was forever applying functional medicine methods, seeking
unusual situations. He treated the whole person, considered genetics, diet,
familiar stress sources, and toxic substance exposure. Every time we talked,
he asked if anyone needed help. After learning of Howie, one day, I called and
said, "Look, I've someone who's hypersensitive contacting many things." So we
stopped by Howie's real estate office. I declared, upon entering, "I'm making
tea." My backpack had an assortment of teas for showing, selling, or drinking.
There was a particular tea formula that wouldn't hurt anybody.

"I have to be careful because of sensitivity. I'd better have only half a
cup." Howie answered. So, that's what he got. He damn near passed out after
one sip! "Damn! What the hell's wrong with you?" Those words expressed
extreme surprise.

"I warned you. I'm hypersensitive to everything," he said. Doc had a few
natural items with him. We tried some, and one brought Howie to functioning again. We visited his residence and met his wife, a retired veteran. Military
discipline must have enabled her to tolerate his disease. Bowie had stripped
all the wallpaper before applying special paint. Years later, he stayed a night
with me. My wife asked, "Where are you bedding down at bedtime?" "In the
car." (Our classic Cadillac sat in the driveway.) "Why not crash in the family
room?" I responded. "Skin contact with those materials triggers reactions."
"Well, why in the hell would you sleep in the Caddy?" I asked. "Ah, its seats
are leather. Leather is natural," he said.

What he endured was unbelievable. It's hard when there's that much
impact. It disappointed me when CHL's teas didn't help; some herbs helped

the more he consumed them. His allergies continued, but stayed under control after finding effective herbs. We never got closer to defining his problems in medical literature besides environmental disease.

Our military developing nuclear bombs at nearby bases captured attention for many years. Weapons tests, fifty miles away, loomed as a most worrisome prospect from 1950 into the 1990s. Citywide, we experienced noticeable seismic effects. Most mushroom clouds were visible from the upper floors of downtown buildings. Curiosity about explosions proved the oddest tourist attraction found anywhere. Viewership of visitors for atmospheric detonations grew so large that locals described outsiders' collective culture as bomb fans or members of a spectator cult. Who could resist nuclear light shows turning night into day? Every multistoried edifice had north or east views and capitalized, offering rooftop witnessing, enjoying alcoholic drinks sporting names like "The Gin'n Atomic Cocktail.

A contest at Sands Hotel and Casino, my preferred hangout, crowned Miss Atomic Testing. On July 17, 1962, we were staying for the final atmospheric explosion of Little Feller (in memory of Little Boy that destroyed Hiroshima on August 6, 1945). From my first year in Vegas, there was extreme wariness until 1963, when a Limited Test Ban Treaty with Russia stopped above-ground detonations after the Cuban Missile Crisis. Until then, Vegans saw radiation as an unavoidable danger of the Cold War. If any Americans suffered, we did! After that, experiments continued but went underground.

Fears lessened but never disappeared until atomic attractions ended. Throughout those days, some media addressed determinations of detrimental effects on public health. Government studies estimated that radiation doses released during those months produced 10,000 to 75,000 additional victims of thyroid carcinoma nationally. Childhood leukemia and adult cancers increased over three states near the military test region. Typical winds carried radioactive dust over southern Nevada into Arizona. The radiation winds from the early explosions blew into Utah and a bit into Arizona and not much in Nevada because of the usual wind direction. We used to hear about related sicknesses all the time in those days! Authorities claimed no danger existed. Before too long, children and others housed near involved areas were developing leukemia. As time passed, communities in affected regions had higher rates of malignancies and thyroid disorders. The fact that no records existed of reliable non-governmental study results seems intentional.

In 1968, a design called Boxcar detonated, yielding over 1.25 megatons. This one's bigger than ever. Citizens made vigorous political attempts at ending it. We left, though it was below ground. When legislating failed, Boxcar exploded as planned. Buddies claimed the strip rocked but didn't experience structural damage. Years later, on April 19, 1972, while we crashed on our waterbed, our dog, usually sleeping on the floor, climbed in my face at 6 a.m. She never did that. Her eyes showed terror. We did not perceive what the hell she feared. Then everything started swaying. Vibrations from an underground explosion rattled the hell out of us, creating the weirdest sensation. We never expected violent shaking coming so damn far. Frenchman Flats was 105 km from our home. Lots of residents worked there. There's not much discussion. Really! They continued quietly; it appeared.

Atom bomb testing attracted swarms of spectators for heavy drinking and midnight shows. After blasts, entertainment went until daylight. Overindulgence made conditions perfect for sober hustlers to thrive, so this extended entertainment hours. I never outgrew it. Ending nights doing golf course runs at sunup felt excellent! The best temperatures occurred in the early hours when sprinklers activated. That's good timing for distance work. High school kids came with me some mornings before golfing started at 7 a.m.

One satisfying, lasting relationship was with Gary Meeter. Our link came from a regional Amateur Athletic Union (AAU) event. The National AAU organization governed track and field during the 1960s. They sanctioned competitions, monitored athletes' amateur status, and staged annual National Championships. After helping to coach at Las Vegas High School, I started feeling at home, associating with others like Harry Reid and becoming a founder of the Las Vegas Track Club (LVTC). Add to that volunteering to represent our club at regional AAU meetings. It was great because I'm a world-class schmoozer. Instantly, substantive talks developed with several AAU representatives. An AAU officer said he had somebody to share in my workouts. I searched for partners everywhere, so he got me together with Gary Meeter, a career bellman at the Riviera. He won Nevada swimming and handball championships and had inner strength for demanding practices. He joined in my training, performing like a champion! He lifted weights or swam laps daily. We added distance runs and speed work, started running together and hanging out. We jogged at parks near his home, eventually doing track work for entering the South Nevada AAU Championship mile. He wasn't fast but maintained conditioning.

The extraordinary revelation was his advocating for eating healthy. Nobody understood much about it back then. In 1964, we visited a store selling organic foodstuffs, local vegetables, and vitamins alongside processed herbs. It was my first health food store exposure. He encouraged reading books on nutrition, directing me to Professor Arnold Ehret's ideas. Ehret's book argued we'd be healthier by adopting mucus-less diets. So I latched on to his advice about taking nutritional supplements. For me, joining Gary became transformative. That made me vegetarian. As an El Cortez Coffee Shop graveyard shift server, there was no resisting dipping into fruit for pastries. Deliveries arrived before dayshift pastry cooks reported at sunrise. Other workers stole pricey meat and dairy. What a curious perspective! Bakers squawked when blackberries disappeared. Cooks didn't complain about pilfering meat. Bakers demanded identifying who stole the berries! I realized, "This is amazing! Thieves can take steaks, but don't touch the damn berries!" Protecting produce over meat pointed toward vegetarianism. Fruit warrants more recognition than meat! That's a different view, for sure!

I heard of a city spot for sale and put money into a damn health food store! The organic foods and supplement dynamics were that of running bringing enlightenment and a life-altering change leading to buying an associated business.

I was mentally and physically in a perfect place. It was nice having the world arranged to suit me. Of course, dismaying news eventually hit.

Reading newspapers was an odd thing for me. One day, when glancing at the Los Angeles Times passing through Stardust's Lounge, a notice about Mr. Zimmerman, our beloved high school coach, jumped out. He died two days earlier. What an eerie experience of coincidences! I couldn't explain the impact. After graduating, I had an ongoing relationship with Zim. Opportunities to share college and track accomplishments with him gave me satisfaction. His contributions in that regard were priceless. We met at least once whenever visiting West Chester. He welcomed and supported me when I showed up at his door. Maybe he perceived how important he was to me. Our conversations touched more than track. We discussed nutrition and allowing enough recovery. Those notions prevailed when defining plans.

Another message from a voice from the past was a missive from Bill O'Shields, the Cagey Coach. Letters sustained our relationship since meeting at Cheyney State College's athletic field on a summer day before getting shipped to Episcopal Farm School in 1948. We remained tied over decades; he was a valuable source of support.

Dear Neal:

It was nice receiving your letter. That letter answered a lot of questions: where you were holed-up, what you were doing, how much money you had gotten hold of, whether you were married, where your brother was, and what happened to your track career.

I had seen your brother one day at the shopping center but had not seen him since. I did not think I could circulate around West Chester as much as I did and not see him if he was still in town. But, you can never tell. He is foot-loose and fancy free now, but I knew he was a reserved man and if he was still around I just had to come across him one place or another.

The names on your letterhead tell me what kind of guys you're in business with. All I can say is watch them because they love money. Maybe you have been around them long enough to know them well enough to know what they expect. If you are on the inside of the business, there is money to be made, but it all depends on how trusting you are. However, I gather you know your business and can hold your own. Good!

Now what about the army? Have you given up that deal altogether? Maybe there again, you know the right people. Or, will this new order from the chief about the reserve get your number? What ever you do, do not get into trouble there.

I'm terribly sorry you did not have the opportunity to show yourself what you could do in track with the right encouragement. You had a lot of ability and should have made a good name for yourself in track. You may not like what I'm going to tell you now: you have always lacked self-discipline to drive yourself into the select class of great track runners. However, I hope this one quality will come to you before you get to be an old man. You have a lot of ability which should be channeled into other areas, and one of these days you will be a great man.

Neal, you are something!...it is men like you that make the big money because you aren't afraid to take chances. Taking chances while you are young is alright but when you get older you cannot make too many mistakes because you do not have the youth and time to get it back once you have lost it....

We did very well last year in the State Track meet. We were third and only a few points behind West Chester State University. I had a good boy in the mile and two mile. He doubled in both events and won both: Glenn Allen. He tied the State record in the mile and did close to the record in the two mile. The sprint relay team won the quarter mile relay in record time. We had a good afternoon that day. We had one weak man in the quarter mile but they did a good job passing the baton in that race. As you know you can make up time with good baton passing. We had been practicing all the week and I stood up there with my fingers crossed during the race.

Well, enough…actually, too much. But I wanted you to know what was going on around the ranch and college. We now live on Locksley Road about one mile from the campus. We have 18 acres and a barn, house and other buildings in the place. Come to see us if you come this way.

Stay well.

Coach Bill

His letter set me thinking. Long ago, I recognized possibilities for achievements of which Coach O'Shields often spoke. Subsequent track coaches assumed my path should be as they thought. Conventional coaches, advocating norms of their world, believed what they saw for me was best. Their valued outcomes required measures of conforming beliefs and actions unsuitable for me. That compliance only came through the application (not just ideas or threats) of force (from the dominant culture's weight) combined with relinquishing a unique sensibility of pursuing personal freedom. I'd never give myself up on that. It looked stifling, if not crippling. Others' desires were not inherently rewarding for me.

The vitamin and supplements industry had lots of healers. Some proved honest, designing potions using science. Others sold snake oil. Someone had information touting an herbal products business starting in Colorado. Phone calls prompted me to attend an organizing meeting at their mountain manufacturing site to see if this program fit me. Created by Dr. Philip Chew, they named the enterprise Chinese Herbalessence Ltd. (CHL). Doctor Chew and his wife committed to building a workable business from humble circumstances in the People's Republic of China (PRC). Dr. Chew aimed at delivering healing and rejuvenation prescriptions that have progressed since China's history began. They proceeded by sharing success attracting forward-thinking entrepreneurs to become partners. Through conversations with principals at their initial organizational gathering, I positioned myself to drive the doctor to Las Vegas for a flight.

We chatted non-stop, riding from Grand Junction, Colorado. My interest stayed peaked throughout eight and a half hours of driving. Interstate 70 cut through the desolate landscape along its westernmost stretch, joining Interstate 15. Hills and sharp turns through Colorado into Utah reduced our average speed to 60 MPH. The road sliced through the mountainous desert. The brush-covered ground, supporting bare outcroppings of layered multi-toned wind-burnished red rock, displayed Earth time's creativity. Miles passed unnoticed, as we engaged in flowing conversation. I came to understand that a Chinese Herbalessence Ltd. personal use plan would enhance running while paying for itself. Chew explained his journey:

> I studied traditional Chinese medicine in China before coming to America. My wife, Dr. Pi Mei Yen Chew, a trained physician in traditional medicine, and I came here looking for a substantially improved life. We often worked more than one job at the same time making barely enough money to survive. After several years doing research for a small pharmaceutical company, we buy our own company and start CHL. The idea of franchising with the company comes from observing and exploring different fast food restaurants. My vision is to make a profitable business opportunity available to the American people through CHL without being required to borrow and invest a lot of money.

I toured the automated computer-controlled factory finding everything efficient and spotless. Operations appeared okay. They loaded me with samples to share. Potential customers tried them and gave positive feedback. Favorable responses confirmed why I plunged into selling CHL. My enthusiasm was unbounded. Quality manufacturing served to grow the business at a record pace.

Chinese Herbalessence Ltd. products were good. Kenny and I and others recognized that eating properly was all-important for competing. Everyone tried discovering what foods worked best for training. Colleges, clinics, and labs everywhere joined in evaluating the effectiveness of supplements, so we moved ahead more quickly than before. We, however, had not found "our magic pill." After considerable utilization and self-testing regarding what seemed suitable for powering workouts, better race times, and faster recovery, a preferred combination of basic CHL formulas meeting exercise needs evolved by adding a mix for improving practices and racing.

1. Tiger Tea — A special formula of herbal teas that helps cleanse the blood and stimulates organ functions. This blend of teas is the foundation of my personal nutrition system. Its origins date back to a period in Chinese history more than 2000 years BC. I drink it almost constantly throughout the day by always having a canister of Tiger Tea by my side. For an extra lift on the day of a race, for example, I included an additional tea called Treasure of Happiness Tea. It is especially effective for supporting metabolism. Many of our subscribers use this tea as part of their diet in weight loss programs.

2. Seventh Heaven Foods — An essential formula of the essence of organic fruits and vegetables. They enhance the processing and absorption of foods in the human diet. More than forty different fruits and vegetables are present in this formula. These concentrates bring maximum nutritional benefits for every meal.

3. Fifth Dynasty Herbs — A formula with five different herbal combinations incorporated into one capsule. The herbal combinations are for six of the eleven major systems of the body: digestive system, circulatory system, immune system, respiratory system, nervous system, and cardiovascular system. The various Chinese herbal

combo's emerged from the quest of the Chinese to make the emperor live forever. These five formulas feed and nourish our bodies and, when eaten with the teas and food concentrates, are about all we need in order to stay healthy.

Since 1972, world-class athletic talent ascended to great value for the PRC. Those developments set Traditional Chinese Medicine (TCM) institutes working toward new (rather than traditional timeless) formulations of vitamins, minerals, herbs, or other botanical substances. Some they fashioned for enhancing performance. Milestones included visiting 1980s Guilin R & D and production operations and taking a picture running the Great Wall. Since China's bamboo curtain lowered after President Nixon went to China, runners entering the Middle Kingdom glorified jogging on the Great Wall. That's an image we want to display at home! Kenny counted among the first foreign runners to do it. He toured in 1976, while Mao Tse Tung held leadership with Zhou En Lai. (Zhou died while they stayed in Hangzhou. Sadness over his loss affected everyone.) That proved a great time, launching Kenny's doctoral study. My funding of his research on sports' social functions had significant value. Support for him connected with establishing the Sociology of Sport as an academic discipline. A role financing a noble mission made me proud. Since then, I've waited to go there and run.

Implementing free Asia vacations as CHL sales performance incentives was a stroke of motivational genius. As a star performer, I ranked with executives heading the group. Visiting Taiwan's farms and mainland sites was what our company's vanguard needed. Such exposure added measures of credibility, solidifying my business. It's funny that quite a few incentive seekers gravitated toward me. Members sought to connect because I modeled our products beyond improving everyday life. That was part and parcel of my age group sports success, combined with first-class schmoozing. So this encouraged agents to work harder, qualifying for visiting Asia and learning more.

Our interest focused on personally connecting with where and how centuries-old compositions developed. As our new bus rolled along, I asked our local guides all kinds of questions non-stop. The first query concerned using sprays, insecticides, or dangerous additives. With me leading, we desired answers from field workers. When we stopped at sources, interpreters questioned workers. I could enter fields myself, but laborers didn't speak English. Back at our vehicle, a guide said in her heavy accent, "They told me, 'We don't use any pesticides.'" Learning about safe ingredients made us happy. We needed information. No sense turning gratis educational trips down!

During our free time in Macau, they provided more poker experiences through the Special Administrative Region. The island was a monster gambling locale. From casino and gaming connections, attractions were not unknown. Several close acquaintances went there. Higher concentrations of money were played, and there was more opportunity to win or lose in a shorter period. Loose rules exist for breaking. This island was a dangerous place, too wild for me. The atmosphere is the opposite of the PRC. We saw that upon crossing the border and heading into Shenzhen.

Military guards patrolling hotel floors felt strange. That surprised us, but the PRC hadn't accepted foreigners for long. They deployed significant numbers of People's Liberation Army personnel, maintaining absolute control over all spaces near foreigners. Before an orientation meeting, I snuck to the top of the place! I looked down, and damned if guards weren't up there observing. High caution toward foreigners prevailed, and it seemed pretty scary!

Later, we stopped at a restaurant with several dogs caged outside. So, I asked why. One guide said people could pick out a dog for dinner! None of us did, so who knows? Most of us figured he messed with us, seeing if we'd freak out. Their humor raises that possibility. Kenny told stories about similar experiences at a Kwangchow restaurant. His group's escorts regaled them, proposing even more exotic cuisine. They offered live monkey brains and a delicacy called "Three Squeaks." It featured live mice floating in a bowl of vegetables and spicy sauce. The rodents get eaten whole, emitting high-pitched squeaks on the first crunch. A group member tested our guides, ordering the primate delicacy. Our hosts refused, claiming to fear he would get sick. Such dishes sounded like urban legends, humoring foreign visitors.

They opened sites of past dynasties for guided viewing. Wherever we toured heritage places, locals visited in droves. There is tremendous home-grown tourism, like DC, with droves of citizens and foreign tourists. A jog on the Great Wall took work. Up and down the massive construction, any run demanded much more than ordinary strength and endurance. We spent an afternoon picnicking near Jinshanling's reconstruction. The expanse's restoration continued unfinished. On this picturesque Wall section, it was time to take my photo while running. There was no escaping the oxygen deprivation effects at an elevation over 3000 feet. Some ridiculous inclines confronted me. Struggles to go up and down thousands of steps became absurd. Niko Shavnisky, my Russian buddy, took photographs. Niko saved me, otherwise, by providing alternative healing, perfected before leaving the Soviet Union. Physical issues cropped up from extended travel and Niko's unique treatments delivered immense relief for continuing to run. His specialized therapy was weird but valuable!

At different PRC TCM institutions, the group encountered therapeutics designed for athletes. Experiences and our sponsors contributed descriptive conversations helpful in promoting sales. I had 10,000 members doing business at my zenith. That volume of associates made world travel necessary for helping recruits build customer bases for franchises. Canada developed into a top spot. Vancouver held many road races and cross-country competitions. My running ability always brought customers to associates and attracted new members. Others quickly became convinced that specific CHL items optimized road racing successes—great anytime.

Chinese Herbalessence Ltd. capitalized on my achievements as well. Exemplar health benefits got promoted through write-ups with photos in our monthly magazine. Everyone joined for well-being or wouldn't be in our program. Plenty of capitalists tried making money. Company decision-makers, however, aimed at balancing improving health with a reasonable profit. I always assumed everybody embraced the idea of intelligent eating, helping folks stay well enough to continue lifestyles past those years when marginally healthy people succumbed to early aging!

As guests of Chen Renhong, China's Minister of Health and Traditional Medicine, our visit was the most rewarding among all our tours of foreign lands. It's of immeasurable benefit because of exposure to the origins of China's several thousand-year wellness legacies and theories connected to cultural efforts promoting traditions of physical expression. Each morning, streets, schoolyards, and parks were filled with devotees of all ages doing Tai Chi or Wushu. Music often accompanied these flowing movements. Each day, organized and well-led neighborhoods exercised while classical folk songs played over loudspeakers. We witnessed pre-world war culture (ancient exercise, arts, and food, including diet-enhancing substances and remedies) supporting modernization and economic development. This dual theme set the tone for our meeting discussions. Emphases remained constant, whether conversing with government representatives, school officials, or township leaders producing herbs.

To investigate the crop's purity, I stepped into coiffured rows of herbs and uprooted some to bring back. It wasn't noticeable if any authorities objected. On arriving at Honolulu airport, drug detection patrols stood out. Curious, I asked a cop why he didn't go through any bags. He said particular canines only sniff for drugs. So then, another damn dog stopped me. It took nothing to spot those greens once that officer emptied my bag. Fast thinking described them as tea. Customs used this dog to check for food, but not drugs! There are laws against smuggling fruits and vegetables into Hawaii. Inspectors okayed my stash. Once home, samples got shipped to a Florida lab for evaluation. Lab tests found no sprays. All of CHL felt good!

I established relationships involving forward-looking people when stopping at PRC institutes and factories. Most of them helped as resource conduits for pursuing better nutrition. We worked with researchers, creating herbal combinations having desired benefits. Though experiencing significant results from previous concoctions, two more entered regular consumption.

1. Exercise Promise — This is a combination of ingredients, including Manchurian Ginseng, that have the ability to improve endurance

throughout long periods of high-intensity running. I experience enhanced energy production and increased transfer of energy to my legs when racing.

2. Sports Perfection — I use this combination of four herbal extracts that, primarily, increase blood flow to working muscles when racing. Simply put, muscle efficiency improved in terms of energy use and elimination of lactic acid. My most notable results, however, are in terms of shortened recovery time.

Championship performances improved after I became a vegetarian anchored by CHL products. The same applied to a special signee, Christine Kennedy. We connected at Reno, Nevada's 15K race. She stood out (though less than five feet tall) at their expo, intensely involved in discussing protein, carbohydrate, fiber, vitamin, and mineral intake for athletic improvement and overall health. Attendees kibitzed about additives, so I entered presenting ideas featuring CHL's program. That excited her to befriend me. We've worked together since then. Kennedy's age-group accomplishments soared. She became the oldest woman breaking three hours in a marathon at 2:59:39. That can happen when seniors work as hard as she did.

Meanwhile, plunging deeper into business endeavors, Gary Meeter introduced me to his world of magic based in his parent's comfortable home. These friendly folks provided dinner whenever I was around. His dad was the head cartographer responsible for Las Vegas' City maps. The smaller population made his father fill empty map spaces by printing quotes from locals. One map had a quote saying, "I'd rather live rich than die rich," NEAL CHAPPELL. I got a charge out of showing it! On visiting Meeter, seeing his room floored me. What a mass of materials! Instruments stacked from floor to ceiling formed an extensive collection of illusionism kits and props. Buying such tools ate up all his money! He purchased everything possible for performing that he found!

Gary gave brilliant performances! He used "Gary Darwin" as his stage name. Predictably, he was destined for Vegas' Magic Hall of Fame. His mission was to get me hooked on magic. We practiced outside the Riviera Hotel while waiting for bellman work. For several years, he pushed delving into sleight-of-hand arts to a peak, bringing me along for shows. Darwin performed in the Thunderbird's Lounge when not doing bellman duty. I learned various finger moves that helped protect me at poker. He also did quick drawings of patrons entering the Riviera. Most famous personalities signed his artwork. It was a real milestone when we started Darwin's Magic Club in 1973. In the beginning, we met at different spots Wednesday nights. Meeter grew into "president for life." My role became taking groups of acquaintances to sessions and supporting shows, which qualified as acts of civic dedication. That grew out of a multidimensional relationship with a Hall of Fame magician—a great guy to boot. Lance Burton, a famed long-standing illusionist at venues, supported Darwin's project as Las Vegas' monument to the art. By the time Gary's parents died, their entire house had filled with Darwin's collectibles. Lance remodeled the home as an accessible museum for devotees.

For sure, the "Sin City" attracting people in the late '50s to early '60s, existed as an accommodating place for outlaws and racketeers. Such characterizations didn't depict me. However, there was an affinity for that environment. The primacy of mob interests influenced socio-economic structure growth. Changes brought opportunities for living a satisfying life and maintaining an open, unaffiliated position as an independent gambler. The desire to live a quasi-legal existence that didn't engender outright lawlessness or organized crime participation held sway. I sought substantial income without owing any "big boys." Being a devoted distance runner, the freedom to train when and where I felt meant so much! I didn't see myself as most did. Some folks woke up thinking about jobs, what family activity to do, fixing cars, etc. These things define their existence. Devoted runners think, "What time do we train? Or "What workout is right today?" People don't structure their lives around something other than work. They believe employment and earning money are more critical than exercise.

Funny that our high school classmates recognized that running was our driving force during our days of innocent youthful desires! Our (Kenny's and my) contrasting focus was chasing our coach. All purposeful endeavors went into improving our times, not getting married or making money. It's going up Mount Everest(s), as West Chester High School's 1956 yearbook described our destiny.

Upon establishing a Tahoe training site, an idyllic lake and mountain terrain became additional incentives for daily long runs. The Tahoe Mountain Milers, a small dedicated community of runners, found me. Even though a tiny group, they held club-oriented runs. Reno was close, and connections with the Silver State Striders Running Club grew solid. There was no problem going between race locations, even for time trials. Silver State Striders put on several marquee events each year. We started the Las Vegas marathon in 1967, as I recall. I watched, inspired when Nick Kitt, who also trained with us in San Jose, finished as the first American. He trailed two imported professionals. Las Vegas Sun newspaper supported that first marathon and sponsored the Canadian and Turkish pros. Nick didn't run for a living. He dealt cards, working at different joints. When our newspaper dropped sponsorship, the LVTC owned it before the Rock 'n' Roll outfit bought the rights from a guy who took over from us. This event woke the town to embrace serious exercise. This race strengthened each year, becoming part of their circuit. Now, thousands show up every December. From our small start, there were frequent events after launching our club. Weekly low-key and periodic high-powered competitions stimulated training hard until I joined Kenny in competing for Saratoga's West Valley Joggers and Striders. A nationally competitive master's club membership elevated reasons for achieving the best form possible. These commitments made winning championships imperative. While going between Nevada homes, I trained and called on everything I'd learned from Iglói. Performing became more critical when I walked away from gambling after 1998.

An almost inaudible knock sounded at my condominium door on a warm December day. There was a doorbell, but this visitor tapped gently. I opened, looking at an enormous fellow's broad smile showing chipped teeth. I was not friends with anybody like this. Faces with heavy eyebrows, flattened noses, and jagged scars would not be difficult to recognize anywhere.

The conversation was brief. I said, "Yes?" He said four words, "You've made enough money!" Next, a long pause ensured I heard him. He turned slowly without swiveling his neck, and walked away. That view framed his massive broad back and this encounter felt like my retirement ceremony.

What a relief! Prospering playing poker to that point and finishing with mind and body intact deserved celebrating! Finally, life became totally about running.

CHAPTER
FOURTEEN

Politics and Sport

The argument that politics and sport are
not connected always was a lie.

Kenny:

Enrolling at San Jose State College (SJS) in 1964 meant waiting a year before competing. I completed B.A. requirements by attending summer sessions, accepting track and cross-country scholarships, and continuing graduate school. Exposure to some professors furthered my enlightenment during an entire year there, primarily by displaying personal contradictions. Professors of Sociology, Psychology, and History, who had progressive intellectual reputations, proved not committed to human welfare to the extent they tried presenting themselves. There were high-sounding words and no commensurate action. They proved elitists' and were proficient in talking the talk but never walked the walk opposing structural injustice. I looked for more. But an inclination to generate liberal expectations was a personal problem. My continuing romanticism needed mastering, and that's the self warranting future monitoring and changing eventually sought through campus rebellion. Later, in the throws of personal activism, at least one faculty member helped. Those giving information and records unveiling questionable administrative practices deserve commending. The ensuing two years from 1964's summer session proved to be preparation for becoming a social activist.

I entered the Social Science master's program and joined the 1965 cross-country team. Successfully testing into a school crossing guard job meant attending night classes. In August 1964, the traffic control position served well because it paid enough to maintain myself without affecting my training or studying. I did that between morning and afternoon duties, reviewing more before school. Crossing guard work proved serendipitous when Lee Evans (future Olympic Champion and 400-meter world record holder) and Linda, his girlfriend, crossed King Road at Ocala attending William C. Overfelt High School. We met mid-summer when Big Sims, my roommate, and I arrived at Calero Reservoir near Morgan Hill to go fishing.

The Evans brothers parked just before we arrived. They assembled their equipment as we exited Big Sims' 53 Oldsmobile. My roommate was a master at ridiculing and verbal putdowns, while I'd mastered instigating such repartee. So we questioned the brothers' angling intentions and doubted their "poop butt" ability. Arguing that they didn't know how was a hurtful but friendly insult. Severe frustration from withering ridiculing provoked the youngest brother's odd defense, "I might not be good at fishing, but I can run." It was bizarre to hear that. Big Sims and I laughed nonstop through our two-hour foray while landing catfish hand-over-fists. When Overfelt opened in August, that same kid, with Linda, his girlfriend, crossed King Road twice daily at my station. We recognized each other and chatted. Whenever we met, we discussed school and running. Lee asked me to watch his first race when track season started, and it was an impressive show with a junior year preseason 440 clocking 48.8. At home, I let my roommate know the boy didn't lie!

Meanwhile, my full-time Master's studies progressed (spring 1966) while I finished NCAA eligibility. B.A. degree requirements wrapped up in

December 1965 but got put off until June. Through the 1966 season, I won every dual-meet 880 and fulfilled scholarship obligations. I met academic objectives, and my competitive running career ended, bombing out at the NCAA Championship (Indiana U.). Track goals became subordinate to finishing graduate work, finding a long-term job, and living daily. The future promised even better when Big Harry (Edwards) completed his Master's at Cornell University, accepted a Sociology position, and arranged a paid assistantship with him, providing me with education-related graduate assistant employment. Things moved along smoothly until December.

Daddy died on December 16, 1966. It hit very hard. There were regrets and crying for my failure to connect upon reaching maturity. Many apologies, sitting unspoken, went undelivered. Mom said he kept working after falling ill. His union organizing and hopes that the labor movement guaranteed a just and fair society shaped his core being. My father died experiencing none of the socio-economic changes for which he strove. Even when too sick to work, Daddy hobbled two and a half blocks to the bus station, drinking coffee with construction laborers starting work at 6 a.m. Evenings, he met workers returning home. Daddy's work life was remarkable. I longed to understand this dynamic. Anxiety disrupted months of seeking to understand him and fostered an awakening. I felt a need to pursue activities connecting me with my essential father—his dignity manifested through hard labor. To honor his struggle by producing activism embracing us both became my desire. These thoughts pointed to changing the future.

Studies I missed while attending Daddy's funeral left little time upon returning to San Jose. It was already weeks into the spring semester. Beyond June's graduation, reflections on him moved to the forefront. Thoughts must turn into action. Data analysis, experiences, and thinking stimulated internalized promises to act against continuing racism where I lived, studied, and worked. Irrefutable consciousness awakened the realization that discrimination connected to the college was never tolerable before or after arriving. I promised that youngsters returning or entering wouldn't stay helpless facing racial discrimination as associates and I had in prior years.

No one ever acted to stop racist practices from repeating or continuing. But, it had become a conscience-rooted demand to no longer leave girls and boys facing oppressive conditions alone.

A transformation occurred to that extent when meeting Harry strolling through the serene, sun-drenched campus. We sat chatting beside idyllic ivy-draped Tower Hall. Conversation covered prospects and concerns for the remaining summer leading into fall. A few minutes went by before we jointly gave voice to desires to oppose prejudice and white privilege awaiting unsuspecting young brethren. When thinking about addressing problems, an understanding arose that produced corrections requiring provocative and irrevocable actions, expressing our humanity! Since discovering shared visions, we planned more discussions clarifying aims and commitment. The analysis yielded plans starting the fall semester different from usual. Public attention required engagement by presenting the administration with proven issues and corrective demands officials couldn't question, deny, or ignore. That's why young people entered a changed environment: formulating political action, disruption, and protest. The Revolt of the Black Athlete (*The Revolt of the Black Athlete, The Free Press, 1969* (TROTBA, PP. 42-43.) explained developments:

> Our rather casual conversation centered on the old and the new aspects of life at San Jose State for Black students. After talking for about an hour, it dawned on us that the same social and racial injustices and discrimination that had dogged our footsteps as freshmen in San Jose were still rampant on campus—racism in the fraternities and sororities, racism in housing, racism and out-and-out mistreatment in athletics, and a general lack of understanding of the problems of Afro-Americans by the college administration.

> Our first move was to approach the administration. We were promptly referred to the Dean of Students, Stanley Benz. It did not take him long to make it crystal clear that, where the interest and

desires of the majority whites were concerned, the necessities of Black students were inconsequential. At this point, we felt that we had no alternative but to move into the public arena. So we called a rally to commence at noon on the opening day of classes for the fall, 1967, semester. We had circulars printed and placed them in all the college's departmental mailboxes. These circulars essentially served notice that the rally would be held and that the topic would be the elimination of racism at San Jose State College. We invited all faculty members and officials.

The rally began on time with, at first, only about thirty-five Black students and a hundred whites in attendance. The faculty was sparsely represented and only a handful of the college's more than fifty administrative officials were present. But as the rally gained momentum, more and more people came out to see what was happening. At its height, there were over 700 people in attendance, including the president of the college, Robert Clark, and representatives from various Black community organizations. As soon as it was clear to us that no more people were coming, we outlined a list of demands and stated publicly what our strategy would be if our demands were not met. We, in effect, declared that we would prevent the opening football game of the season from being played by any means necessary. Most observers felt that this was an inconsistent and self-defeating strategy. Why stop the football game? Why attack the only area that had granted Black people full equality?

Our strategy was basically a simple one. First of all, we recognized something that perhaps the casual observer did not—that athletics was, in fact, as racist as any of the other areas of college life. Second, we felt that we had to utilize a power lever that would bring the community and student body, as well as the administration of the college, into a pressure situation. We had seen, all too often, the spectacle of Black people demonstrating, picketing and marching against groups, organizations, and institutions of limited concern to people in positions of power. We therefore decided to use something more central to the concerns of the entire local community structure—athletics.

What activity is of more relevance to a student body than the first football game of the season? What activity is of more relevance to a college town after a long and economically drought-stricken summer than the first big game? And what is of more immediate importance to a college administration than the threat of stopping a game that had been contracted to include a $12,000 breach of contract clause and the cancellation of all future competition commitments if the game were not played? The faculty also was deeply involved in the affair; particularly the faculty of the Department of Men's Physical Education and Inter-collegiate Athletics for some of the Black athletes had threatened to boycott the game if the Black students were forced to try to stop it.

Our rally spawned the United Black Students for Action (UBSA), an African-American student union moving the institution toward a racial bias-free environment. Some faculty members provided help, while their minority cohorts stayed away. They didn't support confronting authorities, and none positively responded to issues. A few days later, UBSA presented demands. They required publicly transparent proceedings to eliminate white-only rentals and apply existing college standards of housing and groups benefiting from the college. One requirement demanded, "ALL housing must be open to ALL students." Another sine qua non included holding organizations accountable, whether local or national, for behavior violating the institution's purposes. For everyone's well-being (following school moral and ethical codes) Intercollegiate Athletics had to reverse practices upholding discriminatory treatment and exploiting minorities. Professor Edwards, a UBSA Coordinator delivered the list to school and city officials at a public forum.

Controversy ensued when UBSA threatened to stop an upcoming football game against the University of Texas at El Paso (UTEP) if demands weren't honored. Promised picketing evoked warnings about impending deadly stadium rioting. Every Black joining UBSA guaranteed minority players were boycotting games. Reports from San Francisco Bay Area law enforcement warned that various radicals (Black and white revolutionaries and white nationalists alike) planned violence, torching the stadium, preventing playing the game. Both school presidents (UTEP and SJS) agreed, canceling without time to satisfy demands. We understood that shutting down events caused the college and local businesses to lose revenue. While hurting businesses does not end racism, it highlighted that sport's efficacy was generating power, forcing ending exclusionary practices near campus.

Meanwhile, Tommie Smith, San Jose State's most renowned world-class sprinter, attracted many derogatory articles. Simple statements, raising Mexico Olympic boycott possibilities, triggered a death threat deluge. Such attention stimulated expanding sports issues as much as possible, giving impetus to attack oppression across the globe using sport. Here's some mail:

Dear Nigger Smith and all your nigger friends,

If you are all so fast why don't you run back to Africa where you belong.

Let's see if you all can out run my bullets to get there. Sincerely, Your Master

Dear Niggers,

You should be happy that we white people let you go to school in our wonderful country. You should obey your white leaders and not cause any trouble. We know you are too stupid to listen so we can't wait until you make trouble again so that we can shoot you. I'm just a friend trying to help you dumb black niggers.

Your friends, Joe and Ed

Tommie's student status allowed him to access Edwards' counsel. He had genuine concerns regarding racist attacks promising violent, deadly acts. Discussions between us, including Evans, acknowledged threats of physical danger since our youth. The current risk brought no more concern than we had tolerated all along. People stating murderous intentions using members' names heightened typical daily threat-infused conditions. Discussions continued about possibilities for the following year's Olympic Games. A resolution advocating a boycott prevailed at the 1967 National Conference on Black Power (NCBP) in Newark, New Jersey, signaling the idea was spreading and gaining momentum. Contacts including John Carlos, Lew Alcindor, Otis Burrell, Mike Warren, Lucius Allen, and others showed powerful sentiment opposing systems mistreating people of color. Various sources showed that "not only track… athletes, but Afro-Americans dominating other arenas thought seriously about shunning the 68 Games, dramatizing slavery ingrained American injustice. Indeed, some announced sacrificing as early as September 1967." (TROTBA, PP. 49-50.)

Due to Black marquee talent inquiries, Harry had called together noted activists near San Francisco. October 7, 1967, Edwards hosted them at his home. The proceedings went as expected:

In attendance were George Washington Ware, field worker for the Student Non-Violent Coordinating Committee; Tommie Smith, who at the time held eleven world track records; Ken Noel, the co-planner of the Black student revolt at San Jose State College; Jimmy Garrett, an excellent organizer and chairman of the Black Student Union at San Francisco State College; and Bob Hoover, Black political activist and counselor at San Mateo Junior College. Out of this meeting came the Olympic Committee for Human Rights (OCHR) to do the planning for pursuing an Olympic boycott. It was decided also that the best way to initiate the mobilization was to call for a workshop and invite as many Black athletes as possible to attend. The workshop's task was to formally spell out the direction the Olympic boycott phase of the revolt is to take. The segment of the revolt dealing specifically with mobilizing athletes to boycott the 1968 Olympic Games is designated the Olympic Project for Human

Rights (OPHR). Other plans also are proposed—such as the organization of rebellions on various college campuses, the boycotting of racist athletic clubs, and so forth—but our immediate concern is the Olympic Project for Human Rights. The site chosen for the proposed workshop is the Los Angeles Black Youth Conference, which has as its theme "Liberation is coming from a Black thing." This conference, like the original resolution proposing an Afro-American boycott of the Olympic Games, issued from the actions and resolutions of the 1967 National Conference on Black Power. This fact, along with the wish of the organizers of the mobilization to get as many segments of the Black community involved in the revolt as possible, made the Black Youth Conference a "national" base from which to launch the rebellion. The dates for the conference are November 22 and 23, 1967. The time lapse between the organizational meeting and the scheduled date of the Olympic boycott workshop meeting allows the organizers over a month to get relevant information to as many Black athletes as possible and also to urge them to attend. *(Harry Edwards, (TROTBA), PP. 50-51.)*

Enlisting student-athletes for attending a national assembly looked simple. Logistics, however, proved complicated. Discounting expenses and long-standing athletic department barriers to contacting students existed. Communicating with male and female athletes at hyper-paternalistic Historical Black Colleges and Universities (HBCUs) was out of the question. Mail funneled through administrations and departments was a common practice at Negro institutions. Traditional Jim Crow-governed practices forced HBCUs to screen correspondence so that charges only received what administrations allowed, staving off issues of de-funding by state governments. It was simple violation of students' privacy by opening letters. When notifying athletes by phone to expect mail, we found items did not get delivered or fell open by accident. Failed deliveries happened 100%. Intercepting private correspondence never stopped the athlete's growing interest in using the fact that America depended upon the athletes' talents: ready tools for lifting themselves to pursue racial justice.

The Black Youth Conference (TBYC)

Acceptance within the overall civil rights movement helped sustain our project. Opponents couldn't write the campaign off to demagoguery by a single disgruntled ex-athlete troublemaker, Harry Edwards. Most establishment news intended to undermine our efforts that way, and early regular reporting went at him as a mind-corrupting demagogic figure misleading ignorant, innocent, docile followers. These "boys" could never understand exploitation by respected institutions unless an outside individual's unfounded self-serving negative influence had tricked them. Such a statement is rendered a lie by our experience and confirmed by news reporting. Inside information created leverage, forcing concessions from the college. Particular documents showed practices of misusing federal money by the athletic department. They exploited Blacks by allocating disadvantaged student grants to replace sports team scholarships. (Years prior, we abandoned identifying as Negro, using Black.) Athletic administrators conducted operations whereby scholarship athletes signed checks facedown. Transactions occurred by hiding actual money distributions. Grants provided more than needed for NCAA scholarships, and those controlling used the extra amounts for other purposes. Athletes were cheated, demeaned, threatened, and rendered impotent by the process. University bureaucrats usurping their property (grant money) each month denied them citizenship and human rights. The institution confiscated their federal money and converted it into department funds without as much as a thank you. Black athletes existed at the mercy of grifter officials, brazenly acting openly in their presence as they stood powerless. It was a monthly dehumanizing event. When Lee (Evans) complained, it disgusted us enough to go directly to Dick Egner, a San Jose Mercury News reporter. He produced a series of exposing articles forcing resignations and disciplinary actions. That says so much for not having to mislead victims against institutional abuses. More revelations revealed the presence of college-based F.B.I. informants.

No surprise since gutlessness marked them as spies.

A prime vehicle for transitioning from an isolated fringe at SJS was becoming the featured workshop at the National Black Youth Conference's (NBYC) program scheduled for November 22 and 23 (1967) at southwest Los Angeles' Second Baptist Church.

We drove Harry's camper to LA, not knowing what to expect for the workshop reception. The New York Times, Los Angeles Times, Christian Science Monitor, US News and World Report, Life, Time, Newsweek, Sports Illustrated, New York Times Magazine, Saturday Review, and Saturday Evening Post published about developments. Coverage heightened TBYC publicity. The initial focus touted the keynote speech by James Forman, the Student Nonviolent Coordinating Committee's (SNCC) Director of International Relations. To our satisfaction, the boycott symposium drew significant interest. Possibilities for top performers declining to go to Mexico, protesting racism, had appeared throughout the nation since 1960.

In an environment increasingly experiencing nonviolent demonstrations confronting second-class citizenship and increasing Black consciousness and Nationalism, 1968's Black athlete activism was an idea whose time had come. Reporter's efforts at circumventing a ban on covering the workshop and identifying elite athletes signaled national interest. "Negro and white reporters hovered outside Second Baptist Church buildings. They attempted to uncover numbers of people attending, the exact meeting room, and whether they could attend." (TROTBA, P. 52.) We felt managing press coverage by limiting access was best for reducing commentary attacking us. Adverse establishment reporter reactions descended since bringing world-class performers on board. The Olympic Committee for Human Rights (OCHR), the OPHR governing board, accepted Black reporter coverage and tape recorders, cameras, or other means, recorded proceedings verbatim. It reduced opportunities for news operatives to influence attendee behavior and meeting processes. The following *The Revolt of the Black Athlete* excerpt recounts workshop dynamics:

The conference started on time, as did the Olympic boycott workshop. In attendance were Tommie Smith, Otis Burrell, Lew Alcindor, Lee Evans, and other world-class athletes who were almost certain to make the 1968 United States Olympic team if they chose to enter the trials. Also present was a host of less famous athletes from both the college and high school levels. By way of starting the proceedings, I introduced myself as chairman of the workshop and then gave a brief half hour resume of the factors prompting consideration of a proposed boycott of the games. The racist, political, and economic aspects of athletics in America were set forth and then the workshop was thrown open to discussion from the floor. First to speak was Tommie Smith. Briefly, in a five-minute speech, he outlined his reasons for supporting the move to boycott the games. Lee Evans spoke next in a similar vein. Then Otis Burrell took the floor to state his unequivocal support of the proposed boycott. But perhaps the most moving and dynamic statements in behalf of the boycott were those made by Lew Alcindor. His brief and memorable words drew a five-minute ovation from the more than 200 persons who packed the upstairs Sunday school room of the church. "Everybody knows me," big Lew began. "I'm the big basketball star, the weekend hero, everybody's all-American. Well, last summer I was almost killed by a racist cop shooting at a Black cat in Harlem. He was shooting on the street--where masses of Black people were standing around or just taking a walk. But he didn't care. After all we were just niggers. I found out last summer that we don't catch hell because we aren't basketball stars or because we don't have money. We catch hell because we are Black. Somewhere each of us has got to make a stand against this kind of thing. This is how I take my stand—using what I have. And I take my stand here." *(TROTBA, PP. 52-53.)*

The gathering had dissenting voices: mostly notable former professionals. They were "old school." They viewed past sports successes as the single place they received fair treatment, an arena for becoming rich and famous. They believed representing America in international competition was the highest possible privilege, despite ongoing racism. An emerging message sent a definitive signal, and we moved beyond archaic sentiments forever. The following resolution drafted by T.B.Y.C. established a powerful voice in making the point:

RESOLUTION DRAFTED AT BLACK YOUTH
CONFERENCE, LOS ANGELES, NOVEMBER 23, 1967
OLYMPIC BOYCOTT
HARRY EDWARDS: CHAIRMAN

Whereas: The United States has failed to use its power—governmental or economic—to effectively alleviate the problems of 22 million Black people in this country, Whereas the United States has openly and flagrantly carried out and endorsed acts which have operated—by plan—to the detriment of Black people in this country,

Whereas the United States has engaged in acts which constitute a direct affront and humiliation to the basic humanity of Black people in this society,

Whereas the United States has hypocritically put itself up as the leader of the free world while right here in this country we have 22 million Black people catching more hell than anyone in any communist country ever dreamed of.

Whereas the United States government has acted in complicity with other racist elements of this society to strip Black athletes of their prestige and athletic status based upon mere racist whim,

Resolved: Black men and women athletes at a Black Youth Conference held in Los Angeles on the 23rd of November, 1967, have unanimously voted to fully endorse and participate in a boycott of the Olympic Games in 1968.

New York Athletic Club
Whereas the NYAC has worked effectively and meticulously to maintain within its ranks only white Christians,

Whereas the NYAC has had neither an interest in nor any use for Black athletes or athletes of various religious back-grounds until that period of time just prior to the NYAC indoor meet,

Whereas the NYAC has used Black athletes in particular to make this meet a financial success for decades, Black track and field athletes have unanimously voted to boycott anything even remotely connected with the NYAC.

South Africa
Whereas the United States has seen fit to allow the travel within the political borders of this country of persons from countries where Black people can neither enter nor escape the slavery thereof,

And whereby the presence of these foreign persons, their participation in any aspect of social, political, or economic activity in this country, and the complicity with which the United States functions in conjunction with such persons all represent an affront to the basic humanity of Black people in this country, Black men and women athletes have voted unanimously to boycott any meet in which participants from two countries in particular might be in participation. These countries are: 1. South Africa 2. Southern Rhodesia. *(TROTBA, PP. 55-56.)*

Anticipated immediate criticism and ridicule arose among white commentators. They labeled unanimous votes "mob rule." As the foremost domain fostering equality, those touting sports castigated athletes favoring anti-racist resolutions. Some participants received hostile reception upon coming home, lost jobs, and others had advancement opportunities removed. Also, threatening racist letters packed the office mailbox, and telephone calls promised death. Out-and-out racists' instability was the least of worries.

Men in suits followed everywhere, driving unmarked cars. We joked about whether they protected or intended to kill us. On one occasion, they followed Big Harry to an annual department party at the Sociology chairperson's house. James, Harry's brother, and I rode a minute ahead. En route, we pulled into a side street, waiting for the Jaguar. We'd follow him, arriving at Rudoff's together. We delayed pulling out when his sedan crossed because another car followed. Seeing two pale-faced agents in a generic Plymouth tailing startled us. One gray suit looked much older, with wire-rimmed glasses and white hair. The driver was younger; his dark hair cut the same.

We exclaimed, "Oh, shit!" as we rolled out behind them, creating a three-vehicle caravan. At Rudoff's, the unmarked car stopped behind the Jag, and I pulled in, not entirely blocking them. They sped away when we exited the VW intending to ask them to join us. It's possible they wanted their presence known. There's little opportunity to escape the constant pressure filling these spaces. FBI surveillance accompanied every move.

Respite from Project pressures spurred occasional Lemoore, California, pheasant hunting trips. These outings brought relief while defeating weak press challenges, government and private institutions voicing opposition claiming sport is apolitical. We had an ideal outlet through Richard (Pops) and Dora, Tommie's parents. Lemoore's their home turf. His father tended farms for miles around over decades before 1968. These parents brought a large family to freedom from slavery's Texas cotton plantations. No one matched pops' hard work, honesty, and trustworthiness.

In those years, Pops pulled cotton rapidly before machines replaced those scarred and knotted hands squeezing like huge vise-grips delivering bone-crunching handshakes. His years spent sweating, bleeding, and toiling under the sun made local landowners wealthy. Smith's family earned open access to all the area's fields and orchards. Through them, there was unrivaled hunting. That helped by temporarily shedding pressures and intensifying struggles. Pheasant dinners and bonding with Tommie's family were revitalizing during days stolen away from heated politics. Fresh-picked Lemoore croplands contained unlimited game birds. We saw them running through plowed rows, harvested acres still holding scattered sparkling spots. Dark green-headed birds, featherless red facial skin circling eyes above a white ringed neck, feasted on scattered cotton seeds blanketing the rutted ground. Giant harvesting machines stripped white fiber puffs from thin, hard-dry plants while spreading cotton seeds.

Those glorious mornings followed an early arrival at Smith's. The tiny house fit a large big-hearted family producing generosity, kindness, and righteousness by the ton. Tommie got there first. Big Sims, Big Harry, James (Edwards), Lee, and me spilled from my van, finding breakfast waiting. Such gestures lifted tremendous pressure off our shoulders. Relief sensations flooded over us well before hunting started. After breakfast, Smith's sisters put caldrons of water heating over backyard fires. The water was hot when we returned to clean bulging game bag contents. Pops led the way. That first hunt taught us to give him a wide berth. For anyone near him, any pheasants flushed, he downed. We had 12-gauge pump-action shotguns holding three shots. Pops used an ancient 410 single shot. If two birds rose, Pops bagged both. When a rabbit broke out, he nailed that, too. It was uncanny. I never figured out how that worked! Since limits are six each, he was home before anyone else plugged one.

Before we limited, Pops' plucked and dressed birds got stored in the freezer for future consumption. Each unskilled hunter contributed two dinner birds. Luscious breasts go well complimented by cornbread, collard greens, beans, and rice. Wash it down with sweet iced tea, yes! Few morsels equal the "breast of pheasant," capturing an animal's essence. Such feasting harkened to moneyed landowners and European royalty dining on "game birds" since the 10th century AD. Back then, poor people eating prized wild game meant peasants poaching.

Relaxation, laying aside intense political struggle, was rewarding—too brief, but stress-reducing. Back working in San Jose's battleground, any effort using attention and influence generated from amateur athletics took us into uncharted territory. We had to sustain activities garnering athlete and citizen ally support while keeping OPHR's progress at the forefront, getting news coverage. Harry gained an invaluable adviser: Louis Lomax, a renowned author and activist with strong ties to Rev. Dr. Martin Luther King, Jr., Southern Christian Leadership Conference President, and Floyd McKissick, Congress of Racial Equality Director. Lomax evolved into Harry's mentor. We expanded the scope of operations, enhancing credibility by involving notable figures. December 15, 1967's New York City press meeting constituted OPHR's most meaningful step following the NBYC. Lomax, McKissick, and King spoke, stating that the Olympic Project essentials were:

1. Restoration of Muhammad Ali's title and right to box in this country.
2. Removal of the anti-Semitic and anti-Black personality Avery Brundage from his post as Chairman of the International Olympic Committee.
3. Curtailment of participation of all-white teams and individuals from the Union of South Africa and Southern Rhodesia in all United States and Olympic Athletic events.
4. The addition of at least two Black coaches to the men's track and field coaching staff appointed to coach 1968's United States Olympic team. (Stanley V. Wright is a member of the coaching team but he is a devout Negro and therefore is unacceptable.)
5. The appointment of at least two Black people to policy-making positions on the United States Olympic Committee.
6. The complete desegregation of the bigot-dominated and racist New York Athletic Club. *(TROTBA, PP. 58-59.)*

Martin Luther King's and Floyd McKissick's embrace, representing the dominant civil rights organizations, elevated OPHR's importance. An imperative became proving our activism's potency by executing unprecedented actions impacting sports. We imposed a boycott against the New York Athletic Club (NYAC) by attacking their February 15, 1968, winter track fest at Madison Square Garden. It was the world's most featured indoor track invitational. The NYAC had long been known for its lily-white organizational structure and anti-Black and anti-Semitic policies. Success opposing The Garden proceedings depended on facing the OPHR. If they abandoned discriminatory procedures, eliminating our reasons for protesting, we would fail. That thwarts forcing change bolstered by supporters, institutions, and organizations. That these racists continued to refuse to do the right thing was vital. (That makes raising the specter of violence at Madison Square Garden (MSG) strategic. They'd stand fast, fearing judgment as bowing to threats.) Before completing the strategy crippling the New York Meet, I had to get through a deadly crisis entering 1968. That was easier said than done. An assault on the NYAC was paramount starting the New Year.

New Year's Eve, December 31, 1967

Mary and I dropped by 70 North 11th Street for New Year's Eve. Plans included an early dinner and a mellow drink. Dinner at the Fourth Street Steak House suited our budget, style, and taste, fashioning a quiet spell. Next, we'd settle into watching television while deciding what beverage fit the evening, greeting January 1, 1968. Neither of us ever drank Champaign or even wine. It was either brandy or whiskey. Southern Comfort topped liquor ideas, perfect for celebrating. At nine o'clock, TV shows bringing in 1968 commenced. It was time to buy a half-pint. We welcomed leisurely walking two blocks down Santa Clara Street, crossing to the southwest corner of Tenth Street. Within thirty minutes of strolling, covering the distance, we entertained a contemplative opportunity to explore the past, present, and future. Our path went south on Eleventh Street to Santa Clara, crossing Eleventh to Tenth. After crossing Santa Clara, we passed the corner pharmacy, stopping at F & P Liquors. Phil handled the cash register. He was a short, gray-haired, thin reddish-faced older guy, maybe fifty, that befriended my roommates,

Big Sims and Arturo. They visited him, talking more than buying alcohol. Phil enjoyed conversations covering national and world politics. While purchasing a libation, Mary and I bantered, exchanging expectations and concerns about facing another year. At the liquor store, customers entered and departed. So Phil followed behind us, chatting. At a good point, retracing steps east, we turned, walking home.

Two guys, wearing trench coats like my blue Air Force raincoat, except one's black and the other tan, rounded the corner. I sensed hostility across the distance between us and shifted Mary clear to the outside left. As they drew near, both moved over, angling to block me. All stopped when the leader stood face to face. He had olive skin, heavy eyebrows, dark eyes, and a multi-day stubble beard that made him darker. It covered his face, extending down past the collarbone. They looked like my suburban Philadelphia town's Sicilian gangsters. Once our eyes locked, the front guy said, "I'm gonna kill you." A .38 caliber pistol pointed, touching the bridge between my eyes. The barrel's face, framing the hole, shined like a mirror. Its body was black, metal, with plastic handle grips.

The same weapon graced the kitchen table at home. I told Mary, "keep walking," as I wanted her out of the line of fire. I mistakenly envisioned an argument or a fight, not summary execution. No right words were a condemned man's insightful response when the killer spoke, and I said, "What do you want to do that for?"

I heard, "Cause I feel like it!" What can you say? Both hands rose beside my head, palms facing front. Then, pivoting forty-five degrees, my right foot swung forward, moving away, leaving these executioners. As they followed to the corner, vehicles heading east on San Jose's major thoroughfare didn't move, even though stoplights continued cycling. Complete silence descended as a life-and-death drama played. No horns blew; no one called out to help or questioned the unfolding capital crime. Spectators froze, witnessing a murder.

So, it's New Year's Eve, and Mary stands amid San Jose's busiest thoroughfare, urging me to cross, leaving these gangsters standing indecisive, hesitating. Her voice pierced the air, "Ken, come on!! Come on!!" The smaller assailant pulled the other guy's sleeve toward the liquor store. I turned my back, crossing Santa Clara past stunned drivers. Mary, still waiting, grabbed my arm, and we proceeded home. I sought to deprive them of firing with me facing them, and they'd decline the dishonor of shooting from behind. My life hung on that bet! The thing I wouldn't give them was to run in fear. Traffic flow resumed, and it felt good, once again escaping untimely death. Thirty seconds later, relief changed to intense anger at getting threatened. Our decision to go out unarmed produced surging anger. Mary argued for leaving it. But I was outraged enough to race home and return for a shootout. Three patrol cars streamed to the scene, lights flashing and sirens screaming. Suddenly, multiple police vehicles converged on the intersection. I jumped into their path, stopping one, telling them what had happened. That much law enforcement response evaporated all desire for payback. They received a call reporting two shooters. When leaving F & P, Phil saw us getting accosted. He observed the killers and called the law. That played out doubly fortunate because the gangsters planned to rob him. Later, the radio said cops caught two armed robbers during a high-speed chase south on Tenth. They'd robbed a grocery at William Street and shot the owner before encountering us. The incident was another life-changer. My not bringing my .38 saved me immeasurable grief. Had the threat occurred with it drawn under my coat courted disaster for everyone. I could fire before they knew. Life after that would have been different if surviving, but not better. Since then, when the sun goes down, there's no leaving home on New Year's Eve.

The New York Athletic Club (NYAC) Boycott

Once into 1968, the immediate task was completing our strategy attacking the NYAC indoor invitational. We deftly went at them from three fundamental levels. First, there was publicizing that organization's racist character. Next, identifying practices directed at excluding Negroes and Jews for dignified athlete participation. The last step was calling a Press Conference in New York. Jesse Gray, New York City's rent strike leader, SNCC's H. Rap

Brown, CORE's Roy Innis, and Omar Ahmad, 1966 Black Power Conference co-chairman, attended. The OCHR released a detailed summary covering particulars surrounding boycotting NYAC's event:

"We are here to finalize the first step in our drive to realize a boycott of the Olympic Games by Black Athletes. The intransigence of the NYAC in its refusal to even admit the problem of racism in its ranks, much less take steps to rectify it, is, we believe, indicative of the present demeanor of White America toward taking real steps to deal with racism in this society. We see, through this protest, that it isn't just racist individuals we are up against. It's a racist conspiracy involving many of the would-be great institutions of the Society. In this case, we are confronted not only with racism in the NYAC, but also a racist conspiracy involving the AAU and the Directors and Supervisors of Madison Square Garden.

The AAU has paid (partially or in total) for the transportation, aid, and other expenses of Foreign Athletes brought in by the NYAC at the last minute in an effort to break this protest. The AAU has given its approval of this meet, as it has given its approval to all past meets, even though it has been well known for years that the NYAC was a White racist organization.

The supervisors of Madison Square Garden allowed the NYAC to hold its racist functions in the facility for years and thus have perpetuated a racist function in this society.

1. We are taking a number of steps of our own to rectify this situation.
2. We are initiating a number of legal actions against the NYAC
3. We shall picket what remnants of a track meet the NYAC may be able to put together.

We shall white-list any and all universities and colleges taking part in the NYAC function and we shall move on them accordingly. (*TROTBA PP. 67-68.*)

The project's next step was lobbying potential participants. We gained leverage for sufficient commitments not to compete through an alliance network, reaching many community levels and institutions. Marshall Brown's calls, as an eastern AAU Official joining our causes, covered vital ground.

"Edwards, Noel, and their supporters did what they could to organize the New York boycott from their base in San Jose. Edwards says they establish telephone contacts with a number of New York-based organization and individuals... A Black AAU official named Marshall Brown served as Edwards' East Coast connection and personally called many of the athletes and schools that were scheduled to be represented in the field. He enlisted college, high school, track clubs and other east coast interests, exceeding expectations." (Race, Culture, and the Revolt of the Black Athlete by Douglas Hartmann)

Puissance extended by contacting foreigners, raising critical international attention for this racist social and athletic club. Among those informed were the touring Africans and Russians.

The third part of building the NYAC boycott involved marshaling minorities and allies, and mounting a massive demonstration. Contacts with Omar Ahmad, H. Rap Brown, and Jay Cooper, Columbia University's Black American Law Students Association chairman, provided perfect connections bringing large numbers to picketing MSG. As predicted, nearly five thousand protestors mobilized, and picketing encouraged competitors and spectators to stay away.

I took responsibility for halting buses shuttling entrants onto the arena's grounds. My position prevented several passenger coaches from entering. While blocking the entrance, one lead driver edged within less than an inch. Standing straight, I could have kissed it. That was weighing getting crushed against commitment to our cause. There would be no difference if the operator's foot slipped, catapulting the bus, or if done intending to kill me. We'll see if my willingness to give my life overcomes another's choosing an unfortunate accident where they are not held responsible. He expected I'd retreat at the last moment. The decision not to yield occurred well before being positioned for falling under the bus. No telling if the driver noticed the solemn look on my face. I faced a giant machine, a mechanical device operating without consciousness of self or others. Built into the equation, hopefully, a destruction line it wouldn't cross. That's where it stopped. Athletes, coaches, and bus passengers, had seen enough. All reversed, returning to their hotels. My stand sent the marching protesters into frenzied cheers. It elevated energy to a capability for storming MSG.

A mounting enthusiasm point grew where circling again could trigger rushing inside, destroying everything and everyone. We'd grown too close to a course that planning deemed undesirable. We felt the demonstrators' visceral passion, which enabled us to recognize reaching a dangerous stage. I had visions of leading a destructive frenzy. Confrontations weren't unusual, but this was the first tasting blinding mass mob rapture intoxication. Sensing increasing aggressiveness, we huddled the leaders checking strategy, and decided to end protesting before it could turn violent. Before chaos let loose, Harry stepped up, calling the masses together, and delivered a speech declaring victory. We left Madison Square Garden satisfied from hard-fought, activist engagement.

Omar Ahmed felt accomplishing our goal made finishing the night in a "safe-house" necessary. There were distinct possibilities nefarious law enforcement awaited. Civil disobedience raged so hotly that New York's radical Black leadership felt it needed safe houses to stay alive. Such stunning success made Omar insist we join Rap Brown underground. We wormed through abandoned homes, apartments, alleys, and cellar mazes and used coded door knocks and passwords to arrive at Rap's sanctuary. The remaining night disappeared while talking. Before dawn, Omar slipped us out to

Kennedy Airport for San Jose.

On February 16, 1968, the Palo Alto Times (Palo Alto, California) head-lines announced:

"NYAC MEET FLOPS: BOYCOTT DOESN'T"

This headline typified nationwide media responses. From there, we moved forward, confident of our strategy and realizing OCHR's demands. Once crippling NYAC's meet, our program efforts centered on educating athletes and others concerning sports' critical societal functions and employ-ing any inherent power. People could understand this quest as a worldwide effort to end racial discrimination. Our focus shifted to attacking white colleges' deplorable conditions for minorities and promoting similar strug-gles worldwide, including among Mexico City students.

Those involved could instigate positive changes regarding teams, staff, department operations, institutions, and systems' practices with heightened awareness. OCHR proceeded by sanctioning the University of California at Berkeley, the University of Washington (UW), and UTEP (White people say blacklisting. Black activists call it whitelisting.) Attacking U.C. Berkeley, 50 miles north of San Jose, was a logical jumping-off point. They elected to send a white relay team to New York (NYAC meet) rather than supporting nonwhite teammates. That triggered a general revolt. Student dissent flour-ished, demanding the athletic director, track coach, and football coach resign. OCHR threatened to do everything possible to dissuade Berkeley recruits. With mounting protests, marked officials left, and the University developed plans to admit more Blacks. They hired minority staff for basketball and football. As usual, such victories usually produced casualties. No NFL teams drafted football star Bob Smith, a student leader and star senior running back. Attempts to get similar improvements at UW and UTEP gained less than at Berkeley. They all hired minority staff and instituted Black studies.

John Carlos (aka Juan-Los) was a stalwart recruit advocating change at white colleges and universities. One of the world's top sprinters, he moved from East Texas State College to San Jose. The world record-breaking sprint-er's enclave spurred San Jose's recognition as "Speed City." Ever since, creating Speed City gets attributed to Lloyd "Bud" Winter, SJS track coach, through distorting history. Speed City's start, integrating sprinting talent fueling international scale activism, raised expressing Black Power from the campus and the community. Lee and Tommie instigated it. Our newest arrival, Juan-Los, a flamboyant and accomplished sprinter, elevated Speed City as much as anyone. In the same breath, his presence cemented San Jose as a sprinters' utopia—a track Shangri-La.

Reputations and contacts that resident runners cultivated throughout the country tied that entire population to SJS's Black student organization's civil rights role. They created a vital spirit and importance for socio-politi-cal purposes, engulfing its best sprinters. That dynamic drew others. Those pursuing greatness moved where world-renowned athletes, and brave social warriors, influenced change that's the force behind creating Speed City. From spring through the summer of 1968, every 100, 200, and 400-meter sprinter, possibly making the American squad, visited San Jose's resident sprinting contingent. They came because Ronnie Ray Smith, Kirk Clayton (60-yard dash record), Sam Davis, Frankie Slayton, Bob Griffin, and marquee OPHR figures wielded significant influence. Jerry Williams, George Carty, Larry Walls, Billy Gaines (50-yard dash record), and Martin McGrady (600-yard and 660-yard dash records) completed the list. Our record-breakers spoke of OPHR's aims and values impacting the world's best.

While raising the social justice awareness of sprinters contending for spots on the national squad, the organization concentrated on the strategy and tactics of keeping thoughtful coverage consistently in the public eye. Our success could be measured substantially by politicians' criticism of the OPHR and the substantial counterbalancing of positive responses from national magazines. We felt our determined effort at building the OPHR led to the Organization of African Unity's (OAU) move to pursue a ban on the apartheid Republic of South Africa. They threatened to have Black Africa boycott the 1968 Games. The convergence of our connection with the OAU and the international ban on South Africa and Rhodesia broadened our power base. The union magnified the march toward our success and kept the OPHR visible at the forefront of fighting racism worldwide. Several letters came from our brethren in Africa with thanks for the OPHR's work. Our combined forces were victorious in banning South Africa and Rhodesia from the Games, and a significant factor was our proposal to establish an alternative All-African Festival. Never before had Black America and Black Africa united to fight racism, achieving common goals on the world stage.

Work raising social justice awareness among Blacks seeking Olympic team spots got shouldered by OPHR representatives. Meanwhile, we concentrated strategy and tactics on keeping public awareness through thoughtful coverage. Conservative politicians' criticism represented successfully resisting white supremacy. Global recognition spurred the Organization of African Unity's (OAU) moves pursuing banning the apartheid Republic of South Africa. They threatened a Black African withdrawal from the Games. The convergence of OAU connections joining bans on white-ruled southern Africa broadened our power base. Union partnership magnified keeping the OPHR front and center promoting anti-racism worldwide. Africans sent letters thanking us for our efforts. Here's a typical one:

March 5, 1968
Professor Harry Edwards
San Jose State College
San Jose,
California

Dear Professor Edwards,

We refer to your statement of protest against the readmission of South Africa to the Olympic Games, which you made at the Press Conference at the American Committee on Africa dated February 4, 1968.

Your views and support for our struggle against apartheid give us tremendous encouragement that all is not lost regarding public opinion in the U.S.A. We hope that your attitude to our struggle especially in the sphere of sport will gain the support of more and more Americans. Accept, Sir, assurances of our highest esteem.

Yours faithfully,
Alfred Kgokong
Director of Publicity & Information
African National Congress (South Africa)

For the OCHR, ushering goals over the finish, remained. Two Central Valley track meets foretold Los Angeles' team selections. Pre-Olympic plans sought packing Fresno's West Coast Relays and Modesto's California Relays. An OPHR sympathizer flood showed cultural heroes' influence when taking a stand. Plans succeeded such that "at the West Coast Relays ... one reporter dubbed the day "Black Saturday." (TROTBA, P. 98.) Fresno's Relays and Modesto's got swamped by our people on successive weekends. "Sisters" and "brothers" occupied every available stadium space. For the US trials, organic unity manifested among Black athletes. Each planned to win US team positions. They broke from traditional victory ceremonies and refused official handshakes and medal presentations. After the shot-put awards, the US Olympic Committee (USOC) eliminated formal champion presentations. Immediate consensus for demonstrating was wearing black armbands recognizing oppressed people across the planet. Several athletes, including future professionals, announced they would be boycotting Mexico City. Track and field athletes continuing competing meant increasing effectiveness and realizing demands. So, getting San Jose's contingent, among others, reversing decisions and winning spots for Mexico City had more importance. They needed general agreement planning actions there. All eventually agreed to accept different expressions. Everyone should do as they see fit without regrets or recriminations. Any non-traditional behavior served the purpose.

But nothing significant could occur unless they won medals. It was time to temper political efforts and finish competition preparations.

On September 1, 1968, Harry's boycott project concluding statement at NCBP's Philadelphia convention highlighted our accomplishments. Broad achievements were:

- A number of racist organizations changed or closed.
- The plight of Black people in America gained unprecedented international recognition.
- The second-class status of all Blacks, including the wealthy and the famous, had been made undeniably clear.
- Through sport and the relationships between athletes, a cooperative relationship was established with Black Africa.
- The myth of the benefits of sports for Black people was debunked.
- The pervasiveness of racism and white nationalism in all areas of sport was made undeniably clear.
- Sport was transformed into a way of educating people as to the true character of racism in the society.
- The true nature of the Olympic movement as a tool of oppression, white nationalism, and racism was clearly exposed.
- It demonstrated that it was possible, valuable, and necessary for Black people to use every avenue at their disposal to cleanse the society of the forces behind their humiliating and degrading status.
- The Black athlete was no longer a pawn and a tool of white nationalism and a racist society, but had become a viable political force for Black people.
- The accomplishments of the OCHR were achieved without bloodshed or the luxury of expending vast resources. *(TROTBA, PP. 179-180.)*

He noted that much work remained to change America's hyper-lucrative collegiate, amateur, and professional sports business institutions. In this way, the project organizing committee's formal boycott role ended, and individual plans for Mexico City awaited determination.

"In summary, this phase of this political movement originating out of the 1966 Black Power Conference has been a success....

"Black Power!"
Professor Harry Edwards, Chairman, Olympic Committee for Human Rights
Kenneth Noel, Chief Organizer, Olympic Committee for Human Rights *(TROTBA, P. 182)*

The first productive opportunity where OPHR adherents could express commitment, befitting world-class human beings, came after Tommie's 200-meter victory, and Carlos finished third. They each raised a black-gloved fist in a shocking history-making display while the U. S. anthem played. Their act's dramatic air overwhelmed and overshadowed any protesting others delivered while dominating the sprints, the 110 hurdles, and the long jump. Beyond the 200 meters demonstration, little remained that anyone could do as starkly powerful, representing their spirit of sacrifice and the boycott project's aims.

Others expressed resistance differently, but none approached the impact of the 200 victory salute. I was thrilled to witness such courage calling for social justice, and ending minority oppression, utilizing the most critical sports stage! It was seen all over the world. Fear of rejection careening at Lee, if not matching magic accomplished by Tommie's and John's "silent gesture," plagued me. Failure to do something dignified, causing a lifetime Olympic ban, distanced him and his partners. Not similarly performing and facing the same fate invites labeling as weak and cowardly, a more significant personal load following the mind-blowing action and his mates' expulsion than any other athletes. Lee favored leaving Mexico, accompanying John and Tommie. They convinced him to stay. Even suffering extreme emotional strain from Avery Brundage and USOC attacking his compatriots, he won a record 400.

(It lasted decades.) Evans, anchoring the 1600-meter relay, set another world record. (This record stayed the same as his 400.) All US 400-meter runners protested during these medal presentations, but nothing dramatic or irreverent. In many Black people's eyes, Lee paid with annihilated esteem for not matching Smith and Carlos.

Any recognition for his exceptional 400 and 4 x 400 relay performances disappeared under failed attempts mounting demonstrations bearing relevance approaching Tommie and John. Few people knew about the pressure of dedicating performances to his grandmother, who died at 93 in 1993, his great-grandmother, great-uncle, and great-grandfather. Their family survived because his maternal elders, gathering wood in a Mississippi forest, hid and watched whites lynch his great-grandfather and great-uncle (Turners). They were preachers teaching congregations to read the bible, leading to a double lynching. The women immediately walked to Delhi, Louisiana, where Lee's grandmother's sister lived. They survived and continued building a family. That's the major spiritual force behind his accomplishments and being a principal OPHR member.

Among those favoring Carlos and Smith, they accepted mild militancy for everyone but Evans, who failed to grasp human progress's unforgiving demands, hopes, and fears accompanying such moments. Indeed, no actions may be available given the magnitude of consciousness already unleashed. There's no meaningful response other than two heroic world records. I grasped the internal pain he'd find if not matching or exceeding Smith-Carlos' gloved-fist declaration. He'd face more significant prolonged agony than expulsion from Mexico and a historically colonialist and imperialist complicit International Olympic Movement. After his compatriots' iconic and historical sacrifice, he fought off suffocating badgering by coaches and US officials. They were all over him to quash other powerful expressions. No athlete ever faced such pressures. Lee, nonetheless, excelled at handling supreme athletic challenges. After victories, collective individual and relay team demonstrations failed to deliver show-stopping bold or rebellious acts provoking authorities or capturing people's imagination and admiration.

Panther berets and fists half-raised smiling don't rate high as anti-racist, anti-colonial, and anti-imperialist actions. It failed at provoking martyring reprisals.

The responses that Lee faced from people wanting more struck me as unfair, at the least. Remember, Black athletes forged their way to Mexico together, supporting each other. What sports or political accomplishments occurred if they didn't have each other remains for speculation? I wouldn't separate individuals based on the impact of expressing Blackness. I'm not evaluating demonstration fervor. It shouldn't be a "who's Blackest" contest. Yet, when considering other people's determinations, that's what happened. Judging every individual's performance and relevance remained an issue over fifty years later. When inquirers revisit the event, some prior-era athletes use the opportunity to revise and upgrade their contributions. I've had little doubt they believe reconstructed versions are more exact than prior ones. My judgment holds that overall participation also mattered immensely. Revisionist tales continue to be crucial for a particular individual's self-regard. If it serves families, friends, or new and born-again admirers' increasing regard for them, so be it!

I'm satisfied having had a minor role contributing to those events and later developments. There's no value in judging individuals. All expressions supported the OPHR. It's ok that response expressiveness varied. Our goal was to change society's paradigm for the role of Black athletes. We intended to develop expectations (especially in judgments and consensus) whereby perceptions as "world-class," "elite," and "outstanding" no longer settled on athletic performance alone. The goal: making it a dictate that achieving the highest recognition required demonstrable civil rights, human rights, and community grounding. New era stature, becoming an operant condition, reached greater heights among the masses. It has brought an enormous increase in the amounts of money commanded for athlete contributions. The degree of consciousness-raising meant that old political postures no longer sufficed. The value of new elites extended well beyond playing field performance and transmitting ideology sustaining the prevailing social structure.

Black people embraced proposals that elite Blacks refuse to perform without just compensation or support systems built into enterprises seeking their services.

Parts of changing the paradigm included challenging the earlier generation's leadership. That redefines Jesse Owens, Jackie Robinson, Joe Louis, and others as diminished models in the new or next era. Old opinions' influences couldn't prevail given current developments. It also elevates other voices to paramount relevance, such as Jim Brown, Bill Russell, Kareem Abdul Jabbar, Otis Burrell, Arthur Ashe, Muhammad Ali, and other new-era figures (Smith, Carlos, and Evans). (Harry calls this era activism's Third Wave.)

Reviews and revisionist history have recently criticized our efforts regarding not including women as prominent actors. Questioners always present presumed insights, not considering whether a workable possible playing field exists. They never define the extent of BLACK FEMALE ATHLETE INACCESSIBILITY deliberately maintained by restrictions (denying free speech and actions) at paternalistic Negro schools under the color of Jim Crow or fashioned by the USOC. Restrictive practices guaranteed that communication by telephone and mail would fail. Male team members might have contacted women teammates, but no Southern institution males joined. There's no reason to expect more participation than men at institutions kept politically and economically impotent by deadly white supremacist rule. Many HBCUs survived choking on racist state legislatures' fickle whims. (The Dean told students that when I attended Texas Southern University. The Administrator warned students of the school's economic survival jeopardy if it did not maintain a pristine public image. Demonstrating opposition to the status quo was the worst.) No sense in us spending sparse resources non-productively.

Struggle in the trenches executing strategies is necessary for those defining what could and should have been. Reviews introducing actions or potentials formulated years later needed more ground combat-level experiences necessary for counting as realistic expectations. Direct actor involvement was more complicated than seen from high altitude. (Explaining hand-to-hand combatant experiences must fall short when not told by engaged troops. That's an automatic weakness, especially when combatants stand available to talk.) Determining whom to involve occurred having no resources and no ability to penetrate Jim Crow terrorizing power anywhere. Such constraints were clear and undisturbed, ruling southern states. There was no chance representatives could work productively and safely there! It's out of the question! My experiences living in Pensacola, Florida (1957 to late 1960) and Houston in 1964 made that clear. (My wife has said the problem was that self-respecting women didn't want anything to do with us unsavory characters. And she doesn't blame them.) Scholars have yet to investigate government, F.B.I., CoIntelPro, and USOC operations keeping female athletes from connecting with the men. One example is the decision to severely isolate the women's track team at a training camp in New Mexico's Chihuahuan Desert. Researchers should study documents showing how the USOC selected the Alamogordo US women's team site. The reasons, arguments, and conditions they created tell an essential story.

Another layer of struggle warrants consideration. Since founding the project, we weighed having women athletes at the forefront. Gender considerations, however, bumped against significant philosophical differences concerning safety. That's because while we peacefully protested as long as practical, such views being hard and fast positions were in other people's imaginations and assumptions. Original OCHR members, save one, weren't wedded to nonviolence. Socialization shapes individuals having different steadfast convictions. Some personal histories unfolded within environments where daily violent behavior prevailed for survival. We stayed armed because threats of getting killed dogged us. Inside sources informed that Hoover's FBI and Counter Intelligence Program (COINTELPRO) planned violence.

Under those circumstances, involving women loomed problematic. (Any political correctness demands diminish, never appear or disappear.) It constituted an avenue leading to program destruction for those committed to succeeding by "any means necessary." The way to get thrown off balance was if opposition could attack women associated with our project. While not thinking of our personal safety, we wouldn't similarly endanger Black women. Deadly potentials came from different angles. For example, a situation arose involving meeting a regional revolutionary socialist group's representatives. We knew they frequently prevailed with purposes through aggression. Their local contingent demanded a confab with Black student groups seeking to usurp controlling anti-racist activity at SJS. For receiving the brunt of lethal police attacks on Bay Area protest cadres, they wanted college groups catering to their needs, like funding and memberships. Catholic allies granted permission to use a Newman Center basement room.

We lined tables and chairs facing each other. James, Big Sims, Nigger Bill, Home Boy, Tim, Esteban, Aq, and I awaited the revolutionary delegation's arrival and represented UBSA and the OPHR. Seven radical group representatives entered. Their briefcases concealed firearms. Our valises (containing pistols) lay on the tables. The joint conclusion from the discussion, listening, expressing respect, and declining proposals, was neither group benefited from pursuing a different relationship than the current mutual acceptance. Women were excluded since a shootout seemed imminent. Organizational behavior might constitute chauvinism, but women were discriminated against and not chosen for gunfighting. We wouldn't expose them to racist attacks or physical or verbal confrontations. Turning the other cheek did not fit as a strategy. That demanded courage above an average measure. It's where chauvinistic decisions avoiding exposing women to the front lines rested. Expatriate Sociologist Don Dansby's opinion speaks volumes:

> "The events coming down were not determined by paternalistic young Black men, but a hostile and dangerous environment. This is a situation where the why and what come into play. It's easy to answer both questions."

A psychologist might see a dominating combined activist and masculinity element in our movement as a response of oppressed males to accumulated feminizing and emasculating experiences via racism and colonizing practices that make deference necessary for survival. Embracing the status quo in any sense equals deference. The origin of this need is a complicated 400 years deep, and it is a phenomenon that Fanon identifies by analyzing colonized peoples' rebellions. A measure of hyper-masculinity, rejecting feminine considerations, characterizes some political struggles pursuing goals "By Any Means Necessary."

Harry returned to complete doctoral work at Cornell after concluding leading OPHR operations. I put everything into finishing an SJS Social Science Masters Degree and a Sociology Master and Ph.D. at Berkeley.

CHAPTER
FIFTEEN

UC Berkeley

Our education necessitates freeing one from
oneself. Otherwise, our intelligence has no birth.

Kenny:

Throughout 1969, UC Berkeley remained dominated by student unrest, battling Free Speech and Anti-War Movements. The Third World Student's Strike added another progressive force. I enrolled, as it all converged in January. Professors moved classes to locations off-campus chosen by us. It was an almost overwhelming era. My life got complicated; commuting from San Jose, teaching at San Jose State (SJS), and working with Bill Stevens and with students, faculty, and administrators, establishing Black Studies.

SJS kept pace in implementing changes pushed by San Francisco State University's and U.C. Berkeley's Third World Liberation Fronts. Pressure eased nearing year's end when leading area schools approved establishing Ethnic Studies departments. By 1972, changes progressed when a National

Association for promoting national scholarship focusing on ethnic college and university curricula development formed. Four years had passed since Mexico, and Munich's Olympics fast approached. Lee Evans was a Fulbright Scholar and an OPHR mainstay. He trained to run on the next U.S. Team after getting a Master's Degree. Whether anyone planned to protest awaited an on-site answer. Everyone knew race relations improved, increasing opportunities for Blacks securing sports-related positions, but positive change had been nominal. We needed more.

1972 Olympics

Much to our pleasure, remnants of the 1968 boycott carried forward. Although, no Tommie Smith or John Carlos emerged this time to create history-making demonstrations. Vince Matthews placed first, and Wayne Collett finished second, running 400 meters. They acted out concern about Black people's plight on the victory stand.

> ...Matthews and ... Collett stood with hands on hips and talked during the anthem in a protest of U.S. civil rights policies back home. The protest drew the ire of the International Olympic Committee, which banned Collett and Matthews from the rest of the Munich games and cost the sprinters a shot at gold as members of the favored 1,600-relay team. Collett said the protest had nothing to do with anti-American feelings and has long been misunderstood as an act of unpatriotic behavior... "I love America," he said. "I just don't think it's lived up to its promise. I'm not anti-American at all. To suggest otherwise is to not understand the struggle of Blacks in America. (*Peter Yoon, "Munich Olympics: 30 Years Later- A Difficult Reaction", New York Times, Sept. 7, 1972.*)

Mathews' and Collett's actions weighed as heavy as did a communications disaster in Germany that caused two US sprinters to miss the 100 final. (Not to mention Palestinians massacring several Israeli Olympians.)

Unfortunately, the failures of our sprinters disturbed Black participation even more because Coach Bakerson, Black Assistant for Sprints, failed to manage their preparation. At Texas Southern University, his coaching wasn't professional. He represented, rather than developed, athletes. His ultimate value came as a response to the Black human rights project's demands. Our Olympic Project for Human Rights opened opportunities for minority coaches and administrators. None held positions on National Teams or an all-white U.S. Olympic Committee. While I cared about our sprinter's disqualifications, I didn't regret the tremendous poetic justice wrought when Negro Coach Bakerson failed responsibility. Two Black sprinters removed from representing racist America existed as his tenure's shameful irony. He opposed 1968's OPHR, tried stopping athlete involvement, and constantly talked against protest efforts. A letter to Tommie Smith documents his view. He spoke of "the Negro athletes."

Dear Tommie,

I hope that this letter finds you in good health and doing well after the hectic pace in Tokyo. I am sorry I did not have the opportunity to talk with you before you got through customs at San Francisco. There was so much confusion and rushing that I saw you only through the glass door leaving with your wife.

I am trying to get both feet on the ground here at Western Illinois University, but I am certain it will take me a whole school year to get straight. Perhaps you know already that I was selected as one of the Olympic coaches in Chicago a few weeks ago. Coach Payton Jordan will be the head coach and he has already asked me to take charge of both relays and the sprinters and quarter milers.

I don't think it is necessary to tell you how proud and gratifying I feel about being one of the coaches, especially when I will have the chance to be associated with and to work with the greatest track athletes in the world. It is with pride and humility that I accept this challenge to work with the athletes and to represent the United States before the world next October in Mexico City.

Being one of the coaches and knowing you as I do, I have become very concerned lately about a few articles that have appeared in the newspapers on the West Coast and in *Sports Illustrated* in regards to a possible boycott of the Olympic Games by the Negro athletes. Many times interviews are not reported correctly by newspaper men, therefore, I thought I would write to you, Tommie, to really find out what's going on. I am confident that you will level with me on your thinking, and I shall do the same with you.

My feeling is that a boycott by the Negro athlete of the Olympic Games would be a disastrous mistake, not only for the individuals who might boycott, but for the United States in general. We fail to realize that we are Americans first and Negroes second, and boycotting the Olympic Games for "Black Power," "White Power," "Green Power," "Yellow Power," or any power was senseless and stupid. I realize as well as you do that there are still many injustices to our people in this country and that these injustices should and must get corrected, and I sincerely believed someday they will be corrected but not by exploitation of one group by another group, and especially by a group called "Black Power" who have lost the sense of "fair play" and the original objectives of the civil rights movement in this country.

In my humble opinion, the "Black Power" group in this country does not truly represent the 19,000,000 Negroes. It does not even represent 5 per cent of the Negroes. I am certain that the movement leaders are not sincere in their beliefs when it is a known fact that they agitate and provoke other people to destruction while they flee the consequences. Again, I say, Tommie, we as Negroes do have grievances but we do not need spokesmen who are poisonous propagandists, who capitalize on our real grievances for their own personal gains.

You and the rest of the great Negro athletes can show the world how well you can perform despite the many injustices that we face in our country. I have been all over the world and have seen, lived, and talked with many people, and when you come down to the final nut cracking, the United States is a damn good country to be a citizen of.

I am looking forward to having you as a member of both relay teams for Mexico City. Please feel free to lay it on the line with me when you answer my letter. I have talked with Ralph Boston and a few other of the top athletes and they all have told me that in their opinion a boycott would serve no definite purpose.

Take care of yourself, I shall be looking forward to seeing you at some of the big meets next year. Please give my best regards to your lovely wife Denise.

Sincerely,
Coach Bakerson
Track Coach

In Bakerson's biography, a missive I wrote is reprinted.

Dear Stan

I don't know the level of your awareness of the situation in the U.S. or the world, but your letter seems to indicate that your mind is at least partially open. Therefore, I'd like to get this word in before you completely put us down.

It is apparent that you have been thoroughly deluded by your seeming success in the track game. But I think that should you evaluate your position; it can be seen in the final analysis that you are merely a tool in a bizarre game of international prestige. You say that you are proud to be one of the coaches again and maybe you should be, but the truth is that you along with many other Negroes are from another era of the existence of the Black Man—an era of accommodationists and outright Uncle Toms. You see, Stan, the tenor of things has considerably changed and is continuing to change, as to the role that Black people must play in the continued existence of Racist America.

You are right, an Olympic boycott would be a disastrous mistake, but it is the White Man's mistake, for he has allowed a situation to develop which makes a boycott necessary (not just desirable). And in this we cannot neglect the role of the gutless Uncle Toms that have never stood up as men.

Yes there are many injustices left in this country and they are the same ones that have always been and always will be until the Black youth (athletes in particular) call it to a halt. The times are by now too numerous to count. These things cannot be denied so you are wrong. We are not Americans first, we are people first, and we catch hell because we are Black people not because we are Americans.

So in reality no Blacks should perform in any capacity for the glory of this country and only an ignorant Uncle Tom would sincerely coach on a staff of bigoted racists and a team that promotes and reinforces the racial conditions in America. It was a very good tactical move for them to have you head coach a year or so ago and as a staff member now. You know they would have left themselves wide open for a boycott if they hadn't. (They would panic if you said you couldn't do it now.) Think about this—your job is to keep the niggers in line (sprinters and quarter milers). Well maybe they have been able to fool you again but that's about as far as it goes.

It's true that Black power does not represent the 20 to 35 million Blacks in this country, but neither do you or people like you. And even more important, you do not represent the Black athlete. If as you say "We Negroes have grievances" when are you going to voice yours? Let's show the world not only what great athletes we are but also what great MEN we are.

Its time to see how well that team and nation can function without us. Stan, there has to be some serious changes in order for the team or the nation to survive.

Sincerely Yours,
Kenneth Noel

After the events of 1968, athletes needed enlightenment on the perils of relying on token coaches. Stan couldn't give them adequate support during any world event. In an anti-racist struggle for equality, anyone calling themselves "Negro" deserves suspicion regarding whose welfare they sustain. He was not there for them. If given an opportunity, I would have warned them. Eddie Hart (the world's best sprinter) and I attended Berkeley. Unfortunately, our paths never crossed. Any shame visited upon Coach Bakerson is justice from years of exploiting athletes, including fudging on per diem, discovered when I competed for Texas Southern. Pleased after the 1972 Games (with empathy for Eddie and Rey), I sent a letter congratulating their coach— thanking him for creating his imaginative boycott. (He didn't mention my second letter or give it to George Wright, his biographer.)

Further damning behavior accompanied his coaching failure's aftermath. He failed to be responsible and lied by not telling his men truthfully about their situation in real time. Rey Robinson, one runner involved, recounted that story, interviewed by Lance Pugmire, a Los Angeles Times writer. His reporting said Robinson got contacted in the Olympic village when their coach appeared, saying he and Eddie Hart had better hurry. It turned out their competition had proceeded before Stan encouraged getting there. He knew it when alerting them. Actions, though, didn't convey the situation's gravity. Efforts hiding failure included acting like they could get there in time, knowing they couldn't. Coach Bakerson is known as slick. This maneuver allowed claiming victimhood, joining his tardy runners. He let them go on their own when shepherding them to their competition was his duty. Honest coaches would accompany their athletes through layers of disappointment and frustration. That, however, requires courage to admit responsibility. As a weak gesture, Stan accepted blame without consequences.

China

By the summer of 1975, I floundered in developing a concrete compelling doctoral dissertation topic, needing something inspiring and energizing to capture my imagination. An opportunity came because the Symbionese Liberation Army (SLA) surfaced using its slogan, "Death to the fascist insect that preys upon the life of the people." The bold kidnapping of Patty Hearst on February 4, 1974, led to subsequent developments dominating the news. (She joined her captor's bank robbery after a Stockholm syndrome-type conversion.) After Patty Hearst's brainwashing into joining them as Tania, SLA units pulled off robberies and deadly police standoffs. Those still alive, including Hearst, disappeared "underground." Authorities killed most members, continually searching for SLA remnants. FBI agents thought Jack Scott, a radical leftist writer sympathizer, managed political fugitive transporting operations.

When Berkeley Professor Harry Edwards, noted for launching the Sociology of Sport, learned Scott's FBI entanglement created an opening, he moved me into that spot. It presented an ideal dissertation path. Original research on a unique modernizing society like The People's Republic of China (PRC) offered an exciting prospect. It was a time-limited exploration covering 21 days, and only thorough preparation allowed for adequate investigation. Once Edwards helped, everything came together. Possibly collecting sufficient information, a comparative study of sport as institutions in different societies—The People's Republic of China and the United States solidified.

Our government prohibited citizens' direct access until 1980; this necessitated flying from Vancouver, Canada, to Hong Kong. PRC southern region entry uses rail from Shenzhen to Kwangchow/Guangzhou, formerly known as Canton.

Subtle signs showed our China travel companions had personal issues while discussing individual plans in a Vancouver motel. Indicators of impending conflicts surfaced, threatening our mission. The first faulty commitment indicator appeared when several stated they intended to video-tape everything. Such revelations signaled they intended to disregard dedication to maximizing our ROI. All of us received explicit instructions not to bring video equipment. They didn't discuss that restriction when Big Harry reminded everyone about the directive. Harry and I noted their response, discussing how such attitudes might eliminate forging more meaningful relationships with hosts on our trek. There was a faint hope of meeting Mao and quoting him in publications. (These idiots didn't see the value of that possibility.) China's Customs agents would confiscate video cameras when we arrived there. That's what they did, sending equipment ahead to pick up on exiting through Shanghai. They permitted only still cameras, home movie cameras, and tape recorders.

Hong Kong airport presaged challenges of tolerance and expectations for some. Using the toilet presented a supreme olfactory survival test. The smells, sounds, and sights of human waste elimination processes overwhelmed us. There are no signs of cleaning maintenance for thousands of daily uses. Our Kowloon YMCA overnight stay was more enlightening by taking a ferry to see Hong Kong. Out away from brightly lit commercial areas, we encountered aggression from young street people on venturing into neighborhoods. It's best to catch the ferry back allowing more rest for the next day's mainland journey. Four days touring Kwangchow was an appropriate start because local presenters credited the city's early 19th-century activities, led by Sun Yat-sen, for beginning their revolution.

Our primary escorts greeted us at the YMCA. Most communication inside China goes through three national guides. In six cities, Kwangchow, Hangzhou, Jinan, Shanghai, Tientsin, and Beijing, factories, schools, health care centers, neighborhoods, athletic facilities and parks, and communes, and additional help added local dialect interpreters. National guides comprised Mr. Wang, a middle-aged man, Yi Yuan, and Pi Mai Yen, young women. There's no doubt these women specialized in high-level detailed visitor communication. Mr. Wang observed and supervised them. The women's styles contrasted, reflecting their personalities. Yi was tiny and stern, if not cold or harsh. She was a no-nonsense Communist Party member. Pi's cherubic features projected friendship, gentleness, and warmth. I sought closeness with them, finding their contrasting manner helpful when fashioning balanced perspectives regarding interpreting observations in discussions. On our first night inside, the group came together again, reviewing plans for a successful three weeks. Once again, as in Vancouver, all parties expressed goals. This time, we posed needs that might require others to adjust. This second planning session showed overall weak preparation, goals, and objectives. Some people's aims seemed superficial, juvenile, if not silly. "Radical" leaders desired to video their adventure, intending to hawk it in U.S., Canadian, and English markets. They neglected to prepare otherwise. They sought fame as America's first athletes to run on the Great Wall. They'd planned to sell their Tarzan reprise documentary at home. That I was the only distance runner was ironic. Video exercising on the Wall, as something glorious, escaped me. Before the discussion ended, we laid out our dissertation project design.

We compiled more than 400 questions to pose throughout our travels. Data collection included recordings (8mm movie and cassette audio recordings), notes of officials, administrators, teachers, students, workers, entertainers, and athletes' responses. Materials analysis would wait for the return home. We were conducting original research on China's sports and ideology. Our engineering a promising doctoral study showed unforeseen seriousness. The shock on others collapsed their "western radical superiority" air. Unexpected preparedness hit hard, raising blood pressure and causing the Guardian leader's nose to bleed. His retreating move also worked since subsequent events destroyed possibly conceding group members any educational value.

After discussing preparing to bulldoze our colleagues in pursuing our project, we looked around inside the hotel. It seemed odd, but People's Liberation Army (PLA) personnel patrolled our floor. Soldiers walked past while others stood near our leadership's door. Two talked and then turned, walking by us. My thought was the army's making sure nobody disturbs us. After deciding to ask Manchester newspaper's appointed leaders what they knew, it hit on entering their wing. Marijuana smoke from behind doors, including Phil's, instantly triggered rage. Such a volume of arrogant ignorance was unfathomable. If Phil knew cronies smuggled weed, somebody deserved an ass-kicking. They crassly jeopardized our project—access to information for my doctorate.

I had invested the money my family needed. These people exceeded the highest-order assholes! I burst through Phil's door, confronting him lying with toilet paper stuffed up both nostrils, stopping gushing blood set off by earlier stress. I ordered, "Get the fuck up! Explain your fucking role! Do you have marijuana? Did you know people carried pot? Did you know someone had weed leaving Canada?" I spoke carefully, exaggerating my diction. There was no latitude for misunderstanding. Phil backed into a corner. He lied, denying knowledge. A stress-induced nosebleed probably prevented getting sent home because he wasn't high. If there had been smoke in his room, the ensuing fight would've finished our tour before it started. After I demanded he clean up his cronies, we cooled off in our room. I appreciated that Harry's professorial sensibility held sway at 6' 8" and 280 pounds. If disagreements got physical, the Hosts could only jail or deport us to end repeated assaults on these "Ugly Americans."

Later, Phil sought to smooth things over. After avoiding getting physical, we were relieved enough to say it was OK as long as nothing else happened. Already adjudging, different tours existed—ours against theirs, they reduced to subjects for observation. Tolerance required our plan to take precedence over anything others wanted. It dictated every stop, dominating all meetings. We controlled every setting's discourse through deft questioning and exercising comprehensive command in every situation. To further ensure productive outcomes, we engaged Pi and Yi in a way that promoted reliance on each other. They granted us more freedom with people and institutions than the larger group. After each day's group outing, we went with them, checking sites missed on earlier forays or getting additional exposure to valuable informational items, taking pictures, or strengthening commentary. The pair spent evening off-hours discussing daily progress in our room until bedtime. It created invaluable opportunities for validating each day's data collection. In a unique gesture, they gave feedback on our analyses. Our unprecedented personal interaction meant they learned about sport and society as we learned of China's sports from them. Soon, they voluntarily gleaned additional commentary by soliciting clarification of points and answers in writing following some meetings. As learning advanced day by day, our guides progressed, increasingly grasping the insights we sought from city to city. That helped them facilitate sessions with various Party leaders, promoting communications flow.

Before long, exposure to Chinese society affected our group. Curious reactions happened. Dominant responses from the "China effect" appeared midpoint of visiting Hangzhou, our second city. Some acted very insecurely, paranoid, or ill. They expressed "ugly American" attitudes. Popular readings about the PRC or viewing them admiringly across the Pacific as pro-China thinkers weren't enough. In-person experiences presented quite another proposition. Daily observations indicated needing nothing from the U.S. Did our "radicals" underestimate China's accomplishments? Their sense of white supremacy orientation became exposed. It shattered more each day. Their dilemma didn't go unperceived because a similar struggle churned inside us. But, as Blacks, effects had comparatively mild impacts. Continued interaction exposed how programmed we are into revering our culture. Stark contrasting values were impossible to ignore. Society's ideals are so ingrained by socialization; only encountering contrasting cultures like the People's Republic uncovers the deepest held beliefs forming our self-concept in our core being. I always considered myself more Black than influenced by the broader culture. Therefore, I deceived myself regarding a concrete "American" within. We saw socialization's depth vis-à-vis our China exposure. None of us handled it well. So, ugly outbursts accompanied irrational acting-out by various disturbed individuals occurred too often. Exposure to Shanghai, the next city, brought change and interupted some individuals' mounting disintegration.

Several travelers' aberrant behavior came under rigid restraint upon landing at the airport. The DC9 prop plane set down at midnight. This flight reprised 1950s airline transportation, fitting 1920s-style hotel accommodations. We dwell in history. A representative city gang waited with buses to the Peace Hotel. Several locals rode standing (with vacant seats, we assumed they were attempting to intimidate us) while others occupied cars fronting and trailing our convoy (weird, too). Unusual sternness, impatience, and aggravating attitudes came from most resident personnel. Overtly grudging acceptance seriously differed from earlier stages. Their business dress and temperament seemed uptight, as if restraining anti-foreign feelings. Tense interaction set the tone for three days of touring. Though other destinations had generous warmth, nothing very welcoming existed here. When queried, Mr. Wang called the seaport troublesome for eliminating colonization's decadence, so increased restrictions held sway.

Given an autocratic atmosphere, our welcoming agent's refinement stood out. His Mao hat sat cocked at an angle. (Blacks call this style "ace-deuce.") An overcoat hung from his shoulders like a cape. His effeminate manner and tone appeared upper-class British. This interpreter, in knowing Western literature, frequently utilized literary quotes. Discussions about European (classical) and contemporary music exhibited a devil-may-care attitude toward threatening conservatism's presence. Harry labeled him "the Count." Under dismissive "Shanghai mafia" views, they treated the itinerary as strictly business. No alteration or flexibility is allowed. When asking state and school officials follow-up questions, proceedings advanced with mafia types insisting first replies sufficed. Most noteworthy for Shanghai, gangster dynamics aside, were volumes of people on streets day and night and synergy with the gentleman designated "Count de Shanghai." Considerable relief swept over us upon leaving for Tsinan (Jinan)

In departing Tsinan (Jinan), headed for Tientsin several days later, heretofore repressed criminality of our associates' disturbed deep sensibility. Eastern region accommodations all displayed implements of their colonizer's legacy. Rooms proved uniquely enjoyable because furnishings remained from pre-revolution European domination. Accouterments (soap trays, ashtrays, tea boxes, water glasses) adorning rooms were pre-1949 vintage. Jinan must be the coldest place on earth! I froze wearing all my outer clothing (multiple pairs of socks, three layers of jeans, an equal layering of jerseys, and a ski jacket)! It was wise to borrow a 25-pound Bear Coat. Everyone did that, but they couldn't find Harry's size.

We longed to move on to Tientsin, away from freezing. The time crawled, sitting without the train leaving. After over an hour, they directed us to gather our baggage. Outside, we saw our bags lined up. That they deposited our stuff on dirt meant something was astray. Not fathoming it, I presumed rail lines heading north had issues, or we were diverting, taking alternative transport. We collected our belongings for boarding other carriers. Would it be by air? Yi requested specific tourists open their baggage. The exposed luggage containing looted objects was astonishing. Towels, soap bars and trays, ashtrays, carved tea boxes, and fine glassware that had survived since the 1920s. The Americans robbed their chambers. In disbelief, I pondered, seeking what twisted values existed between us. Why are they like that with no shame? I couldn't envision behaving as they did.

Two went beyond minor theft by stealing bear coats. Explicit instructions were to lay them on our beds. Out of respect for others, ordinary people would be too civilized to commit outrageous acts against their generous providers. Our degenerates couldn't be embarrassed. People could borrow coats in any city. They embraced each other's Americanism. After such an incident, anxieties triggering childish behavior dominated. Our hosts ramped up their performance, exceeding expectations and further testing outlooks. Beyond Shanghai, conditions improved every day in becoming more connected with our guides. Unexpectedly, while treatment couldn't bring more satisfaction, information access increased. (Repeatedly, the Chinese proved the master's of hosting.)

We expected they protected tours from unpalatable facts, otherwise living under modernization. They provided fine accommodations. Our attentive shepherds circulated through crowds, tuning into hostility voiced toward foreigners. Many elders survived unbearable European and Japanese exploitation, and individuals suffered emotional and physical scars. Anger boiled, even under improving conditions. It happened at Tientsin's Physical Culture and Sports Center's college hockey game. After arriving, locals gathered, holding discussions. Our escorts suspected trouble was brewing, and they insisted on leaving without dithering.

Even reacting fast, racing for the bus became necessary to escape our pursuers. I saw a venerable man hobbling on his cane. He attempted running while brandishing that stick and depended on it for assistance while decrying our existence. Later, someone characterized him as outraged by our presence, spurring chasing us. Older generations suffered harsh occupying invasions. Comrade Yi pointed out generations must die out before such reactions end. Tientsin's eruption was the only time we faced an emotional expression toward colonialism's legacy. Their recent history included harmful exploitation by Europe and America.

By now, Yi got vexed by certain characters' transgressions. Two errant actors dropped out on reaching Shanghai. These characters removed themselves from facing Chinese success rebuilding after Japan's invasion and their revolution. Both sought plush Hawaiian playlands where they could indulge themselves. They mentioned sunbathing and drinking brewskies. Our hosts hospitalized more miscreants in Tientsin (soft incarceration) with respiratory conditions. They left some behind, planning to reconnect when exiting the People's Republic. Others flew to a Beijing hospital for polite imprisonment (hospitalized) until leaving. Most of us continued traveling, suffering significant respiratory trouble. Hospitalized folks returned, rejoining us for a final day before leaving China. They told stories of remaining hospitalized even though they recovered. It never struck them; hospitalization equaled incarceration. They didn't notice how happy they were when set free for less than twenty-four hours.

Our Beijing conference with China's Minister of Physical Culture and Sport, including his executive staff, constituted the crowning point. He was the leading person responsible for sports. After his remarks, Harry and I took command of questions and answers. Our approach built bottom-up for defining social functions and cultural value of sport and associated activities. Focused on confirming and validating our operating theories through national authorities, we constructed several questions for top meetings. Government Ministers more than accommodated, giving exact answers. They allowed extra time to go to great lengths to show their understanding, acceptance, and pleasure. Lengthy sessions satisfied our data collection needs. They surpassed our greatest expectations. Indications grew that highest level officials valued our mission as scholars. It's odd, but no Americans tried joining us. Away from the tour, guides offered separate privileges, excluding others. An evening visit from Yi and Pei signaled possibilities for more than ordinary opportunity, information, and connection.

We arrived hoping to earn an in-person audience with Mao Tse-tung. It required extraordinary laudable work. I'd guarantee that our possessing marijuana destroyed any possibility. There's no way to overcome such failure. It became imperative to rise above these degenerates—separating ourselves and our mission from them. We sought special recognition at every turn, and guides took extra steps to ensure getting our needs met. After seeing the Great

Wall, Comrade Pi offered a special tour around Beijing. With her leading, we roamed widely, enjoying an intimate perusal. On a second Forbidden City visit, she took us into areas off-limits for foreigners.

Harry and I confidently awaited the tour's concluding banquet. Others expressed similar optimism, but we're sure ours differed, not knowing their reasons. There was confidence in understanding our hosts, their thinking, and their uses of symbolic arrangements. It made them history's foremost diplomacy experts. They'd lay out the banquet hall, position tables, and employ seating arrangements in presenting their evaluation regarding our tour. Two positioning aspects speak to performance. A pointed indicator was who sat at each table. Order of placement provided another sign with our host as the key figure.

Chen Xitong, Beijing's Mayor, hosted. When tours go well, representing foreign delegation leaders usually sit with the highest-ranking officials. So, if our Guardian-designated leading member wasn't beside our host, we didn't do well. Once that was decided, strategically placing individuals at each table with PRC officials showed their evaluations, and our predictions, appeared accurate. They had seven large round tables arranged with one dominating. (They could have taken a similar but less conspicuous approach with a long table.) Several others, however, formed subgroups driving home their view. Comrade Yi directed Professor Edwards and me to sit with her at the Mayor's table.

Harry sat on Mayor Xitong's immediate right, with me on his left. Placement put the Professor as our leading person. Since I sat on the Mayor's other side, I ranked second. I understood seating us both, making their determination emphatic, but I was uncertain about evaluating my place. Yi, second-ranking national guide, sitting on my left, elevated me above commonplace status next to Mayor Xitong. There's added significance from her as a Communist Party Member. An even higher-level Party Member flanked Harry. Pei, ranking 3rd on the national team, was across from the Mayor. (We considered a position opposite the host had to be complimentary (submissive), thus neutralizing stations opposing a dominant one.) Phil,

Guardian's leader, graced a table beside Mr. Wang, head guide. Poker faces acted as though arrangements had neither rhyme nor reason. Farewell honors recognized the staunch appreciation shown for China. Efforts ensuring our visit benefited the PRC and us by exchanging volumes of knowledge impressed. Later presenting our work and experiences and educating others paid off on their investment. Future activity included completing our study and communicating conclusions. Observations comparing respective societal institutions achieved common goals. Reasonable calculations indicated analysis and writing would require three years. By September, signs hinted that changes in China would affect our study if only covering 1976's information. Broader relevancy demanded collecting data addressing trends for future developments. It meant returning to repeat an improved design protocol.

Two years later, we returned to the PRC, heading the US-China People's Friendship Association National Sports and Recreation Tour. Youxie, an organization created to promote relations with people of foreign countries, hosted 1978's format, mirroring 1976. Ideals proclaimed for Youxie were forming closer ties between the American people and China's people. However, this one visited the Northern provinces' major cities, including Shanghai, Beijing, Shenyang, Changchun, and Harbin, Manchuria.

This second time around we interviewed top national officials; Huang Chung, Vice Minister in Charge of the Physical Culture and Sports Commission, and Ho Chen Liang, Vice Secretary-General of the All-China Sports Federation. We hoped to avoid drug possession and use difficulties that occurred in 1976.

This tour's composition had notable changes. Professor Edwards took charge and selected those going. Our collaboration continued, and I expected his selections would do better than Guardian's previous bunch. On paper, it appeared all signees had sufficient maturity. Several, it turned out, had trouble accepting China's success, and they became ugly Americans, as happened years before. Those disturbed by society's improving conditions rejected modernizing China through varied aberrant behavior. Acts included:

- Drunkenness.
- Interfering with late-night street traffic.
- Early morning skinny-dipping in public ponds.

Aside from daily data collection (question-and-answer sessions, voice recording, photos, movies, and taking notes), long train rides from Beijing through Shenyang and Changchun to Harbin added exceptional quality. Two days' rest in Luta (Dalian) allowed enjoying a seaside resort.

Professor Edwards, Mr. Huang, our lead escort, and I shared a sleeping compartment. His gigantic head on a tiny body caused him to be affectionately nicknamed "Big Head Huang." Sharing close quarters provided ideal uninterrupted access for confidential discussions on substantive matters. Exchanges bolstered our analyses through reviewing with him. He was a perfect knowledgeable sounding board who had answers. He arranged unprecedented intimate time together that generated greater confidence in completing dissertation information collection and executing a worthy project by the journey's end. Arriving there brought tremendous relief and heightened anticipation. I understood finishing at Berkeley was a matter of time. When leaving Harbin for Beijing, I wanted to end this tour early to start writing. In the concluding days, we were permitted to explore the capital before flying to Shanghai and departing, and the final hours included seeing Mao. Of course, he was dead. His memorial-resting place occupied Tiananmen Square's southeast corner. Our interpreters said few foreign delegations earned such an honor. Our tour's presence enabling their visiting Mao's memorial was extraordinary. It was moving beyond words for our female escorts. They thought China honoring our group allowed them to pay their respects. Everyone exited Memorial Hall floating on air all afternoon, examining the Forbidden City before moving to Youxie's grand dinner. There's no curiosity about not performing well. Arrangements would be different than in 1976. We were not eager for validation. That vanished, traveling by sleeper train to Manchuria and back with Mr. Huang and waiting to go home and write up our research.

Interspersed between Youxie and government representatives spanning a thirty-foot table, we positioned for the honorary dinner. Layout signaled general acceptance, and there were no identifying fractures. While thinking there's nothing more to learn, Wang Bingnan, President of the Chinese People's Association for Friendship with Foreign Countries, transformed an embarrassing event into humor, deftly executing diplomacy. It delivered a valuable life lesson.

The evening began with drinking generous glasses of plum wine, Tsingtao beer, and Mao-Tai, potent liquor made from sorghum. Before serving food, toasts offered by Big Harry triggered reciprocal toasts by Youxie representatives. No tour members present could handle that kind of alcohol consumption. Speech and actions became error-prone. One noted psychologist hit his alcohol limit in no time. The world-renowned teacher fumbled, reaching for another Tsingtao beer, splashing it everywhere, and froze with embarrassment. I watched as Youxie's representative knocked over his beer, and his deliberate fumble became an immediate point of camaraderie. Everyone has accidents. An accomplished diplomat relieves guests of feeling clumsy. With that, a relaxed, wonderful feast ensued. Two years earlier, farewell ceremonies had no alcohol, possibly making an additional point. Maybe it meant they didn't trust our weed-smoking group to handle drugs with dignity. That, too, was wise.

Doctor of Philosophy

Mom visited California in the summer of 1981. I was submitting documents for finishing Berkeley. She accompanied me through collecting signatures, official document stamping, and filing forms. It had been quite a journey for her through years of childhood illnesses, life-threatening accidents, and years of delinquency, criminality, rebellion, and Black Power involvement. She survived.

Meanwhile, I regained the scholarly promise shown starting elementary school and abandoned favoring athletic achievement upon entering Junior High School. I pursued the degree because I could and it was not related to

pursuing an academic career. I took no particular satisfaction from graduation exercises. Mom and I relaxed in the Sociology Department's Graduation
auditorium. They called out my name. Those on stage received diplomas,
hoods, recognition, and applause. Sociology's Chairman said he'd seen me
there. I stayed silent, electing to get my certificate by mail. I'm not sure what
my mother thought. With five college degrees, I never donned caps or gowns
receiving graduation honors.

On Big Harry (Professor Edwards): I consider having been friends since
1961 - close friends since 1964, over fifty years. He's a physical, artistic, and
intellectual giant. Most people know him from academic pursuits and political activism. The unseen force behind his public persona is never on display.
People won't believe his kind, generous side. He's a world-class comedian, an
unparalleled actor and entertainer, an unconquerable debater, and a fierce,
ruthless combatant. The combatant surfaces, especially when confronted
with any bullshit that's not his own. I've seen the complete package. Some
demonstrations were frightening. He's attacked adversaries; destroying them
to an extent I couldn't escape feeling acute embarrassment transference. I
often came away beaten worse than defeated opponents. I believe his size and
apex intellect demands a take-no-prisoners approach for opponents. Those
presenting opposing arguments or competing with research on subjects don't
show warranted caution and respect, constituting foolish, insulting behavior.
Hence, there's no quarter when demolishing opponents. He feels most have
not received sufficient destruction commensurate with their presumptive
opposition.

I (irresponsibly) presented early chapter drafts for review without applying his standards to my dissertation committee. While others on my committee accepted these sections, he didn't. A merciless face-to-face critique said
everything. No reason for rejection went unstated. Judgment afforded no
attention to possibly insulting me; there's no allowance for friendship or
sensitivity. I got the point. I performed carelessly, knowing his standards,
and failed to meet them. On leaving his office, looking up and invoking god's
witness (a genuine desperate act for non-believers), I vowed, speaking out

loud: "i will never give that motherfucker a chance to kick my ass like that again." He supplied the best reminder of steadfast professionalism. That's what friends are for; we should always embrace such qualities. Re-educated, I presented a finished product written acceptably.

Legacy

While completing doctoral work, a notice arrived for our 25-year class reunion of 1956 West Chester High School graduates. I didn't attend other gatherings - 5th, 10th, or 20th years. This one offered possible energizing respite from my current oppressive schedule. It was a chance to see Black classmates who didn't live in West Chester. Most were close friends through 12 years in school. We struggled for dignity together, living among racists. It was an excellent venue for telling survival stories. But most made plans for a separate celebration. Handfuls attended prior "white" reunions, coming away dissatisfied. They tasted an old familiar sense of not belonging, carrying over from the fifties. It was an estrangement, eventually welcomed. I would check both reunions, starting with the white one.

Three things punctuated 1981's (white) reunion. First, an enormous banner proclaiming the undefeated 1956 Cross-Country Team winning the League Championship stretched across the banquet hall's entrance. (The place had been off-limits for Negroes during our youth under Jim Crow.) It never registered as such an outstanding senior year event, then. Classmates never directly expressed it meant something to them. I always considered the championship meaningful only to our teammates and coaches. My role in producing an exceptional accomplishment for the graduating class had practically zero personal value after 25 years. For a second curiosity, I had two white classmates as friends, Neal Chappell and Jack Williams. There were superficial connections with all others. During those years, no fundamental aspects of life became genuine feelings with other mates. Neal, Jack, and I suffered together on tracks and cross-country courses and maintained contact. We cared because our lives came together in dependency when on racecourses. That realization settled the romanticized bonding myth falling on integrated schools' graduating classes coming out of that era. Differing life realities swamped romanticized claims of shared bonding experiences. There was no reason to attend future gatherings without Neal or Jack. Third, while touting successes and class achievements, their Master of Ceremonies announced I was the only member earning a Ph.D.

CHAPTER
SIXTEEN

Born Again: Competition

*There are rebirths that are myths and those
that are real. Local, national and international
records show the manner of ours.*

Kenny:

We traveled a circuitous route back to lives dominated by competitive running. This journey resumed after 16 inactive years. Family, work, school, and doctorate requirements filled those days. I needed satisfying recognition of my core identity with which I struggled. An answer to "Who am I?" went unresolved. Time and energy got swallowed by teaching, fatherhood, and doctoral student responsibilities. With everything included, something was missing. I ignored a noticeable absence of adequate exercise for the longest time. The way forward was starting jogging, using my understanding of intense national-level training as a college athlete and Iglói disciple.

Satisfaction surfaced once workouts began. Comfortable sleeping was accompanied by rediscovering self, raised consciousness, and a more relaxed mental state. I had confidence in making crucial decisions concerning the future I'd been reticent to make since 1969.

I stopped teaching after a prolonged struggle with fashioning a manageable balance when teaching demands and scholarship became too difficult over long periods. I wanted the Berkeley Ph.D. but felt uncomfortable lecturing before large groups. Teaching requires working too hard for minimal professional adequacy. In education, my closest friends and my brother-in-law worked hard, but they also stood out as gifted teachers. That's not me! Minimal adequacy in an occupation requiring presenting complex ideas to large classes meant fooling myself that it was for me. Those situations brought a hefty dose of unnecessary stress. With the Ph.D. pocketed, I could decide what I wanted to do. I needed an income from employment that demanded only eight hours, with no at-home tasks. In 1979, my former roommate, Arturo, steered me to an electronics industry job at GTE Sylvania in Mountain View, California. An entry-level stockroom position earned the same as an instructor at San Jose State College (SJS). Stockroom jobs had low intellectual demands. The greatest benefit of the new job was leaving mental energy for dissertation work. I spent several hours writing before and after stockroom duties. Not having to prepare for the next day helped. I devoted weekends to writing because each week finished unburdened. Fortunately, I got a hiring interview with Jack Cunningham, GTE's component materials manager. He considered me because we attended West Chester High School in Pennsylvania. Helen, my youngest sister, graduated with him behind me. They were freshmen when I finished. Calculations predicting what the new job allowed proved spot-on. I didn't mention two Master's degrees and U.C. Berkeley doctoral student status on the application and avoided being classified as overqualified.

Within thirty days, scholarly effort improved. Within six months, I began operating their satellite stock location alone, including defining hours, break periods, and lunch. The office provided unlimited stationery supplies and top-of-the-line copying/printing equipment. My days soon started at 4 a.m., writing until work hours kicked in at 7:00. Ph.D. research and writing in the office came before and after duties. Quiet off-hours yielded surprising numbers of quality pages. Soon, the stress felt from researching, lecturing, and writing while an SJS instructor disappeared.

On The Road Again

During lunchtime walks, I saw joggers leaving the main plant at noon. Once it was clear they ran every day, I timed their return. They stayed out for an hour. Their older leader, thin with a trotting horse's gait, looked like an experienced marathoner. I spent ten days observing them and built interest in daily running again. To join GTE's noon group made sense. Unsure how far they ran or at what pace, I was too insecure to approach them. I shadowed the group, delaying starting, then maintaining their speed, following unseen after giving them a healthy head start. Their workout lasted sixty minutes from Whisman Boulevard through Mountain View. After circling Rengsdorf Park's small grass patch, they reversed, traversing busy streets, except inside the park.

Runners comprised two women and eight men with varied body types, leaving and returning together. After twenty days, I let them get several minutes ahead before erasing the deficit. Within weeks, I caught up. If they went slow, there's no problem. When the tempo increased, it was easy to keep pace. Deep inside, I wanted to be sure I could stay with John Armstrong, their leader, at his fastest speed. They grew impressed with my ability. A retired Navy Commander, Armstrong was well-respected in the West Valley Joggers and Striders (WVJS) running club. He ran marathons in under three hours. Before long, I could push him to his limit. We talked about joining WVJS to train with them.

West Valley Joggers and Striders

At 45, I hadn't run after an 880 for SJS in the 1966 NCAA finals at Indiana University. I uncovered new possibilities for competitive running when joining the West Valley Joggers. My school running mate, Neal, wanted to belong, and we envisioned competing again. Early training with WVJS remained casual. After I turned 50 (in 1988), workouts elevated my interest in age-group competitions organized by the USA Track and Field Federation (USATF).

Neal came on board after participating in founding Las Vegas' Club (LVTC), specializing in low-key fun runs. When reaching 50, he bought a second home near Lake Tahoe, qualifying him for Pacific Association (PA) USATF membership. PA territory extends from Oregon's border to San Luis Obispo (central California), spreading eastward beyond Reno, Nevada. After dominating bay area roads through 1989, we sent our fifty's team to Tacoma, Washington, for an 8k National Road Championship. We brought five legendary PA competitors, including Sal Vasquez, Tim Rostige, Bill Meinhart, Roger Bryant, and John Finch, overwhelming the field with the first three finishers and taking the team title with seven of eight spots. Neal finished sixth, and I came in eighth. Sal ran away with the individual crown. That's the first time our club financially supported competing outside the State. With so many legends, withholding help was impossible. That group dominated the Pacific Association (PA) Grand Prix following Tacoma.

Neal:

Northwest business interests made buying Lake Tahoe property imperative. I conducted business from Vegas before spending summers in Kingsbury, a mile from the water. Because of investments and selling Chinese Herbalessence Ltd Health Food and Herbal Products (CHL), southern Nevada digs weren't sufficient for operations. There's little need to be there. Before retiring, other opportunities caused me to turn away from living off poker. I attacked expanding health food enterprises, seeking recruits from Seattle to Vancouver, Canada. My CHL active growing down-line members required mentoring, improving product knowledge, recruitment, and sales techniques. My business' rapid growth required attending CHL headquarters informational meetings and corporate conferences. They had conventions, seminars, and awards gatherings. An ability to travel to various places for business reasons fits. Things went well because travel requirements routed me through San Jose. I had many friends there. Gambling had provided wealth but shifted toward less comfortable work. There was little trouble with running as maintaining sanity, focus, and stability. Kenny provided an immediate base for selling herbs combined with practical distance training.

San Jose was the perfect stop on Seattle, Vancouver, or Hawaii travels. But creeping into prominence was a burgeoning real estate enterprise. With Rudy, Ed, and their cohorts in Las Vegas purchasing "fixer-uppers," remodeling them to sell, I was collecting healthy profits after recovering original investments. I advanced funds to receive a percentage after expenses. Nevada's real estate opportunities required traveling between southern and northern locations and deciding to buy property. Managing projects positioned me to buy one.

I used houses when traveling. Construction crews were involved with purchasing and sales deals. They occupied some while doing repairs. Part of the compensation was living rent-free. I traveled, selling CHL for months on end. Sometimes, not paying while in a remodel was convenient. Real estate business kept growing until house deals required more attention. I found one property worth buying at a rock-bottom price. When this particular Kingsbury, Nevada location wrapped up, fixing to sell morphed into realizing I should name my price and grab it. Attractions for owning property near the Lake were significant. A home in PA territory made sense. Relocation offered significant benefits when so involved with running, allowing me to live near casinos. Mountain property allowed intense training for endurance-enhanced fitness. Rewards from living there came fast. Workouts triggered tremendous performance boosts as an elite club career blossomed.

Unlimited trails through forested hills were an invaluable feature. Cushioning pine needle layers accumulating over centuries covered trails carved by animals. They are ideal footing for long runs or 10K pace long intervals. My favorite trail starts yards from the front door. I have plotted a circuit and marked distances. Logs track times on mountain paths equating with races. Calculating expected performances is effortless. Knowing how many training days it takes to dominate our age group each year was essential. Data allowed for declining with aging—what's behind performance dropping. I hadn't been sure and was studying numbers. Southern Nevada wasn't ideal for year-round training because of the unbearable summer heat. In Tahoe from June until December snow eliminated Vegas' summer heat problem. This second home at altitude was perfect, and adaptation only took two weeks of daily runs. After that, there's a steady improvement toward racing goals by hitting indicative times at key trail mileage points. I call one "Route 30" because parts used to be US Highway 30.

Kenny:

In 1993, I turned 55—the youngest in that age group. This was the time to try marquee races! There was no 5K better than Carlsbad! The runner's community dubbed it "World's Fastest Five Thousand." The course's profile doesn't engender that designation. Attracting the world's fastest people and producing world marks makes it so. Preparations went well for the epic undertaking. 17:30 at Davis' Turkey Trot bodes well. My mile was a shock when they yelled, "5:20!" I saw Neal ahead hit his split at 5:10. I'm never that close through any 5 K's first mile. Performances show conditioning improvement. Based on Carlsbad's 1992 age-group results, the top three seemed reasonable. At that pace, a 55+ victory was within reach. This race is not a mundane competition. The setting has a full-blown equipment manufacturer-supported Expo. Pre-race dinner guests were running legends and currently leading distance runners. Sebastian Coe, England's hero to 800-meter guys like me, attended as Honorary Race Director. He sat beside me, eating with the Kenyans and Mexico's 10K champion. On Friday, I stayed with Rasheed Salahudin, a 1960s San Jose campus struggle coconspirator. Saturday, we drove from Imperial Beach, south of San Diego. Norm Saucedo (WVJS) met us to attend the participants' dinner. Norm allowed me a bed in his motel room. The next day was it.

The moment of truth arrived when my friend appeared at the starting line. I wasn't expecting to see him, even though he said he'd come. In warm-ups, I toured the first loop. With three hills and two 180-degree turns, it was far from flat! Good news, the masters lead off! Neal went out fast at the gun, with me trailing. Planned negative splits caused not pushing the first half's inclines. The second half continued at a hard tempo but not fast enough to make the podium. I passed two old fellows finishing 200 meters downhill but only ran 18:20. Pre-race calculations showed placing required going under 18:00. Twenty seconds over sufficiently discouraged me—no need to bother with awards. So, we hung out with Norm while I cursed and complained about my poor performance. We watched the elites and marveled at their times.

Seeing four Africans running 8:06 through the first 180-degree turn at 2 miles was a thrill. Unbelievable, I thought! That took my mind off my failure. Deena Drossen ran for a new mark with a thrilling performance for the elite women. She punished the opposition with unmatched splits from the 2K point to the end. They had nothing left coming home. Watching her gave me a sorely needed sense of satisfaction. What an effort! That made the trip to Carlsbad worth it! Quite a few running equipment vendors had booths, giving terrific discounts on everything. We shopped for a few hours until Norm insisted on looking at the results. It was getting late with the sun descending to the ocean horizon and darkness shading in from the east. People were slowly dispersing from the Expo. So, we quickly looked at the list of top finishers on the information board at the awards table. It was utterly amazing to see my name in third place for 55+. My friends were beside themselves because I made a complete nuisance of myself by complaining nonstop about running so poorly. I was that kind of fool! Hallelujah! Even the third-place award for the Carlsbad 5000 was something to behold—a highly recognized symbol of achievement for broken-down road warriors.

With the trophy held tight, I eavesdropped on animated conversations, looking for someone going to San Diego's airport. Sweatz (Neal) and I could wrangle hidden opportunities in most environments, finding what we needed. Zimbabwe's Philemon Hanneck, who ran 13:22, winning as an elite, commanded immediate transportation to catch an evening flight. The sponsor's van had room. How can you beat that? Riding and conversing with Hanneck was terrific. The event manager drove and tried hogging the conversation, and I guessed he felt entitled as an essential person. Although never a talker, there's no way I would allow that guy to ask Hanneck more questions or make more comments than me. WVJS should know Hanneck, who went to school in Texas. He told his life story. I had an award, eliciting West Valley members' collective envy, and an airport ride absorbing stories that'll make them doubly jealous!

My routine blood antigen test readings moved upward, beginning in 1997. Reading levels rose, suggesting growing cancer. Other reasonable causes exist for changes but need proving. Everyone expressed puzzlement because typical symptoms weren't present. I have been undergoing yearly exams since 1983. Doctors performed digital rectal probes, affording minimal dignity, using gloved fingers to feel for prostate abnormalities. The idea was early disease detection, then treatment preventing death. An enlarged organ plus frequent urination are typical problem indicators. Not having those symptoms or others, I'm asymptomatic. Plenty of possibilities come with being Black, the high-risk demographic. There are lots of reasons to consider I had it. That's where PSA tests get their value.

Over twelve weeks, antigen readings increased from 3.1 to 8.5. Finger checks never showed that. With significant progression, exams should detect tumors or other irregularities. Blood tests measure a protein called prostate-specific antigen. Malignant cells elevate protein production, causing measurable PSA increases. With rising scores, tissue biopsies come next. My case qualified as unusual. (As part of the unique nature of things, I add that, at one point, three doctors made inconclusive digital checks during a pre-biopsy hospital visit. I noted men increasing in age did individual rectal searches as they all witnessed.)

With an ultrasound probe inserted rectally, a needle penetrates the intestine's wall, plucking prostate pieces. They pulled bits in batches. The first two out of five seemed proper and tolerable. Midway into the third extraction, my thoughts questioned if we needed more. Discomfort increased with repeating the procedure. Over two plugs are unnecessary torture. For that moment, I didn't care "bout no cancer!" By the end, I settled into extreme discomfort. Lab tests showed initial samples had no abnormalities. It's unfortunate because next comes more biopsies. However, removing material until identifying cancer or more tissue plugs becomes useless doesn't seem sensible. My misfortune was nine more sessions, pulling five samples, but the results from batch number nine confirmed cell mutations. Diffusion made finding cancerous cells difficult, as they hadn't formed a mass. Pain mounting through fifty incursions left me unsettled toward more sampling. Remaining upbeat throughout wasn't easy.

With the disease confirmed, we needed to decide on a treatment. No options qualified as desirable, and each choice had drawbacks. I spent days weighing options—surgery, radiation therapy, or chemotherapy. While mulling over choices, friends directed me to a Black support group, and I phoned their leader to check out what they did. That call determined they were not for me. When he said, "We should pray," I hung up.

Which procedure least affects what continues as most meaningful in life? I wanted a treatment least impacting competing, and I chose surgery to avoid abnormal physical decline. Nine months passed, and age-group world relay marks fell with me, leading off. The National 10K Cross Country followed two National Road Racing Championships, and Sweatz's performances make losing impossible.

Neal:

The 50+ team easily won 1996's Cross-Country Nationals held locally at Stanford. Kenny and I are 58 and 57; we're "over-the-hill" as 50s. Other than Sal Vasquez, the squad was under 52.

Fast-forwarding to more teammates hitting 60; we began preparing to break division global records. Initial success came in the Distance Medley Relay on August 8, 1998, in West Valley College's stadium. An account by Walt Van Zant graced the "WVJS Quarterly Newsletter."

Ken Noel, Norm Saucedo, Gene Antonides, and Karl Misner broke the distance medley relay (800 meters/400 meters/1200 meters/1600 meters) world record on 8/8/98 by seven seconds to the cheering of their fellow club members.

8/8/98 - 60+ Distance Medley Relay World Record

Our 60+ team of Ken Noel, Norm Saucedo, Gene Antonides, and Karl Misner took a shot at the 60+world record for the distance medley relay (800, 400, 1200, 1600) of 13:24 on this Saturday morning and successfully broke it by 7 seconds.

Ken Noel ran the opening 800 leg. His goal was to run 2:30. The charged atmosphere of 50+ fanatics cheering him on must have gotten him excited as he ran the first 200 meters in 33 seconds and his first lap in 71.9. This has to be the case because Ken is known for his ability to run at an even pace over the course of a race and finish strong. Even though he wisely slowed down to 38.9 seconds for the second 200 meters, this first lap took its toll as he dropped to a 79.6 on the 2nd lap to finish in 2:31.5. Our planned goal of 2:30/1:10/4:00/5:40 would bring us in 4 seconds under the record. So, Ken missing his goal by 1.4 seconds was no big deal.

Norm Saucedo ran the 400 on the 2nd leg. Norm has been injured for several months and, so, was far from top form. But, he is such a good runner that his teammates felt that he could manage a sub-70 and he did with a 68.0. This put us 0.6 seconds under our goal after two legs.

Gene Antonides, who had recently run an atrocious 5:56 mile, ran the 1200. Since his terrible mile, Gene had run a 5:40 mile and a 2:25 800. Plus, he easily strode through a 4:07 1200 on Wednesday night as part of our interval workout. Thus, he felt confident that he would run his goal of 4:00 for 1200. Gene, who normally starts slow and finishes fast, blasted out with a 76 first 400. This appeared to tire him but Gene later stated that he felt fine as he drifted to an 84 second 400. And, Gene was right that he felt okay because he finished with a 76.5 for a fantastic 3:56 1200. This is the equivalent of about a 5:25 for the 1600. Not too bad for an aging runner. So, our 60+ team was 7:36 after 3 legs as compared to a goal of 7:40.

This apparently got Karl (Mizner) very excited. He whizzed through his first lap in 75.7 before starting to fizzle. He ran his second lap in 86.1 to come through the 800 in 2:41.8. This put him 12+ seconds up on the team goal and 16 seconds up on the record. However, the grim reaper grabbed a hold of his legs during the last two laps. He ran his 3rd lap in 91 as compared to his goal of 85. This left the team 10 seconds ahead of the record pace. Thus, it was obvious to most observers that the record would be broken. However, Karl surely suffered a lot during that last lap as his tight legs struggled to an 88 second interval. This gave him 5:41.4 for one mile and the team a final time of 13:17. Thusly, the world record of 13:24 was soundly broken.

Ken Noel 71.9-79.6 = 2:31.5
Norm Saucedo 67.9 = 1:07.9
Gene Antonides 75.9-83.9-76.4 = 3:56.2
Karl Misner 75.7-86.1-91.1-88.5 = 5:41.4
13:17.0

A new world's best led us into the PA road slate. As 60+ mates logged sequential wins, we looked forward to me becoming eligible. Current results at 59 say I'll go undefeated well into the future. We expected to set world marks and win USATF championships. World Masters' website listing shows the 4 x 1500-relay time as no challenge. Equal distances we'd clocked with ease guaranteed to smash such a soft standard. Having a WR under our belts boosts confidence in contesting other global bests. With that accomplishment, we challenged the 4 x 1600 world listing. A 4 x 1500 recap appeared in December 1999's newsletter.

After that, we went after the 4 x 1600 on August 28. The stretch between attempts gave enough rest, allowing for honing preparation. We expected benefits from finishing Northern California's schedule from practice sessions and preparing for relays. Walt's write-up describes our record run.

VOL XXIX-#3 WEST VALLEY JOGGERS & STRIDERS SEPT 1999

Congratulations to 60+ runners Neal Chappell, Ralph Poole, Ken Noel, and Gene Antonides. They recently broke the 60+ records for the 4 x 1500 relay and the 4 x 1600 relay. They broke the 4 x 1500 record by nearly three minutes and the 4 x 1600 record by 4 seconds.

8/18/99 - 4 x 1500M 60+ World Record

This evening, August 18, 1999, our 60+ team of Ken Noel, Gene Antonides, Ralph Poole, and Neal Chappell broke the 60/69 world record for the 4 x 1500 meter relay by nearly three minutes. The former record was 24:03.3 and they ran 21:11.1. It took a couple of hours just to get the relay in motion on Wednesday night, August 18, 1999. We had hoped to make the record attempt on the West Valley College track. However, they had not completed resurfacing the track. So, we went over to Saratoga high school. Alas, they had no inside rail, which is a requirement for world records. So, we tried the new Archbishop Mitty High School track. It had the same problem as at Saratoga. Our final stop was the San Jose City College track where we struck pay dirt. Some parts of the railing had been removed but we reconnected the removed pieces, cleared the myriad of joggers from the first lane, and got ready for the record attempt. We needed to average 6:00 per runner (6:26 per mile pace) to break the record. Ken Noel led off and opened with an 80 first lap. This took its toll as he faded to an 87 and 89 before finishing with a 67 on his final 300 for a time of 5:25.0. This put us 35 seconds up on the record. Gene Antonides was our second runner. He ran his first lap in 86 but faded to 93 on his second lap. However, he recovered to run 89 on the 3rd lap and a spectacular 57.5 on his final 300 for a time of 5:25.4. Now we were 70 seconds ahead of world record pace with our two best runners coming up. Ralph Poole went out fast, covering the first lap in 78 seconds (not bad for a 63-year old). He dropped to 89 and 90 on his second and third laps before finishing with a final 300 of 62 for a time of 5:18.9. Neal Chappell started the final leg in near darkness. He blazed through the first lap in 74. He slowed considerably during the second lap but his 83 was still an excellent split as he passed 800 meters in 2:37. Neal then ran an 85 on the third lap before finishing with a 60 for the last 300. His time of 5:01.8 was the best of the quartet.

Splits:
Ken Noel 1:20-2:47-4:18-5:25.0
Gene Antonides 1:26-2:59-4:28-5:25.4
Ralph Poole 1:18-2:47-4:17-5:18.9
Neal Chappell 1:14-2:37-4:02-5:01.8
8/28/99 - 4 x 1600M 60+ World Record

Ten days earlier our 60+ team easily broke the world record for the 4 x 1500 meter relay. This morning the same foursome of Ken Noel, Gene Antonides, Ralph Poole, and Neal Chappell went after the much more difficult 4 x 1600 record, which was held by the Tamalpa Running Club 60+ team, our arch rivals in San Francisco.

The record of 22:37.1 is an average of just over 5:39 per 1600. A 1600 is about 10 yards short of a mile. The running order of the team was Ken, Gene, Ralph, and Neal. The 50+ team running against them included Rich Stiller, Jake White, Dick Chimenti, and Danny Moon. Ken Noel led off the relay on the San Jose City College track shortly after 8AM. Rich Stiller, the 50+ leadoff runner, set an even pace, which Ken stayed with for the first three laps before running his last 400 in 82 seconds to finish with a 5:45.25. This was his best time of the year. Gene Antonides and Jake White started together on the second leg. Gene, who has not recovered his former form since incurring an injury earlier this year, went out at a slow pace. So, Jake took off and grabbed an early 10-yard lead on him. After two laps, Gene had lost 14 seconds to the record pace (Ken had already lost 6 seconds). The club members present were worried. Fortunately, Gene got his act together and gained back 4.5 seconds during the last half of the run. He finished about 5 seconds in front of Jake after concluding his 5:48.5 1600 with a blistering lap of 76.6. We were now 15.6 seconds behind the record pace. It took Dick Chimenti a little over a lap to catch Ralph Poole on the third leg. Ralph had planned to run his first two laps in 85 each. Instead, he opened with a pair of 88s. This left us an additional 6.5 seconds behind the record pace. We knew that Neal would gain a lot of time for us during the final leg. However, if Ralph lost much more during the last two laps, it would be impossible to get the record.

Fortunately, Ralph had saved a little for the final two laps. He picked up the pace and finished in 5:41.2. Our time after 3 legs was 17:15.2. Neal Chappell needed a 5:21.8 on his final 1600 to get the record. Our final 50+ runner, Danny Moon, said that he could handle 80-second 400s for the first three laps. However, this was not good enough for Neal. He opened with a 77 before slowing to an 81. His third lap was 83.5. So, he was 4:01.6 with 400 meters to go. He needed a final lap of 80.2 to get the record. Neal was up to the task as he ran his last lap in 75.9 for a final time of 5:17.5. The team had broken the world record by 4.4 seconds.

Splits:
Ken Noel 1:27-2:56-4:23-5:45.3
Gene Antonides 1:31-3:04-4:32-5:48.7
Ralph Poole 1:27-2:56-4:21-5:41.2
Neal Chappell 1:17-2:38-4:02-5:17.5

Kenny:

That we'd passed the baton to Neal behind the calculated pace embarrassed us. A record elated, but we didn't help our anchor. I apologized. As we jogged through City College's campus, I said, "Sorry we left you overcoming such a burden from less than supportive performances." He responded, "You carried us (he and I) through our early career. Now I can carry us the rest of the way." We intended to win the 1999 USA Cross Country 60+ individual and team competitions with the Grand Prix Series. Write-ups appeared in the March 2000 "Newsletter":

VOL XXIX-#4 WEST VALLEY JOGGERS & STRIDERS NEWSLETTER DEC 1999

Neal Chappell, Dave Norlander, and Ken Noel were the members of our winning 60+ team at the National Masters 10K XC championships. Neal was the #1 60+ runner in this race, Sue MacDonald was the #1 45+ woman runner, and Gail Campbell was the #1 50+ woman runner.

Neal Chappell, who turned 60 in May, finished his 1999 season in a blaze of glory. He won the 60+ division at the Pacific Sun 10K, the Clarksburg 5K, and the Davis 5K. Then, he led our 60+ team to the National 10K XC Championship at Long Beach by beating all of the 60+ runners. Dave Norlander and Ken Noel were the members of the winning 60+ XC team.

Neal:

Lengthy coverage by our 60+ chronographer describing Long Beach's race got refused. Walt Van Zant, a WVJS founder and "President for Life," rejected reporting from the scene without explanation. Here is Kenny's submission that Walt dismissed:

At Long Beach, we were fully aware of who was our real competition. It's Russ Kiernan, Jim Moore and Bernie Hollander from the Tamalpa Running Club based in San Francisco. From the inception of our club (WVJS) as an Amateur Athletic Union (AAU) registered team in 1970, our two clubs are the most friendly and most bitter rivals. Because of year-round weekly competitions on northern California roads and cross-country courses, we know all of their runners as well as we know our own. The same can be said for them. Individually, Tamalpa's threesome at the 1999 10K National Cross Country Championship was better than two of our runners. Individually, Russ, Jim and Bernie will out distance Dave (Norlander) and Ken (Noel) in any given race. Dave and Ken are about on the same level with Dave being a shade better in longer races like 10Ks. Neal (Chappell) is the deciding factor that our bitter rivals have to overcome to win this National Championship. In order for that to happen, we know that Neal would have to run the worst race of his life. Anything near a normal performance will be enough for him to win the individual title and our group to win the team championship.

It was your usual gathering of runners at the starting line on a picture perfect sunny California morning. Lots of familiar faces were there from the northern California running clubs. There was time, in bumping into Jim Moore (a 60+ Tamalpa runner), for a customary exchange of summaries of our trials and tribulations, and our aches and pains since the last competition. Jim is just the friendliest of people and unmatched for being a good runner who's humble. Our teams lined up next to each other and waited for the sound of the starter's gun. Our team (WVJS and Tamalpa) styles contrasted because we always start at a faster pace than they do. That means we will be in front of them for a while until they catch us in the middle. The outcome is decided by what happens from that point to the finish. Actually, Neal can decide the outcome for the team championship long before that. How teams place with regard to winning the team championship is determined by the combined finishing times for a club's first three runners. It seems that from the start Neal is very determined to ensure that we win the team title. Over the first mile, he's at the front keeping pace with the 40 and 50 year-olds. At the midpoint, there is a 180-degree turn and, with that, everyone sees how fellow runners and their opponents are doing. As Neal's teammates, we can see how far ahead he is and can time the gap back to Tamalpa's Russ Kiernan. To everyone's surprise, Neal is already in front by 2 minutes. More importantly, he is moving away. Neal is running with much greater determination than we had ever seen from him. We yelled our encouragement across the fairway to him, but it was entirely unnecessary. Since the other Tamalpa team members had yet to catch Dave and me, the team championship would go to the WVJS team as long as no one faltered. With a little more than a mile to go, Dave started inching away from me and eventually settled in some 50 yards ahead. At that time, the trailing Tamalpa pair caught us inside a mile from the finish. It was too late to take a major bite out of the time advantage that Neal provided. By now, he was 4 minutes ahead. WVJS mission accomplished!

Kenny:

With Ralph Poole leading, we dominated each outing and achieved our goals, including winning PA's Road Series. A club blurb summarized:

> Our 60+ men finished first. They won five of the races. Our top dogs were Ralph Poole, who finished first and won $150, Neal Chappell, who finished 4th, and Dave Norlander, who finished 7th. Our top team participators were Bill Floodberg with 10 races, Ralph Poole with 8 races, Ken Noel with 7 races, Ed Reyna with 7 races, and Gene Antonides with 6 races. World Record Holders in the "Seniors" (age 60 +).

The 60+ team's season ended with mixed feelings. Ralph retired from competition, owning two 60s world records and Grand Prix individual and team titles. On a sad note, Karl Mizner, who anchored 1998's distance medley (World Record), had a deadly brain tumor. His condition reminded our group of life's fragility. We benefited from temporary fortunate circumstances. Frequent visits with Karl pulled at our hearts when witnessing his deterioration butting up against his runner's strength and willpower. His is the loneliest place because there's no stopping declining or altering courses with progressing conditions. We did our best by steadfastly recounting triumphs. Karl was meaningful in so many ways. His death came on July 18, 2000.

Neal:

I kept winning, including the 2000 Nationals described in WVJS's story.

> Saturday, 11/4/2000
>
> Neal Chappell finished first in the 60+ division of the National Masters 8K Championship on November 4, 2000. However, I do not believe that he got credit for the win because of a problem regarding date of birth verification. He has now shown a USATF

official his birth certificate. So, maybe he will eventually get credit for the win. VOL XXX-#3 WVJS NEWSLETTER Dec. 2000

The US cross-country was at Columbia Point, Tri-Cities golf club in Washington. Its 13 hours of driving from Kingsbury. Friday night, I found motels booked. Their State high school finals were Saturday at Columbia Point. That's why hotels sold out. I used nearby gym locker room facilities, resting and cleaning up, so it's all good! I slept in my van in the golf course parking lot. The noise of people arriving awakened me to line up on Sunday morning. I can't say I was awake when off and running. I always loved groomed fairways. Columbia Point is like that. If given choices, they offered ideal surfaces, easy on the legs. I can't picture a more scenic 8K. We overlooked the evergreen banks of the Columbia River curving westward along Washington's southern edge. Its best feature was no demanding hills, neutralizing leg speed advantages. That's true because I out-kicked Tom Weddle from Minnesota down the last stretch. In other finals, I had gone against this guy, but he's never bested me. Results from the Midwest to California proved he ruled a wide area. Better sprinting beat him. These runs were more satisfying when accompanied by teammates. It's easier if Kenny's present, but Columbia Point is difficult to get to from San Jose. At least with events outside California, there's only a minor concern with verifying ages. When bay area rivals are present, maybe those issues received attention. No PA Association teams came.

The Pacific region admin hasn't relented in rejecting birth dates on applications. They ignored hospital certificates and passports. My opponents always tried to win by disqualification. Regardless of what I did, disputes got raised. Somewhere petty bureaucrats with miserable lives ignore documented evidence of birth. It was funny but sad.

Kenny:

Questions about Neal's birth continued causing minor concerns. We saw it as a "running" joke whenever someone broached the question. Often, accusers had serious looks and acted as if uncovering an elusive capital crime.

When everything is said and done, more pressing concerns prevailed. Of great consternation was Jutta's health. She's my training partner after Vicky and David García moved to Las Vegas. Vicki trained with me starting at GTE. Before leaving here, she recruited (and convinced) Jutta to take over. Vicki understood I'd suffer without another female partner. Jutta was ideal. She was German, born during World War II, and approaching six years old when Germany surrendered. She lived through the Allied Occupation. I learned that her family had rooms in a building housing Black American soldiers. Judging from conversations recounting WWII's aftermath, sharing living space with Blacks was positive and memorable. I guessed such youthful experiences influenced our connecting as well as we did. Jutta was talented and committed, full of competitiveness. Aggressive cancer attacked her ribs again. I never thought she'd take sick, dying before me. An opportunity to speak at her memorial allowed me to tell people about the unique person I knew. I sought to do this by expressing what she meant to me. I made a statement, hoping it was clear enough.

In Memory of Jutta McCormick

First of all, what I know about Jutta comes from thousands of miles of running together … with a fair share of those miles being logged in the dark with flashlights showing the way along the trails at Rancho. What I know about her also came through a friendship forged in the heat and fire of burning lungs and burning legs during hundreds of track workouts and long runs on Sundays going over the "Mother of all hills" on Canon Drive. And, yes, what I know about Jutta comes from the hundreds of hours of conversations over coffee at Peete's, Whole Foods, and Picadilly. Those were special times and there were many of them. Those were special times and they were too few.

Most of our talks were about family. If I were to pinpoint one thing about her, it would not be Jutta the runner. It would not be Jutta the most focused and fierce competitor I have known other than Sue Francis. It would not be Jutta, the Lab Administrator at Stanford, who strongly believed in equal opportunity, that is, that brilliant students, renowned professors, and school officials have equal opportunity to bring her no-nonsense stance to the surface. That failure to observe the no-nonsense rule would bring her wrath down upon them equally. No, even though these are qualities to be cherished and remembered, they are not the qualities of Jutta that I would single out.

I was most impressed with and impacted by the tremendous wealth of love that she expressed for her family. Without having met Lonnie, the love that she expressed for him made him a special person to me. You have to say, "With this woman loving a man that much, he's got to be all right."

From the way she talked, it was clear that having the two boys served to expand the wealth of love within her. I was fortunate to see the

455

process of expanding the wealth of love repeated when Maggie and Elizabeth were born. As an outsider looking in, I could see that wealth of love surfacing over and over again. I must confess to making it a point, during each run or in our discussions over coffee, to inject something that would cause her to express her love for each of you. It was a selfish thing on my part because I really enjoyed seeing how she felt about you. Not just hearing the words, but seeing that feeling within her. It was so real and wonderful. It speaks to what each of you has given her. This is what I will remember. There is more, but this is what I will remember.

There is the intellectual and cultured side of her that I came to know...

But her expression of love for you is what I will remember.

There were long discussions of political issues, classical music, and literature.

But her expression of love for you is what I will remember.

I will remember that together with her, you made for her all of the love that she could possibly hold.

This is my witness.

Jutta wanted cremation and her ashes scattered on our favorite Rancho San Antonio Park trail. Her family asked me to lead them to Jutta's favorite location at Rancho. That would be our reflective stop returning from Wildcat runs, topping the steepest incline. There's a horizon spanning a panoramic South Bay picture. Soft, warm breezes swept over us as the sun's rays shot their warmth through us whenever pausing. We enjoyed peaceful moments amid bird songs. Family members shared, carrying her remains. They invited me to bring her to the hill's crest over the last 100 yards. We returned her to the soil after I explained what she liked about the spot. I spoke, reminding them that a Great Blue Heron had landed beside us just before we journeyed up the hill, standing until we left. I was sure this spiritual messenger came on schedule, lifting her spirit from the earth and transporting it into the universe. What an uplifting sign!

Neal:

You might say that I'm a running legend throughout Tahoe territory. I've logged long miles cruising natural paths and golf courses along the water's edge. Visibility includes racing over South Tahoe High School's track, moved from Echo Summit's 1968 Olympic Trials. If not in these places, I serve at charity events or conduct activities connected with the Tahoe Marathon. The most crowd-pleasing Marathon event is their historical 3-mile fun run. From the beginning, I've been organizing and leading that part. The low-key event ranked high among attendees as the most satisfying overall experience. The setting's magic touched everyone. Local Tribune stories portrayed my contribution:

> Who better to lead marathoners on a historic run on Thursday than longtime running phenom Neal Chappell of Stateline? Chappell added to his running resume last weekend by winning the national masters road racing championship for participants 65 and older. His winning time in the 10k in Paso Robles, Calif., was 42 minutes, 25 seconds. "I ran 2 seconds faster than last year, I can't believe it," Chappell said. The national 10k champion will lead entrants for this week's Lake Tahoe Marathon on a 3-mile historic run from the Horizon through Kahle Meadow to Nevada Beach at 5 PM Thursday. "It's a fun run, so we don't go too fast," Chappell said.

Write-ups don't portray escort activity as a platform for communicating area history and environmental protection needs. To commune with nature imparts spiritual uplift to running. My sacred duty is to publicize those feelings; Marathon Festivals serve that purpose.

I've had great partnerships with folks at the Tahoe Tribune. They publish an article each year covering my running. No one knew about breaking two age-group records upon reaching 60, and I imagined that might set them off big time! Matto' Nein, the Tribune's writer, printed an excellent review of my recent career.

NEAL CHAPPELL ENJOYING LIFE ON THE RUN

By Matto' Nein - Tribune Staff Writer

He says running is the root of athletics. And for Neal Chappell, it's a way of life. The South Lake Tahoe resident has seen it all as a competitive runner. He's run with numerous Olympic greats. He knows such iconic track figures as Tommy Smith and John Carlos from the late and mid- 60s' and just recently he won two national titles. On November 14, 2000, in Tri Cities, Washington, Chappell added the National 8K Cross Country Championship as his latest national title in a long and illustrious running career. Almost exactly one year previous, on November 29, 1999, Chappell won the National 10K race in Long Beach both coming in the master's division. "I've been running my whole life," Chappell said. "Now that I've finally won national titles, my buddies give me a hard time about taking so long to do it."

His journey has taken him from the Santa Clara Valley Youth Village (SCVYV) where he trained under Mihály Iglói and connected with Jim Beatty and others as an up and coming middle distance runner. While training with the SCVYV team, he attended San Jose City College (SJCC), where he became a junior college All-American

in the half-mile. During his two years at SJCC, Chappell associated with such personalities as Harry Edwards, who became a
renowned Sports Sociologist. Harry was a sophomore at San Jose
State College at the time. This all occurred for Neal after a stint of
running at the University of North Carolina following graduation
from high school.

We continued working out and competing, using Mihái's teaching into
our 70s. When knowledgeable people learn we trained with Tábori, Beatty,
Schul, and Grelle during our heyday, they want comments on the coach's
legendary demands. It isn't easy to demystify the program. His coaching
served a small group well and not others. Top-performing disciples never
detailed their journey. In-depth depictions of trials, tribulations, and bringing
rewards with Iglói are rare. Few good explanations cover his method. We
recommended interested persons read such articles as "How Iglói's Magyars
Trained" by Derek Parker as the most sensible. (There's no such thing as too
much pain when surviving their workouts.)

I remember, in the 1950's, a televised track meet featuring the Mihály
Iglói coached Hungarian's Sándor Iharos, István Rózsavölgyi, Sándor
Rozsnyoi and László Tábori. They reigned supreme through 1955
and up to the Hungarian Revolution of 1956. Half-a-century later. ...
I am still inspired by the outstanding achievements of these wonderful athletes and their charismatic guide. ... I was impressed by the
sheer quantity and quality of sessions tackled by Iglói's athletes.
A typical day's training for Rozsavlogyi included : 10 x100m in
20 seconds(50m jog recovery) + 10 x 300m in 45 to 48 seconds
(100m recovery) + 5 x 600m in 1.40 (200m recovery) + 10 x 100m
(50m jog recovery) + 10 x 300m (100m recovery) + 10 x 100m in 15
seconds (50 m jog recovery) .... Grueling work-outs like these made
me realize why Hungarian m-d runners were ... outstanding....
...I learned Iglói's training programs were systematic, with every

session carefully planned ... to each athlete's individual needs. They blended the art and science of coaching. .... Repetition distances were mostly 100, 150, 200, 300 and 400 metres with longer runs used sparingly.... (Ed. Note, one session, said to have taken place on Xmas Day 1955 by Iharos, was 2 x 1500 at 3:43.....the World Record was then 3:40.8). ...Iglói... believed it important to train close to race pace as often as possible. Iglói reckoned too many longer, slower reps would hamper speed development by impairing the contractile efficiency of his athletes' white, fast twitch muscle fibres, which are responsible for stride rate. .... He kept oxygen debt low so athletes could emphasize good running form, technique, style and relaxation at speed. Flexibility of approach was an Iglói trademark. He had an uncanny ability to tune into his athletes' thoughts, moods and physiological requirements. He never planned training sessions too far in advance, preferring to work from day to day, depending on environmental conditions, how the athlete felt, etc. If he believed athletes needed more stamina, he programmed longer sessions as this extract from Iharos' diary reveals: Tuesday- 5 x 400m in 56.8 to 57.6 (recoveries not mentioned); Wednesday-25 x 100m (50m jog recovery); Thursday- 15 x100m (50m jog recovery) + 10 x 300m in 45.0 seconds (100m jog recovery) + 6 x 600m in 1.37 (200m jog recovery); Friday-40 x100m (jog 50m recovery); Saturday- 14 x 100m (jog 50m recovery) + 6 x 150m (recovery not mentioned) + 5 x 100m (50m Jog recovery); Sunday (am) 12 x 100m with fast finishes: (pm) 5k race.

Iglói's unique personality and ability to motivate athletes was a major element in his coaching.... Iglói confirmed his greatness by taking his skills to America and succeeding in a vastly different social and economic environment. He produced excellent results with men like Jim Beatty, and his methods influenced Bob Schul, Jim Grelle, Billy Mills and Jim Ryun in the 1960's....

BMC News Autumn 2004 Vol 3 Issue 16 British Miler's News

Kenny:

While attending several schools, having successful careers, and running, we gradually figured out sport's role in society. We've watched increasing sports activism as the public recognizes athletes' protests during Olympic festivals as positive. Acceptance is broadening in America and the world. As members of The Olympic Project for Human Rights (OPHR) (co-founded by Harry (Edwards) and me), athletes stood to empower African Americans. Their stance became a motivating symbol for San José State University because Tommie Smith, Lee Evans and John Carlos were student-athletes. Their political involvement shows young people must create positive social influence. Since 2005, campus organizations have collaborated with academic departments and school administration, promoting campus-wide awareness and defining OPHR's significance as part of the University's heritage. Institutionalizing activities commemorating the Olympic project's creation and the 1968 Protest became imperative for demonstrating that everyone should make an impact today. San Jose State introduced Legacy Week in 2007, drawing on valuing social justice activism. SJS faculty and staff established the week as a sanctioned effort. The initiative's goals are:

1. to make social justice issues more central to the campus mission,
2. to develop community,
3. to encourage critical thinking about our complex societal issues, and
4. to have students begin to explore how their field of study or future career can play a part in finding solutions."

(http://as.SJS.edu/cccac/index.jsp?val=cccac_legacy_month)

They didn't establish a celebratory week to let people enjoy feeling good based strictly on past student and faculty actions. Their purpose, scope, and objectives aim to propel students and others into doing more than just being intelligent, involved citizens. Students get challenging encouragement to pursue more than expertise for high-paying jobs. Embracing the support of social justice and fostering solutions to issues are consistent themes. With that focus, the University exceeds expectations. Of equal importance was the atmosphere for implementing future meaningful programs. As of October 17, 2005, when they unveiled the Smith-Carlos statue, they fostered confidence the administrative aims are advancing toward new developments connected to the OPHR. I had been skeptical before.

Health advocacy comes with progression as a runner and scholar. Beyond 1998's surgery, I have had PSA testing twice a year. Prostatectomy data project problems would not return for a decade or more. Medical studies suggest 5 to 10 summers before revisiting cancer. March 17, 2009, Dr. Tsang broke the news: the disease returned as projected. Seven days later, radiation started. I understood some cancer always escapes removal with any procedure. Cells remaining may stay insignificant indeterminately. As I learned, errant cells migrate back to their home area, even when removing the prostate. They become a detectable danger when enough gather, producing measurable test readings. Radiation treatments ended on June 23, 2009. Dr. Tsang confirmed its effectiveness during July's visit. September's PSA test reconfirmed the results. Radiation, however, took its physical toll.

Over six weeks of getting zapped, I tried continuing to exercise. I fought against earlier training levels declining by holding onto the pre-radiation regimen. By week four, movement slowed in losing the battle. Week five reduced me to slow walking. After that, I had no energy. Lost bowel control brings particular uncertainty. Days can't start until the bowels clear. It was difficult training my intestines to empty before 10 a.m. each morning. I preferred exercising early before activities required leaving home. Six years passed until mileage at increasing paces improved. Varying tempo jogs went well enough, hinting that competing again is possible. The knowledge from Iglói half a century ago never proved more valuable. Confidence moving forward came from possessing that history.

Neal:

Annual Penn Relays trips helped to keep me involved with track and field. Decades-long emprise and running dedication have kept us going. An academic gathering during Penn's carnival linked to interest in politics and sport. From 2002, when in Philadelphia during relays' week, we attended the University of Pennsylvania Africana Studies Department's Race and Sport Colloquium. This sports symposium, at Wharton Business School, occurred during the Relays. Its purpose was to hold public-spirited informative discussions featuring scholars, writers, and athletes. We conversed thoughtfully with Professor Edwards, Tommie Smith, John Carlos, and Stephen A. Smith. Gene Zubrinsky (Zub), a former 1960s world-class high jumper, travels with Kenny and me each year. Camille (Zubrinsky) Charles, his daughter, was Walter H. and Leonore C. Annenberg Professor. Ken Shropshire headed the Forum under Camille. History with Zub, including stints as roommates, gave us access as VIP guests. Connections included dining with the colloquium's principals. From the beginning, we had friendships with guest speakers. 2013 featured Wyomia Tyus, 1964 and 1968 Olympic sprint champion. Zub is close to Art Simburg, her first husband. He's known Tyus beginning at San Jose State. We looked forward to insightful discussions because she's a Black female who, winning the 100-meters and 4 x 100 relay, starred at Mexico's Games. Recent forums sought to reframe the 68 OPHR Boycott movement by today's expectations. Questions probing women's low profile fueled criticism ambitious moderators pursue when possible.

Like the OPHR-instigated demonstrations, political action prompted programs at educational institutions to draw attention to athletes influencing change. Tyus fielded those types of inquiries at most speaking engagements. We wanted thoughts on Black females not getting asked to become boycott demands advocates. Various commentators and scholars pursued elevating their own status with "gotcha" questions pointing to presumed "mistakes" diminishing boycott project accomplishments. They desired to produce personal acclaim. Their mindset was to place themselves as the 1968 Olympic Project's intellectual heirs. That's notably the case when they attempt reframing efforts by today's correctness requirements. Ambitious participants sell similar criticisms when given a chance. That happened with Penn's 2013 Race and Sports Program.

Kenny:

Tyus spoke at Penn's 2013 Forum about not having an identified role in the Olympic Human Rights Movement. She felt we ignored women, took their support for granted, and did not invite them to join. As positive recognition for Smith-Carlos' victory stand demonstration expanded nationwide and worldwide over the last two decades, our interest in trending questions about Black women athletes not getting recruited to OPHR roles grew. The three of us observed that program directors used gender-oriented criticism as a strategy, creating a niche for them and attaching to a social movement that has accrued value for more than half a century. As with any popular long-term political action, women participated in the OPHR. Two members were women we married in 1970.

Smug, cavalier stances surfaced as program moderators fashioned self-righteous positions. They acted as if they discovered something nobody else realized. Half a century later, they affected postures of knowing what should have happened. Claims instigating such authority when they weren't present are puzzling. They never dealt with powerful opposing institutional forces confronted during socio-political struggles, circumstances, occurrences, and conditions. The possibilities of things being different if they were involved are irrelevant. Better ideas have functioning validity when creating projects in real time. There's no way to know what specific organizers could or shouldn't do with their energy, resources, or capabilities when projects meet overwhelming opposition, political and economic power-induced isolation, and containment. Should activism develop into organized change efforts, despite the resistance of everyone with power, but getting accepted many years into the future—that, maybe, speaks for itself. If their aim is for participants to abandon the dreams that they struggled mightily to achieve, then good luck. They deserve lofty praise if producing enduring historical effects. Ideas combined with actions must generate exceptional lasting value. Personal approaches to emerging interests applying political correctness measurements to our organization were always receptive and resistant. There's one organizing limitation I hadn't spoken about before. That's enlisting associates to take part in life-threatening undertakings. While we never mentioned methods, we hadn't embraced non-violence. Appearances of being non-violent prevailed, but we carried deadly weapons everywhere.

Authorities knew we were armed. Police contacts showed their secret list of every Black San Jose citizen owning rifles, shotguns, or handguns. Everyone's name appeared. Some information came from gun sales. Shooting range registries from Milpitas to Gilroy were another source. Those surveillance measures maintained against San Jose's Blacks weren't surprising. Whether that practice has remained should be made public. Cops never disclosed their surveillance practices. We recognize that encounters with violence mean fights to the death. We wouldn't ask anyone (especially women) to join under those conditions. Active members volunteered with that understanding. Physical danger existed, so we adopted an attitude of preparedness. We didn't consider bringing women into that cauldron but, otherwise, accepted all volunteers. Deft avoiding emotional confrontations made us de facto non-violent. We were okay with that public image.

At Penn, when Wyomia said, "Being women was a factor (in not being involved in the OPHR) because we were never asked," the moderator surged forward, displaying his eagerness. "That's the point I wanted to get at! I'd like to know a lot more about that!" he said.

The thrill coloring his outburst caught notice. We'd seen this reaction at other forums. There were desires, fledgling views, and hopeful expectations that an unaddressed chauvinistic truth existed about excluding Black women from the Project front lines. In some instances, we heard pronouncements that Black women runners had an angle on the boycott scholars use for gaining recognition in promoting athlete activism—receiving academic notice. We saw their hunger, but attempts at discovery weren't yielding noteworthy results. That was my view when observing some discussions. This moderator thought Black males' politics at Echo Summit (trials) should have received the same attention among Black women at their high altitude camp in Los Alamos, New Mexico. Wyomia expressed how not being included played out.

In her eyes, the camp administration prohibited open communication without discrimination. There was mail, which coaches filtered, and facility phones, unavailable for use as athletes might desire. People talked if they saw each other. That's it! Early on, OPHR principals contacted several women. If I remember correctly, most communication went through Lee Evans. His friends were Madelyn Manning, an 800-meter specialist, and a few others. These women wanted to get involved.

The lack of travel and communications resources left the project without sufficient offensive and defensive capabilities. Operations made it off of Harry's teaching salary, and communicating beyond in-person conversations relied on his office telephone. Although the United States Olympic Committee (USOC) feared Blacks joining forces, we had no funds to overcome their contrived barriers. Sympathizers within the USOC said they figured if women committed, men would respond by maximizing participation. Women's isolated training lowered the potential for boycott involvement reaching critical mass. That was among the goals we wanted to pursue but couldn't finance. We did what was possible on an Assistant Professor's salary battling the Olympic Committee's and FBI's budget. Wyomia offered a sobering summary of confinement at the women's facility.

In her eyes, Los Alamos was abominable (compared to the men's camp). This stark geographic isolation for women raised questions of intent. She thought USOC mistreatment resulted from sexism. Disparity, however, applied double for Black women. **She didn't associate the specter of OPHR recruiting or racism with the USOC's strategic control over Blacks by isolating all the women.** They housed males near Lake Tahoe without restrictions. The women's team got nothing in comparison. Life would have been different, particularly in connecting with civil and human rights movement participation, if men's and women's camps had been equally located, especially for Blacks. Separation (physical, communication, political awareness) between the sexes prevailed, so women did not know what the men had in mind or were doing. If this was USOC's aim, their plans delivered desired results. The Olympic Project failed to connect with female athletes, Black or otherwise. Wyomia expressed regrets:

> "When I look back at my career and think about the sixties and what was going on, we were out of it because we were women, and we were Black women. So much didn't happen for us for these reasons. So many things would not come our way and people would not talk to us. Coach Temple kept us focused and not mired in the issues of the day. The only way we knew anything about the Human Rights Project was when the reporters told us something that the men said or did and asked what we thought about it." (From my personal recording at 2013 Penn Forum)

Some women thought that Barbara Ferrell had OPHR contacts in Los Angeles. That wasn't so. Indeed, most Black females in track lived sequestered at southern Negro Colleges, but Barbara had no more association than they. Wyomia says, "We felt taken for granted. The presumption was that we would go along with the men."

The misogynistic USOC view was Black women couldn't make their own decisions. (History says that has never been the case,) US Team processes curtailed freedom to act or speak out. External pressure came from the USOC, the coaches, and the managers. Communication meetings for Black team members occurred in Mexico City, and people decided what they would do. Wyomia recounts:

"The thing I thought I would do, with no discussion with anyone, was to wear black shorts when others wore white."

She and her relay members wore black shorts, showing solidarity with Tommie and John. Most interesting was her reaction to watching their medal ceremony. She captivated us, describing a remarkable personal experience. Her voice, presenting internalized descriptions from 1968's experiences, transported us there:

When they went on the victory stand and did the salute, I was totally and completely flabbergasted! My eyes got so big! I couldn't believe it! The stadium was just silent for what seemed like the longest time. It was an eerie and bone-chilling feeling! Then there was an eruption of people yelling and beating drums! I couldn't believe I was there! I was there and doubted it was me! How could this be me seeing and knowing what's happening? It was scary having the feeling that they could be me—that I am them! We are all brothers and sisters! We love and respect each other more than any thing. And I was in total shock when they came off the stand and into the tunnel! Then, people were yelling at them! I just said, 'Oh, my God'! Should I even be watching this, I thought?" That's my memory! It was wow! You first heard people yelling good things. Then, people were saying, "How could they do that to their country?" I had a level of fear for their safety and future that can't be measured.

Hearing her voice and internalizing her description was as much as getting transported there as I could imagine.

Neither Big Harry nor I went to Mexico because FBI connections warned of plans to make us victims connected to the Tlatelolco Massacre. There, wonton slaughter concluded student-led demonstrations, with the army and Mexico City police killing over 300 protestors before the Olympics, and hundreds disappeared without a trace. We communicated with Mexican students starting in 1967 and avoided getting implicated as foreigners influencing what everyone labeled "the Mexican Dirty War."

We knew that anyone representing the USA had protection from deadly conspiracies concocted by American and Mexican secret agencies. In Wyomia's mind, Black track athletes felt there was nothing they could add as captivating expressions once their compatriots finished. From introspection, conjuring demonstrations approaching our 200-meter runners' impact, a single possibility occurred to me—self-immolation. That's an ultimate sacrifice used by Buddhist priest expressing commitment to fighting for universal human welfare. We didn't want to make points with such finality. The stances the iconic activists' took in Mexico City resulted in their status increasing over half a century. When all questioning and misgivings got answered, accepted, or dismissed, I don't think their success in highlighting human rights issues could diminish in the world's eyes.

CHAPTER
SEVENTEEN

Homegoings

*With money, and especially without
money, the lasting value is friendship.*

Neal:

April 16, 2014, I woke up with the damn hernia nagging! It's been sitting in my groin for years and nagged during last February's National 8k. Injuries weakened me, yet I performed as expected, and my time captured second for the 70s age group, even though I'm the oldest at 74. The soreness was mentally distracting, climbing brutal hills. Our minds play tricks sometimes. Though it's not crippling, an operation was in order. Surgery meant not attending 2014's Penn Relays at month's end. There weren't enough recovery days. Difficulties with hospital appointments eliminated traveling. It's better to do it before leaving Vegas and another beautiful Lake Tahoe summer. It snowed there today, which sounds weird, too. Undergoing hernia surgery now meant I'd do Brea, California's National 8k, when turning 75. That made for odds favoring finishing first. With the damn hernia repaired, I wouldn't worry. There are ten months of preparation ahead.

At my advanced age, I do moderate training. Workouts are only enough for winning local or regional contests. I peruse past results to calculate possible victories and adjust the work. Practice designs sustain estimated winning paces according to course lengths. Strategies avoid over-training and flaming out. Most of all, it promotes longevity and remaining injury-free. Last year (2013), I did 38:19; anything close wins my age group. I've run this event before, encountering problems with organizers accepting registration birth dates. Issues date back 15 years when rival clubs raised questions. The identity of those lodging objections continues to be undisclosed. When turning 60, I dominated the Super Senior competition without effort. Somebody didn't like my margins of victory. They thought I was still a 40-something. Who wants to look old? My hair was full of color in those days.

Body strength from training makes my back straight; I stand tall, carrying myself. Detractors qualified as old-ass haters. Eligibility protests lodged more than once succeeded on one occasion. When winning consecutive US Road Racing 10Ks, a letter disqualified WVJS's team and me. We won back-to-back National Club crowns. Disqualification mattered little because USATF notices meant nothing regarding keeping the winner's medals. Pacific Association President Irene Herman had several proofs of my birth. She had seen certificate copies more than once and knew that claims against me were bogus. I tried settling these issues by emailing her for help. The national administration kept requesting proof (2015). Hater's shenanigans did not affect my preparation for coming races. Records of conditioning before Brea illustrate our take on hard days, alternating with easy running before a national competition. We projected how Iglói would do it. Kenny helped with planning and adjusting intervals and communicating daily.

Sunday, February 1, 2015 - 1 mile warm-up + 10 x 100 meters easy speed + 1 x 1 mile at race pace (7:56) + 2 lap jog + 1 x 1 mile at race pace (7:53) + 2 lap jog + 1 x 1 mile at race pace (7:58) + 2 lap jog + 1 x 1 mile at race pace (7:55) + 2 lap jog warm down + 10 x 100 meters easy speed	Warm day, calm winds, didn't feel up to doing another mile. Wanted to average 7:50
Monday, February 2, 2015—4 mile easy run + 10 x 100 meters easy speed	Warm day, Felt great And rested
Tuesday, February 3, 2015—7 min warm-up + 10 min stretching + 10 x 100 meters 1 easy speed and 1 good speed + 1 x 1 mile in 7:16 (lap splits 1:48, 49, 50, 49) + 2 lap jog + 1 x 1 mile in 7:17 (lap splits 1:49, 50, 49, 49) + 2 lap jog + 1 x 1 mile in 7:21 (lap splits 1:47, 50, 53, 51) + 2 lap jog warm down + 10 x 100 meters easy speed	Felt wasted after two, but went on to do another surprised by the fast first lap.
Wednesday, February 4, 2015—4 mile easy run + 10 x 100 meters easy speed	Warm day, no aches or pains
Thursday, February 5, 2015—10 min warm-up + 10 x 100 meters good speed + 1 x 800 in 3:22 (lap splits 90, 92) + 1 lap jog + 1 x 800 in 3:24 (lap splits 92, 92) + 1 lap jog + 1 x 800 in 3:25 (lap splits 91, 94) + 2 lap jog warm down + 10 x 100 meters easy speed	Not tired after two, but felt it on 2nd lap of #3. Great weather!
Friday, February 6, 2015—4 mile easy run + 10 x 100 meters easy speed. Average 9:10 per mile for total of 35:40 without trying. Right now, I predict to average 7:45 per mile for 8k for a finishing time of 38:44. Certainly at my max on the intervals.	Warm day, calm winds, all around good feeling

Saturday, February 7, 2015—4 mile easy run + 10 x 100 meters easy speed. Average 9:15 per mile. Able to keep the pace steady and concentrate on relaxing.	Warm day, calm winds,
Sunday, February 8, 2015—10 min warm-up + 10 min stretching + 10 x 100 meters 1 easy speed and 1 good speed + 1 x 1 mile in 7:00 (lap splits 1:42, 46, 56, 46) + 2 lap jog + 1 x 1 mile in 7:08 (lap splits 1:44, 47, 49, 48) + 2 lap jog + 1 x 1 mile in 7:08 (lap splits 1:47, 48, 48, 45) + 2 lap jog warm down + 10 x 100 meters easy speed. Surprised that the times are that good.	Wind on last lap of last mile. Struggled Used indoor spikes. It helped.
Monday, February 9, 2015—4 mile easy run + 10 x 100 meters easy speed	Warm day, calm wind, no aches
Tuesday, February 10, 2015—10 min warm-up + 10 x 100 meters good speed + 1 x 800 in 3:24 (lap splits 92, 92) + 1 lap jog + 1 x 800 in 3:24 (lap splits 91, 93) + 1 lap jog + 1 x 800 in 3:24 (lap splits 94, 90) + 2 lap jog warm down + 10 x 100 meters easy speed	Times are inching down. Great weather!
Wednesday, February 11, 2015—4 mile easy run + 10 x 100 meters easy speed	Warm day, calm winds, no aches or pains
Thursday, February 12, 2015—10 min warm-up + 10 min stretching + 10 x 100 meters 1 easy speed and 1 good speed + 1 x 1 mile in 7:06 (lap splits 1:43, 48, 58, 47) + 2 lap jog + 1 x 1 mile in 7:02 (lap splits 1:44, 45, 47, 46) + 2 lap jog + 1 x 1 mile in 7:05 (lap splits 1:46, 47, 47, 45) + 2 lap jog warm down + 10 x 100 meters easy speed.	Times are inching down. Great weather!
Friday, February 13, 2015—4 mile easy run + 10 x 100 meters easy speed.	Warm day, calm winds, good feeling

Saturday, February 14, 2015—10 min warm-up + 10 x 100 meters good speed + 1 x 800 in 3:24 (lap splits 92, 92) + 1 lap jog + 1 x 800 in 3:24 (lap splits 91, 93) + 1 lap jog + 1 x 800 in 3:24 (lap splits 94, 90) + 1 lap jog + 1 x 800 in 3:26 (lap splits 94, 92) 2 lap jog warm down + 10 x 100 meters easy speed	Wind on last lap of last mile. Struggled with that. No aches or pains. Running in flats.
Sunday, February 15, 2015—4 mile easy run + 10 x 100 meters easy speed. Able to keep the pace steady and concentrate on relaxing.	Warm day, calm winds,
Monday, February 16, 2015—4 mile easy run + 10 x 100 meters easy speed.	Warm day, calm winds
Tuesday, February 17, 2015—10 min warm-up + 10 min stretching + 10 x 100 meters 1 easy speed and 1 good speed + 1 x 1 mile in 7:42 + 1 lap jog + 1 x 1 mile in 7:22 + 2 laps jog + 1 x 1 mile in 7:10 + 1 lap jog + 1 x 1 mile in 7:25 + 1 lap jog warm down + 10 x 100 meters easy speed.	No aches or pains. Running in flats..
Wednesday, February 18, 2015—4 mile easy run + 10 x 100 meters easy speed.	Warm day, calm winds, feel good
Thursday, February 19, 2015—10 min warm-up + 10 x 100 meters good speed + 1 x 800 in 3:25 (lap splits 92, 93) + 1 lap jog + 1 x 800 in 3:28 (lap splits 93, 95) + 1 lap jog + 1 x 800 in 3:28 (lap splits 94, 94) + 1 lap jog + 1 x 800 in 3:25 (lap splits 93, 92) 2 lap jog warm down + 10 x 100 meters easy speed	Warm day, calm winds, good feeling
Friday, February 20, 2015—Complete rest.	
Saturday, February 21, 2015—Complete rest.	

Sunday, February 22, 2015—National 8K Championship. Mile 1 = 7:38 Mile 2 = 7:24 Mile 3 = 8:23 Mile 4 = 8:24 Mile 5 (.96 mile) = 7:10 Total of 38:59 Good for 1st Place 75 age group.	Cool morning with a threat of rain.

My strategy employed negative splits, matching the final month's training for maintaining prior division-winning paces. On average, five minutes per kilometer is fast enough, and this course is not for tackling alone. Richard Chimenti, my WVJS teammate, has run well. We started together, helping each other past halfway.

Fast starts were regular, pushing me beyond my comfort zone for the first five minutes. Dick dropped behind as I went over the hills, feeling no deficit. Chimenti wasn't fairing well. He fell off on the second series of rises. After 3K, I went on alone. It wasn't so trying once a cluster of women made contact. It felt possible to keep going and have something left for the finish. One woman passed with eight minutes remaining, drawing attention. She eased in front, so the Bib number identified her as 65 (or more). As a 75-year-old man, I stayed close and let her pull me. Synchronizing our strides relaxed me, conserving energy by drafting behind her. On seeing the finish and going to hard tempo I passed the woman ending in 38:59. That's 4:52 per kilometer. The last 1.5k clocked 7:10. An interval program mirroring Iggles brought results within an acceptable error margin. It's difficult judging how much rises hurt, but they did. There's another individual title and third place for teams on my résumé. With Dave Norlander and Dick Chimenti, WVJS garnered 3rd among 70 to 79 opponents. A rewarding day came from diligent work! My thoughts shifted toward what run came next.

Place	Bib	Athlete Name	City	State	Age	Gender	Finish Time
211	4816	**Neal Chappell**	Stateline	NV	75	Male	38:59
231	4779	**Roland Cormier**	Jackson	NJ	75	Male	41:38
235	4817	**David Norlander**	Los Altos	CA	75	Male	42:37

From experiences and awareness to document it, we followed Iglói's methods (while tempering up-tempo intervals due to age), training ourselves since 1962's LATC dismissal by executives. Under his influence, we filled our notebooks to study his directives, internalized nuanced definitional expressions for intervals, and kept the faith. Championships and world records came after turning 60 with more US titles in my 70s.

My last victorious 8K National came in 2015 because the USATF moved it to Virginia Beach, Virginia. The Noels, Kenny's family, had their 2010 reunion there. He praised the new location as beautiful under any circumstances. Now that I'm old, I won't travel great distances for competitions, as long airplane rides prove too taxing on an ancient runner's legs!

Kenny:

Cohort members kept slipping away one after another. We've reached a tenuous phase. One death of particular significance was Tom Brown, who meant so much to us on and off the track. His inspiration went back to high school when watching California performances from the east coast. Our friendship required me to share what a vital person he was. Relatives didn't know him in ways we did, particularly relating to track, and they deserved to hear a full appreciation of his importance. My narrative for his funeral presented a courageous friend and inspirational runner. Alas, I couldn't attend his memorial services; Genara, his oldest of three daughters, read our friendship story, describing strong individual relationships from an immeasurable passion for running and distinctive brotherhood spanning our lifetimes. People widely

hailed this sentiment in response to announcing Thomas' death by distrib-
uting testimonial copies within the old runners' community.

Tom Brown: A Wonderful Friend

I have a story to tell about Tom Brown and his importance in my
life. 56 years ago, when Thomas and I became friends, I told him the
basic story of a connection I had with him that came before we ever
met face-to-face. However, I never talked to him about the story's
deeper meaning. That is what I want to do right now. Sure, Thomas
was already important to me before the moment when we met and
became friends in 1960. He was important to me well before we ever
met. We were the same age and we were both runner's and ran the
same events. We lived on the opposite sides of the country. He grew
up in a small town on the west coast and I grew up in a small town
on the east coast.

As a high school senior in 1956, Thomas was part of the greatest high
school half-mile race in history. In the 1956 California State Track
and Field Championship, Jerry Siebert finished first and eventually
represented the United States at the 1960 and 1964 Olympics. Tom
Brown finished fourth in the 1956 California State Championship
race, but his time was exactly the same as the third place finisher.
All of the times in the race were exceptional! According to George
Wright, a noted author and track and field analyst, "Many people still
consider the 1956 meet the greatest State Meet ever. There have been
a number of really outstanding State Meets, yet I feel the importance
of the 1956 meet was the performances across the schedule represented a major breakthrough in talent, performances and depth. We
should see Tom Brown as part of the process of raising the level of
talent in high school track and field for the future."

From my perspective, the top performances in Tom's half-mile race were amazing feats because they were 10 seconds faster than I had ever run. I had no idea that high school runners could run like that. When I learned about that race and heard the names, I thought Siebert and the others, those are white boys, and Tom Brown is a Negro name. You might wonder why that was important. It was extremely important because I grew up in a segregated town, even though it is in the north and within a stone's throw of Philadelphia, Pennsylvania. Under the conditions of segregation, I had the desire to be a valued citizen of the larger society without ever having the feeling that I'm a valued person by birth. I had the desire to achieve great things without ever getting the sense of being able to achieve great things sufficient to lift me to the status that white people receive at birth because of growing up in a racially segregated environment. In Junior High School, I consciously abandoned the path to academic success to focus my efforts on running as my best route to public recognition and acceptance. Thomas showed me, as a Negro high school runner, that I could have similar noteworthy achievements. The only difference between the two of us, that I could see, was that he was in California. Therefore, in my simple mind, all I needed to do was go to California. In 1956, Thomas became my hero before I ever met him. His achievement planted the idea of coming to California in my mind. On arriving in San Jose to join the Santa Clara Youth Village track team in October 1960, after 4 years in the military, Thomas was the first Black person that I met. After spending time at Modesto Junior College where he met his wife, Joyce, he was already a member of the Youth Village team. He was training with and running with several members that would break world records and win National Championships and Olympic Championships over the next few years. It was not surprising to find him training with such a talented group of runners. Thomas had come to San Jose after receiving a track scholarship to attend

San Jose State College. San Jose State was a National track power at the time.

On hearing of Tom's passing, Ben Tucker, a Hall of Fame runner at San Jose State, said, "I remember Tom Brown very well. I called him Long Lean Tom. You and Tom were the only two brothers on the Santa Clara Youth Village team. You guys certainly inspired me during my days at San Jose State; knowing I was not the only Brother running middle distance. Sorry to hear of his passing, he was truly a pioneer in his day and was one of the rare Black middle distance runners during his era. You guys demonstrated to me that I could be a successful middle distance runner."

Lot's of factors led to my coming to San Jose, but the very first direct influence in bringing that about was Tom Brown. The vision of my own capability generated by Thomas' performance at the 1956 State Championship is born out with my experiences after coming to California. With the help of Thomas and his family in the early 60's (I lived with them in 1962 and 1963), I had as much success as anyone can have in track (1964 NCAA 880 Champion) and education (Ph. D. from UC Berkeley). I can't say that any of that would have happened without Thomas and Joyce. I was fortunate to talk on the phone with him every month in recent years. We called each other whenever a major track meet was on television. Most recently, it was the Olympics. I will miss him over the rest of my days.

Kenneth Noel, Ph.D.

The journey to here had many trials yielding great rewards. Sustained running over fifty years has brought home the person adrift on the violent racist landscape amidst exploitation and discrimination for so long. It's very much like being born again. The effects are spiritually satisfying, which was missing for some time, but no more. It seems now we might quietly run to the end of our active lives. That's how we'll recognize it's over. As discussed many times, the final curtain comes down soon after running ends. The increasing questions are who can show up for the upcoming social run? Who can attend the next club workout, PA, or national event? It is no longer so much about winning. The struggle is getting to the starting line, breakfast, lunch, dinner, or the next workout or race—not to mention Philadelphia gatherings with our brethren.

Penn Relays meeting reconvened in 2017 after skipping 2016's cold rainy weekend. That we avoided less than ideal weather matters, considering our fragile state. At least twice recently, we all landed home suffering upper respiratory afflictions, laying us low for months. Enough of that! 2017's predicted perfect weather held. We prepared to complete the trip, touching the usual bases.

Neal:

The dominant motivator changing my life was running. The same consideration applies to Kenny, particularly considering how it kept him from prison.

In 2002, we inaugurated attending the Relays Carnival. Paul Drayton and Mel Pender organized a veteran athletes banquet honoring Olympic and Relays' veterans as Relays guests. Travel from Vegas wasn't easy, with few direct flights. Over the past, it worked the same for Kenny flying from San Jose, California. However, Terry Qureshi, an American Airlines pilot, provided tremendous help. Terry considers him their family member, so he flies everywhere for free. Terry's mother, Naseem, served as Kenny's assistant at a Silicon Valley electronics company until retiring in 2003. Trips were for meeting comrades from the track as far back as 1960 following two days in West Chester, revisiting our first eighteen years' haunts.

There's always a romantic aura, if only from the Revolutionary War heritage displayed everywhere. In concert, the environment pictured an ideal distance running setting. Nature provoked running by featuring paths over rolling hills, winding through dense woods, and along streams bubbling across soft meadows for feeling free. We internalized the spirituality of it. Value-shaping experiences fed desires to return home. This environment surely seduced us, though we developed similar reverence from different vantage points. Half of my early days were spent in Thornton, an enclave surrounded by wooded hills with few residents, primarily relatives. It offered pure country living with summers spent fishing and swimming. Snow sledding filled the winters. Kenny grew to appreciate the countryside while hunting and fishing. He followed Gerald, his brother, swimming in the Brandywine River, flowing through the Brandywine Battlefield outside town. They knew enough about George Washington's and Lafayette's days in the area. Connections with the natural environment similarly shaped our consciousness. Love of the outdoors carried forward. Early worldviews developed while immersed in nature's realm and fed into becoming lifelong runners. We continued appreciating the significant shaping of our small-town roots.

Three acts remained mandatory when at home. An afternoon at Henderson High School with Hester (Dorsey) Davenport came before all else. She graduated with us and is among our favorite people. Whether she knows it, her role makes her our remaining personal tie to West Chester High and our schoolboy history. She is the only Black in town with whom we sustain a connection. We lace up our shoes every time to jog the old Montgomery Street cross-country course, and it's an excellent way to recount triumphs.

1955 was West Chester High's first undefeated XC season. They've developed homes on land along the old route. We found houses and kids with threatening dogs on streets where undeveloped roads had gone through hillocks. Unfriendly animals make us walk. Traffic crossing Goshen Road out and back has become treacherous. 2.5-mile races ended with a lap on the cinders. We planned jogs to arrive at the stadium while girls and boys' teams had a rest day before competing at Penn. On each visit, team coaches let us meet with their charges. Talks recount school days, reinforcing that sufficient work leads to better performances and scholarships. We hope our stories encourage lifelong running. There's a special feeling when proselytizing our passion.

While Jack Williams (JR) remained close, contact with former class-mates got scheduled. He was the straightest of straight arrows. JR and Kenny became co-captains. Jack relished the "Cap'n" title because he considered such roles as honors beyond words. One captain needed to handle interactions with other teams in a dignified manner. Kenny couldn't do that because he never accepted or respected any pretense of civility or authority. When things got thorny or contentious, he injected maximum grit and determination. With JR, there was a lot to discuss. Heart trouble stopped his running long ago, so now he coaches. His Tatnall girls' team took several Delaware championships. He possesses an abundance of good stories concerning his charges.

Recent decades saw local governments expand. Educated professionals created unprecedented uptown business growth accommodating their young, affluent lifestyle. WC became a yuppie enclave—where young folks interact on balmy nights and weekends. Athletic stores and running clubs supported significant exercise increases. It can't be all bad!

We sign up for races during every return. On April 23, 2006, we did a 10k traversing multiple neighborhoods. It was the "11th Annual Chester County Race Against Violence." After picking up prizes, a conversation started with two middle-aged Black women. Both ran, and one bagged an award. How or why a discussion on race got initiated between us escapes me. While discussing WC's racist past, the trophy winner identified herself as the first Black child to integrate High Street School, the old neighborhood's white elementary school. Of course, we knew differently because Helen, Kenny's sister, and Leonard Yates, Big Joe Yates's younger brother, did so in 1951, well before the Brown v. Board of Education 1954 Supreme Court decision ordering desegregation. Leonard didn't last, but Helen stayed until junior high. The young woman's claim prevailed without our arguing. Her version resulted from the Borough's disgraceful segregation record not being taught at any level. With care, the conversation concluded, and we avoided diminishing her sense of civil rights accomplishment. I should have let her call Helen for an accurate history. Valley Forge Historical Park's 10K Revolutionary Run is another annual event. Steep hills forming Washington's Revolutionary Army camp are challenging since we don't train for them. They gave magnificent awards—American Revolution-themed artwork—worth the effort!

Our relocation to unfamiliar places, challenging situations, and reuniting in California demanded adapting new survival practices. Our determination to venture out spawned inner strength for making a way in hostile settings. These occasions required pursuing our passion (running) and embracing unknown climes. It demanded perseverance to succeed without established support or reasonable prospects for food and housing while not knowing anyone before arriving. Any struggles stood out when meeting school associates like Connerly, who never left WC. He settled for security at home, maintaining family resources, and ensuring social stability and economic comfort. Those staying hungered to hear about travels, difficulties, adventures, narrow escapes, and successes. They prized others' less secure lives more than their own. They never realized it's not too late to pursue unusual experiences. Conversations and musings never intimated they'd venture out.

Searching for memories of how desiring to run consumed me, becoming my focus; no extraordinary external forces were working. Positives included Donald's achievements coupled with Bill O'Shields', Cheyney College's legendary track coach, encouragement. To return east meant staying at Donald's near Thornton, and Cheyney College lay one mile north. Their campus setting reminded me of my relationship with Cheyney's legendary track coach. His attention gave me a track-related confirming influence from nine years old forward. Cheyney University's new stadium is now named for Coach O'Shields.

I saw running fast over long distances afforded regular escapes, if not total relief, from confinement at Episcopal Farm School (EFS). Valued harriers could exit residential compounds to venture into open spaces on surrounding trails. Fresh air and cruising outside farm boundaries mile after mile on runs had great rewards as a multifaceted positive outlet. In contrast to farm and boarding school restrictions, what an uplifting thing! How could anyone survive without that? There's constant hunger to escape, and it breeds personal discontent. When eventually escaping for good, I left feeling heightened enthusiasm for running. I entered West Chester High

School (WCHS) through Jack's, my oldest brother, intervention and found a team matching my drive to run in spades. He signed me into WCHS and delivered me into a typical teenage environment for the first time. There's coaching, talented personnel, and facilities propelling me away from EFS's oppression! Their student culture provided great recognition. Several cousins there made transitioning easier.

With little thought, I felt I needed to be there. Free at last! For sure, that's what my brother wanted when he tore EFS's shackles from their grip on me. In becoming substantially free, I radically changed my sense of self-worth. Once arriving, my main interests became establishing track and cross-country connections, no matter what. I had no idea it would take on a lifetime of meaning. I did not know how WCHS interactions could influence life's unfolding directions (twists, turns, difficulties, and rewards).

An excellent example was eventually embracing the burgeoning health food movement and its growing body of knowledge and practices. Healthy lifestyle choices have gone with competitive running for over 65 years. A national championship win at 75 showed my path's sensibility. Refined nutrition's importance as a performance enhancement tool came much earlier than for most. I'm confident of having maximized performance over many decades. So far, so good! Not giving up running for pointedly lucrative or secure economic prospects makes me proud. Happiness is staying true to myself and cultivating my runner's DNA. Other people thought it best to sacrifice personal freedom and accede to popular athletic arrangements. They favored becoming elite under obligation to traditional authority's management, judgments, and rewards. Bill O'Shields expressed disappointment when I left college to follow Coach Iglói.

Most noted runners from our day stopped after college. Those guys did it based on limited goals. Our ideas and values weren't so conventional. We didn't rely on establishment support, caring enough to continue beyond most others. It's more to us.

My transfer to WCHS elevates track and cross-country involvement to new levels. Commitment growth went on a steep ascent, morphing into a passion. Mr. Zimmerman, our coach, corralled me three days before 1954's fall classes. Kenny and Jack Williams met me on the first day. I skipped second grade in elementary school, so although we're juniors, they're older. Kenny had followed JR into competing at the highest level. He entered the tenth grade as the District Junior High School Sprint Champion. Performing at West Chester was different and new. Jack had wiry and springy legs. His bouncy stride combined with better endurance. Kenny was Black and thin with a sprinter's speed.

Count me as blending their characteristics, possibly passing as a dusky complexioned mulatto, if warranted. We formed the team's robust nucleus and immediately collaborated as equals, building teams. Academics were Cap'n Jack's passion. Partnering athletically with him, we embraced running more than other pursuits. I was the person envisioning an undefeated senior season. The goal, for sure, drew us together above and beyond high school sports. It set a course sharing devotion to the same passion. When we met, JR had more distance talent. He set the standard for progressing to competition leaders as seniors. That's how we became WC's original undefeated harriers. Four sophomores (Pete Giunta, Bobby Harris, Jerry Stine, and Don Austin) who had guts joined, rounding out our supporting cast. They learned to stay close behind. We did well enough, winning every dual meet and several championships. One junior ran fast enough to join us seniors on the 1956 4 x 440 relay and win at Penn. Those Relays' awards stood above all others. It's a pinnacle of accomplishment.

WC treks became routine after Zubrinsky suggested joining a Philly meeting of athletes. A stop at Cagianno's News Stand on Church Street was imperative. Mike delivered worthwhile news. He was a dependable gossiping classmate. His business at Gay and Darlington Street's intersection is vital to staying abreast of classmates dying. Someone dies between each trip. Every departure draws us closer to the inevitable event. Friends' passing makes focusing on running and Penn visits more critical.

Annually returning east celebrates being lucky and doing well with opportunities given past tenuous teenage circumstances. My return to WC never sought to resolve needing places to grow and prosper, running track and cross-country at the highest level. It pulls on me, constituting a weak force. Interest in high school distance teams continued beyond 1955 –1956 because the ultimate intention was to launch a long-standing culture. Those following us continued unbeaten. We accepted responsibility, as missionaries, for addressing teams since 2005. After 1956, I followed the school teams' fortunes.

Zim is the top among those worth remembering. His support made us unique at the school. With his mentoring, we had freedom other schoolmates never experienced. We did the cross-country course until the day's classes ended. Physical Education for the last period enabled extending runs into after-school practices. There was pride in being "Zim's Boys." At North Carolina (UNC), summer visits with hm allowed sharing my athletic improvement. That was great!

For Zim's final season, we intended to express our appreciation for him. I often wondered if my maternal father's absence influenced the motivational purpose in getting coached by Zim and if my stepfather never filling that role meant anything. It's doubtful he ever cared for such a bargain. Yet, Harvey proved an exceptional provider for Mom. Zim was a father figure for his teams. Acknowledging me at the first football pep rally (1954) hit me as an unexpected personal confirmation. My mother never got to watch me run. Zim was always there. My thought is teenagers must run for someone other than themselves! Kenny's mother and father attended track meets but didn't tell him or discuss events. Jack's father died long ago. We've added visiting Zim's grave since his burial at Birmingham Lafayette Cemetery south of the Brandywine Battlefield.

Recent years in West Chester yield at least two notable events, essential memorials confirming our legends at WCHS. We felt the school's sports complex on Chestnut Street should have Mr. Zimmerman's name with Mr. Butcher's for the track. They didn't dedicate the complex to Zim, but named the grounds for Mr. Butcher. Even before WWII, Walter Butcher maintained all the fields. He had known the Noels four doors away on Minor Street. He embraced us to the extent of grooming the cinder oval more than the preset maintenance required. For him, its care was personal. He witnessed and cheered our accomplishments on his prized surfaces. Even then, we considered it as belonging to him. He treated every yard with utmost care! West Chester East's stadium became Harold I. Zimmerman Stadium for whatever reason. It's satisfying that one WC school stadium complex has Zim's name. It isn't where he held sway while becoming revered in Pennsylvania. Naming the complex where he presided is not a struggle we wanted. West Chester cannot outgrow his significance. Two days get allocated for doing stuff around WC. Wednesday and Friday work best. We reserve Thursdays for attending Penn's Forum on Sports and Society at the Wharton School on Chestnut Street. The forum proved a much-appreciated academic sidebar for east coast treks. Forum presenters explore subjects fueling extensive discussions at Friday night banquets.

2017 involved a University evening radio broadcast discussing sport and society. An opportunity arose when we lunched with Carlos (John Carlos) at the Study Hotel. He and Charlene, his wife, scheduled the interview and insisted Kenny take part. He had done no prior talks but agreed to go on air. I was comfortable relaxing in the studio, listening, and sipping herbal tea. It would be fun discussing 1968's Olympic Project for Human Rights. I've often heard conversations addressing it in San Jose during OPHR's ascendance. Maybe something different will come out now. Shows could be on slates for future visits if it goes well.

I took notes while observing. Professor Shropshire's introduction called them "Doctors" right away. He invoked scholar status, making their words worth listening to. It sounds unusual because my friend rarely used his academic title. When he used it, instances were at two funerals, informing families that their deceased relative helped him reach an intellectual pinnacle (Ph.D.). They could take pride as the deceased's relatives while discovering something noble involving their departed loved one that speaks well for their family.

This broadcast conveyed how typical student experiences could produce

Smith's and Carlos' iconic Mexico City presentation. I couldn't tell if the questioner intended to characterize both subjects as young men experiencing sudden transformation into activists or as predisposed toward activism. Kenny recounted being an ordinary student when he stated,

> "We were commonplace students, up to a point. We did all of the things that most young people do. We were like every other student going to school and participating in different aspects of the civil rights movement touching us. We went to classes, attended meetings and discussions, thought about how to bring change and make life better, and joined in campus and more massive demonstrations to help promote our points of view. What I'm afraid of is that people will look at what happened with the Olympic protest and political demonstration in Mexico City and think it was because we were different and not everyday people. What we recognized was that all of us had the same stuff inside. The same possibilities were there for all to use."

That's a familiar perspective coming from many shared experiences. We were victims facing discrimination in San Jose, and many others struggled to survive. Positive or negative outcomes depend on which side the coin landed on, with the customs, norms, and social practices playing out. The difference from most is we were athletes. I see nothing unusual regarding his quest for change using sport. It progressed reasonably, focusing on the realm where we invested earnest desires for meaning, acceptance, and value. Arriving there is natural when critical thinking joins self-awareness. It's using average minds in the best way and not just for particular folks. People and their institutions can never be perfect, making social activism a human responsibility. There's a charge of contributing to humanity, warranting an elevation of individual effort. World-class athletes' gifts come with obligations to give back to humankind. It doesn't involve doing great things in one fell swoop. It can be something small.

Carlos explained, in response to questions about joining the boycott project, "I was in a town called Commerce, Texas. I knew I had come to the wrong place, and I knew I should be in a big city, and I found San Jose."

Carlos's brief response instigated Kenny to inject perspective on environments informing personal development, which he suggested Carlos and Smith use when giving talks. He said,

> I think it helped that the people in our core group came from widely different environments. It was good that Carlos came from New York, a big city, and experienced the oppression of Commerce, Texas and East Texas State College. It was good that Harry came from East Saint Louis, Illinois, a virtual hellhole for Black people. I was from a small segregated town near Philadelphia, and that offered another way of looking at the world. Tommie Smith and Lee Evans were products of the farm fields in California's central valley. All told, a vibrant mix of backgrounds came to the table with their perspectives at San Jose State in 1967 and 1968.

He pointed out qualities endemic to places with different characteristics created helpful perspectives when blending, informing, and fueling political movements. Shropshire endorsed some vague popular notions. His presumption was clear when he addressed Carlos, "I assume the reason you left a college in Commerce, Texas, was coming to what was called or was soon to be called Speed City?" Intriguing that he rejoined "or was soon to be called" identifying the political hotbed in San Jose. Did "Speed City" come before or after Carlos arrived? The statement from the professor seemed curious; knowing the title for the college's "Speed City to Civil Rights" project existed for several years, suggesting Speed City started after WWII. What he understood of project inaccuracies was another question.

One conversation issue was whether Speed City became a coherent social phenomenon predating OPHR's founding. Was it created as a continuous progression of SJS administrations' history of intended accomplishments?

Or was it produced by pursuing change that institutions opposed? A proper mix of yes and no answers notates the real story. OPHR created conditions warranting international acclaim with no local institutions supporting its development. It was an organic Black Power magnetic attraction that makes "Speed City" a worthy label for the creativity of the Black community bonding using athletic excellence. Carlos responded by fielding the interviewer's assumptions:

> I don't think I left ETS as a result of Speed City. I was never in it just to run. I used to go to the library at ETS to read the newspaper, and I was aware of the movement that was going on in sports at that time to bring awareness of the plight of people of colour to the forefront. And, that's what was going on in the city of San Jose. I always said that these guys were the explosives. Lee, Tommie and those guys that were running track, but I like to consider myself as the wick that brought the fire. I was the missing component, as some would say. How can you even imagine the existence of a place called Speed City before I came?

They clarified Speed City's growth from the OPHR, not the reverse. Penn's radio show informed listeners as well as entertained them. October (2018) is Mexico's Olympics 50th anniversary, and a good guess is more public talks belong on 2018's schedule.

Saturday at Franklin Field meant basking in the stadium crowd's competitive, excited, communal atmosphere. We evaluated talented youth for continuing as world-class performers with every race. Our younger representatives must keep leading competition across the world. Performances were always great, while seldom meeting exaggerated expectations. As veterans, we're never satisfied. The Brothers of the Wind imprint on awards symbolized human progress as a relay. Succeeding generations improving on the track is imperative.

During school days, choices for productive lives were sparse compared to colleagues. Two weeks before entering his senior year, juvenile court dictated

Kenny's next move. His release on probation caused leaving upon graduating. Before I knew it, he had entered basic training at Lackland Air Force Base near San Antonio, Texas, and the judge banned him from returning until he was 21.

I searched for colleges, and all attempts at admissions came up empty. Not being in school allowed working on banking tuition funds. I wanted to keep running, and that made UNC my choice. Little else influenced my decisions. Jim Beatty's presence was their big draw from the awe of witnessing his 1955 and 1956 Franklin Field victories. My wish to run overrode doubts and misgivings regarding college. From instilling personal discipline and determination, running made venturing into unlikely realms more likely, plus without anxiety. At every stop, physical ability meant security. Ready-made comradeship guaranteed acceptance in any runner's group. A welcome waited on moving from WC to UNC at Chapel Hill. An equal reception occurred on traveling round-trip to California. After Carolina, I paused in Miami and went from Miami to various California locations. The ultimate spot for this distance-running professional gambler became Nevada. At UNC, circumstances landed me under Iglói. His open embrace solidified my training commitment, and constant reliance on running prevailed. Requirements and impact (physical, mental, and social) helped me progress through it all. Pontificating regarding benefits was right. Perhaps more significant for me was realizing reasons to embrace it early in the game, welcoming them without effort or concern. From discussions comes my list of rewards from running. These dictates, for me, were integral to daily life. The rigors of hard training made it easy for me to step out of my comfort zone when encountering other kinds of challenges.

1. The rigors of hard training and high-level competition taught me that I could set goals for almost anything, and then achieve them.
2. One of the things to learn was that my level of desire to be a runner required a willingness to seek diverging paths and choose scarier routes over the safer ones without trepidation.

3. It was necessary to recognize and understand the extent to which running was critical in shaping my identity.

4. It was essential to acknowledge and realize that running can be a tool that a person can use to manage and cope with the stresses and strains of modern urban life.

5. It was necessary to recognize and understand that running could be a way of meditating, soothing and revitalizing the human spirit.

6. It was essential to know and understand how important running was for me as I developed personally and professionally beyond being concerned only about running.

7. It was necessary to recognize and realize that there is power in running in terms of its impact on willpower and mental resilience in stressful situations and conditions.

8. It was necessary to recognize and understand that there is power in running in terms of getting healthier and physically stronger, and promoting the desire to be that way.

9. It was necessary to recognize and understand that running can bring a large measure of stability to daily life. For me, all things existed to support my running schedule and its physical demands. That process constitutes my definition of the "good life". That was the way it has been since 1958 or 1959. Running as I do fosters a level of stability that is reliable beyond measure. I knew what I needed to do with my life every day and I knew why everything needed to be done and when. I knew what external conditions and influences to manage. I know if what I'm doing is of benefit or what has to change for that reason.

10. It was necessary to recognize and understand that running was the most constant force in the course of my life day after day, from place to place, and in making all manner of social and economic decisions. The telltale question was how does something relate to my ability to run every day?

11. From a life of running, I have a firm grasp on what are the norms for

every step. If life was good, the evidence was that running was good. We manage what we do to that end.

How our lives changed remained an obvious question while seeing West Chester's friends. When exchanging narratives, all they sought was hearing from us.

CHAPTER
EIGHTEEN

Speed City

*Satisfaction finishing the last days links
to all the expressions of courage.*

Neal:

Kenny and I recently discussed developments following 1968's Olympic project. Fifty years of activism, pushing change, including Harry's work founding the Sociology of Sport, led to the creation of San Jose State's (SJS) Institute for the Study of Sport and Social Change (ISSSC). Recently, the University claimed its pre-1967 sports were intentional forces for positive reforms, birthing the OPHR. It was on our minds because Mexico's Games semicentennial approached, and developing plans for international commemorative activities were ongoing. SJS prepared for increased 50th-anniversary attention as the home of operations for Tommie Smith, John Carlos, Lee Evans, and the 1967 - 1968 Olympic project. From efforts started in 2005, school-connected researchers have fashioned a history, incorporating an activism saga into photo and material displays. Their presentation is the "Speed City: From Civil Rights to Black Power Exhibit and Legacy Project." Although receiving attention for decades, nicknaming their track program "Speed City" going back to the early fifties is questionable.

Kenny:

We found it curious that those invested in the Speed City Legacy project went to great lengths in crediting San Jose State for fostering consciousness on its campus before 1960. In the years after World War II, minority athletes performed with distinction. That's their basis for suggesting a relationship between years of Olympic involvement and our protest organizing. They shaped their story, implying 1967's Black student uprising started because the school organically became fertile ground, embracing and nourishing activism against discrimination. Because of institution nurturance, activists blossomed to become celebrated worldwide. SJS, backing them, allowed Smith, Carlos, and Evans to lead their historical demonstrations in Mexico City, garnering universal recognition. School administrators hold that going back to WWII; the college deserves appreciation for what happened. Without dwelling on this issue, based on experiences, the academy did not contribute to Blacks' moral courage or consciousness to conduct organized protests. Events occurred despite the administration's existence. History shows that school representatives encouraged going along, continuing the status quo. They accepted racism, never recognizing or opposing racism before students rebelled in 1967. Nothing produced or sustained by faculty or administration in prior years fostered awareness or recognized and confronted American society's failure to live up to its values. No one spoke of current racist practices' wrongfulness. White people never openly discussed changing Jim Crow's unwavering oppression, but everyone knew of systemic injustice.

Neal:

I was alongside Kenny, experiencing the racial hatred he and others endured, so I know there's no reason to doubt. I was there when we encountered discrimination. The school can't take pride in acting against racism unless eschewing honesty. Only fools go along. Stooges and lackeys got on board for their fake anti-discrimination ride through history. Outside classrooms, integration only applied to playing fields, and in ways less than complete. There was nothing near total participation outside of athletics. That failure does not deserve recognition as pursuing professed equality. We don't understand why 21st-century changes don't stand as what counts in moving the institution forward. The best approach is being honest when looking back. It's not good having institutions of higher learning engaged in redefining questionable history using acclamation declarations.

Kenny:

We flat-out rejected self-serving false narrative propagators' posturing. Their storyline romanticizes Bud Winter and pre-sixties Negro runners as precursors for 1967's human rights efforts. SJS's and Bud Winter's relationship with the Santa Clara Valley Youth Village (SCVYV) was an underexposed development. After the spring semester, SJS's runners competed for Santa Clara until fall.

If we put aside those facts for a broader view of track phenomena in San Jose's Seventh Street complex, the facility warrants being called "Long Distance City." During the early stages of San Jose attracting a series of world-class speedsters, America's distance era was in full swing. Mihály Iglói, among the world's greatest distance coaches, worked with Coach Winter on sprinting techniques. Bud came to him because he had innovative theories for training dash men. Bud incorporated those ideas into his methods. I tried listening to discussions but couldn't catch any helpful conversation. We'll never find out.

Neal:

Future scholars should capture the tale of Iglói's men on the SCVYV Team influencing the popularity of exercise in the U.S. They produced many exceptional performances by Americans. László Tábori, Jim Beatty, Jim Grelle, Max Truax, Bob Schul, Jerry Siebert, and Billy Mills are a few making my point. Jack Marden, an excellent SCVYV member in his own right doing 5000 meters or more, still lives in Saratoga, and he knew Santa Clara Valley's charitable Catholic organization well. Kenny and I had standing invitations for Sunday dinner at the Marden's, a prominent local family. That was an absolute lifesaver. Even though we trained in San Jose for two years before moving south to launch the Los Angeles Track Club, many accomplishments came. As we understand it, distance achievement builds on an aerobic base. Now, at least two of us stand among those (maybe the only ones left) still carrying the torch Iglói and Father Schmidt ignited with the Santa Clara Mission's athletic promotion. We still followed as Iglói commanded, "Hard training must make!"

We are reaching marks signaling approaching the finish of our long run. We intend to continue road races with a handful of achievements ahead. Recent events opened opportunities to do more with past participation in things connecting politics and sports. As elders, our example supports the running community, encouraging working out. No day passes without folks expressing appreciation when seeing us logging miles on runs through communities. Blowing horns followed by encouraging shouts are typical. Inquiries about our exercise volume are regular conversations with strangers wherever we go. We remain anchored by a commitment to daily runs. Goals to improve performances aren't pressing concerns. We expect to win titles by doing enough work because everyone our age is within reach. Testing ourselves in competition remains an exciting prospect into our 80s. 5K and 8K races are where we are now, although 800 meters look challenging.

Kenny:

Those partnering with San Jose State to create a narrative for the "Speed City" phenomenon produced plenty of revisionist history. As an inventive exercise, they framed "Speed City: Roots and Legacy Project" and a show called "Speed City: From Civil Rights to Black Power." It has appeared in San Jose's Pacific Hotel Gallery at Happy Hollow History Park and Museum of Art. Elements of SJS's Legacy Week activities promote a false narrative through an annual celebration. If anyone wants to contrast our argument, check the programs mentioned. It's good to evaluate a university's sports history. I caution against assigning positive causality when later actions defy mainstream norms, long-accepted thinking, and behavior.

After they completed collaborations, concerns surfaced for 1960s era Black students around efforts shaping the story purposed to make the institution look good. It shows producers avoiding incorporating significant sources, declining a more studied approach. In that case, reasonable, reliable research depth, breadth, interpretation, and presentation get left wanting. Analysis weakness and deliberate contributor misrepresentations cause missing out on producing a more fact-based account. To this date, I declined to voice comments criticizing, and encouraged expanding interviews to improve data integrity by using more eyewitnesses instead of hearsay and conjecture.

Questionable intent was unfortunate because correct information exists from writers like Sports Illustrated Magazines' Mark Mulvoy. In his article "The Boys from Speed City Burn Up the Town" (June 17, 1968), he joins others writing SCVYV stories, introducing "Speed City." Some commented that Tommie Smith and John Carlos created that popular name for SJS's Spartans. Statements like, "San Jose State star sprinters Tommie Smith and John Carlos ... who coined the nickname 'Speed City' for the Spartan's program." (From 'Speed City—A lesson in righteous protests' (NBC Sports. com) do not help. Other problems of weakness and discovery exist because many of those interviewed who described events, conditions, issues, actions, and results were not involved. People who took part are still alive and able to lend their voices. Interviewees belied events by speaking as if they were there, although they were not. They've tried convincing folks that their contributions were from direct participation. That's why current popularized versions stay vulnerable to characterization as revisionist.

Now I offer my perspective. Speed City grew out of the Civil Rights and Black Power movements. SJS Black student social activism and the Olympic Boycott intertwined in 1966, 1967, and 1968. It was a product of our politics (characters, relationships, and activities), not college athletic recruitment aims. The forces behind its creation were two scholars with ideas embodying human rights and sport. A partial list of principals includes Smith, Evans, Carlos, Jerry Williams, Kirk Clayton, George Carty, Ronnie Ray Smith, Billy Gaines, Sam Davis, Frankie Slayton, Bob Griffin, and Martin McGrady. Why shouldn't people know Tommie came here to play basketball for Stu Inman? Bud Winter was an internationally renowned sprint coach, but Tommie chose San Jose for additional reasons.

Lee Evans' family was here after leaving Fresno, California. He attended Overfelt High and didn't enroll in SJS just because they recruited him. As a freshman, Bert Bonanno, Winter's protégé, had him at San Jose City College, exerting influence there. A valuable version of the story is possible owing to Bert's view. Stan Dow's mentoring had been vital since high school. Lee leaned toward coming to run with Tommie but verged on attending USC. Vern Wolfe, a prior SJS assistant, headed that perennial power. As one of the last points, I recruited Lee to SJS, sealing his transfer when his mother invited me to dinner to tell them why he should stay in San Jose. I was a UBSA organization leader, involved in recruiting minorities and financial aid distribution. I promised unwavering support to succeed at everything he did. Many more family members and loved ones encouraged his staying at home. In particular, it mattered that his success continued in front of them.

Tommie's and Lee's prominence in our boycott movement attracted more sprinters. With their friend Art Simburg, they were unparalleled recruiters for expanding San Jose's sprint corps. Simburg did a yeoman's task, riding Greyhound buses across the country and contacting potential Olympians from other states face-to-face. His relentlessness was effective. Deeply involved in building a world sprint capital, he relates to the process in a documentary, *Black Power Salute*.

"Around the scene, Bud Winter was always considered the best sprint coach globally. But, it was not until Tommie came, and sprinters began to come afterward, that the Speed City aspect developed where there was an avalanche of the top sprinters in the world there.

"Tommie and Lee became the foundation for what would later become the Speed City Team."

We knew personal plans for a future as a track and field business manager for ex-Olympians were part of his motivation.

Each new arrival increased incentives for more to come as word spread. Possibilities for connecting and joining other great sprinters with activist notoriety were waiting for them. In San Jose, they were becoming the greatest acquiring political cred, not only elite performer credentials. An Olympic Boycott effort makes identifying the interdependence of politics and sport inexorable, causing Black people to challenge individuals to earn their allegiance through more than world-class performances. It heralds a new day's social dynamic.

I'm sure knowledge that dash men comprising San Jose's sprinting corps did not have scholarships isn't widespread. Predominant financing for all Blacks came from government grants demanded by UBSA, the OPHR, and others. They were not relying on Athletic Department funds. In taking Olympic Project connected athletes' economic situation further, we should recognize they included runners, not in school. Legacy Program developers didn't uncover personal backgrounds or income sources related to nonstudents' involvement and produce questionable scholarship. Researchers should find information on stalwarts like Gaines and McGrady. I see these truths standing against administration claims promoting itself. More coverage of nonstudents' economic situation improves study quality. That is not their only glaring omission. They should have covered Santa Clara's AAU Club's representative champions, national champions, and major record holders. I'd love to access the contents of Santa Clara University Library's Archives & Special Collections materials from SCVYV operations. Contents of "Box 4: Santa Clara Valley Youth Village Track Team, 1953 - 1968, & updated" and "Box 5: Santa Clara Valley Youth Village Track Team, 1956–1968" call for studying. Without analyzing these documents, essential story elements are missing. Scholars must survey those resources when generating acclaim for

SJS, as responsible for creating sprinting's epicenter in San Jose from 1966 to 1970.

If there was a suitable complex location for bringing track activists together, including nonstudents, it was the south campus—not the main campus. Quasi-academic looks at sprinters affecting activism, and the Human Rights Movement is flawed. Black student involvement in Civil Rights and Black Power Movements was the most significant impetus for the world's top sprinters gathering in San Jose. The best approach to understanding this era is promoting social science-driven studies. I hope to see complete and accurate analyses so that the OPHR continues influencing at the highest level for generations.

EPILOGUE

The Tyranny of Pre-existing Negative Social Conditions, Their Mitigation and Our Survival

Pre-existing conditions are not only medical health terms. Aren't they any conditions that warrant changing before contact with people?

Kenny and Neal:

Sociological research on types of organized oppression and domination, such as colonialism, shows that, in time, these systems fracture when becoming untenable. Such governance (authoritarian) affects those entering down-trodden populations under enslavement or colonization, foreign control (in effect) of social, economic, and political environments, limiting choices, make up debilitating pre-existing conditions. They come as difficulties people face because of occupation, income, education or status, or their lack, and are manifestations of inadequate resources. It remains so for the impoverished, the homeless, the disabled, financially deprived students, racial minorities, or others needing government help. In a racist society, oppressed members experience an adverse order of processes at birth or subjugation for which damaging outcomes are characteristic. When applying a "prudent person concept" to social contracts for newborns or new arrivals to follow norms for the good of everyone, intelligent persons seek dissolution or redress of hate-driven practices. Neal's life was fraught with contradictions and constraints accompanying being born into an impoverished, underclass family with no mobility. Kenny navigated through similar incongruities, restrictions, and obstacles maintained for descendants of formerly enslaved people. He found that socio-economic strictures of race stratification prevent forming meaningful connections for improving one's station. In societies, helpful contacts are crucial for inclusion as members. From the outset, normative dictates degrade oppressed people, working against them, blocking or inhibiting access to integration and personal growth avenues, which would otherwise lead to maximizing potential.

There's an overlay of malicious injustice blunting and belying values extolled by America without regard to real life. The hateful attitudes and behavior of prejudiced folks Neal and Kenny encountered together were unsurprising. Their experience was a persistent systematic denial of full participation because of discrimination from infancy. In psychology studies, they learned that every instance of success denying humans' dignity poisons the psyche of everyone involved—those denied and the deniers. It happens to individuals, families, and others before they forthrightly grasp or interpret interactions. Humans who get refused a sense of worth often respond with forms of rebellion stemming from estrangement or alienation. Restrictive regimes guarantee a scarcity of opportunities for learning skills, positively guiding one's fate when facing dehumanization. One outcome is that while bulwarks for restraint make life difficult, imperfections and variations in worldview, progressive stances, and heightened consciousness of different individuals and groups make it possible for oppressed persons to survive, escaping physical, mental, and social diminishment (social loss, little motivation). We aimed to defeat harmful purposes by finding and pursuing less-traveled paths forward.

Beginning with school, we got exposed to repeated disparities between indoctrination with American ideals and experiences with other socializing instruments, including contacts in schools and on the streets. They caused realizing the bankruptcy of authority across the board. Socialization instigated internalizing disadvantageous norms disposing rejected people to accept discrimination and, yet, racist or class ideologies never went unquestioned in our minds after our primary grades. It took only learning to read, which happened before kindergarten. From there, conforming was a questionable proposition bending toward non conformity.

Promotions of assumptions of significant opportunities, as essentials for acceptance applying for everyone, were sinister features in traditional education. While we both drew toward hoping for a secure future, we recognized it hadn't worked for us as it was automatic for most of our white schoolmates. Small measures of hope are at play. As a tiny stratified town, West Chester was perfect, with visible inconsistencies in values and social mores inescapable. Skillfully dealing with disconnects between ideals compared to reality, by any means necessary, was an innate logical development. Part of moving forward means developing an extensive arsenal of resistance behaviors. Among valuable forms is passivism, cooperation, or assimilation. Another collection of behaviors worth possessing include passive resistance, violating norms, social activism, and anti-racism. A third set of approaches falls under "any means necessary." This mandate includes lying, cheating, stealing, physical assault (possibly killing in self-defense), and property and personal destruction, including suicide (the height of which is self-immolation). In coping with systemic wrongfulness, dismissing actions directed against oppression aren't wise. They are behavior based on attitudes toward survival, expected from people's essential intelligence.

Institutions supporting and guiding everyone's progression from infancy are corrupt, predisposing against positive possibilities. Our readiness to use methods transgressing norms in seeking prosperity became standard with our outlook and employed in our arsenal of tools for coping. We did not differ from most other youngsters growing up imbued with America's founding tenants. Violating customs was common under a constitution's false proclamations of freedom, etc., except for Blacks, other people of color, natives, people experiencing poverty, and disabled people. With rights never granted in their entirety, the deep desire for them never ends.

Wherever conditions warranted changes, our ability to respond with actions matching or exceeding others suffering from an array of paradoxes made up a spectrum. Too often, reactions were self-destructive. (They arrested Kenny, for example, after his junior year of high school—resulting from his counter-productive response in defending Black friends attacked by white boys.) Under aberrant Jim Crow controls, most nonconforming behavior was natural, though ineffective in the larger society. Any elevated antisocial conduct was symptomatic of unmet needs warranting societal reforms or restorative corrective actions. As long as institutions were derelict in delivering support-affirming services, they eroded the social fabric. Jim Crow practices were never worthy of acceptance or allegiance from aggrieved persons.

Tyrannized people expressing themselves against oppressors are no mystery. Dissent's level (scope, intensity, and proliferation) showed that society was not working as needed. Their panoply of expressions includes objectionable, detrimental, violent, and passive behavior. A consistent flow of achievements, positive interactions, and confirmations of outstanding athletic ability from success on the track was a balance but didn't transform the outside world. Frequent exposure to injustices causes our shrugging off encounters with prejudice, going ahead with conventional and unconventional measures for succeeding. When necessary, we sought alternative measures for achieving goals. Constant searches for new directions speak to the point. We enrolled in twelve colleges, completing eight degrees. Without benefits parlayed from running, outcomes could have been less desirable.

This story of two boys bonded by a love of running recognizes longstanding diabolical beliefs and paradoxes they must overcome. Numerous clashes with active and passive purveyors of social and cultural negativity occur when they venture away from home. Conflicts and upheavals from such circumscriptions are typical across the planet, characteristically spawning rebellions and revolutions by subjugated victims going back several hundred years. Such problems bring inevitable failures in confused or confusing societies with multidimensional exploitation. We were not immune to repressive machinations. Sustained efforts against detrimental inequitable requirements were inevitable and reasonable for improving everyone and everything.

While moving forward with resolve represented by this story of questing for human value in two lives, we cannot see the ending of the dark forces plaguing America. Gun violence, mass murders, assaults, rapes, and other acts against women; burglaries, and robberies, and the unrelenting advance of the prison-industrial complex frame this point for us. Adverse encounters affecting victims, near-victims, and masses of uninvolved populations have undeniably been outgrowths of unaddressed societal flaws. This timeless dynamic applies to most oppressed people experiencing focused degradation, heartbreak, and survival challenges in a race, class, gender, ableist, and sexual orientation-conflicted culture.

Our early endeavors focused on personal welfare—we were not concerned with others suffering equal difficulties. Advancement beyond that approach with personal growth, embracing the discipline and drive demanded by an aspirational lifestyle for world-class running, plus continuing high-level exercise until such physical viability ends, represents more than seeking individual gains. By embracing our humanity, we can heal and become well. Obama's era was a landmark indicator of the movement toward uplifting improvements, and his election triumphed over some of our heritage's worst elements. We see it as part of a positive continuum but not a fundamental change. Whether focused on political, social, economic, spiritual, or athletic realms, the triumphs we speak of are accomplishments of the mind. That all humans are Brothers of the Wind, no matter if they run and no matter where they exist, is a lesson moving around the world in fits and starts.

We became teachers at one apex of consciousness of our roles in life. Once becoming a partner in Chinese Herbalessence Ltd's supplement organization, and after buying a health store in Las Vegas, Neal embraced teaching about healthy lifestyles. He developed a philosophical foundation for his business, articulating it at length to management, his sales team, and customers. Educating employees and customers on diet and exercise, living well, and succeeding in life, was best for building his enterprise. His entrée into the healthy food movement fits well with a dedicated physical training regimen. It is helped by demonstrating running as a concrete expression of a healthy lifestyle. He believes our bodies heal themselves with proper nourishment and stimulation. His approach is not limited to eating organic farm produce. It includes supplementing diets using herbs possessing nutrients that are too limited otherwise. Settling in Nevada immersed him in mentoring others to improve their physical well-being. He teaches that the way to accomplish this is through eating better, avoiding forms of animal protein, and regular exercise.

During a parallel period, Kenny conducted courses on family and intergroup relations at colleges in San Jose. By then, his studies aided in framing understanding his own life related to encountered intergroup concerns. His vision for engaging people and advocating for change came directly from personal history, military and college experiences, and concentrated studies. After becoming an activist JC student in 1962, his social protest activity paused until 1967, when founding the UBSA and Olympic Project for Human Rights (OPHR) (with Harry Edwards). Our organization is widely heralded for influencing future directions of sport and athlete performance, benefiting society beyond the playing fields as never envisioned before. The acclaim of induction into the California Hawaii State NAACP's Legacy Hall of Fame in a 2023 ceremony has recently graced the OPHR leaders. Specifically, the Hall of Fame "honors outstanding community leaders who have fought tirelessly to advance civil rights." They note that the impact of our legacy makes California and Hawaii a better place for all.

We have a few concluding insights:

- The best that anyone can embrace for the greatest good is a lifetime of activism without necessitating a decisive win.
- Amy Bass determined with her doctoral dissertation, looking at San Jose's Olympic Project for Human Rights, "It's not the triumph, but the struggle."
- An infallible principle of the OPHR's adherents, "There are no final victories." (Harry Edwards)

If you're interested in contacting us, please send an email to:

kennethenoel@gmail.com and **nealchappell@hotmail.com**

ABOUT THE AUTHORS

NEAL CHAPPELL has been a successful vitamin and Health Food entrepreneur and an esteemed professional poker player. At the gaming tables in the Tahoe and Vegas Casinos, he is Tahoe or Vegas Slim. As an avid runner since his teenage years, he successfully competed at all levels of the sport from high school through college before graduating from Nevada Southern University in Las Vegas (now UNLV). That was after being one of their top runners and establishing the University's Track and Cross Country Program as a student and coach. Neal has been an unbeatable performer in age group competition, consistently winning individual National Championships over the past 30 years. With Ken Noel, he anchored several Age Group Relay Teams to World Records and National Club Team Championships for the West Valley Jogger and Striders (Saratoga, Ca.).

KEN NOEL has a doctoral degree in Sociology and was a college instructor before joining a friend in developing a successful Silicon Valley Startup Company. During a lifetime of competitive running, he won an NCAA College Division National Championship. Much later in life, he garnered three Age Group Relay Records on the track, a National 8K Road Racing Championship, and three National 10K Road Racing Championships on teams with Neal Chappell, his lifelong running partner.